D1121107

An Introduction to

MENNONITE
HISTORY

An Introduction to

MENNONITE HISTORY

A Popular History of the Anabaptists and the
Mennonites

Second Edition

Cornelius J. Dyck, Editor

HERALD PRESS
Scottdale, Pennsylvania
Kitchener, Ontario

Library of Congress Cataloging in Publication Data

Main entry under title:

An introduction to Mennonite history.

    Bibliography: p.
    Includes index.
    Summary: A history of Anabaptist-Mennonite
thought from the sixteenth century to the present,
with a description of Mennonite life and thought
around the world today.
    1. Mennonites—History. 2. Anabaptists—History.
[1. Mennonites—History. 2. Anabaptists—History]
I. Dyck, Cornelius J. II. Title.
BX8115.I57   1981   289.7   81-1958
ISBN 0-8361-1955-X (pbk.)   AACR2

AN INTRODUCTION TO MENNONITE HISTORY
Copyright © 1967, 1981 by Herald Press, Scottdale, Pa. 15683
    Published simultaneously in Canada by Herald Press,
    Kitchener, Ont. N2G 4M5. All rights reserved.
Published 1967. Second edition 1981.
Library of Congress Catalog Card Number: 81-1958
International Standard Book Number: 0-8361-1955-X
Printed in the United States of America
Design: Alice B. Shetler

    86 17 16 15 14 13 12

Forward Through the Ages

Forward through the ages, in unbroken line,
Move the faithful spirits, at the call divine;
Gifts in diff'ring measure, hearts of one accord,
Manifold the service, one the sure reward.

Forward through the ages, in unbroken line,
Move the faithful spirits, at the call divine.

Wider grows the kingdom, reign of love and light;
For it we must labor, till our faith is sight;
Prophets have proclaimed it, martyrs testified,
Poets sung its glory, heroes for it died.

Not alone we conquer, not alone we fall;
In each loss or triumph, lose or triumph all.
Bound by God's far purpose, in one living whole,
Move we on together, to the shining goal.

—Frederick L. Hosmer, 1908

Contents

List of Maps and Charts

Abbreviations

1. AIMM   Africa Inter-Mennonite Mission
         (formerly CIM)
2. CPS   Civilian Public Service
3. CIM   Congo Inland Mission (now AIMM)
4. EMEK   European Mennonite Evangelism Committee
5. HPC   Historic Peace Churches (Brethren,
         Friends, Mennonites)
6. IMO   International Mennonite Organization (Europe)
7. IMPC   International Mennonite Peace Committee
8. MCC   Mennonite Central Committee
9. MCSFI Mennonite Christian Service Fellowship
         of India
10. MEDA Mennonite Economic Development Associates
11. MWC   Mennonite World Conference
12. PAX   Peace program under MCC
13. SEDA Service for the Development of
         Agriculture (Zaire)
14. SMO   Swiss Mennonite Organization for
         Relief Work
15. TAP   Teachers Abroad Program, under MCC
16. USSR Union of Soviet Socialist Republics

Preface

This is a history of Anabaptist-Mennonite life and thought from the sixteenth century to the present, written particularly for young adults. The progress of scholarly studies of Anabaptism and the growing unity among Mennonites around the world seem to call for a book which describes in simple terms who the Mennonites are in relation to their sixteenth-century ancestors, and in relation to each other. It is intended to introduce students, church study groups, and others to the basic historical and doctrinal developments through 450 years of Anabaptist and Mennonite efforts to be the faithful church.

The preparation of the manuscript for the original volume published in 1967, as well as the preparation of this revised volume, has been a project of the Institute of Mennonite Studies, which is a research agency of the Associated Mennonite Biblical Seminaries (AMBS) of Elkhart, Indiana. The chapters of the original volume were submitted to the present editor by the writers in preliminary form to allow him maximum freedom in achieving a relative uniformity of style. In the present revision process the editor was granted authorization by the writers to undertake any revisions he considered necessary. The original writers were not involved in the revision process except in the reading of certain sections of the new manuscript. Appreciation is expressed here for this fraternal act of trust and cooperation.

The revisions made in the first eight chapters are not major, including primarily a catching up with recent historiography in Anabaptist studies. Some new material has been added. These chapters were originally drafted by the following: John H. Yoder, 2, 3, and 8; John S. Oyer, 4; Walter Klaassen, 5; William E. Keeney, 6 and 7, and the editor, 1. More changes have been made in chapters 9, originally by Ernst Crous, now deceased, and 10, originally by Frank H. Epp. Chapter 11 is largely the work of the editor with some indebtedness to J. C. Wenger, while chapter 12 is largely the work of J. C. Wenger with some indebtedness to the editor. The remaining chapters must largely be attributed to the editor, except for part of 15, originally drafted by Frank C. Peters, and parts of 18 and 20, originally drafted by Walter Klaassen and William E. Keeney respectively. The editor, of course, continues to remain responsible for any errors of fact or interpretation or omission.

The purpose of the revision was, first of all, to describe the rapid changes which have been taking place in the "Mennonite world" in Africa, Asia, and Latin America, as well as in Europe and North America, in the past decade. Not only were the statistics out of date, but many other changes have occurred in most of the groups described. Other concerns had to do with historiography, with the place of minorities among Mennonites, the role of women, greater sensitivity to discriminatory language, attention to inter-Mennonite activities, the need for a different kind of bibliography, and other details.

In addition to the appreciation already expressed to the coauthors, it is a pleasure to express my indebtedness to Paul N. Kraybill, editor of the *Mennonite World Handbook* (Lombard, Ill.: Mennonite World Conference, 1978), which relieved me of much tedious correspondence and placed a wealth of material at my disposal. My use of it may have been less inhibited because it was my privilege to have a small part in bringing it to birth. The efforts of Jan Gleysteen and Paul M. Schrock of Herald Press in selecting photos and shaping appropriate captions are gratefully acknowledged. Appreciation is also expressed to the administration of AMBS for significant support of the project, to James M. Stayer, Amos Hoover, and a host of other friends who have given good counsel, to Sue Yoder for patient and efficient typing of the manuscript, and to Wilma, my wife, for editorial help and quiet confidence.

Cornelius J. Dyck
Elkhart, Indiana

An Introduction to

MENNONITE
HISTORY

Chapter 1

The Church Before the Reformation

THE REFORMATION was a sixteenth-century movement in Europe to reform the church. Sometimes October 31, 1517, is given as the date of its beginning, since on that day Martin Luther posted ninety-five statements about the church for discussion at Wittenberg University. The problems which brought about the Reformation were spiritual, social, economic, and political in origin and combined to bring about radical changes in the life and thought of the Western world. In some ways these changes marked the end of the Middle Ages and a beginning of the modern era.

At the center of this movement was a strong desire to reform the church. All through the Middle Ages the voices of councils, clergy, kings, and lay people had been crying for an end to the corruption of the institutional church. Those who saw greed as the biggest sin urged economic reforms. Those who deplored the scandal of incompetent and often immoral clergy urged reform of the priesthood. And those who saw the pride and power of the pope as the root of all evil called for more church councils to exercise control. By the year 1500, many proposals for reform had been heard, but there was little agreement about how these might be carried out. All, however, seemed to agree that reformation meant a return of the church to its first-century apostolic purity. In this sense the Reformation was a backward-looking movement. Somewhere along the way the church had fallen and it now needed to return to a virtue it had once possessed. A brief look at the church before the Reformation will help us to understand more fully the dramatic events of the early sixteenth century and their influence upon us.

Persecution: Soon after Pentecost the church which Jesus Christ had founded suffered persecution. The baptism with water and by the Spirit was often followed by the baptism of blood—martyrdom. Hated by the Jews and suspected by the Romans as "enemies of the human race" (Tacitus), suffering became part of the new life in Christ for His disciples:

> They were stoned, they were sawn in two, they were killed with the sword; they went about in skins of sheep and goats, destitute, afflicted, ill-treated—of whom the world was not worthy—wandering over deserts and mountains, and in dens and caves of the earth. Hebrews 11:37, 38.)

But "the blood of martyrs is seed" (Tertullian). By mid-second century the *Epistle to Diognetus* reminded the persecutors that they were fighting a losing battle: "Do you not see that the more of them are punished, the more do others increase? These things do not seem to come from a human power; they are a mighty act of God; they are proofs of His human power; they are a mighty act of God; they are proofs of His presence." Fifty years later Tertullian answered critics of the faith with the words, "We are but of yesterday, and we have filled everything you have—cities, tenements, forts, towns, exchanges, yes! and camps, tribes, palace, senate, forum."[1]

The church indeed seemed to be almost everywhere, from Rome to Asia Minor and India, from Europe to North Africa. It included men and women of many different cultural backgrounds. Some of its leading teachers and writers, like Tertullian, Cyprian, Augustine, and others, were Africans. Some of its major leaders, as in Montanism which tried to restore a declining emphasis upon the Holy Spirit, were women. But the church was also adapting to its environment and being changed by it. There were still occasional persecutions in the third and early fourth centuries, but political leaders found many Christians increasingly cooperative and congenial. By AD 173 army life had become so attractive and Christianity so much a part of society that young Christian men began enlisting in the Roman legions. Christians began to use the courts to settle disputes among themselves. Many gained prominence in social and political institutions. Increasingly, becoming a Christian came to be the acceptable thing to do.

Constantine: This trend toward the total acceptance of Christians into society received dramatic reinforcement when Constantine became emperor of Rome early in the fourth century. Christians were now the royal favorites while non-Christians were soon persecuted. Those who had suffered grievously under Diocletian's unexpected persecution a few years before could now draw on state funds to build churches and to support ministers. Sunday was decreed a public day of rest and worship, combining a pagan celebration with the Christian desire to celebrate the resurrection of Jesus as Christ and to distinguish themselves from the Sabbath-keeping Jews. As emperor, Constantine wrote letters of instruction to the clergy, though he himself was not a baptized Christian, and enforced the discipline of the church with the power of the state. He called the clergy together at state expense to consider basic issues of the faith and sometimes chaired their meetings personally.

Why he did all this is not clear. He had seen that the church could not easily be destroyed by persecution, he needed an appealing state religion to unify the empire, and he may himself have been attracted to the Christian faith. Whatever the reasons, from that time on church and state went hand in hand. Though they were to quarrel often in the centuries to come, no one seriously questioned this *Constantinian synthesis* for over 1,000 years. A Christian society into which all persons were born as citizens, and baptized in infancy as Christians, seemed to be the fulfillment of God's plan for mankind.

The church now faced the enormous task of making society Christian and absorbing into its own life the masses of people who had become members without knowing it. This already

hopeless undertaking was doomed to certain failure soon after it
began by the infiltration into the Roman Empire, and therefore
into the church, of thousands upon thousands of Goths, Vandals,
and other tribes from the North. By AD 500 all of Italy was
under the rule of their king Theodoric (d. 526). Much of Northern
Europe was ruled by Clovis (d. 511), who became a Christian because, like Constantine, he believed that God had given him victory in battle. Externally the church prospered. Some of the old
glory of the disintegrating Roman Empire came to be associated
with the papacy. As spiritual successors of the Apostle Peter,
and political successors in Rome of the emperors who had moved
to Constantinople, the bishops (popes) of Rome soon became the
most powerful men in Europe. They had the most income, the
largest armies, the best scholars, and the most influence since
the people believed them to be the only authorized representatives of God on earth, following in the steps of St. Peter.

A double standard: There were those, of course, who
protested against this secularization of the church. Hermits
arose to live in lonely and desert places, torturing their bodies to
liberate the spirit for communion with God. Monks banded
together to build monasteries in which they could escape the sin
and temptation of a wicked world by giving themselves in prayer
and fasting. Similarly, convents were built for nuns. But instead
of calling all Christians to imitate the dedication of these men
and women, the church made saints out of these few. Instead of
leading to a general repentance, the lives of these few stimulated
the developing double moral standard. By a system of "spiritual
bookkeeping" the excess merit which these saints were assumed
to possess was transferred to those who seemed unable to or did
not want to live a godly life. Soon lay people were not expected to
live on the same moral and spiritual level as saints or clergy.

Attempts at reform: There were many persons who tried to
renew the life of the church in these centuries and with some
success. Protestant preoccupation with the Reformation of the
sixteenth century has tended to overlook these movements.
Among the reformers was Benedict of Nursia (d. ca. 547) whose
deep spiritual concern led to the founding of the Benedictine
Order, a renewal movement which has continued to this day. His

Rule gave guidance to the worship and work of monasteries and convents throughout Europe and did much to improve their quality of life. Early in the seventh century Gregory the Great prepared new forms of worship and sent missionaries to England, which led to a return missionary program from England to the continent under Boniface in the eighth century. One of the greatest forces in expanding the institutional church through force of arms, but also deepening its life through education and numerous reforms, was Charlemagne (d. 814). With the help of his Benedictine adviser, Alcuin of York (d. 804), clergy training was undertaken, preaching encouraged, church discipline initiated, mutual aid encouraged, monasteries reformed, and a vast network of schools established in much of what is now known as Western Europe. So great was his influence that he is referred to as the founder of the "Holy Roman Empire" which was to last for a millennium, from his crowning in Rome on Christmas Day 800 to the time of Napoleon.

Other reform movements came upon the scene. In the tenth century the monastic reforms of Cluny touched most of the monasteries of Europe, and in the eleventh priests were forbidden to marry, in order to prevent them from being a hereditary caste with inherited power and wealth. In the twelfth and thirteenth centuries the Franciscans, Dominicans, and other priestly orders arose to teach, preach, and serve among the people. And in the thirteenth century Innocent III convened a council to reform the church, while Thomas Aquinas hammered out a theological system which attempted to pull together all the traditions of the church into a meaningful faith. So impressive did all these developments seem even to later historians, that they called the thirteenth the greatest of all centuries, the century of faith.

Yet none of these reforms turned the church decisively in a new direction, and the external power of the church over the world continued to increase. By the ninth century, for example, almost one half of the land in Europe was under the control of the church, which therefore increasingly considered itself responsible for the total welfare of the general public. It became ever more difficult for the church to limit itself to spiritual affairs while leaving secular things to the authorities of the state. By the twelfth century the authority of the church was almost universal and little happened without its consent. Princes and statesmen, bankers and scholars were subject to its will. As the moon shines only by the reflected light of the sun, so the glory and power of the state is only a reflection of the greater glory and power of the church, it was said.

The Crusades: But the very "success" of the church became its undoing. Under an illusion of pious grandeur, Pope Urban II launched the Crusades in 1096 to recover the Holy Land from the Turks; instead of fighting each other, let Christians fight against the enemies of God. The sword became the missionary instrument of the church. All who went to fight were assured full remission of the penalties for their sins, and tens of thousands went in repeated waves until the thirteenth century. There was even a children's Crusade in 1212. The wealthy, and those who could not go, were able to buy indulgences granting the same remission of sins as those who went received, a development which was to become the direct cause of Luther's protest in 1517.

The Crusades brutalized the life of the church. In 1208 Pope Innocent III even declared a Crusade in Europe itself against the Cathari of France. When a Crusader asked how he might know the heretical Cathari from true believers, he was told to kill them all, for the Lord would know His own and would sort them out at the pearly gates.

Other problems of the church: To the heritage of the Crusade was added the burden of rising nationalism, which brought grave financial problems for the church. The papacy went bankrupt. From its highest point in 1200, the prestige of the papacy fell to an all-time low in 1300. To the financial chaos was added the burden of division. For seventy-three years, from 1305 to 1378, the papal court was in a "Babylonian Captivity" at Avignon in France and at the mercy of French kings. When it returned to Rome, there were suddenly two popes and then three popes excommunicating each other, all claiming to be the only representative (vicar) of Christ on earth. Though councils were called and the division finally healed in 1417, even the simple-

For more than twelve centuries the church was the dominant power in Western Europe. **The cathedral complex of Bamberg** recalls the day when the church owned 50 percent of the land and employed 15 percent of the population.

minded were under no illusions about the spirituality of the church. The clergy were often ill-trained and greedy, or simply hungry. While the rich could purchase heaven itself, the poor seemed consigned to purgatory or hell because they could not pay for the services of the church.

At the heart of church life was the sacramental system which had grown up around the simple teaching of Jesus and the early church. There were now seven sacraments: baptism, confirmation, penance, the mass (Lord's Supper), marriage, ordination, and extreme unction. In each of these the ritual itself became more important than faith and obedience. It was believed that water baptism saved the infant from hell and that in the mass the bread and wine became the actual flesh and blood of Christ. Extreme unction became the last rite to prepare for death, instead of a prayer for healing, as taught in James 5:14-15. The spiritual had become almost entirely objective and mechanical.

Late medieval piety: There were, obviously, also people who had a deep personal faith. There were faithful, dedicated priests. There were skeptics who didn't care about faith. But most people relied on this sacramental system for their salvation. Plagues, wars, and fear of death made most people long for a guaranteed escape from hell. Helping the sacramental routine were woodcuts on religious themes which people unable to read could hang on the wall and venerate. There were also Bibles for those who could read and their number increased rapidly with Gutenberg's invention of movable type. More popular, however, were the relics of saints and pilgrimages to shrines. In 1509, Frederick the Wise, Prince of Saxony, had 5,005 relic items on display. The viewing of each was said to give one hundred days' remission from purgatory. A grand total reduction of 500,000 years of purgatory could be obtained at Wittenberg. At Halle over three million years could be secured. Among these relics were hay from the manger at Bethlehem, twigs from the burning bush of Moses, the thumb of St. Anne (mother of Mary), a part of the diaper of the baby Jesus, and a feather from the wing of the archangel Michael.

Great trust was placed in the help of saints. Every ache and pain was believed to have a saint to guard against it—St. Vitus guarded against epilepsy, St. Denis against headache and rabies, St. Margaret against insanity, and so on—an unending host of helpers for those in need. None were called on more often than Mary, for whom veneration increased enormously in the twelfth and following centuries. Folk piety had to have a sinless Mary to intercede for them with the sinless Christ. Mary was considered the second Eve—as the disobedience of the first Eve had made the coming of Christ necessary, so the obedience of the second Eve (Mary) had made it possible. The line between fear of death and hell, miracle, and superstition was thin. The devil and his seduction became a dominant theme in literature, art, and conversation. He was a real competitor with God for the soul of the sinner. Some people, of course, did not care but many were afraid. They thought that the end of the world was near, and God seemed far away; they longed for a personal rather than an institutional church relationship to God.

One objectionable feature of the medieval church was **the selling of indulgences**—the pardon of one's sins in return for specific sums of money. The practice was questioned by thinking Christians, but the church took no action on their concerns, since the system provided a steady source of revenue. The wild claims made by Johannes Tetzel, shown here, led to Luther's break with Rome.

Preparing the Way

The Reformation did not come unannounced, though the way in which it shook the foundations of Europe was unexpected. The influence of the Crusades and of the Renaissance, the rise of nationalism and its clash with the international papal church, the corruption of the clergy and the church, the growing restlessness of the common people all became signs that a major storm was about to break.

Not least among these signs were men and movements which helped to prepare the way for the spiritual breakthrough which the Reformation was to bring. Consciously or unconsciously the reformers of the sixteenth century stood on the shoulders of these men and movements. We think, for example, of Francis of Assisi (d. 1226), who became a living reproach of the greed and wealth of the church, and who recaptured in his own life what it means to be a disciple of Christ. We think also of Girolamo Savonarola, who was hanged in Florence in 1498, because of his powerful, prophetic preaching. And there were many others!

Among these others were three men and two groups of men whose thought and work were particularly important in preparing the way for the Reformation. The men were Peter Waldo, John Wyclif, and John Hus; the groups of men were the mystics and the humanists. Waldo, Wyclif, and Hus were men of deep conviction. They were also men of action. The mystics and the humanists were not activist reformers, but their spiritual and intellectual leadership prepared the way for the men of action and created the kind of climate in the minds of the people which made reform possible. We turn now to a brief discussion of these pioneers.

Peter Waldo (d. ca. 1218): In 1176, the song of a minstrel stirred a deep longing in the heart of Waldo, a rich merchant of Lyon, France. Upon asking a theologian for the best way to God, he was quoted Matthew 19:21: "If you would be perfect, go, sell what you possess and give to the poor, and you will have treasure in heaven; and come, follow me." A new life began for Waldo with this verse. He sold his property, resolving to be as poor as Jesus and the apostles had been. His wife and family

Peter Waldo (12th century), a rich merchant in Lyon, France, sold his business to finance the translation and distribution of the Scriptures. His followers became known as Waldensians. **John Hus** (ca. 1369-1415) initiated a reform in Czechoslavakia. The Council of Constance decreed his burning at the stake. The invention of printing by **Johann Gutenberg** (ca. 1400-1468) was a major factor in spreading the concerns for church renewal among the people. This prepared the way for **Martin Luther** (1483-1546) who initiated the Reformation by posting the ninety-five theses on October 31, 1517.

received enough to support them. Then he began to study the New Testament, memorizing favorite passages, and reciting them to whoever would listen, together with his own interpretation of the passage. Within a year he was joined by others and the group eventually became known as Waldensians. They called themselves the *Poor in Spirit,* and asked the Third Lateran Council in 1179 for permission to preach as laymen. This was denied, but they felt compelled by God to continue nevertheless, and severe persecution followed for almost 700 years. Relative freedom was granted them in Italy (where the largest groups came to live) only in 1848.

At the heart of the Waldensian reform movement was a love for the Scriptures and a desire to put into practice in their own lives what they read in them. They studied the Bible together in small-group meetings. In their writings the Word of God is called

> ... salvation for the soul of the poor, a tonic for the weak, food for the hungry, teaching for the true, comfort unto the chastened, the cessation of slander and the acquisition of virtue.

> Even as they who are assailed by the enemy flee to a strong tower so do the assailed saints betake themselves to the Holy Scripture. There they find weapons against heresies, armor against the assaults of the devil, the assaults of the flesh, the glory of the world.[2]

Because they placed special emphasis on the New Testament and obedience to the words of Jesus recorded in Matthew 5, 6, and 7, they became known as the Sermon on the Mount people. And, because they were convinced that the Scriptures held the answer to people's problems, they traveled all over Europe two by two, preaching, witnessing, and suffering for the sake of Christ. The neglect of the Scriptures in Roman Catholicism was to them a certain sign that the church had fallen from the faith.

The Waldensians were not Protestants before the Reformation, but Christians who took the Word of God seriously. They rejected the mass, purgatory, and participation in warfare as unbiblical, but continued to practice infant baptism. They believed that all Christians, whether men or women, were called to witness to their faith by living it and preaching it. So effective were they in this lay witnessing that long before the Reformation a Roman Catholic leader wrote, "One third of Christendom if not more has attended illicit Waldensian conventicles [meetings] and is at heart Waldensian."[3] Numerous attempts to link the Anabaptists historically with the Waldensians have failed, but through them the spiritual soil was being prepared for the events of the sixteenth century.

John Wyclif (d. 1384): A man who prepared the way for Martin Luther and other reformers much more than the Waldensians was John Wyclif, the "Morning Star of the Reformation." Wyclif, a professor at Oxford University, became a reformer only in the last decade of his life. He had long believed that the church should be poor as were the apostles and that Christ had given it authority over spiritual matters only. When he met representatives of the pope at Bruges in 1374 and found that they did not agree with him, he gave up all hope of reform through councils and clergy.

On his return to England he called upon the king to reform the church, by force, if necessary. At the same time, however, he urged that the Scriptures be made available to all people as the only certain ground for reform. "Holy Scripture is the highest authority for every Christian and the standard of faith and of all human perfection,"[4] he said. Because his hope for reform rested in a recovery of the Word of God by the people, he trained persons to memorize long passages and recite them as they traveled through the country. These "poor preachers" or "Lollards," as they were called, were really traveling evangelists in England.

In the meantime, Wyclif's own biblical studies led him to reject the pope as necessary for the church, The church, he said, is made up of those whom God elects for salvation. He also rejected the papal interpretation of the Lord's Supper as being the actual flesh and blood of Christ, saying that the bread and wine are symbols or signs of the work and grace of Christ. He considered indulgences, which were taken to forgive sin, to be the work of the devil, and he taught that priests should marry. The work of the clergy is acceptable before God, he said, only if they themselves lead holy lives; those who did not should be removed from office by the state.

Because he had powerful protectors among the nobles, who wanted him to succeed for their own selfish interests, Wyclif died a natural death. Later, his bones were dug up, burned, and cast on the River Swift, often the practice with heretics. His books were also burned. Nevertheless, he, like the Waldensians, had pioneered in the recovery of the authority of the Scriptures over the life of the church. He had drawn attention to the corruption in the church and pointed to solutions. He was one of the greatest English preachers before the Reformation. Later, in 1572, a picture was painted in Bohemia showing Wyclif striking a spark, Hus kindling the coals with it, and Luther holding up the flaming torch. A monument to the Reformation in Worms, Germany, shows Luther surrounded by four men, Waldo, Wyclif, Hus, and Savonarola.

John Hus (d. 1415). The central events in the life of Hus are quickly told. As a professor at the university of Prague he became a major leader of the reform movement in Bohemia. In this he was guided by the writings of Wyclif, but he placed less reliance on the reforming ability of the state, and he developed a deeper understanding of the nature of the church. With Wyclif he urged the study of the Scriptures by the people and argued from them without rejecting tradition as strongly as Wyclif did.

His preaching and reform proposals were extremely popular. Because he attacked the papacy, the corruption of the clergy, and other problems of the church—especially the sale of indulgences—he lost the support of the bishops and of King Wenceslas. He went into hiding with friends in the country and continued his reform writing. During this period he wrote his treatise on the church. The church, he said, is not where the pope is, but where two or three are gathered in the name of Christ. Similarly it is not the pope but the Holy Spirit who gives unity to the church. Nor does the pope have any power to include or exclude people from heaven. This power of the keys is held by the believing church under the guidance of the Holy Spirit and consists in preaching, witnessing, counseling, church discipline, and the Lord's Supper.

Because he was accused of heresy and rejected the authority of the pope, Hus repeatedly declared his desire to defend his views before a general council of the church. When such a council convened at Constance to end the schism in the church, and he was asked to appear before it, he went. Though his friends warned him of the dangers to his life, he said:

> I confide altogether in my Saviour. I trust that He will accord me His Holy Spirit to fortify me in His truth, so that I may face with courage temptations, prison, and if necessary a cruel death.[5]

Emperor Sigismund issued a safe-conduct guarantee for him, but after his arrival in Constance he spent most of his time in prison. Instead of presenting his teachings to the council fathers, they put him on trial for his life as a heretic. Pope John 23, who was a wicked man and had reportedly been a pirate before his ordination, pressed for his condemnation. His fate was sealed. From his prison he wrote:

> It is better to die well than to live ill. One should not flinch before the sentence of death. To finish the present life in grace is to go away from pain and misery. He who fears death loses the joy of life. Above all else truth triumphs. He conquers who dies, because no adversity can hurt the one over whom iniquity holds no sway.[6]

He was given one last chance to recant, which he refused. Then they put a paper crown on his head with three demons on it and the words, "We commit your soul to the devil," after which they took him outside of the city and burned him to ashes. The date was July 6, 1415.

So effectively had John Hus prepared the way for the Reformation that 105 years later Martin Luther said, "We are all Hussites without knowing it." During that 100 years, however, bloody Hussite wars devastated the land as his followers struggled for religious and political independence. A crusade was eventually launched against them. Most of them finally made their peace with Roman Catholicism, but some continued separately as the Bohemian Brethren, known today as the Moravians. One of their great early leaders was Peter Chelcicki (active 1420-60), who taught many of the principles the

Anabaptists were to emphasize a century later.

The Mystics: Influencing the thought and work of these reformers, and of the entire Middle Ages, were the mystics— men and women who cultivated an inner, personal religion and practiced the presence of God. The mystics sought union with God. Personal, firsthand experience was for them the final authority in matters of faith. The church with its priests, sacraments, and traditions was not rejected. All of its rites and ceremonies could, in fact, help the mystics along in their spiritual pilgrimage, but they were not really necessary. God could be known best, they believed, through self-denial, contemplation, and spiritual insight. The key to the knowledge of God was love.

There were almost as many kinds of mysticism in the Middle Ages as there were mystics. In Bernard of Clairvaux (d. 1153), who has sometimes been called the father of Western mysticism, we find a man of orthodox Catholic theology who could lose himself completely in the love of God, yet who was also one of the most active church reformers of all time, giving himself completely to the service of others. Hugh (d. 1141) of St. Victor near Paris was much more intellectual by inclination, yet his mysticism is apparent, for example, in his description of the three levels of faith. On the lowest level the Christian believes what the church teaches because the church says it is true; on the second level he believes it because his reason tells him it makes sense; and on the highest level he believes it because he knows by inner experience what the church and reason have already told him to be true.

Of great importance in the development of Luther's thought were the German mystics, Master Eckhart (d. 1327) and John Tauler (d. 1361), as well as an anonymous book called *A German Theology.* Luther was not a mystic, but the writings of these men and the *German Theology* mirrored the longing for God which he himself felt and which drove him unrelentingly to find a gracious God. These mystics wanted to remain faithful members of the Roman Catholic Church, but the corruption within it shocked them. They wanted the church reformed and believed this could only come about through a deeper commitment to the inner voice and work of the Spirit. Their utter abandonment to the will of God is reflected in Luther's later willingness to face any threat regardless of the personal consequences for himself.

In the Netherlands mysticism was particularly at home among the Brethren of the Common Life, the most famous of whom was possibly Thomas à Kempis (d. 1471), who is believed to have been the author of *The Imitation of Christ*. In contrast to many earlier mystics, the Brethren of the Common Life were serious and able students of the Bible. They tended to take its message literally and personally, as a result of which following in the footsteps of Jesus became their highest goal. This piety came to be known as the *devotio moderna* or new devotion. During the fifteenth century the Brethren established many schools which soon gained an excellent reputation for piety and learning. Both Erasmus and Luther studied under the Brethren, but neither seemed to enjoy the experience particularly. The influence of the schools was clearly evident, nevertheless, in the later work of both.

The humanists: It is possible that humanism did more to prepare the way for the coming of the Reformation than any single man or movement in the later Middle Ages. Humanism was the life and spirit of the Renaissance, the fourteenth- and fifteenth-century recovery of the ancient culture of Greece and Rome. Humanism was this-worldly, calling on people to shift their gaze from heaven to the earth around them. It rejected many of the irrational superstitions and customs of the age. It expressed itself in a flowering of the arts and sciences—the poetry of Dante (d. 1321) and Petrarch (d. 1374), the sculpture of Donatello (d. 1466), the architecture of Alberti (d. 1472), the painting of da Vinci (d. 1519) and Michelangelo (d. 1564), and a multitude of other creative masters. Humanism was inspired by a new spirit of freedom and inquiry which found ample moral and financial support in the papacy as the great patron of the arts.

The humanists north of the Alps generally had a stronger religious concern than those in Italy, giving themselves more to biblical studies than to classical sources. As Christian humanists they were also concerned with the problems of the

church, though they did not usually participate in action programs of reform. Their tools were a pen, a critical intellect,
satire, humor, and thorough scholarship. Humanist circles could
be found in most of the major universities and cities, and
everywhere they were respected, hated, feared, and loved. In
these circles and throughout Europe, no one was more respected
than Desiderius Erasmus (d. 1536), the "prince of the humanists." As a young man Luther almost worshiped Erasmus,
writing to him, "Where is he in whom Erasmus does not control
the inner thoughts, does not teach, does not rule ...?" But by
1524 he called him a babbler and a skeptic and felt he was undercutting the Reformation. And yet in some ways the old saying
that Erasmus laid the egg which Luther hatched is right.

Erasmus and Luther had many things in common. Both deplored the corruption of the clergy and the papacy; both emphasized the central place Scripture should have in the life of the
church; both taught the importance of Christ for the believer.
Nevertheless, the two men were very different. Erasmus was
scholarly and polite; Luther could be vulgar and dogmatic.
Erasmus believed reform could come to the church without
destroying its unity; Luther was a man of action ready to die for
his faith. Luther came to be a reformer because of his personal
search for faith. Erasmus had more of a detached scholar's
interest in Reformation issues. There were also basic differences
in understanding the faith. Luther saw salvation primarily as
grace, Erasmus primarily as imitating Christ, though both
stressed the importance of faith. Luther held man to be a
miserable sinner, while Erasmus, together with all humanists,
stressed the fundamental goodness of man. Luther might be
described as crying, "Back to the Bible," while Erasmus might
have asked, "What is the Bible?"

In all of this Erasmus represented the best in humanism.
The Reformation would not have been possible without the humanists' recovery of the Scriptures and of biblical scholarship.
Their sharp pens goaded the church to act where the actions of
the reformers often caused a reaction. The humanists added
spiritual depth to the church by stressing the inward and personal dimension of faith, where the reformers were often forced

to quarrel over doctrine or external church issues. Yet all of the major reformers had a humanist education and were scholars in their own right—Luther wrote much more than Erasmus, and during his university student days was known as "the learned philosopher"—but at a given point each of the reformers became deeply and personally involved in the life and problems of the church. How the humanists' vision of gradual reform through education, criticism, and patience would have worked out we will never know.

The Lutheran Reformation

The Lutheran Reformation centered in Wittenberg, Germany, where Martin Luther was professor of theology at the university from 1512 until his death in 1546. His road to becoming a theologian, prophet, and reformer had been a stormy one because of his own inner struggles of faith. He had learned that Christians must love God and do good works in order to be saved, but he could not love God—he was afraid of Him—and he was constantly seeing himself as a sinner. All the well-meant counsel of friends did not change this. God was angry with him, he said, and would send him straight to hell if he should die.

In desperation he finally became a monk, as he later said, "against the wishes of my father, of my mother, of God, and of the devil." Surely he would find peace as a holy man and learn to love God. His doubts continued, however, though he fasted and prayed more than other monks. His studies led him deep into the Scriptures and he became an effective and popular teacher at the university. It was while lecturing on the Book of Galatians and then Romans that the final breakthrough came for him. One day, while studying in his little tower room, he discovered a new meaning of the words of the Apostle Paul in Romans 1:17, "He who through faith is righteous shall live." God is not angry with man; He loves him, not because of what man does for God, but because of what God does for man in Christ. Man is justified by faith in Christ, not by good works. After discovering this Luther could finally say, "Now I felt myself newborn and in Paradise. All the Holy Scriptures looked different to me. . . ."

This experience of the grace of God was at the heart of

Luther's zeal. He now became an extremely busy man, preaching, writing, counseling, and traveling. He was summoned to Rome to be tried for heresy, but he remembered the fate of Hus and did not go. Consequently he was excommunicated and later placed under the ban of the empire, meaning that anyone could kill him as a heretic, but he was a man of the people and they loved him. He defended his faith before Emperor Charles and had to flee for safety to Wartburg castle, where he translated the Greek New Testament into German because he wanted every German, including every simple plowboy, to be able to read the Bible. Later he translated the Old Testament also. After his return to Wittenberg under the protection of Duke Frederick the Wise, he sent teachers and ministers to the churches to help the clergy, who were poorly trained and knew little about the gospel. He wrote catechisms for use in the churches and many hymns, including "A Mighty Fortress Is Our God." Soon the gospel was singing its way into the hearts of the people who had never sung in church before. He knew their spiritual needs and wanted to share with them the answer he had found.

Opposition to Luther's work did not come only from Rome. Among his own friends were those who disagreed with him, as we saw in Erasmus. Another critic was Andreas Carlstadt (d. 1541), a man who said many things close to what the Anabaptists were to say a few years later. He urged Luther to give more attention in his preaching to the importance of following Jesus in life, since many people took the Reformation emphasis on grace to mean that works were not important so long as they believed in Christ. He also rejected the swearing of oaths, and instead of the sacramental interpretation of the Lord's Supper, whereby the bread and wine were taken to have saving power in and of themselves, he began to celebrate the Lord's Supper as a memorial service of what Christ had done on the cross. He forbade others to call him doctor, saying that all are equal in the church of Christ. All of this greatly distressed Luther, but did not change his program.

Thomas Müntzer (d. 1525), whose reform demands went much further than those of Carlstadt, gave Luther a great deal of trouble. He had become a pastor at Luther's suggestion, and was an able speaker, but his program for social reforms soon seemed revolutionary to Luther and the princes. When this brought him into conflict with them, he began holding meetings in homes. Persons from the lower classes of society felt particularly attracted to his messages about equality and freedom.

Among those attending the meetings were three men who came to be known as the Zwickau Prophets. Zwickau was the name of their hometown, and the prophet role was ascribed to them because they had moved from Bible study to spiritual visions which they freely shared with others. In 1521, in fact, they went to Wittenberg to show the Lutheran reformers that they must rely more on the Holy Spirit. Some of the Wittenberg men, including Carlstadt, were deeply impressed by them, but when Luther heard of their work he returned quickly from his hiding place in the Wartburg and sent them scurrying. Following this incident Müntzer was reported to have said that he would not trust Luther even if he had swallowed a dozen Bibles, to which Luther replied that he would not trust Müntzer either, even if he had swallowed the Holy Spirit, feathers and all.

Gradually Müntzer succeeded in gaining a large following among the peasants, who saw in him a man who could help them gain relief from the oppression of the nobles. He organized many of them into an armed force, using a red cross and unsheathed sword as banner emblem. Soon armed uprisings were occurring everywhere as the peasants took justice into their own hands. In doing this they thought they were simply helping to fulfill the divine plan for society as they had learned to understand it from the preaching of Luther and his helpers. A military showdown came on May 15, 1525, at Frankenhausen and thousands of peasants were killed by the well-armed nobles. Müntzer himself was captured, tortured, and executed several days later. These events are known as the Peasants' Revolt.

Carlstadt, the Zwickau Prophets, and the Peasants' Revolt closed Luther's mind to the Anabaptists when they appeared in 1525. He lumped together as fanatics all those who felt that his Reformation had not gone far enough. One of his favorite terms for them was *Schwärmer*, meaning a person driven by impulses and emotions rather than by common sense.

The Anabaptists actually rejoiced at the work Luther had done but called it a halfway Reformation. They did not find the Bible teaching his sacramental understanding of the Lord's Supper nor baptism as having saving power, but they were particularly disappointed in his definition of the church as being wherever the Word of God was preached and the sacraments rightly administered. To them the church, according to the New Testament, should consist of believers only. These would voluntarily join the church, instead of being brought in through infant baptism. By their free decision they would bind themselves to witness and to discipline as the body of Christ. While Luther had brought many changes and had, above all, restored the gospel as grace, they felt that he had left unchanged the really basic problem of the church which had come when Constantine merged the church with the state.

It will be noted in the following chapter that Ulrich Zwingli also relied on the state to reform the church. Because of this the Swiss Brethren were finally forced to go their own way. Their intention was not to begin a separate movement, but to complete what Zwingli had left unfinished. The persons and movements which prepared the way for the Reformation, therefore, also helped to prepare the way for Anabaptism. Anabaptism cannot really be understood without seeing its development in relation to these movements. The history of Anabaptism is also a part of the universal history of the church through the ages. The history of the Christian church begins with Christ, not in the sixteenth century!

Chapter 2

Anabaptist Origins in Switzerland

SOUTH GERMANY and SWITZERLAND had no city which served as a center of the Reformation movement in the way Wittenberg served Lutheranism in the North. The major South German and Swiss cities were independent states with their own laws, commerce, and religious interests. Because of this the persons who arose from among these people to renew the church, and whom history has called *reformers*, had differing emphases from region to region. In their own way each of these led in the process of church reorganization, dealing with the authorities of the cities and Roman Catholic opposition as best they could.

With all these variations, however, the one man who was strongest and most respected among these first-generation reformers was Ulrich Zwingli (d. 1531), of Zurich. Zwingli first became known through his criticism of the system whereby an endless stream of Swiss youth was sent to the great military powers of Europe as mercenary soldiers. He was also a good friend of Erasmus. Zwingli was a popular preacher as well, as a result of which he left his small parish at Einsiedeln in January of 1519, to be installed in the prestigious church in Zurich itself. Here he startled his listeners by preaching day after day directly from the Bible, beginning his sermon invariably at the place in the Scriptures where he had ended the day before. As he did this, he became increasingly independent of and critical of the traditional practices of Roman Catholicism even as Luther was criticizing them, but he was not greatly influenced by Luther in this. His own studies and biblical preaching led him to these new conclusions.

By the middle of 1522 it had become clear that Zwingli and others of like mind were coming to demand such radical renewal measures within the church that no bishop or other church authority would support them. How then should they go about reforming the church? The answer was given by Zwingli himself in November of that year, when he resigned as priest of the Roman Catholic Church and rejected its authority over him. Hereupon the Council of Two Hundred, which was the governing body of the city of Zurich, immediately reinstated him in his old position but under their authority. Formally speaking, this action of the government in calling a preacher marked the beginning of the Swiss Reformation and of the state church.

Such action naturally brought criticism upon the council for having appointed a man whom the Roman Catholic Church considered a heretic. To clear themselves of this accusation and to give a formal justification to their action, the council called a disputation in January 1523, to clarify the issues. According to the customs of the time a disputation was a formal debate carried on according to accepted standards, which included impartial chairmanship and record taking. The theses which Zwingli was willing to defend were published ahead of time, and invitations were sent to all concerned, including the great Catholic universities and the bishop of Constance, in whose diocese Zurich belonged. Zwingli's intention was to show that these theses were according to the Word of God. But no real debate developed, since Johannes Faber, sent to represent the bishop, denied that the council of Zurich (a political body of laymen) was authorized to serve as umpire in theological matters. Therefore, since no one had shown the Zwinglian proposals to be contrary to the Word of God, the council reconfirmed his appointment and instructed him to continue to preach nothing but the gospel truth.

In 1522 **Ulrich Zwingli** (1484-1531), pastor of the Grossmünster in Zurich, broke with Rome, but was immediately reinstated under the authority of Zurich's city council. **Christopher Froschauer,** pioneer printer in Zürich, took an active part in church reform. In 1529 he completed a beautifully executed German Bible, several years ahead of Luther. His Bible was long a favorite with the Anabaptists.

Both of these actions—the hiring of Zwingli in November, and his formal reaffirmation by the council in January—were conservative decisions in their intention; they simply allowed him to continue his preaching. And yet they were of revolutionary importance since they represented a declaration of independence from the control of the Roman hierarchy and a seizing of the right to name ministers by the local political authority.

The State Resists Reform

As Zwingli's preaching and the consequent process of reformation went on, the council found it increasingly difficult to accept all the implications arising from this rediscovery of the gospel. For example, Zwingli had taught that the taking of interest was unbiblical, though he also stressed the importance of obeying civil authority. Wilhelm Reublin, a Zurich priest, and Conrad Grebel strongly supported the teaching against interest (tithes). Consequently the Zurich area peasants appealed to the council to be relieved of this heavy burden which was a kind of tax, but the council would hear nothing of this and ordered them to continue paying interest to the city and the monasteries as usual.

In late summer of 1523 Zwingli began to spell out more clearly how the traditional Catholic mass might be replaced with an evangelical communion service. To demonstrate the rightness of his teaching that the mass is not a sacrifice but a commemoration, and to cast light on the further radical demand of some of his disciples that all paintings and statues should be removed from the churches, a second disputation was held October 27-29. But the council feared the consequences of doing away with the mass. This would not only seem sacrilegious to other cantons in the Swiss Confederacy but would jeopardize Zurich's political and economic relationship to them as well. Thus it became clear that the council was in no hurry to permit external changes in religious practices, even though the theology of the Lord's Supper had been clearly stated by Zwingli and accepted as valid by the people and the council.

In December Zwingli finally decided to go ahead himself in his own congregation with a biblical celebration of the Lord's Supper in both kinds, i.e., with the cup no longer reserved only for the priest. In a memorandum to the council he announced his intention to celebrate such a Lord's Supper on Christmas Day, 1523, adding that the preachers would "stand condemned as liars before the Word of God" if they did not go through with this. But the council refused to agree. Zwingli was obliged to submit a second statement nine days later in which the threat to go ahead with his own Protestant communion service was withdrawn, and the decision was again left in the hands of the council. Thereupon the council decreed that there would be no change at all in the mass at that time. Zwingli accepted this indefinite delay rather than jeopardize his working relationship with the council.

The Dissatisfied Minority

Because of these delays and compromises a feeling of dissatisfaction began to arise within the circle of Zwingli's most devoted disciples. They had been critical of certain remainders of Roman Catholic practice in the draft of a new reformed order of worship which Zwingli had published in August. They had objected to the continued wearing of robes by the clergy, believing that this supported the idea that the mass was a sacrifice, and they had objected to the use of prescribed songs and prayers other than the Lord's Prayer in the liturgy. Zwingli had accepted these criticisms, changing his proposals at some points and defending others; the fellowship among them remained open.

After discussion of the mass in the October debate, however, these disciples were much less willing than Zwingli to see the council left with the responsibility of determining how the Reformation was to be carried out. The record of the debate reports:

> Conrad Grebel rose and thought that the priests should be given instructions, since they were all present, as to what should be done about the Mass; [the disputation] would be in vain, if something were not done about the Mass. . . .
>
> Zwingli: My Lords [the Council] will decide how to proceed henceforth with the Mass.
>
> Simon Stumpf: Master Ulrich: You have no authority to place the decision in the hands of My Lords, for the decision is already made; the Spirit of God decides.
>
> Zwingli: That is right. I shall likewise preach and act against it if they decide otherwise. I do not place the decision in their hands. Nor shall I pass judgment on the Word of God. . . . This convocation did not have the purpose of deciding for or against the Word of God, but to ascertain from Scripture whether the Mass is a sacrifice or not. Hereafter they will deliberate as to the way in which that may be done most appropriately and without disturbance.

Simon Stumpf, a priest in the country town of Höngg, was one of Zwingli's devoted followers. Conrad Grebel was the son of an upper-class Zurich family, who had spent his youth aimlessly in the universities of Vienna and Paris until Zwingli had led him to a strong personal commitment to the cause of the gospel. The exchange quoted above marks the first sign of their doubts about whether the state would be an adequate tool for reforming the church, but they accepted Zwingli's explanations for the time being.

With Zwingli's December compromise on the mass, however, these disciples realized that they were really in opposition to Zwingli who agreed that the Reformation should go no faster than the state was willing to put it into effect. Looking back on the October disputation with the perspective of later developments, Grebel was now able to say that the essential compromise had already been made then: "The Word was overthrown, trampled upon, and enslaved by its most learned heralds." In mock debating style Grebel set forth the thesis: "Whoever thinks, believes, or says that Zwingli is performing his duties as a shepherd, thinks, believes, and speaks impiously." From this point on, Grebel and his friends became increasingly distrustful of the council as a source of initiative in purifying the church.[1]

A Last Attempt

Little is known about the group of disappointed disciples of Zwingli from December 1523, to the fall of 1524. We know neither how many there were nor what they did. Only two known developments are certain to have fallen within this period—the idea of a basic change in the political organization of Zurich, and a growing conviction against the practice of infant baptism.

Political reorganization: In considering the halfheartedness of the council and Zwingli's unwillingness to move ahead without its support, these disciples concluded that the best way might be to get a sympathetic council elected. Conrad Grebel and Felix Mantz seem to have proposed to Zwingli that the friends of the Reformation might constitute something like a political party. They were confident that if Zwingli were to challenge the population of Zurich publicly to take sides for or against the Word of God as he was preaching it, the majority would be on his side. This majority could then elect a properly disposed city council and the Reformation would again move forward with state approval. This proposal met Zwingli halfway. It did not ask him to act against the state, nor did it say that the state would have no business carrying out the Reformation as long as it acted according to the Word of God. Yet by making the membership of such a "Reformation Party" voluntary, this proposal would in effect have created an independent religious institution and would, therefore, have begun to break the bond between church and state.

Zwingli had two objections to this proposal. On the one hand, he was still confident that the council could be trusted to move ahead responsibly, though slowly, with the Reformation program. A more basic reason was his growing fear of the divisive social effects of asking individuals within society to make their own decisions. The result might be Roman Catholic worship in one part of Zurich and Protestant worship in another, thus destroying the unity of the city and with it of the church. This, in turn, would dishonor God by casting doubt upon His sovereignty and upon the clarity of His revealed will.

Baptism of infants: In the early days of the Reformation Martin Luther and Ulrich Zwingli, together with many of their lesser colleagues, could not avoid challenging the Roman Catholic practice of infant baptism. As a sacrament with its own effectiveness regardless of the attitude of the infant, this practice was believed to purify the child from the stain of original sin, making salvation certain in case of early death and predisposing the infant toward a mature Christian life. The Reformation principles challenged this understanding from both sides. From the perspective of the individual the reformers defined faith as a personal response of trusting obedience and repentance. It must be genuine and personal to meet the conditions for salvation. They insisted that no church ceremony (sacraments) could have saving value.

In looking back on these events from our own times we need to remember that when questions were raised about the rightness of baptizing infants it was not clear in anyone's mind what else could be done in its place. One might have suggested that baptism be postponed until the child was three or four years of age and could have some consciousness of what was happening to him, and could remember it. Or one might have suggested that parents should at least cease these baptisms immediately after birth and wait for light about what to do in their place. No one, in any case, thought that the only possibility was to *rebaptize* as adult believers those who had been baptized in infancy—which, of course, meant nearly everyone in Europe at that time, except the Jews.

Early in 1523 Wilhelm Reublin was preaching so vigorously against infant baptism in Zollikon and Witikon that he was jailed. The fact that he was able to do this in the villages around Zurich rather than in the city itself indicates the relative freedom of the country folk from the authority of the city government though they were politically subject to it. Reublin was joined in this work by Hans Brötli. The positive response to this preaching was due to religious as well as social and economic factors. People living outside of Zurich resented paying the city tax and the city council's control over their parishes. The people wanted to elect their own clergy. A strong anticlerical feeling prevailed. Anabaptism seemed to support many of the aspirations of the peasants.

Autumn 1524

The first real explanation of the thinking of Reublin, Grebel, and their circle on infant baptism, and the first sign of them as a self-conscious group of persons rejecting Zwingli's leadership, is found in three letters written by Conrad Grebel and his friends in September of 1524. Having abandoned their hope that Zwingli himself could be won to take initiative in leading the Reformation, they wrote to three major Protestant leaders—Martin Luther, Andreas Carlstadt, and Thomas Müntzer. Both Carlstadt and Müntzer were in the process of separating themselves from the Lutheran movement because of its lack of progress as they had hoped. Only the letter to Müntzer has been preserved, but we do not know whether he received it. We know of no responses to these letters. Erhard Hegenwald wrote to Grebel on January 1, 1525, but specifically mentions that he had not seen his letter to Luther. He was personally acquainted with Grebel, but held Luther's views. There was contact with Carlstadt in Basel in late 1524 and Felix Mantz became instrumental in publishing some of his writings. His influence on Mantz and Grebel is under further study.

The primary concern expressed in the letter to Müntzer is for recognizing the Word of God as the only authority in matters of church reformation, in contrast to Zwingli's caution and "forbearance." They had read some of Müntzer's writings criticizing unreal faith and superficial religious practices and had come to believe they would find an ally in him. At the same time they clearly rejected the position which they had just heard that he held, that physical violence could be used to further the cause of the Reformation or in the interest of social justice for the peasants. Consequently their letter stated that

> ... the Gospel and its adherents are not to be protected by the sword, neither are they thus to protect themselves.... True Christian believers are sheep among wolves, sheep for the slaughter; they must be baptized in anguish and affliction, tribulation, persecution, suffering, and death; they must be tried with fire, and must reach the fatherland of eternal rest, not by killing their bodily, but by mortifying their spiritual enemies. Neither do they use worldly sword or war, since all killing has ceased with them.... [2]

In addition, they made two points on baptism—that it means the entrance of the believer into membership and into the discipline of the Christian congregation and that it reflects the personal experience and commitment of the believer:

> We understand that even an adult is not to be baptized without Christ's rule of binding and loosing. The Scripture describes baptism for us thus, that it signifies that by faith and the blood of Christ sins have been washed away for him who is baptized, changes his mind, and believes before and after; that it signifies that a man is dead and ought to be dead to sin and walks in newness of life and spirit, and that he shall certainly be saved if, according to this meaning, he lives his faith by inner baptism; so that the water does not confirm or increase faith, as the scholars at Wittenberg say, and [does not] give comfort [nor] is it the final refuge on the death bed. Also baptism does not save....

By "Christ's rule of binding and loosing" they meant the instructions of Jesus in Matthew 18:15-18, according to which

Christians are responsible to one another for counsel, admonition, and forgiveness. Baptism thus also meant committing oneself to give and receive counsel, which a child cannot do. The further meaning of baptism as a symbolism of washing seemed meaningful to them only if the spiritual reality to which it points is there. Apart from this, they held, water cannot purify, reassure, or save.

A Breakthrough

By December 1524 agitation around the question of infant baptism had become a problem which would lead to social difficulties if left unchecked. The city council, therefore, instructed Zwingli to meet once a week with all those who rejected infant baptism until the matter could be resolved. After two meetings on successive Tuesday evenings in December the talks were broken off by Zwingli because "it would be dangerous," i.e., because he feared discussion with those who did not respect his spiritual authority would only make matters worse. When the discussions were thus broken off, Felix Mantz submitted to the council a document in which he asked the members of the council themselves, as a group of Christian leaders, to renew the conversation since Zwingli himself was impossible to work with. The council responded by calling for a public meeting on January 17, but the announcements calling that meeting already showed that there was no intention to deal with the matter as an open question:

> As some are mistakenly saying that young children should not be baptized until they come to maturity, our lords; the mayor and the small and the Great Council of the city of Zurich announce that all ... should appear next Tuesday....[3]

Consequently the outcome of this pseudo-disputation was never in doubt. The council ruled that children should continue to be baptized and that any parents who persisted in refusal should be expelled from Zurich lands. This decision of January 18, 1525, meant that force would now be used in persecuting religious minorities in this area.

The small circle of seekers for a more faithful Reformation

The **city of Zurich** today with the river Limmat in the foreground and Lake Zurich and the Alps to the south. The twin-spired Grossmünster is Zurich's major landmark. The **Neustadtgasse** stands immediately behind the Grossmünster. Somewhere on this street, in the house of Felix Mantz, the first Anabaptist baptisms took place.

had no more time now for further careful study. Baptism had
not been their first concern, and it was not the central one, but it
was the point at which the line had been drawn by Zwingli. They
had one week to choose between compliance and exile. Under the
pressure of this choice before them they met in the home of Felix
Mantz, near Zwingli's church, on the evening of January 21 to
consider what they ought to do. There are several accounts of
what happened next. The best known of these is found in the
Hutterite Chronicle which was begun by Caspar Braitmichel in
his old age (d. 1573). Two other accounts are of particular
interest to us because both incorporate in Dutch translation a
letter written from Klettgau, Switzerland, possibly as early as
1530, to a group in Cologne in response to their inquiry about the
origins of the new movement. If the early date and place of
origin of the letter can be fully documented it would constitute a
more reliable report than the one in the *Chronicle*, written far
from the actual events in time and space. Since this last account
is readily available in numerous publications the following is a
translation of one of the other two accounts, written in 1615,
most likely by a Mennonite in Friesland. The early letter which
it incorporates reads, in part, as follows:

> Therefore, dear brothers, since you have asked us about the be-
> ginning of the brotherhood of the Swiss brethren, it was about the
> time when men wrote the year 1522 that Ulrich Zwingli, Conrad
> Grebel, a nobleman, and Felix Mantz—all three very learned men,
> experienced in the German, Latin, Greek, and Hebrew languages—
> came to discuss matters of faith, and discovered that infant bap-
> tism is unnecessary, also not known as a baptism. Thereupon the
> two—Conrad and Felix—believed and confessed that one must, ac-
> cording to Christian order, be baptized according to the words of
> Christ: he who believes and is baptized shall be saved. This led to
> disunity among the three, and Ulrich Zwingli did not wish this, but
> said that it would create a disturbance. But the two previously
> mentioned men held that one could not ignore God's command be-
> cause of that.

> Meanwhile it happened that a priest with the name of George,
> of the house of Jacob, who was called George Blaurock because he
> wore a blue coat, also came with a particular zeal he had towards
> God's will. He was held to be an ordinary and simple priest but

with a godly zeal in matters of faith, who through the grace of God which was given him acted in a strange manner. He came to Zwingli and talked to him about the faith, but achieved nothing. Thereupon he was told that there were others who had more zeal than Zwingli. These he sought out and came to them, namely, to Conrad and Felix, and talked with them and they became united in these things.

And it happened that they were together. After fear lay greatly upon them, they called upon God in heaven, that he should show mercy to them. Then George arose and asked Conrad for God's sake to baptize him; and this he did. After that, he baptized the others also. [Grebel or Blaurock? If Grebel, who baptized him?] After this, more priests and other people were added who soon sealed it with their blood. So also the above-named Felix Mantz, who was the first; he was drowned at Zürich. Wolfgang Uliman was burned at Waltzen with ten others including his brother, who was his companion. He was the seventh. After him a cleric named Hans Pretle [Johann Brötli] who was also our servant in the land. And thus it spread through persecution, as with Michael Sattler and many of his relatives. Thus also Melchior Veit, who was George Blaurock's companion, who was burned at Dracha.

Thus you have the facts about what happened at the beginning. Later many things happened, so that many ran disorderly. But the sure foundation of truth remained. The Lord knows his own. Let those who call upon the name of the Lord forsake unrighteousness. And so you have the account of the beginning concerning which you should have no doubt, for we have most surely experienced it.[4]

The action taken that evening was spontaneous under the deeply felt pressure of the presence of the Holy Spirit. There had been no advance calculation that "the way to make the break would be to baptize adults," and no strategic weighing of whether this was the right time to make the break. The significance of this act lay not so much in the proper practice of baptism itself, as in the creation of a new, visible church body distinct from the established church controlled by the state, as was true of the all-inclusive establishment of medieval Catholicism. Thus the prayer meeting and events of January 21 came to be the formal beginning of Anabaptism as a visible believers' church with emphases distinct from both Roman Catholicism and emerging Protestantism.

Chapter 3

Persecution and Consolidation

THE JANUARY 21 meeting which led to the first baptism had already taken place under the threat of persecution. Members of this group were soon called Anabaptists or *re-baptizers*, though they themselves preferred simply to be called *brethren*. Instead of trying to resist the decree of the council against them, the Brethren now made plans for sharing their newfound convictions with others. The first church meeting was a missionary meeting. Each of those persons who had to leave the city of Zurich returned to some place where they were known and could expect people to listen to them. For some, especially the tradesmen, this meant going northeast to St. Gall, northwest to Basel, or southwest to Bern—cities in which the stirrings of the Reformation had already begun to be felt. For others it meant taking refuge in rural areas where the repressive measures of the city government would be enforced less severely. Thus Hans Brötli and Wilhelm Reublin went northward into the area between Zurich, Waldshut, and Schaffhausen. Others went eastward into Appenzell, and west into the area ruled jointly by Zurich and Bern and, therefore, not rigidly controlled by either. In the course of the spring and summer of 1525 small groups of sympathizers were established in most of these places.

Hubmaier at Waldshut

Situated on the north side of the Rhine, just 32 kilometers from Zurich, was the small town of Waldshut. It was an Austrian possession under the rule of the still solidly Catholic Holy Roman Empire. Its nearness to Schaffhausen and Zurich, however, had nevertheless brought it into close contact with religious developments in the Swiss cities. This contact was increased significantly by the arrival of Balthasar Hubmaier in Waldshut in 1521. As a south German priest and doctor of theology, he was well known for his popular preaching in Regensburg and his service at the University of Ingolstadt. While he showed no special sympathies for the young Reformation movement upon his arrival, he soon became a close friend and co-worker of Ulrich Zwingli in Zurich. In 1523 his sympathies for the Reformation cause were so outspoken that Waldshut itself became suspect in the eyes of the Austrian government.

Though he considered Zwingli both his friend and colleague, Hubmaier was less his disciple and intellectually more independent than were the younger men in Zurich. Nevertheless, he shared Zwingli's low opinion of infant baptism in 1523-24, and his concern for a pure church order according to the Bible. He was left out of the late 1524 discussions in Zurich which led to the January 18, 1525, decision of the council and the baptismal meeting of the Brethren. Hubmaier considered himself a friend of Zwingli's, but rejected infant baptism. In the spring of 1525 Wilhelm Reublin, while preaching in the countryside east of Waldshut, also began to convince some members of Hubmaier's church in the city itself, and several received baptism. In the Easter season, Hubmaier and most of the members of his congregation were baptized upon their profession of faith. This was the first time that an organized church joined the Anabaptist cause. It was a political as well as a religious act. The Austrian authorities feared, perhaps with some reason, that Hubmaier and the city government might scheme to take Waldshut out of the Empire and annex it to the Swiss cantons. In any case, no Protestants or Anabaptists could be tolerated for the sake of political unity. Waldshut, however, was prepared to defend itself with the full support of most of its citizens, including Hubmaier.

In the following months Hubmaier produced a flood of literature on baptism and the church. Most of his pamphlets, however, were not printed until later. The first and most complete statement of early Anabaptism on the question of baptism, called *On the Christian Baptism of Believers*, was written by Hubmaier. It was written after Zwingli had refused to answer his letter inviting the reformer to a debate with Hubmaier on the subject. It is an analysis of the major biblical texts on baptism as taught and practiced by John the Baptist, by Christ, and by the apostles. He concluded that everywhere baptism followed only after some kind of preaching or instruction, and after faith in the message heard had been expressed. The book does not deal with rebaptism, since he considered the infant baptism of the Roman Catholic Church not to be baptism by biblical standards. The simplicity, clear biblical basis, and blunt statement of the case make this 68-page booklet a classic. In later writings Hubmaier further elaborated his conviction, drawing upon statements from church fathers and theologians of all ages to support his position. He answered the anti-Anabaptist writings of Zwingli and Oecolampadius, the state-church pastor in Basel, and drafted orders of worship in keeping with his vision of the committed, disciplined church of believers.

In December Waldshut was seized by the Austrian forces of the empire and recatholicized. Hubmaier managed to escape.

The Brethren in St. Gall

In these early days the cause of the Reformation in St. Gall was carried by two laymen: the weaver Hans Kessler and the humanist scholar and medical doctor Joachim von Watt (Vadian). Both of these men, though not theologians but self-educated in matters of faith, led in Bible studies and encouraged renewal in the absence of strong clerical leadership. Late in 1523 their movement was strengthened with the coming of Lorenz Hochrütiner, who had been banished from Zurich under the charge of having removed images from churches. The Bible reading movement in St. Gall had experienced tension even

From Zurich the Anabaptist movement spread into the neighboring canton of **Appenzell.** Our first martyr, Eberli Bolt, personally won more than 1500 members to the movement and for a few years the entire area was predominantly Anabaptist. By 1528 all of these had been captured or forced to flee to Moravia. The Zurich government instituted the death penalty for Anabaptist heresy in December 1526. First to die under the new law was Felix Mantz, drowned for his faith in **the Limmat at the Schipfge** on January 5, 1527.

before they heard of the first baptisms in Zurich. Whereas Watt and Kessler favored a slow evolution within the church, Hochrütiner and Wolfgang Uolimann were calling for a more radical rejection of all traditions, even refusing to use the church building which had been offered to them for Bible reading meetings by the city authorities.

It was, therefore, no surprise that a division took place in St. Gall when news of the Zurich baptisms reached the Bible reading group. For a time it seemed that the more aggressive Anabaptist party was the stronger. It had weighty friends, if not actual baptized members, on the city council. On Palm Sunday, 1525, Conrad Grebel himself was present when a group of persons numbering perhaps two hundred publicly paraded down to the Sitter River for a mass baptism.

The movement was even more successful in some of the rural areas surrounding St. Gall, especially in the small canton of Appenzell, where the villages had a high degree of autonomy. Here it was possible for a whole village, being both a political and ecclesiastical unit at the same time, to vote to expel a Roman Catholic priest or even a Zwinglian preacher, and replace him with an Anabaptist. There was certainly an element of political and economic interest involved in this development. Since Anabaptism was opposed to the legal requirements of the tithe and to the support of ministers through compulsory taxation, there were those who saw in the movement the possibility of economic relief and even revolutionary social changes favoring the peasants.

It was also for this reason that the developing sympathy for Anabaptism in St. Gall and Appenzell called forth such a strong reaction from the authorities. Hans Krüsi, the most active leader in the villages, was seized at night by the troops of the bishop of St. Gall and taken to Lucerne where he was executed. After a public debate the council of St. Gall imposed a fine on those who persisted in their Anabaptist commitment. The effect of these measures was that those whose enthusiasm had been superficial quickly returned to the official church, while the convictions of those who were committed to the movement became stronger. For decades the Anabaptists of St. Gall were marked by an especially radical emphasis. It is reported that some of them refused to use medicine when the city was struck by a plague in 1530. They were also stricter about Christian simplicity of dress and about nonresistance than were other Anabaptists. Still others, especially among those who had first belonged to the movement and then withdrawn from it under pressure, seem to have justified various kinds of misbehavior on religious grounds. They either claimed that the true believer was free from the law, or that they had received special visions and revelations.

Suffering Comes to the Believers

We have seen that persecution began even before the first baptism since the threat of banishment was announced January 18, 1525. The first imprisonment of Anabaptists in Zurich was in early February. Prisons, fines, and sometimes torture were standard procedure for prisoners. Release from prison came only when the prisoner would promise to forsake the Anabaptist meetings. By March 1526 life imprisonment sentences were being imposed. Wherever Anabaptism became known similar measures were initiated.

The first death penalties were inflicted on Anabaptists by the governments of Roman Catholic cantons, who executed them simply as Protestants, rather than specifically as Anabaptists. Thus Hippolytus (popularly called Bolt) Eberle, who had apparently joined the fellowship at St. Gall in April or May 1525, was executed just a few weeks later in his home canton of Schwyz. He is also known as the first Protestant martyr, since the authorities of the canton did not distinguish between Protestant and Anabaptist heresy. The first death penalty at the hands of a Protestant government was the drowning of Felix Mantz in the Limmat River in Zurich on January 5, 1527. The official grounds for these extreme measures included more than the simple offense of baptizing, being baptized, or attending Anabaptist meetings. The authorities held that the real reason for execution was either sedition, i.e., a refusal to obey the government injunction not to baptize, or perjury, i.e., returning to Anabaptism after having promised to forsake it. Thus a religious offense was transformed into a civil one.

By early 1527 the Zurich Anabaptist movement was severely threatened with disintegration. Of the original leadership circle, Conrad Grebel had died of illness, and Felix Mantz had been executed. George Blaurock had escaped execution only because he was not a citizen of Zurich, and was not able to return. Other leaders were widely scattered, facing dangers and problems for which they were not prepared. Under the mounting pressure of persecution the movement was threatened on two sides from within. On the one hand was a widening circle of those who were sympathetic with the Anabaptist message, especially its criticism of the abuses in the established churches, but who excused themselves from the high cost of full and open identification with the movement. Perhaps this caution was covered with an argument to the effect that true faith is spiritual and not bound by outward forms. Thus they could give inner assent to Anabaptist teaching without suffering for it. On the other side were those whom the pressure of persecution and religious enthusiasm could push into emotional moral excesses in the name of special revelation or heroic faithfulness.

Consolidation

It was in response to these needs that a group of Anabaptist leaders met in the village of Schleitheim near the Swiss-German border later in February of 1527. We cannot tell how the meeting was called nor how long it continued. Tradition tells us that Michael Sattler was the author of its conclusions. George Blaurock could have been there. We may assume that Wilhelm Reublin, who was working closely with Sattler at that time, attended. But little as we know of the organization and attendance, it is still no exaggeration to say that it was this meeting, and the conclusions which it reached, which fixed the identity and saved the life of the young movement. The meeting provided continuity with the legacy of Grebel, Mantz, and Hubmaier, but a new dimension was also added through Sattler, who came fresh out of the Freiburg Benedictine monastery and its support of peasant grievances against church and state.

This was not a representative meeting to which delegates

came each to vote for the position of their supporters, and whose conclusions represented a minimum to which they could all agree without changing their minds. The persons who gathered at Schleitheim came together in disagreement and confusion, testifying later that during the meeting the Holy Spirit had led them to agreement and common convictions.[1]

> ... we ... make known ... unto all that love God, that ... we have been united ... and (the praise and glory be to God alone) uncontradicted by all the brothers, completely at peace. Herein we have sensed the unity of the Father and of our common Christ as present with us in their Spirit. For the Lord is a Lord of peace and not of quarreling....

The first result of this common conviction was the recognition that the Anabaptists were not in spiritual unity with those who had a different understanding of "spiritual liberty." To some at that time "spiritual liberty" meant the freedom of fanaticism and licentiousness; to others the freedom of the conformists to continue in the state church with its sacraments, civil oaths, and the bearing of arms. In their meeting at Schleitheim the Brethren rejected both of these alternatives:

> A very great offense has been introduced by some false brothers among us, whereby several have turned away from the faith, thinking to practice and observe the freedom of the Spirit and of Christ. But such have fallen short of the truth and (to their own condemnation) are given over to the lasciviousness and license of the flesh. They have esteemed that faith and love may do and permit everything and that nothing can harm nor condemn them, since they are "believers."
>
> Note well, you members of God in Christ Jesus, that faith in the heavenly Father through Jesus Christ is not thus formed....

In the first three articles substantial agreement was recorded on the meaning of church membership, being defined in their understanding of baptism, the ban, and the Lord's Supper. *Baptism* is only for those who

> have been taught repentance and the amendment of life and [who] believe truly that their sins are taken away through

Christ, and to all those who desire to walk in the resurrection of
Jesus Christ and be buried with Him in death, so that they might
rise with Him; to all those who with such an understanding
themselves desire and request it from us....

Obviously no child could "walk in the resurrection," but only
those who had counted the cost. And these had to take the initiative in asking for baptism. Baptism was a covenant not only
with God, but also with the congregation, whereby the members
pledged to help each other in the life of obedience through admonition and, if necessary, the *ban*. The *Lord's Supper* was to be a
celebration only of those who were in full unity with the fellowship: "Whoever had not been called by one God to one faith, to
one baptism, to one Spirit, to one body, with all the children of
God's church cannot be made one bread with them...."

The fourth article defined the principle of separation from
the world of darkness and unbelief in specific terms appropriate
to the situation:

... everything which has not been united with our God in Christ is
nothing but an abomination which we should shun. By this are
meant all popish and repopish works and idolatry, gatherings,
church attendance, winehouses, guarantees and commitments of
unbelief, and other things of the kind, which the world regards
highly, and yet which are carnal or flatly counter to the command
of God....

The fifth article provided for local church leadership more
clearly than had been done before by stating that "the shepherd
in the church of God shall be someone according to the rule of
Paul, who has a completely good testimony among those outside
the faith." The faithful are encouraged to support the shepherd
according to his need, and if he is taken from them, either
through persecution or through being sent on a missionary
assignment, he is to be replaced immediately: "Should this
shepherd be driven away or taken home to the Lord through the
cross, that very hour another shall be ordained in his place...."

In the last two articles of agreement, the relation of a Christian to the state is dealt with through a discussion of "the sword"

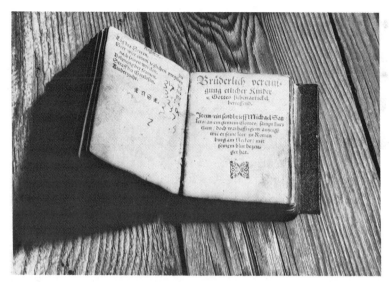

In response to violent opposition from without and differences of opinion from within, the Swiss Brethren met at Schleitheim in February 1527 to draw up the seven articles of the **Brotherly Agreement.**

and the swearing of oaths. Both articles are longer than the preceding five and enter into considerable detail of argument. The special emphasis given to these themes likely indicates both that they were subjects concerning which Anabaptists were especially criticized and threatened by the official churches, and that they were issues concerning which it was less clear to some of the members what position they should really take and how to explain it. The argument is based on a radical simplicity in following the words and example of Jesus, but this simplicity does not avoid the challenge of detailed argument with the opposing positions. It became clear that those who belong to Christ can neither resort to violence to achieve their objectives, nor swear by the name of God to confirm their own good intentions.

The Schleitheim meeting saved the Anabaptist movement in at least two ways. The very fact that this meeting took place successfully and was able to define the position against both conformists and fanatics made of Anabaptism an organized body able to meet its problems and survive instead of degenerating into a mere flurry of radical enthusiasm. On the level of doctrine, the position defined here was simple, biblical, complete, and consistent enough that a simple Christian could understand it, testify to it, and suffer for it. The seven articles of agreement are sometimes referred to as the *Schleitheim Confession of Faith* (1527), the first such confession among the Anabaptists. It is closer to the intention of those who were present, however, to call it a *brotherly understanding* as they themselves did.

As indicated earlier, it is believed that Michael Sattler was the primary drafter of this statement of the faith. Soon after the meeting he was arrested together with thirteen other Anabaptists, and subjected to a merciless interrogation and tortured. When he was given the possibility of hiring an attorney to aid in his defense, he declined on the ground that this was not a legal matter but simply a defense of the faith which he, as a believer, must always be ready and willing to do himself. Nine charges were filed against him, including the charge that "he has forsaken the [Benedictine] order and has married a wife," as well as the charge that he intended to overthrow both the Roman Catholic Church and the civil order. Sattler responded briefly to each of these charges, concluding with the statement:

> Therefore, you servants of God, in case you might not have heard or read the Word of God, would you send for the most learned [men] and for the godly books of the Bible, in whatever they might be, and let them discuss the same with us in the Word of God. If they show us with Holy Scripture that we are in error and wrong, we will gladly retract and recant, and will gladly suffer condemnation and the punishment for our offense. But if we cannot be proved in error, I hope to God that you will repent and let yourselves be taught.

The response given by the authorities was that the "hangman will debate with you," and the sentence of death was confirmed.

Because of his great popularity with the people, a heavy guard had to be set around the prison to prevent a revolt in his behalf. On the day of execution his tongue was cut out, he was torn seven times with red-hot irons, and eventually burned. We know very little about Sattler's wife. However, his close companion Wilhelm Reublin wrote:

> On Wednesday Michael's wife was taken out on the waters of the Neckar. She could not be turned away from her faith by any human grace or words. In great joy and strong faith she accepted and suffered death. God be praised! Thus she was drowned.

Heinrich Hug, one of the chroniclers of these events, concluded his account with the words, "It was a miserable affair, they died for their conviction." Four others were executed with the sword, but the agony of those days is seen in even sharper focus with Reublin's further report that:

> The other women and men all recanted at Rottenburg and abjured with two fingers laid in a Bible, and swore an oath: that the blood and flesh of Jesus Christ are in the sacrament of the altar, etc., further that infant baptism is right, etc. And that they hold and believe what the Roman church has established, and that it is correct. . . .

In one sense these developments were a fulfillment of the early Zwinglian vision, but they went further. While Anabaptism was forced into separation by persecution, the Schleitheim articles provided the necessary justification for separatism. The expectations of church and state could not be brought into harmony with the new identity emerging as Anabaptist. The events in South Germany and the Netherlands would further reinforce this separation.

Chapter 4

Central German and Moravian Anabaptism

THE PEOPLE of Europe were excited beyond self-control by the burning issues of the Reformation. Anabaptism was born and bred in that atmosphere, and shared in it. As Anabaptist ideas spread among the German- and Dutch-speaking people of Europe, they were developed by a variety of leaders and took a variety of forms. Anabaptism was not one united movement. It now becomes our task to examine several of the new leaders who arrived on the scene somewhat independent of each other and added their own characteristic touch to the work of the Spirit in the lives of the people of Europe.

One of the most kindly spirits among the early Anabaptist leaders was Hans Denk (d. 1527). Born in Bavaria and educated at the University of Ingolstadt, he applied his humanist training to the work of editing and proofreading in two of the better presses in Basel. Here he became a friend of the reformer Johannes Oecolampadius. Here too he must have absorbed some of the fresh Reformation teaching. Upon the recommendation of Oecolampadius, the city of Nürnberg engaged Denk as principal of its St. Sebald school in September of 1523.

Nürnberg witnessed its share of religious controversy during the course of the next year, and Denk became thoroughly involved in it. Both Müntzer and Carlstadt, who were becoming increasingly dissatisfied with the Lutheran Reformation, visited the town and left pamphlets to be printed there. The Lutheran pastor, who was trying to introduce the Reformation gradually, was disturbed by the growing radicalism. At his urging the city council asked three suspect artists to appear before it in defense of their view of the Lord's Supper. It was believed that they denied the official church teaching of the real, physical presence of the body and blood of Christ in the bread and wine of the Supper. In January 1525, Denk himself was called before the city council because he had associated with one of the artists. The town fathers were especially eager to make certain that the schoolmaster did not dabble in heresy. In a series of meetings throughout the month Denk's views on a variety of religious topics were examined by the council. It seemed to the town fathers that Denk was hedging in his responses to their questions and unwilling to give a clear and direct answer. Their suspicions seemed confirmed in his reply to their question about the Lord's Supper. While not denying directly the physical presence of Christ in the bread and wine, he stressed that the primary question was really whether the person who ate the bread and drank the wine had a living, personal faith. This answer was obviously not satisfactory and on January 21, 1525—the day on which the first baptism occurred in Zurich—Denk was banished from the city for life, threatened with death if he came within fifteen kilometers of the city limits. His property was confiscated, the council said, to provide for his wife and children.

Denk spent most of the year 1525 wandering around Germany. He may have been in Mühlhausen with Müntzer, and he visited with the Swiss Brethren and the Zwinglians in St. Gall. In the autumn of the year he turned his steps to Augsburg where he was able to secure a teaching position again. Within a year, however, the Lutheran pastor there began to attack Denk's religious views and, being unable to reach agreement with him in a series of meetings, Denk abruptly left town in November 1526. It may be that during his Augsburg residence he had been persuaded by Balthasar Hubmaier to accept believer's baptism. There is no evidence that he formed an Anabaptist congregation, but he was undoubtedly responsible for the development of interest in Anabaptism on the part of many. A congregation was established in Augsburg after he left. Among his Augsburg activities was also the baptism of that most vigorous of Anabaptist missioners, Hans Hut.

From Augsburg Denk went to Strassburg, a city with more religious freedom than existed elsewhere, and one in which a number of Anabaptists found refuge from persecutions. Within a month, however, he was deeply involved in religious arguments, not only with Capito and Bucer, the leaders of the Reformation there, but also with Michael Sattler. On Christmas Day, 1526, he left Strassburg to wander down the Rhine, discussing his faith with the local Lutheran pastors in the towns to which he came and, when possible, speaking to the people also. He even tried to convert some Jews, but without success. By February 1527 he was in Worms, where he joined Ludwig Hätzer in producing a German translation of the Old Testament prophets. At the same time he was so busy discussing his faith with others that the leaders of the Reformation in both Strassburg and Basel became alarmed. Consequently the Elector of the Palatinate took firm measures against the Worms radicals, and Denk was on the march again.

In August of 1527 he returned to Augsburg where the Anabaptist congregation had meanwhile become established. Here he met with Hans Hut, whom he had baptized earlier, and possibly several others in religious discussion. This meeting has sometimes been called the *Martyrs' Synod* because some of its members met their death soon afterward. Discussion apparently centered around the role of the "last times" in their evangelistic preaching. Hut agreed not to give undue emphasis in his missionary preaching to the early return of Christ and to the last judgment, both truths in which he believed devoutly. In September Denk was in Ulm, and from there he went to Basel. He was weary beyond measure with the life of a fugitive, and wrote to the Basel reformer Oecolampadius begging for permission to settle in that city. Oecolampadius wanted some form of written word from Denk that would indicate a renunciation of his Anabaptist views, and Denk provided a statement of belief which Oecolampadius published two years later. But it was not a recantation, as the reformer claimed it to be. Denk had not changed his basic position. He had been pained by the sharpness of disagreement between the major reformers and the Anabaptists and wanted to find some way of reconciliation. He remained in Basel until his death from the plague in November.

In his faith, Denk was influenced by medieval mysticism, which he got in part from the anonymous book known as the *German Theology* and in part from Müntzer and Carlstadt. Because of this he believed that God reveals Himself to the inner man in a reflective, nonrational way, as well as in the Scriptures. He disliked the Lutheran reliance on Scripture alone as revelation because Scripture by itself, unaided by the Spirit, leads to a dead legalism. The reader of Scripture, Denk believed, needs the presence of that same Spirit who inspired its authors in order to understand it. It is likely that this was also the reason for his disagreement with the Swiss Anabaptists. Denk was primarily interested in the inner life, life in the Spirit.

Denk also was overwhelmed by the love of God. He praised this love of God so much, wrote a critic in 1525, that he seemed to suggest that all men, even the devil himself, would eventually be saved. Whether he actually taught that the love of God would save all men, regardless of their sin and unbelief, cannot be determined from his writings, but it is clear that the love of God forms the very core of his faith.

He was attracted to Anabaptism by the emphasis on discipleship. "No one may truly know Christ," he said, "except one follows Him in life." He deplored the absence of moral improvement in the lives of most of the new Protestants. This emphasis on moral living led him to join Anabaptism, but he had difficulty fitting into their church life. Dogmatic statements and emphasis upon minor details of the faith distressed him. He was a man born in the wrong century. The early sixteenth century could not tolerate dissent and delighted in dogmatic statements of a most binding and restrictive sort. Because he could not bring himself to agree with statements of dogma, he was accused by the reformers, and one suspects also by the Anabaptists, of hedging, of never committing himself.

Hans Hut

Of all the traveling missioners who visited south Germany and Austria, Hans Hut stands out because of his wide influence. Hut was born and raised in southern Thuringia. For a time he served as sexton in the village of Bibra but soon developed a trade in books to supplement his income as a bookbinder. The pursuit of this trade took him to many parts of Germany, where he became familiar with Lutheran doctrine and promoted it after a fashion through the sale of tracts and pamphlets. But he also encountered more radical ideas. At his trial in 1527 he said that he had first heard attacks against the practice of infant baptism from three men whom he met in his travels. Stirred by this encounter, he studied the Scriptures on the issue and even consulted the Lutheran theologians during one of his trips to Wittenberg, but he remained dissatisfied with the practice. Indeed, he refused to have his newborn child baptized, sometime early in 1524. When the lords of Bibra heard of this they ordered a public debate, the result of which was that those who did not accept infant baptism were told to leave the region.

This event was a turning point in Hut's life. Leaving Bibra with his wife and five children, he began a life of wandering which ended only with his capture and death in Augsburg in 1527. He appeared at the Battle of Frankenhausen which crushed the Peasants' Revolt, in 1525, after having heard some of Müntzer's sermons to the peasants. Though he was captured first by the peasants and then by the lords, he was released unharmed. Müntzer perished after the battle, but his vision of the imminent return of the Lord made a profound impression on Hut. For over a year he wandered about Germany, preaching on baptism, the Lord's Supper, and the end times until he came to Augsburg in May 1526. Here Hans Denk and a friend talked to him about the earnest Christian lives of those who had received believer's baptism. After lengthy persuasion, he accepted baptism himself at the hands of Denk on May 26.

For the remainder of his short life Hut went from village to town in Franconia, Bavaria, Austria, and Moravia, preaching and baptizing. On coming to a town he would begin speaking in any available place with the words, "Go into all the world and preach the gospel to the whole creation. He who believes and is baptized will be saved" [Mk. 16:15, 16] and this is the baptism—to endure anxiety, want, sorrow, and all tribulations in patience." He preached wherever people were—in isolated farmhouses, or in forests, or in homes of workers in the towns. His fiery sermons made an appeal in part because they conveyed his own burning conviction of the imminent destruction of Europe at the hands of the Turks. His critics said he was actually preaching revolution, but he denied this at his trial. He won many to the Anabaptist movement; one historian has declared that he won more converts during the two years of his ministry than all of the other Anabaptist missioners together.

Hut was captured in Augsburg in August 1527, tried, tortured severely, and killed accidentally in his cell. Some claimed that he tried to escape by lighting a fire in his cell intending to call it to the attention of the guards and grab their keys, but that he became asphyxiated in the process. His son declared that a lighted candle, placed by his pallet of straw by the guards when they brought him back unconscious from torture, ignited the straw and killed him. In any event his corpse was carried to the judgment hall and tied to the executioner's cart. The dead body was sentenced to death by burning, and was recommitted to the flames on December 7.

Hut's teaching had several characteristic features which set it off from that of the Swiss Brethren. In the first place, he was much more fascinated with Christ's second coming than they were. He was reported to have specified the exact time of Christ's visitation to be during Pentecost of 1528. Some even said he had counseled his listeners to prepare to destroy the godless after a dramatic battle in which the Turks would crush the flower of European chivalry near Nürnberg. Hut denied these charges, and we have seen that Denk helped him to modify his emphasis on the second coming when they met in Augsburg in 1526. Hut was not the only preacher of Reformation times who stressed the second coming of Christ. Many devout people in those days believed that God was about to bring an end to human history with a decisive act of His own.

A second distinctive feature of Hut's teaching, as found

especially in the writings and court testimonies of some of his followers, was his mysticism. This mysticism, which he learned from Müntzer and the late medieval mystics, is found in an emphasis on personal suffering as the mark of the Christian who truly follows Christ. The Christian must suffer as Christ suffered, and this suffering becomes, in part, a means whereby the Christian is saved from the hell of this world. It is to the last part that the Swiss Brethren would have objected. No Anabaptist denied the fact of suffering for the true Christian, but some would deny that suffering played a role in salvation. By suffering, moreover, Hut did not mean only physical suffering but also mental anguish over sin and separation from God.

A third distinctive feature of Hut's teaching was the emphasis on the sharing of material goods. There ran through his messages, at least as his listeners interpreted them, a note of rebuke to the owner of material goods who did not share these goods in the freest manner with others. He made the sharing of goods more central than some Anabaptists did.

Central German Anabaptism

Anabaptism in Central Germany began with the evangelizing work of Hut. Hut preached and baptized in his native Thuringia in 1526, but he also founded a congregation in the city of Königsberg. When the authorities discovered this movement, some of the new members were executed in February 1527, while others managed to escape with Hut to Austria and beyond. Some also fled north, so that despite persecution, a flourishing movement arose within three years in both Saxony and Hesse. The most vigorous Anabaptist congregation, which furnished leadership and inspiration to the movement elsewhere and thus became a center, was in the small village of Sorga, a few miles east of the town of Hersfeld. Here Melchior Rink was the acknowledged leader and inspiration of the movement.

Rink appeared as a chaplain at Hersfeld in 1523. He and a colleague developed an interest in Reformation teachings, and they began to preach them openly; their sermons included denunciations of the sins of the local Franciscan monks. The anger of the monks and the rebellious, unsettled mood of those people

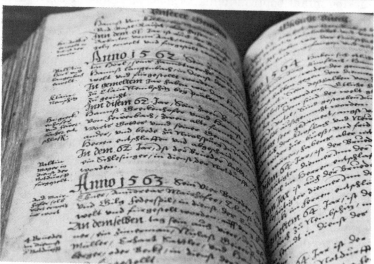

The St. Sebald church and school in Nürnberg. Hans Denk was rector of the school until his expulsion from the city in 1525. **Balthasar Hubmaier,** a Catholic priest from Waldshut on the Rhine, and most of his congregation joined the Anabaptists at Eastertime 1525. Hubmaier died a martyr three years later. The **Grossgeschichtsbuch** (Great Chronicle) of the Hutterites is a major source of our early history. The handwritten original is found in South Dakota.

who heard Rink and his colleague prompted the political authorities to expel both of them. Rink found a pastorate in a village south of Eisenach, aided and probably supervised by Jacob Strauss, a Reformation leader with generally Lutheran inclinations. Strauss influenced Rink toward a more radical position on baptism, including rejection of infant baptism, on Christian communal attitudes on material wealth, and on the prominent role of the congregation in basic church polity. In all of these matters Strauss, and Rink after him, took sharp issue with the Lutheran theologians. In effect Strauss launched Rink on his radical Reformation career. Rink was also influenced by Müntzer and, like Hut, followed him into the Peasants' War in 1525, emerging unscathed in body but changed in spirit. He fled south to the Palatinate, where he met Denk and came under his influence.

By 1528 Rink was back in the neighborhood of Hersfeld, attacking infant baptism in his sermons and winning converts to the Anabaptist cause. Hearing of his activities Landgrave Philip of Hesse summoned him to give an account for preaching the Anabaptist doctrines which had been expressly forbidden by law. Philip gave Rink three choices: to renounce his views publicly, to leave the area, or to submit to a theological examination by the theological faculty of the University of Marburg. Rink chose the latter and was, as expected, found guilty but refused to go into exile as commanded. Consequently he was arrested in 1529 and imprisoned for two years, released in 1531, rearrested in November of that year, and finally sentenced to life imprisonment. He died in prison near the scene of his labors, sometime in the 1550s.

Others succeeded Rink as leaders in Central Germany, including Fritz Erbe, whose imprisonment for sixteen years became a symbol of Lutheran persecution and Anabaptist patience in suffering. No one, however, had the same fiery zeal for believer's baptism that Rink had shown and by the 1540s continuing persecution, flight, and recantations led to a sharp decline in the movement in this area.

To the west of Rink's center at Sorga, within the heart of Landgrave Philip's land, Hesse, a flourishing movement of

Anabaptists was to be found in the 1530s. Able leaders came up the Rhine from the north and courageous missioners from the Moravian Anabaptists, later called Hutterites, visited them. When persecution became too severe some, in turn, went to Moravia. Philip preferred exile to execution as punishment for the Anabaptists, arguing that if all heretics were to be killed he would need to include Jews and Catholics also. Most of the contemporary princes in Germany thought him too mild in his treatment of the Anabaptists, and the movement in Hesse was indeed vigorous. When a group of them, perhaps as many as twelve, were jailed at one place for well over a year, they were able to make a hole in the wall large enough to escape, but most of them remained in order not to alarm the authorities. Those who were at large did not flee, but continued their evangelizing, one of them converting and baptizing thirty persons while he was supposedly in jail.

But for all their zeal, the Hessian Anabaptist leaders who were linked more to the Melchiorites of the north than to the Central German movement, finally gave up and returned to the state (Lutheran) church. In 1538 Philip arranged for a debate between four of them and Martin Bucer, the reformer of Strassburg. Bucer persuaded them that the evil of separation from the one body of Christ, the true church, was greater than the evil of immoral living among the people in the state church. But they had made their point that the Christian must lead a clean and pure life. As a result the state church in Hesse decided to excommunicate those people who did not live morally as Christians should, a victory of sorts for the former Anabaptists.

The Hutterian Brethren

Anabaptism spread from Switzerland and Bavaria into the Austrian lands and the Tirol. Late in 1527 Leonhard Schiemer and Hans Schlaffer were spreading Anabaptist doctrine in the Inn Valley, where Schiemer was caught and executed in January 1528. Both missioners reflected the teachings and evangelical zeal of Hans Hut, by whom they had been baptized and instructed. These men and others worked from Rattenberg and Schwaz east into Upper and Lower Austria, and south into the

Tirol. Blaurock of the Zurich circle baptized converts and established congregations south of the Brenner Pass in the Tirol. It was in this region that he was finally caught, tortured, and burned at the stake in September 1529. Other Anabaptist leaders were Georg Zaunring and eventually Jacob Hutter.

The Austrian authorities were especially harsh in their treatment of Anabaptists. Within the old Austrian holdings the Archduke Ferdinand held a firmer control over his feudal noble-vassals than in the Tirol. But in all regions he struck at the Anabaptists with fury, issuing mandates to the local authorities to ferret them out and destroy them. He appointed special officials to judge those who were caught. He organized bands of *Täuferjäger*, Anabaptist hunters, whose task it was to find them among the people. The punishment was always the same: death. Even the Anabaptist who recanted under torture was to be killed, though the form of his execution was the more merciful beheading rather than the crueler burning.

It was this severity of persecution that gave rise to a flow of refugees into Moravia, which became a promised land for the Anabaptists in the early decades of the movement. Moravia also came under the political control of Ferdinand, in 1526, but the Moravian nobles had a tradition of relative freedom from control by their political overlord. Thus they were not inclined to look with favor on Ferdinand's attempts to bring them under his control on the Anabaptist question or on any other issue. Ferdinand was able to enforce his will in Anabaptist matters in Moravia only very slowly. And for a period of several decades it became a haven in Europe for the persecuted flocks. Austrian refugees fleeing to Moravia made up a large share of the Hutterite communities after the early 1530s.

Hubmaier was one of these refugees who welcomed the relative peace and quiet of the Moravian lands. After unhappy experiences with Zwingli and the other Zurichers, including imprisonment and a forced recantation, he was only too happy to settle down in Nicolsburg, where we find him early in the summer of 1526. There the lords of Liechtenstein, particularly Leonhard, gave protection to the Anabaptists. Nicolsburg had a Lutheran congregation among its German-speaking people and with the aid of the refugees, Hubmaier set himself to the task of converting it into an Anabaptist one. Most of the Anabaptists tried by the courts in Tirol in 1528 and 1529 indicated that they either had been baptized in Nicolsburg or had lived there for some period of time. By late spring of 1527 Nicolsburg was a major center, numbering perhaps as many as 12,000 Anabaptists.

At this juncture the fiery evangelist Hans Hut entered the town. Even before his coming the Anabaptists had grown restless with conflicting opinions on several major issues including the Christian's attitude toward the use of force in political affairs. Hut helped to bring the issues to a head. One of the most pressing issues was that of the war tax. It was brought on by the somewhat feverish preparations of the Austrian political leaders and some Germans to fight the Turks. Should a Christian pay war tax? Hubmaier had always sided with the major reformers on letting the state regulate religious affairs. Consequently he was interested in winning political leaders to his cause in whose lands he and his fellow Anabaptists could find refuge. When those political rulers faced the necessity of levying a war tax, it naturally had to be paid. Hut was far less willing than Hubmaier to support political rulers in any shape or form, but especially when they asked for money to outfit their armies against the Turks. Hut believed that the Turks were being used by God to destroy the political rulers of Europe. Of course the Christian could not pay war tax.

There were other, more important, issues in this Nicolsburg Disputation of May 1527. Hubmaier countered Hut's view of special divine revelations in visions or dreams, as against the more sober view of revelation by Scripture alone. Hubmaier also rejected Hut's prediction on the imminent second coming of Christ; apparently Denk and others had not been successful in inducing Hut to cease promoting his views. Hubmaier did not dispute what seemed to him the fact of the return of Christ, relatively soon; he merely had a different set of calculations on the time of that return. Hut challenged Hubmaier's interpretation of the role of the Christian magistrate in the work of the Lord in view of Christ's imminent return. Hut also joined the band, made up largely of refugees who insisted on a radical sharing of material goods in the form of Christian communalism. No one owned private property in their group. On the other hand, Hubmaier, with his noble backing, felt that the lords of Liechtenstein were generous enough in providing a place of refuge for the Anabaptists without going to the extreme of renouncing title to all their lands and property, if those lords became Anabaptists. Finally, Hut's special form of nonresistance to the Turkish menace (not a biblicist pacifism, it should be noted again) seemed dangerously irresponsible to Leonhard von Liechtenstein, who thereupon imprisoned him. The imprisonment, as well as various brief accounts about the Disputation, tell us that the issues on which there was disagreement were numerous, and that the Disputation itself was acrimonious. A friend helped Hut to escape. But the community remained divided into those who came to be called *Schwertler* (sword-bearers) and the *Stäbler* (staff bearers).

Neither of the two opponents lived long after the debate. Hut was caught in Augsburg in August and died the following December. Hubmaier was arrested a few months after the debate, and his noble protectors proved either unwilling or unable to defend him. Archduke Ferdinand of Austria had been elected margrave of Moravia in October 1526, after the former margrave, Louis of Hungary, had been killed in the war against the Turks at Mohacs. Ferdinand was as determined to repress the Anabaptists in his newly acquired territory as he was in his hereditary Austrian lands. He demanded the life of Hubmaier, against whom he had an old grudge: Hubmaier had been one of the leaders of the revolt of Waldshut against the Austrian overlord. The circumstances of Hubmaier's capture are not known. For the last several months in 1527 until March 1528, Hubmaier was held prisoner in the Kreuzenstein castle. He went through a series of trials or examinations, with the customary use of torture. He also carried on a lengthy conversation with at least one Catholic theologian, an old university colleague and friend, Johannes Faber. Hubmaier could give more ground to a Catholic than most Anabaptists could, on such issues as the authority of the state and the place of works within salvation, but he could not reach agreement with Faber on believer's baptism and on the nature of the Lord's Supper. He decided, therefore, to write an account of his faith to be presented to Ferdinand in an attempt to gain mercy from the archduke and composed his *Rechenschaft seines Glaubens*, but mercy was not granted. He was condemned to death both for heresy and for treason and burned at the stake on March 10, 1528, before a large crowd of people. The executioner rubbed gunpower into his hair and beard as an act of mercy: it would explode and bring quick death. His wife, who faithfully urged him to keep up his courage, showed her own faith and courage when she refused to recant and was drowned a few days later.

With the death of their spiritual leader the *Schwertler* group faded away. Not so the *Stäbler*. Before the Nicolsburg Disputation a number of them had withdrawn from fellowship with the former. Now, in the spring of 1528, Leonhard of Liechtenstein felt he could no longer tolerate religious differences among them and ordered those *Stäbler* who had broken fellowship with the others to leave. Approximately two hundred adults prepared to leave with their families. Outside of Nicolsburg they spread a coat on the ground and "everyone willingly laid his fortune down without compulsion or urging for the support of the needy."[1] They spent three weeks traveling to Austerlitz, where the lords of Kaunitz took them in and gave them a place to live and work. Under their leaders Jacob Widemann and Philip Weber, they increased in number through the addition of refugees.

The years from 1529 to the coming of Jacob Hutter in 1533 were, nevertheless, difficult for this Austerlitz group. Frequent tensions arose because they had not yet developed a thoroughgoing Christian community of goods. The initial action at Nicolsburg had been aimed primarily at meeting an immediate need on the part of those who had nothing at all, but there had also been in it the eschatological urging spirit of Hans Hut. He had received a vision of dramatic events to occur in the spring of 1528 and some *Stäbler* consequently believed it useless to own any property after that time of Christ's return. While their first sharing had been to meet a specific need, they soon moved to sharing both the things they consumed and the work of production as a community. Eventually they were to move to where the community owned everything and gave each person his task to perform as well as his food, clothing, and housing.

In the fully developed idea of community of goods, from the mid 1530s to the present, the single most important factor was that of love for the brother. The Hutterites, as they were to be called, considered their expression of Christian love to be the only true one. There could be no Christian love among Christian brethren who did not renounce all of their private possessions and commit them wholly to the community of brethren; indeed, failure to join with the brethren in community of goods called into question, in the Hutterite mind, the reality of the individual's salvation. Their great leader of the mid-seventeenth century, Andreas Ehrenpeis, wrote: "If Christian love to the neighbor cannot achieve as much as community in things temporal, in assistance and counsel, then the blood of Christ does not cleanse a man from his sins."[2] The Hutterites also used an argument derived from the practice of the Lord's Supper. Just as the grain of wheat and the single grape each lost its own identity completely in the loaf of bread and the wine, so also each member must completely dissolve himself/herself within the larger unity of the community, indeed, without this complete disappearance of the individual, no unity that was uniquely Christian was possible at all. The Hutterites cut at the natural selfishness of the human being and demanded of each member a yieldedness of self, a surrender, which they called *Gelassenheit.* No true discipleship, following after Christ, was possible without it.

The problems which had arisen from a lack of experience in communal living were eventually solved under the vigorous leadership of Jacob Hutter. Hutter, which means hat-maker, came from the Tirol in 1529 to investigate the Moravian lands as a possible place of refuge for his fellow Anabaptists. Both he and a co-worker were favorably impressed by what they saw in Moravia, and soon sent group after group of Tirolean Anabaptists to that haven. Hutter himself remained in the Tirol to continue his evangelical work, but he was appealed to by the

Brethren in Moravia on several occasions to settle differences of opinion among them. The original Austerlitz group that practiced community of goods separated by 1530 from some of the unhappy ones moving to Auspitz. When Hutter returned to Moravia in 1530 to determine where the blame for this split lay, he found the Austerlitz leaders to be most at fault. In 1533 Hutter came to Auspitz, where continued frictions among leaders and mismanagement of the community resources compelled him to remain for two years. By 1535 the community's affairs were competently managed through his vigorous leadership, but several of the former leaders, dissatisfied with his decisions and probably jealous of his popularity with the majority of the members, left Auspitz for other regions.

In that year all the Anabaptists in Moravia faced renewed persecution under the prodding of Archduke Ferdinand of Austria. The communities centering at Auspitz, which had grown larger through the addition of countless refugees from the Tirol and elsewhere, were broken up; their inhabitants were reduced to wandering about under the open skies, and finally to settling in smaller groups on those estates whose lords were willing to wink at Ferdinand's commands. But in the meantime the brotherhood had insisted that Hutter leave them because the civil authorities placed such a high priority on the capture of this leader. He returned to the Tirol in the hopes that persecution would have declined there, but within a few months he and his wife were surprised at night in the home of a friend. Tried in December, he was publicly burned at the stake on February 25, 1536. The measure of his influence on the Brethren in Moravia is evidenced by their referring to themselves henceforth as the *Hutterische Brüder*, from which we derive the English name Hutterian Brethren.

The "Golden Period"

After Hutter's departure the Brethren were led by a succession of very able men, including Hans Amon, Peter Ridemann, Peter Walpot, and Klaus Braidl. The communities thrived, for precisely when the Anabaptists elsewhere in Europe faced fresh and vigorous efforts of the Catholic Counter-

Reformation, efforts aimed at complete suppression, the Brethren in Moravia were permitted a remarkable degree of freedom. From approximately 1555 to 1595 the Brethren flourished; they referred to a part of this period as their "Golden Period." They sent out a succession of missioners to many parts of Europe; most of these paid for their activities with their lives, but they did so with the courage that was in itself a most attractive feature of Anabaptism, helping to win converts. The Brethren added to their number, through converts and through an almost constant stream of refugees from other parts of Europe. New colonies were founded, both in Moravia and beyond the eastern borders into Slovakia, then a part of Hungary. Perhaps they had as many as one hundred communities, totaling from 20,000 to 30,000 members. This was also a period of vigorous literary activity. Braitmichel began the *Geschicht-Buch* (Chronicle) which his successors carried on down to 1665. The Brethren were careful to keep records of letters to and from the brotherhood and of tracts written by and against them. Their organizational skills, developed to the highest degree by the demands of the community life which they practiced, were apparent in the fact that they could organize original materials into a historical account far in advance of their own times in terms of the method used.

What was the organizational pattern of their colonies? The entire brotherhood was under the direction of one bishop *(Vorsteher)*. Each colony *(Bruderhof)*, then, had one or more preachers *(Diener des Wortes)* and several men who managed the economic affairs, including the farming *(Diener der Notdurft)*. Each colony consisted of a series of whitewashed houses grouped around a central courtyard. Here the members, numbering usually several hundred, lived and performed their various tasks, bound less by family ties than by ties of the entire colony. The continuous performance of the same kinds of tasks by the members developed in them an efficiency of operation that made their colonies so economically successful that neighboring peasants complained of unfair competition.

"It was like a big clockwork, where one wheel drives the other one, promotes, helps, and makes the whole clock function." Or "it is like a beehive where all the busy bees work together to a common end, the one doing this, the other that, not for their own need but for the good of all."[3]

Their very efficiency led to tales among the neighboring outsiders about their enormous wealth. Later monetary fines imposed on them by the civil authorities indicate that they were wealthy enough, but persecution and the rigor of their self-imposed discipline kept them from an economic and spiritual laxity which such comparative wealth often produces.

In the course of time the Brethren wrote a large number of rules and regulations, governing how they lived together and how they practiced certain crafts. The most famous of these was formulated in 1651 during the rule of Andreas Ehrenpreis; this *Gemeinde-Ordnungen* is still in use today. The Brethren excelled in the exercise of certain crafts: the making of ceramics, cutlery, carriages, certain kinds of beds, and clocks. Medicinal skills were developed to such an extent that Hutterite physicians and surgeons were sometimes called to the courts of nobles to practice their arts. Any income which a visiting brother gained from his outside employment was to be turned over to the community. Even the occasional coin found on the roadside was to go into this treasury.

Family life was not emphasized in the colony. The children left their parents for the communal nursery-kindergarten at the age of two or three. Here they were under the care of women attendants who devoted all their time to the supervision and training of the children. They were taught a proper cleanliness, how to pray, and how to conduct themselves. From the kindergarten they passed to the elementary school, arranged in what we could call a boarding-school fashion. Children from outside the colony, including some from the families of nobles, were accepted and trained in the Hutterite elementary schools. The quality of the education was high, as evidenced by the later writings of the schools' graduates. Penmanship and spelling were excellent, and knowledge of the Bible together with certain elements of logic used in debate was very high.

By the time the young adult reached his early twenties, he became a candidate for baptism. The ceremony itself was performed after he had undergone a period of instruction; it was based on the candidate's solemn promise to be faithful to God and to the brotherhood. Also while in the early twenties the young people married. Romance was not the basis for choice of marriage partners. The elders brought together all the unmarried people of both sexes and suggested two or three possible males to each girl, one of whom she had to choose. The wedding ceremony followed the assembly by a few days, allowing no time for courtship. Marriage was viewed as one of several human relations which God had commanded humans to enter. The Christian did so, as the Hutterites had it, reluctantly and with no thought for his own pleasure. Marriage was entered into because the Lord had commanded His children to marry in order to multiply.

Extermination

The relative peace of the "Golden Period" came to an end late in the 1590s and in the first decade of the seventeenth century. It was inevitable that persecution would break out against people whom most Europeans thought of as heretical. Cardinal Franz von Dietrichstein led the renewed persecution while, at the same time, keeping Balthasar Goller, a Hutterite physician, in his employ until the latter's death in 1619. A campaign of vilification was pressed against them by the Austrian government in the hope of winning popular support for further suppressive measures. In this campaign they were aided by two priests who knew them well and by two former Hutterites who were urged to show their orthodoxy by denouncing their former brethren. The comparative wealth of the Hutterite communities came under frequent attack, and financial demands for help against the Turks were pressed upon them. In 1605 the Turks plundered the Hutterite colonies and carried off not only material goods but also women and children. One Hutterite wandered in Turkish lands for three years trying to locate and ransom some of his fellow believers, but he had little success and died in the attempt. The events of the Turkish War from 1593 to

1606, and the persecution of their own Austrian government shook these Moravian communities to the core.

The Thirty Years' War (1618-48) was another calamity which struck them. With the Roman Catholic forces victorious in the early part of the war, pressure against the Hutterites became even more severe. In 1622 they were forced to retreat to their colonies in Slovakia, then under the rule of Hungary, with the loss of their land, buildings, and most of their possessions. With these migrations and the loss of spiritual leadership much of the earlier life went out of them. They lost the precision and orderliness of their group life and their self-discipline; the forces of disorder were too powerful for the moment. But in this hour of need another leader of exceptional ability arose to guide them: Andreas Ehrenpreis, who ruled as bishop from 1639 to his death in 1662. Ehrenpreis' greatest contributions were a fresh ordering of the organizational pattern and the direction of a spiritual renewal among them. During this period also began the practice of recording sermons that were preached which, together with the *Gemeinde-Ordnungen* of 1651, are much used today by the Hutterites in Canada and the United States.

After the death of Ehrenpreis a new decline set in. Late in the seventeenth century they abandoned their earlier form of communal living in favor of forms which gave a larger role to private property and initiative. They appealed to the Dutch Mennonites for financial help on several occasions and apparently received some. The internal decay and loss of discipline were too great, however, and in the eighteenth century most of the Hutterites surrendered to the arguments of the Catholic Jesuits coupled with the threat of force by the Austrian government. One of their colonies, far to the southeast in Transylvania, revived in spirit and in numbers by Lutherans who accepted the Hutterite position in the 1750s, decided to migrate eastward into the Ukraine in 1767. A few families from Slovakia followed them in 1782-83 under the leadership of Jacob Walter, but the remaining colonies in these regions turned Roman Catholic.

Despite the internal decay among the Hutterites, the Jesuits did not have an easy time converting them. Many tactics were used to this end. They sent the spiritual leaders among the males to monasteries, where most of them finally gave in. Catholic services were held in the colonies, and the remaining brothers and sisters were compelled by force to attend. Children were taken from the colonies and brought up by dedicated Catholics. For a time in the 1750s and 1760s the Hutterites became nominal Catholics, but met secretly to practice their old faith. By the late eighteenth century it appears that their resistance was completely overcome. They were given the nickname *Habaner* by the peasants, and their descendants still occupied some of the old Slovakian colonies at least until World War II. But the distinctive religious tradition and practice was lost in these regions; it was carried to the Ukraine, and from there again to Canada and the United States in the 1870s.

Chapter 5

Pilgram Marpeck and South German Anabaptism

THE RECORDS of the ancient imperial city of Strassburg on the Rhine reveal that on September 19, 1528, an Austrian civil engineer by the name of Pilgram Marpeck became a citizen of that city. He had come to Strassburg because his life was in danger in his ancestral home of Rattenberg, located in the beautiful valley of the Inn River in Austria. The events of his life leading up to September 1528 can be reconstructed from the sixteenth-century records of Rattenberg and neighboring cities, as well as from some comments Marpeck himself made several years later.

The date of his birth is not known, and the only fragment of information we have about his early life is that, as he himself tells us, he was raised by God-fearing parents in the Roman Catholic faith. To judge from his later social prominence and technical ability he must have enjoyed a good education, most likely in the Rattenberg Latin School. In the year 1520 he became a member of the miners' guild of Rattenberg and was occupied with transporting copper ore from the mines of the city of Kitzbühel, some miles to the east of Rattenberg. Several years later his name appears on the roster of the city council of Rattenberg. As a trusted civic official he was appointed to the post of mining magistrate. This involved legal jurisdiction over the extensive mining operations in the lower Inn Valley. His salary was 65 pounds with a three-pound allowance for the proper dress on official occasions.

Marpeck was moderately wealthy. He was able to make a large loan to the city in 1525, and is known to have owned several houses. He and his wife undertook to pay for the education of three orphan children, which reflects his wealth as well as his sense of social responsibility. Because of his wealth and social standing Marpeck moved freely in the circles of the nobility. His lifelong friendship with Countess Helene von Freyberg, whose castle was near Kitzbühel, reflected this.

Life apparently flowed along pleasantly for the Marpecks for several years after 1525. Pilgram was a member of the inner council of the city, business was thriving, and it appeared that the Marpeck tradition of social standing and responsibility would continue. But it was not to be. The next entry in the Rattenberg records announces that Pilgram Marpeck had been dismissed from his office as mining magistrate but without stating a reason. It was most likely because, as a public official, he refused to aid in the detection and capture of Anabaptists. The date is January 28, 1528. Sometime during the next eight months he left his wealth, home, and station, never to return. His property, valued at 3,500 guilders, was confiscated by the city.

What made a fugitive out of so solid and respected a citizen as Pilgram Marpeck? Only something more compelling than wealth, position, and social prominence could have brought about such a change. Although all direct evidence is lacking, the reason was clearly that Marpeck had become an Anabaptist. He had promised obedience to Jesus Christ even though it demanded the sacrifice of all he had, including life itself. As seen in the preceding chapter, it was dangerous to be an Anabaptist in Austria in 1528. On August 20, 1527, Ferdinand I of Austria issued a mandate against all "sectarians and heretics." He would tolerate no beliefs within his domain that were contrary to those held by the church of Rome. Everywhere Anabaptists were caught and imprisoned and many executed. We know that an Anabaptist congregation existed in Rattenberg late in 1527, because on November 25 Leonhard Schiemer was arrested after serving as bishop of the congregation for only one day. He was beheaded on January 14, 1528. Another notable Anabaptist preacher, Hans Schlaffer, was caught near Rattenberg on December 5, 1527, and executed on February 4, 1528. Marpeck must have known of these two martyrs and particularly the letters Schiemer wrote to the Rattenberg congregation during his imprisonment. If Marpeck was an Anabaptist at the time, he would have been a member of that congregation.

It is likely that Marpeck and his family were among the many Anabaptist refugees who left their homes for places of safety, for to remain meant almost certain death. This was especially true after April 1, 1528, when an even harsher mandate was issued by Ferdinand against the Anabaptists. The Marpecks decided upon Strassburg as their destination. That city had a reputation for tolerance toward Anabaptists and was one of the few such places in all of Europe.

Strassburg

Strassburg was an unusually important European city of the sixteenth century. It was the link between the Netherlands and Italy, between Paris and Vienna, and its location on the junction of two important routes of commerce contributed much to its prosperity. But along those same highways came men with ideas, traveling voluntarily in search of a better hearing or forced to flee by persecution. The range and diversity of the ideas held by the people who either traveled through or settled down in Strassburg is truly astonishing.

But Strassburg was not only a popular and exciting place for overnight stops on the way to some other place. Like a magnet it drew people who, because of some point of view usually connected with Christian belief, were unwanted elsewhere. As a result of political revolts in the thirteenth and fourteenth centuries, the city had become independent of its ruler who, as was so often the case, was both prince and bishop at the same time. A democratic form of government was developed with a complicated system of councils and elected officials representing the two main social groups, the nobility and the commoners. The main center of power lay with the twenty guilds, which were unions of craftsmen.

Wherever the bishops of the church of Rome were in full control they dealt decisively with any dissenters. For many centuries church law had insisted on the death penalty for denial of any church doctrine or for rebaptism. But in Strassburg the bishop had little power and could therefore not significantly interfere in religious matters. Strassburg's tolerant attitude to difference of opinion and moderation in punishing offenders had a long tradition. "He who would be hanged anywhere is simply driven from Strassburg by flogging" was a saying of the day.

When the Reformation began and its main ideas flooded the countries of Europe in the form of pamphlets and tracts, Strassburg was quickly in the middle of things. Because of its reputation for toleration it became a center for printing and distribution of all kinds of Reformation literature. Naturally the citizens did not remain unaffected by what was happening. The insistence of Martin Luther that a person is acceptable to God only through faith and never through the works prescribed by the church of Rome found welcome ears in a city that had already in its own way challenged the big church. When Luther's ninety-five theses arrived in Strassburg in 1518, copies were nailed to the doors of every church and parsonage in the city.

In the same year Matthew Zell came to Strassburg to serve as pastor of the cathedral parish. He was won for the Reformation and began soon after to express his newly won convictions. By 1523 he supported the use of German instead of Latin in church worship and rejected the Roman practice of giving only the bread to the people at communion. When he was denied the use of the cathedral pulpit by the authorities of the Roman church, the powerful guilds came to his aid and built for him a wooden platform from which he preached to congregations numbering as many as 3,000 people. Support was so strongly on the side of reform that the government of Strassburg issued a mandate at the end of 1523 authorizing evangelical preaching. When Zell was excommunicated in 1524 for having married, the government kept him in office. By August 1524 the city authorities took over the responsibility for nominating, installing,

Strassburg, located at the junction of numerous trade routes and rivers, derived its name from the Roman Strataburgum—city of roads. Truly cosmopolitan, it also became a marketplace for new ideas such as Anabaptism. The engineer Pilgram Marpeck arrived in Strassburg in the fall of 1528. Employed by the city he built the **channel dams on the Kinzig,** but was eventually relieved of his job and exiled because of his preaching activities.

and paying the pastors of the seven churches in the city in a manner similar to that of Zürich under Zwingli. In May 1523 Martin Bucer arrived in the city and, because of his talent for leadership and his energy, soon became the chief reformer of Strassburg. We shall hear more of him later in the chapter.

Anabaptists began coming to Strassburg early in 1526 although Balthasar Hubmaier had his book on baptism published there in July 1525. Among the first to arrive were Michael Sattler and Wilhelm Reublin, both belonging to the Swiss Brethren. In November 1526 Hans Denk arrived from Augsburg and had a public debate with the Strassburg ministers. Denk was ordered out of the city, as we have seen, and the council decreed that no more public debates between the ministers and dissenters should be held without the express permission of the council. Several more prominent Anabaptists, as well as other sorts of Reformation dissenters, came to Strassburg in 1526-27.

Matthew Zell exhibited a truly Christian spirit toward the Anabaptists and completely rejected the notion that anyone should be persecuted for their faith. He regarded most of the Anabaptists as true Christians who ought to be commended, not coerced. He publicly stated that he was not in agreement with the oppressive measures proposed by Bucer and city officials. Wolfgang Capito, another of the Strassburg reformers, found himself drawn to the Anabaptists, especially to Michael Sattler. Although he held some views in common with them, he nevertheless agreed that those Anabaptists who stubbornly insisted on their schismatic views were to be punished. It was due mainly to Zell and Capito that Strassburg was the "City of Hope" for the persecuted Anabaptists. Martin Bucer, the chief reformer, also had friendly feelings for Anabaptists at the beginning, due chiefly to his friendship with Michael Sattler, but when the Anabaptists insisted on forming their own fellowship, his attitude toward them became one of total opposition. Although he strongly advocated that Anabaptists be turned from their beliefs by persuasion, he did not hesitate to use violence if they showed no inclination to change. On July 27, 1527, a severe mandate was issued prohibiting all citizens from giving assistance and shelter to Anabaptists. It was put into effect immediately, but the tradition of tolerance in Strassburg made it impossible to win the struggle with the Anabaptists. Even with the expulsion in 1534 of Leopold Scharnschlager, a strong leader and associate of Pilgram Marpeck, organized congregational life continued, although not as strongly as before. The tradition of tolerance made possible Anabaptist conferences in Strassburg in the years 1554, 1556, 1557, 1568, 1592, and 1607.

Marpeck and Anabaptism

After that digression into the history of the city of Strassburg and its attitude toward the Anabaptists, we return now to the story of Pilgram Marpeck. It is clear that he came to Strassburg in order to join and work in the Anabaptist brotherhood. A notation from October 22, 1528, read: "... Pilgram Marpeck from Rattenberg in the Inn Valley, a citizen, with his wife, in whose house the meetings of the Anabaptists took place...." He apparently gained immediate employment in the city, perhaps as a member of the gardeners' guild. And it was not long before his engineering talents were discovered, for he was soon employed by the city as engineer.

Across the Rhine to the east of Strassburg lies the Black Forest. In 1528 as today it contained vast stands of silver fir on the higher elevations of the mountains and beech, birch, and oak lower down in the valleys. But the forests were at least twenty-five to thirty kilometers from Strassburg and the transport of logs over mountainous roads was a laborious, slow, and inefficient affair. It was to solve this economic problem that Marpeck was hired by the city.

His task was to bring the timber from the mountains into Strassburg by water. The Kinzig River divides the Black Forest into its northern and southern sections and flows into the Rhine near Strassburg. This river had been used for generations to float logs into Strassburg, but its usefulness was limited to the springtime when the water ran high due to the thawing snow up in the mountains. Marpeck's assignment was certainly to make possible the use of the river at least for the duration of the summer and autumn. This he accomplished by constructing a system of dams, behind which water was conserved in the spring. When the timbers were ready to float, a gate in the dam was opened, releasing enough water to float the logs down. In addition to the dams he constructed a series of special spillways primarily to bypass the many rock obstructions and rapids on the Kinzig. He did similar work on the Murg River further to the north and on several small streams flowing into the Rhine from the Vosges Mountains to the west. This engineering accomplishment added much to the economic welfare of Strassburg. It was undoubtedly Marpeck's usefulness to the city which made his stay possible, even though he was known as an Anabaptist leader from the beginning. Evidently his work had lasting significance, for generations later the timber brought down the Black Forest was still known as "Pilgramwood."

Martin Bucer and Wolfgang Capito were the most influential Protestant leaders in Strassburg while Marpeck lived there. Capito regarded him highly and seems to have been chiefly responsible for his extended stay. It was Bucer who was determined to get rid of Marpeck. His attitude was prompted primarily by Marpeck's public and penetrating criticism of church affairs in Strassburg, for which Bucer bore the main responsibility. Nor is it altogether surprising that he should have resented and feared Marpeck, for Marpeck was a strong and forthright leader. His theological writings reveal a man of high intelligence, especially when we remember that he was a layman with no formal theological training. Although his writings tend to be wordy and repetitious, they reveal the mind of a man who had struggled effectively with some of the basic religious questions of his day. Evidently he had read much and listened carefully. Even though the Strassburg clergy found his presence highly disturbing, they gave him the testimony that "he had many splendid gifts from God and in many respects manifested a vigorous good zeal." Bucer himself agreed that, although he was a "stiff-necked heretic," he and his wife exhibited a "fine, blameless behavior."

But Marpeck was not content to be the quiet leader of the Anabaptist church in Strassburg. He felt compelled to speak to other Christians about his understanding of the Christian faith. Since Bucer and his fellow ministers were so influential in the city he spoke to them. In fact, during a discussion with Bucer in December of 1531 Marpeck said that the opportunity for such discussion with other Christians was the reason for his coming to Strassburg. This conviction about the necessity to witness to his fellow Christians, however, finally led to his expulsion from the city.

He was known as an Anabaptist leader from the beginning of his stay in Strassburg, but because of his professional skill he had been left unmolested. By 1531, however, Bucer began to get impatient, for Marpeck was influencing not only the common people but also some of higher standing. Bucer's letters to his friends revealed his growing feeling that he could no longer tolerate his presence. Late in 1531 Bucer therefore managed to have Marpeck arrested and put in prison. But his success was of short duration, for Marpeck was released unconditionally, in part due to Capito's intercession, and likely because the city needed his professional services.

This experience did not discourage Marpeck. In fact, it seems to have prompted his next step, which was a request to the council for a public debate with the ministers. He evidently felt that a public hearing would aid the true understanding of the Christian faith. The council, however, remembering the public debate with Hans Denk five years earlier, denied the request, and instead arranged for a private discussion between Marpeck and Bucer before the council and other city officials. The public was excluded, very likely because the council feared that the simple logic of the Anabaptist leader would turn the public against the established order in the city. Capito had left Strassburg for an extended vacation on the insistence of Bucer. Thus the stage was set for the contest. Actually it was no contest because it was like a baseball game in which the manager of one team is the umpire. Under such conditions the outcome was predictable. The council decided on December 18 that unless Marpeck abandoned his opinions and his efforts to "overthrow infant baptism" he was to be banished from the city. He was also warned that if he returned, his reception would be such that he would soon wish he had stayed away.

Marpeck responded calmly and without anger or excitement

to this shattering announcement. He said that he could make no promise never to return since God might lead him back. He also requested four weeks of grace so that he could settle the sale of his property and some financial matters relating to his employment with the city. During this time he wrote a long confession of faith which fills about thirty-five printed pages. To this Bucer wrote an equally long reply, point by point. These documents, as well as the minutes of the debate of December 9, clearly reveal the two main points of difference between Christians of the Anabaptist and Reformed faiths in Strassburg in 1531: baptism and the relationship of the church to the civic government.

It is not enough simply to state their position on these matters, for there were reasons for their convictions. We must try to understand why Bucer defended infant baptism and why Marpeck rejected it; why Bucer felt compelled to persecute the Anabaptists and why Marpeck made a plea for religious freedom. This can best be done by examining how each one understood and interpreted the Bible. Both of them believed that the Bible was the Christian's authority in the church and in private life, but in their interpretation of Scripture they ended up at opposite points on some basic questions.

The Interpretation of Scripture

We begin with Bucer because his interpretation of Scripture and the position derived from it was accepted as the official view of the city of Strassburg. This was the interpretation Marpeck criticized and against which we must see and understand Marpeck's own interpretation. Bucer believed that the Old and New Testaments formed an indivisible unity, with the Old Testament having practically the same authority for the Christian as the New. God made a covenant with Abraham in which He graciously and freely pledged Himself to be the God of Abraham's descendants. This same covenant extended through both Old and New Testaments and on into the present day. Since the coming of Jesus that covenant is better understood. People understand better what God has done and what He wants them to do, but the original covenant has in no basic way been changed or canceled out by the coming of Jesus.

For Bucer, this understanding of the Bible led to a number of important consequences. First, baptism in the Christian church was regarded as the equivalent of circumcision in the Hebrew community. As circumcision was the sign that a person was included in the covenant, so baptism was also the sign of the same covenant. It is the sign that God is gracious and merciful, and desires to be gracious to this particular child. Faith is not connected with baptism, for both sin and salvation begin before there is any faith. Each child is a sinner, having inherited evil from Adam, and because it needs God's grace and forgiveness, it must also have the sign of baptism.

The second consequence of Bucer's understanding of the Bible was that although not all the people in the city of Strassburg were obedient followers of Christ, yet they must all be in the church even as all the Hebrews were included in the Old Testament covenant. That would be like saying that everyone belongs on the team whether they observe the rules or not. God, said Bucer, was the only one who could decide who was a Christian and who was not; man cannot make such decisions. In fact, Bucer held to the idea of special election which really means that God has in His mysterious wisdom appointed some persons to salvation and some to damnation. No one knows what God's choice is with respect to any person. Thus man cannot decide who belongs to the church because even a thoroughly evil person may be elected to salvation. It was assumed that in due course God would draw such a person to Himself, bringing forth the fruit of love. To say, therefore, that such a person may not be in the church is to put oneself in the place of God.

A third consequence had to do with the relationship of the church and the civil government which in Strassburg was the city council. Bucer held that God has two kinds of servants. The first preach the Word of God and tell people what is right and what is wrong like the prophets and priests in the Old Testament. The second, like the Old Testament kings, are responsible for seeing that everyone does what is right and punish those who do not. This meant that all who opposed the work of the ministers whether by evil living or by contradicting their ideas would be punished. An example of how this worked was the petition of Bucer and his fellow ministers to the council in December of 1531 to punish those who contradicted and despised their teachings. There can be little doubt that Marpeck was among those to whom this petition was aimed. Bucer insisted that it was a Christian's responsibility to bear the sword of a magistrate since only the Christian knew what God wanted people to do. He also believed in the support of the council for the sake of those who did not have a sufficiently strong will to do what was right; such weak persons would be helped to do the right by the threat of force. Church and government were thus thoroughly intermixed, and there was some confusion about the responsibility of each. The outcome of such an arrangement was often that the decisions in the life of the church were governed by political and social considerations rather than by the Bible.

The fourth consequence of Bucer's understanding of the Bible was that since Christians had a fuller understanding of God's will than the Old Testament Hebrews, most of the rules and regulations of the Old Testament were no longer binding. The Hebrews needed such external observances as sacrifice and food laws because of their lack of understanding, but in the Christian church only faith and love are required. For the situation in Strassburg this meant simply that there was no definite order in church life. Everyone was assumed to be a member of the church regardless of what they did or whether they wanted to be in the church or not.

We now turn to Marpeck's understanding of the Bible and his views of baptism and the relationship of the church to the civic government that flowed from it. The Old and New Testaments formed a unity for him, but of a different kind than the unity which Bucer found. Marpeck said that Old and New Testaments stand to each other in a relationship of promise and fulfillment, just as today, for example, the pledge of marriage in the engagement and the marriage itself are inseparable, but still quite clearly distinguishable. One is introductory to the other. When Jesus came, the old order was replaced by a new one. The old is no longer authoritative because the new covenant in Christ is of a different nature than the old covenant made with Abraham. The same gracious God gave both covenants, but the old covenant was characterized by a complex system of rules and regulations because, although people wanted to do God's will, they neither clearly understood it nor did they have the strength to do it. It was, said Marpeck, a covenant of slavery. The new covenant, however, is characterized by freedom. No system of regulations is necessary because the people that accept it both know God's will and are free and able to do it because God gives them the strength. Briefly then Marpeck held that under the old covenant people were forced to do right and under the new they are free to do right. From this view followed four important consequences.

First, he believed that God wants all persons to obey Him freely, without compulsion, and that it is possible for every person to obey God if they so choose. Thus Marpeck completely rejected Bucer's doctrine of election; God wants every person to be saved. Because he rejected the doctrine of election he also rejected infant baptism, since an infant cannot freely choose to obey God. Actually infant baptism compels a person to be in the church without giving that person any choice in the matter. Furthermore, before any can freely obey God, they must repent of their sins and believe that God loves them and wants their obedience, but infants can neither repent nor believe. Furthermore, we need not worry about the welfare of innocent babies. They have no sin until they are able to distinguish between good and evil. Since they are not sinners they need no redemption; God has already accepted them because Jesus said, "Let the children come to me, for theirs is the kingdom of heaven." Even the children of Christian parents, once they become responsible, have no advantage before God. It should not be assumed that they are or will be Christians. They too must repent and believe in order to be saved.

The second consequence was that Marpeck regarded the New Testament as the final authority for Christian life in the church. He agreed with Bucer that faith and love were all-important, but he went on to say that only the person who is unconditionally obedient to Christ has true faith and true love. Since in the New Testament baptism clearly follows faith, it must be so today; only those who have faith may be baptized. Jesus commanded His followers to love their enemies. That allows for no exceptions and means that Christians may not participate in war.

Third, since the New Testament is the Christian's final authority, it cancels out the Old Testament view wherever the two do not agree. Bucer appealed to the Old Testament union of church and state, but for Marpeck that was a slavish system. Since freedom is characteristic of the New Testament, freedom in matters of faith must be taken seriously, and this would inevitably mean the clear separation of church and world. To Marpeck not only God's gracious favor but also man's free response mattered. The church is the society only of those who freely choose to be obedient to Christ. Joining the church is therefore not merely the acceptance of God's grace but also a willingness to live in obedience to it. It is not doing people a favor to regard them as members of the church if they do not want to be obedient to Christ of their own free will. Bucer rejected this reasoning because it would inevitably lead to the formation of a new church.

The fourth and final consequence of Marpeck's view of the Scriptures was that he rejected the idea of two servants in the church, the preacher and the magistrate, as held by Bucer. The preacher is in the church to be sure because he proclaims God's love and grace and offers it to people. The magistrate does not function within the church because there only Christ rules over the spirits of members. The magistrate is appointed by God to restrain evil among those persons who have no desire to obey Christ. In practice this meant the rejection of all coercion in matters of faith. No magistrate has the authority even to judge in such matters, much less to force people to accept such judgments. Since God wants a free response from all people, compelling them to believe that of which they are not convinced interferes with God's order. This even applies to children of Christian parents who cannot simply be told what to believe. It applies also to those who hold views that are different from those in power. To use the magistrate to punish dissenters or blasphemers is to admit that the Word of Christ is not able to do what it is said to be capable of, to convert evil men. It is simply contrary to God's order and the spirit of Christ to persecute anyone for their faith or for having no faith at all. Those who do not want to believe should be left alone; they should not be expected to live as Christians when they have no power to do so. Not only did Marpeck state these convictions in his confession, he also appealed directly to the city council to let liberty of conscience and religious freedom prevail in Strassburg.

Marpeck's confession convinced neither Bucer nor the council and he finally left Strassburg in February 1532. For the next decade we know practically nothing of his life. He evidently continued as an important leader among the Anabaptists of Germany, Switzerland, and Moravia, apparently traveling a great deal and writing letters to churches and individuals.

An Invisible Church?

In 1542 he suddenly emerged again with the publication of a little book on baptism. This volume was in fact a careful revision of a work by some Anabaptist preachers from North Germany. Marpeck's purpose in publishing it was that it might help to unite and strengthen the Anabaptist fellowship. While certainly performing this function, it also caught the attention of another dissenter, Caspar Schwenckfeld, who lived not far from Augsburg. He was not an Anabaptist but what one might call an "invisiblist." He believed that what is truly real in life is invisible. And therefore concern about such visible matters as baptism and the Lord's Supper was idolatry because it prevented people from being concerned for what was truly important. Since Marpeck had argued for the importance of right observance of baptism and the Lord's Supper in the church, Schwenckfeld regarded the book as an attack on himself. He replied with a book of his own charging the Anabaptists with completely misunderstanding the Bible and the Christian faith.

The position represented by Schwenckfeld proved a great temptation for the persecuted Anabaptists. Why not, some of them seriously asked, abandon baptism and the Lord's Supper since faith is what really counts? Why not become an "invisible" church so that we will not be persecuted anymore? These questions had already been asked in 1531 in Strassburg while Marpeck was there and he had in that year written two little books against this view. Now he and some of his co-workers took up the task of replying to Schwenckfeld's criticism in a work of about 800 pages. The basic question was again the interpretation of the Bible and especially the matter of the relationship of the New to the Old Testament. There is no need to discuss this argument in detail because it was almost identical to Marpeck's argument with Bucer, which we have described.

In 1544 Marpeck gained employment with the city of Augsburg as an engineer and did work similar to that which he had done at Strassburg. Although efforts were made to prosecute him he remained in his position until his death in 1556.

Throughout his time as an Anabaptist leader and elder he was deeply concerned for the unity of the Anabaptist fellowship. This concern is clearly reflected in the fourteen remaining letters from his hand addressed to Anabaptists at Strassburg, in Switzerland, in Moravia, and in Germany. He writes about the unity of the church. He warns some that although the Christian is free in Christ, no one is free to live a life of sin, and he criticizes others for judging each other too harshly. He urges members separated by misunderstanding to be reconciled, writes very practically about the place of the minister in the congregation, and deals with a variety of other matters.

Pilgram Marpeck was the most notable German Anabaptist leader and theologian. He contributed a great deal to the clarification of the Anabaptist interpretation of the Christian faith. Even today he inspires us with his passion for unity among believers in Christ.

Chapter 6

Anabaptism in the Netherlands

THE HEADWATERS of the Rhine are in Switzerland, but the river flows through Germany into the Netherlands, where it divides into several branches as it reaches the sea. The Anabaptist movement also had its headwaters in Switzerland and, like the Rhine, divided into several streams as it passed through Germany and down to the Netherlands. But Anabaptism flowed in ideas rather than water and through people rather than through hills and valleys.

Ideas are powerful. In a changing society they can be creatively good or tragic. Some people use well the power of new ideas; others channel them to bad ends; still others fear them and try to dam them up and hold them back. The history of the birth of the Anabaptist movement in the Netherlands, from where its people came to be known as Mennonites, is about the flow of new ideas into a society ready for change. This history not only reflects abuse and opposition, but also the creative use of new ideas.

Melchior Hoffman

Melchior Hoffman was the one through whom Anabaptism came to the Netherlands. He was a gifted but uneducated leader, a tanner or furrier by training. Born in Swabia in Southern

Germany in 1493, he emerged as a self-taught Lutheran preacher active in Sweden and the small countries on the east shore of the Baltic. When driven from this area, he went to Holstein in Northern Germany and to Denmark. But after experiencing opposition there also, he went to Emden and then up the Rhine to Strassburg.

Hoffman moved from one idea to another almost as easily as he moved from one place to another. He began as an evangelist for the Lutherans, later moved closer to Zwingli, and then to the more radical Carlstadt, both of whom differed from Luther in their understanding of the Lord's Supper and other doctrines. Nevertheless his own originality and Bible study, especially the books of Daniel and the Revelation of John, led him to develop his own views. In Strassburg he first met the Anabaptists and absorbed many of their ideas into his own thinking, but added other ideas of his own. In the Netherlands this mixture separated, creating in the process one of the darkest moments in Anabaptist history.

In 1530 Hoffman left Strassburg to return to Emden, soon after having become an Anabaptist. Here he found a ready response among those already inclined to reform with the result that about three hundred were baptized. From Emden he also sent lay preachers into the Netherlands and later traveled there himself. In the meantime his continuing interest in prophecy led him to more extreme ideas. Among them was a radical emphasis upon the nearness of Christ's return to set up His kingdom on earth. The prophecies of Leonard and Ursula Jost, Barbara Rebstock, and other visionaries led him to believe that Strassburg would be the spiritual Jerusalem, and that he himself was Elijah chosen to proclaim the coming event to all people. Finding his way back to Strassburg, he acted on his faith in these prophecies by having himself imprisoned. This was to be a necessary precondition to the coming of the kingdom. Obbe Philips, whom we will meet again later, said of these events:

> Thus, through the mediation of this prophecy, Melchior removed to Strasbourg and there began to preach and to teach here and there in the houses of the burghers. Then to be brief, the authorities sent

their servants to take him prisoner. When Melchior saw that he was going to prison, he thanked God that the hour had come and threw his hat from his head and took a knife and cut off his hose [the trousers and stockings were one garment] at the ankle, threw his shoes away and extended his hand with the fingers to heaven and swore by the living God who lives there from eternity to eternity that he would take no food and enjoy no drink other than bread and water until the time that he could point out with his hand and outstretched fingers the One who had sent him. And with this he went willingly, cheerfully, and well comforted to prison.[1]

He remained in prison until his death some ten years later. The prophecies he had so fervently believed remained unfulfilled, but his influence on other leaders in the Netherlands was of great importance for the future of the movement.

The Tragedy of Münster

Among the apostles whom Hoffman had sent into the Netherlands from Emden were Sicke Freerks, a tailor and for that reason sometimes called Snijder, who went to Leeuwarden, and Jan Volkertszoon Tripmaker, who went to Amsterdam. As a people with a long history of freedom, but now suffering under the oppressive rule of Spain, the Dutch were ready to listen to the words of these apostles. The Spanish king, who was also Holy Roman Emperor, ruled with a heavy hand. Because of this and because of the new winds of social change sweeping across Europe, the people were restless and disturbed. They resented the armies which were constantly moving across the land. And a series of floods had destroyed property and killed both livestock and people. The plague also troubled them. In Leiden it was reportedly so bad that people said, "Oh, dear Lord, do not pass us by with the gift of the hot sickness, for we would rather die than live any longer." Disaster and adversity were believed to be signs of the anger of God.

There was also dissatisfaction among the people with the poor state of the medieval church. They knew of the Brethren of the Common Life, who had brought reforms and provided schools where a better religious life was taught. With the coming of printing more people could get Bibles. As many as thirty printings of different translations of the Bible as a whole or in part appeared in less than ten years before 1530. The Sacramentarians too had offered growing opposition to the Roman Catholic interpretation of the Lord's Supper. They rejected the doctrine of the physical presence of the body and blood of Christ in the bread and wine. Already in 1527, three years before the Anabaptists came, the Sacramentarian widow Weynken of Monnickendam was arrested for heresy on this issue. When she was asked, "What do you hold concerning the sacrament?" she answered, "I hold your sacrament to be bread and flour, and if you hold it as God, I say that it is your devil." She was burned at the stake.[2]

With the coming of the Hoffmanite apostles to the Netherlands these yearnings and frustrations found new hope of fulfillment in the teachings of Anabaptism. Not all of the responses were encouraging, however. When Hoffman was imprisoned in 1533, a baker from Haarlem named Jan Matthijs claimed the leadership in Amsterdam, sending twelve apostles out in pairs to convert the people. One pair visited Leeuwarden late that year where they succeeded in winning and baptizing Obbe and Dirk Philips, two brothers who were to become key figures in the early history of the movement. Other apostles reached the city of Münster in Northern Germany and began the countdown leading to the tragedy which was to overtake the city.

Upon their arrival in Münster these apostles of Jan Matthijs found several preachers who were in close agreement with them and ready to have them remain there. This they quickly reported to Matthijs, who moved to the city early in 1534, eager to see the fulfillment of the Hoffmanite prophecy. But whereas Hoffman had claimed Strassburg to be the site of the New Jerusalem, Matthijs used a new prophecy to change the location to his own Münster. Far more important was the change to violence. Hoffman had been peaceful and urged his followers to wait for God to set up His kingdom at the appointed time. The possibility of calling upon His faithful to help annihilate the wicked by force of arms was an option but only at Christ's return. Matthijs now taught that the faithful were to prepare for the return of Christ beforehand by making a place for His kingdom by destroying the wicked. As a result, everyone was soon forced to receive bap-

The St. Lamberti tower on the main street in Münster, Westfalen, still bears witness to the tragedy of 1534-1535. **The three iron cages** once held the bodies of radical Anabaptist leaders put on public display. Most of the male population was massacred; only a few escaped.

tism and join the new community, or leave the city. Military preparations were quickly made for the great battle which would usher in the kingdom.

As might be expected, the bishop of Münster, who did not live in the city, gathered an army with some support from the German princes, and laid siege to the supposed New Jerusalem. This, of course, simply increased the militancy of the Münsterites. When Jan Matthijs was killed, leadership passed to another Jan—Jan van Leiden, whose ideas were even more extreme than those of Matthijs. He proclaimed himself the new King David and ruled with an iron hand. Polygamy was introduced on the basis of examples from the Old Testament and because the battle was leaving many families without a male leader. The besieged group suffered grievously from hunger and disease. The city finally fell on June 24, 1535, through the betrayal of a defector from within.

The Münsterite movement had aroused the hopes of many among the common people in Northwestern Germany and the Netherlands. Now they were not only disappointed at its failure, but even more at the bad name it gave to Anabaptists everywhere. Because of Münster Anabaptists were all now labeled as visionaries and revolutionaries. It was one of those times in history when persecution drove people to extreme action. This extreme action convinced the persecutors that they were right and justified even more severe measures against them.

The Peaceful Anabaptists

Not all of those who became Anabaptists in the Netherlands followed the Münsterites, nor even the more moderate and peaceful views of Hoffman. With Obbe and Dirk Philips, whom we have already referred to, Anabaptism followed another course even under severe persecution. In Dirk the Dutch movement was eventually to have one of its major spokesmen, theologians, and churchman.

Obbe and Dirk Philips were sons of a priest in Leeuwarden. Their education was probably better than the average of the day. Obbe was both a surgeon and barber as was customary at the time. Dirk was associated with the Franciscans and may have had training in theology. They were both baptized by apostles of Jan Matthijs in December-January of 1533-34 and Obbe was immediately ordained as elder. This authorized him to ordain other leaders in addition to carrying other church responsibilities.

Obbe did not accept the revolutionary teachings of Jan Matthijs. He soon gathered about himself a group of potential leaders concerned for a more faithful study and use of the Scriptures. They rejected the use of force, as well as the prophecies which had led to the armed attempts of Münster. But Obbe's spiritual pilgrimage was not yet at an end. Though he worked diligently to restore order after the Münster tragedy, he became increasingly disillusioned with the Anabaptist movement which had originally spawned Münster and now, in reaction, seemed to be becoming increasingly rigid and legalistic in its demands. Because of this he pulled back from the movement in 1539-40, having earlier, however, ordained his brother Dirk as well as David Joris and Menno Simons as leaders. It is probable that he became a spiritualist who practiced an inward religion without openly joining any church. We know very little about him after his withdrawal, except that he lived in Rostock along the North German coast and died in 1568. A confession which he wrote shortly before 1560 to explain why he left the Anabaptists is the only writing we have from his hand.

Dirk worked faithfully with Obbe in opposing the revolutionary Münsterites. As his writings became known among the Anabaptists, they strengthened and encouraged the progress of the peaceful group. He might, in fact, have taken Obbe's place as leader had it not been for another who had risen in the group, Menno Simons. We now turn our attention to him as the most important leader in the first generation of Dutch Anabaptism.

Menno Simons

Menno Simons became an Anabaptist more than ten years after the first baptism in Zurich on January 21, 1525, and about six years after the apostles of Melchior Hoffman began preaching in the Netherlands. He was born in Witmarsum, a small village in the northern Dutch province of Friesland where his parents lived, most likely as farmers. We know that he studied for the priesthood and was ordained by the bishop of Utrecht in 1524, but he knew only a little Greek and no Hebrew. His first assignment was as the second of three priests in Pingjum, a kilometer west of his hometown.

In his later recollections of these early years as a village priest he tells how he spent his time in "playing cards, drinking, and in diversions as, alas, is the fashion and usage of such useless people." He did not engage in serious immoral activities but wasted away his time in careless living. Already in his first year as priest, however, he began to be troubled about the Roman Catholic doctrine of the physical presence of the flesh and blood of Christ in the bread and wine of the mass. It is likely that he had been influenced by the Sacramentarians, of whom there were many in the Netherlands. Since he could not rid himself of these doubts even through prayer and confession, he decided to turn to the Scriptures in his further search. In taking this step, he writes, he was influenced by Luther. This study of the Scriptures convinced him that the church was wrong in its teaching that Christ was physically present in the Lord's Supper.

Soon he began to doubt in another area. To his amazement he heard that Sicke Freerks (Snijder), the apostle who had been sent by Hoffman, had been beheaded in nearby Leeuwarden for having himself rebaptized. This time Menno turned to the Scriptures immediately but was unable to find support for the practice of infant baptism. Thereupon he studied the writings of the reformers Luther, Bucer, and Bullinger. He discovered that while they defended infant baptism, he again did not find their arguments supported by Scripture. Yet despite these doubts he remained in the priesthood. He was, in fact, promoted to become priest in his hometown of Witmarsum. It was there that his reputation as an evangelical preacher increased, for he had much occasion to refute the Münsterite doctrine which was making inroads among his people. He conferred with the Münsterite leaders, and though he respected their zeal and sincerity, he was certain they were in error. He tried publicly to correct these errors through his preaching.

The decisive moment for Menno came in one of the tragic

Anabaptism came to the low countries around 1530 through the itinerant preacher **Melchior Hoffman** who first heard the ideas in Strassburg. **Menno Simons** joined the peaceful Anabaptists in January 1536. Because of Menno's capable leadership the Anabaptists in the north soon gained the nickname, "Mennists" (Mennonites).

events connected with Münster. A band of about three hundred rallied to support Münster and took over a monastery called the Old Cloister near Witmarsum. They were besieged, captured, and many of them were killed in battle or executed. It is believed that one of them, named Peter Simons, was Menno's brother. This event, in any case, moved Menno to action. While he agreed with these supporters at many points, he deplored their misguided zeal. They were like sheep without a shepherd, while he remained in comfort and ease, even building his reputation by opposing them. And so, after much inward struggle, and with the typical deliberateness of his Frisian people, he broke with the past. In a public statement on January 30, 1536, he told of his new commitment to the cause of Christ, and then went into hiding with the help of the peaceful Anabaptists with whom he was most in agreement.

The next year was spent in study of the Scriptures and in writing. It is, no doubt, during this period that he worked out the fuller meaning of the position to which he had come and on which he stood committed until his death twenty-five years later. At the end of this year of preparation, he was visited by a delegation of from six to eight men who asked him to become leader and elder of their people. After hesitating because of the serious implications of this call to lead a persecuted group, he finally consented to serve. He was ordained by Obbe Philips, who had also baptized him earlier.

Neither Traditionalist nor Fanatic

In 1539-40, two or three years after Menno Simons' ordination, Obbe Philips withdrew from the movement, as we have seen. He had grown weary of the struggle against Roman Catholic traditionalism on the one hand, and the fanatical extremism of Münster on the other. Whereas the former seemed to be guided more by tradition than by the Scriptures, those who sympathized with the revolutionary spirit of Münster seemed to read every biblical text in the light of their own visions and expectations. Among these were the followers of Melchior Hoffman, known as *Melchiorites*. In between were the Lutherans and Calvinists, who wanted reform but kept many of the traditions of the Roman Catholic past, and disagreed sharply with the Anabaptists on numerous issues.

To lead the fledgling Anabaptist group through this spiritual wilderness became the lot of Menno Simons. His lot in life was to sift truth from half-truth, oppose error with clear teaching, encourage the persecuted, correct the misguided, and build the young church while himself being hunted as a heretic. In this time of struggle, during the 1540s and 1550s, he had many helpers, especially Dirk Philips. But it was Menno's leadership which saved the Dutch Anabaptist movement from fanaticism and possible disintegration. Because of his leadership those who belonged to the movement were soon known as *Mennists*, or *Mennonists*, and eventually as *Mennonites*.

In a way the most difficult part of the struggle during these years was not that against Roman Catholic persecution, nor against the revolutionary ideas of the fanatics. The struggle was most intense against the Lutherans, Calvinists, and even the people among his own following with whom Menno had much in common. With these it was much more difficult to know where, when, and how to take a stand. The Mennonites agreed with the Lutherans and Calvinists on the major points of Reformation doctrine, especially on justification by faith and the authority of the Scriptures, but drew different implications from these doctrines. For the Mennonites, justification by faith meant that only persons old enough to have a conscious faith and make decisions for themselves could be baptized; and only those whose life showed the results of faith were to be gathered into the church.

In contrast the Lutherans and Calvinists (Reformed) still held to the idea that a society which does not have a common religion is dangerous. They pointed to the Münsterites as evidence of the danger when people are free to choose membership in any church group, or free to refuse altogether. Menno engaged in personal and written debate with the leaders of these state churches in the decade following 1540. Many of the writings we have from his hand today reflect the issues of that period.

The first major meeting was with John a Lasco at Emden in 1544, followed by two lengthy written statements from Menno. The second debate was with Martin Micron, pastor of the Reformed Church in London. When Queen Mary restored Catholicism as the official religion after the reforms of Henry VIII and Edward VI, the Calvinists had to leave England. Some arrived off the coast of North Germany near Wismar in the winter of 1553. The Mennonites, who were themselves refugees in hiding, helped the group when their boat was frozen in the ice and no one else would accept them.

At the insistence of the Reformed leaders a series of meetings was held between them and the Mennonites in February 1554. Micron, who had meanwhile located at Emden, was brought in to participate. Contrary to their understanding, he then published an account of these meetings, forcing Menno to release his interpretation also and publicly answering the charges Micron had made against him. Micron answered Menno and with that both the personal and written debate was closed, but meanwhile the authorities became aroused and Menno had to flee from the region.

Another exchange came with Gellius Faber, who inclined toward the Lutherans, but cooperated with the Reformed John a Lasco in Emden. He had participated in the debate against Menno in 1544, and in 1552 wrote a booklet against the Anabaptists which Menno felt to be so unfair that he had to reply. This answer, which is simply entitled *Reply to Gellius Faber*, tells of Menno's conversion, and discusses his call to the ministry. In addition, it is particularly helpful for understanding how the Mennonites differed from the Reformed and the Lutherans on baptism, the Lord's Supper, church discipline, the nature of the church, and the incarnation of Christ. Both Menno and Dirk Philips were frequently charged with heresy in connection with the incarnation because they believed that Christ had not received his flesh from Mary but from God himself. Only in that way could he have been sinless and established a pure church as his body. To their opponents this seemed to deny the humanity of Christ and, therefore, the incarnation itself.

These debates made it clear that the Mennonites differed with the state churches on two basic issues: the nature of the Christian life and the nature of the church. On the first, they stressed the importance of the new birth and discipleship. Only persons who were repentant and knew by experience the grace of God should be baptized and join the church. Evidence of the new birth was to be seen in the serious attempt to live as disciples who had committed themselves fully to Christ as Lord. Vital signs of this discipleship were love and nonresistance. On the nature of the church they insisted that it must be a voluntary gathering of believers. Church members were to be bound together on the sole basis of their loyalty to Christ and their love for each other. Their life as disciples would separate them from the world. The ban served as an instrument of love to warn and chasten the erring among them. The use of the sword or other instruments of the state to enforce the will of the church was rejected as contrary to the example and teachings of Christ and the apostles.

Batenburgers, Jorists, and Adam Pastor

To the opposition and persecution of these state churches

and of Roman Catholicism was added the pressure of the fanatics. They were not only eroding Menno's work among his own people, but bringing disrepute to the entire movement. Most active among these were the Batenburgers, Jorists, and Adam Pastor. Among these the first were the most corrupt, but fortunately, short-lived. They tried to carry on the violent tradition of Münster, robbing and plundering churches, and seeking to kill all who could not be converted. They adopted the practices of polygamy and community of goods as practiced at Münster. Their influence did not last much beyond 1544, but their evil deeds caused great difficulties for the peaceful Anabaptists who were identified with them.

The Jorists were the followers of David Joris, a gifted and persuasive man who had also been ordained by Obbe Philips. It was Joris who had tried unsuccessfully to gather the scattered remnants after the fall of Münster. His controversy with Menno arose when he began to place increasing emphasis on spirit and prophecy while, at the same time, accusing Menno of living according to the dead letter of the Scripture. Menno felt the authority of the Bible was supreme and wrote very strongly against Joris who he charged would "dare to put your dreams, your fantasies, enthusiasms, rhetorical figures, and other magic illusions ahead of the wisdom of the Holy Spirit, through which the prophetic and apostolic Scriptures have been given."[3] Joris felt that three time periods or dispensations in the history of the human race had been revealed: the age of the Father with David in the Old Testament, the age of the Son with Jesus Christ as the second David in the New Testament, and the age of the Spirit with himself (Joris) as the David of his age.

Because Joris believed that the inner, spiritual life was all that mattered for Christians, he could pretend to be Reformed or Roman Catholic and so escape persecution. After 1544 he, therefore, moved to Basel, Switzerland, under the assumed name of Jan van Brugge, and identified himself as a Reformed merchant who had fled from Belgium. He lived as a respectable citizen and honored churchman while, at the same time, carrying on secret correspondence with his followers in the Netherlands and writing little books for their instruction. After his death on August 25, 1556, a family quarrel led to the discovery of his real identity to the chagrin of his children who had married into respectable families of high Basel society. Because he had been a heretic his body was dug up and burned along with his books. His followers in the Netherlands maintained themselves into the seventeenth century.

The third group to trouble Menno were followers of Adam Pastor, a German priest whose original name had been Roelof Martens, and who had joined the Anabaptists in 1533. As co-worker with the other leaders, Menno ordained him as elder soon after 1542, and he participated in the debates with the Jorists at Lübeck in 1546, as well as in the conferences at Emden and Goch in 1547. Soon, however, it appeared that Pastor did not really believe in the Trinity, having intellectual problems with the incarnation and deity of Christ. He was consequently banned from the church by Menno and Dirk in 1547. In 1552 Menno met with him again to discuss the deity of Christ, but he could not win him back. Menno held firmly to the Scriptures as authority, while Pastor tended to put logic and reason above the Scriptures. Pastor was one of the best educated leaders among the Mennonites, but Menno and his followers believed that reason must be tested and judged by Scripture, not Scripture by reason. A group of "Adamites" continued for some time after Pastor's death in the 1560s.

Thus against both the traditionalists and the fanatics, Menno and Dirk held steadfastly to the Bible as final authority in faith and life. The use of prophecy, the inner word of the Spirit, visions, or reason all had to be checked against the Bible. It was also clear to Menno and Dirk that the Bible had to be understood in light of the teachings and example of Jesus.

And so Menno Simons labored after Obbe left them, to gather and defend the flock, but he did this against great odds. For most of this period he was a hunted man with a price on his head. In 1536 he married Gertrude, about whom we unfortunately know very little. Nine years later he wrote that he "could not find in all the country a 'cabin or hut' in which my poor wife and our little children could be put up in safety for a year or two." Tjaard Renicx of Kimswerd, a little village not far from

Pingjum in Friesland, was executed in January 1539, for having
given shelter to Menno. Only one of Menno's two daughters and
a son outlived him. Menno himself was a cripple in later years,
but we do not know how he became that way.

Despite these handicaps Menno traveled from Amsterdam
to Danzig and perhaps further east along the Baltic seacoast. He
was courageous in meeting his foes, tender in his sympathies to
those in the church. He wrote devotional materials as well as
treatises in the heat of controversy. He made mistakes, was not
always consistent in his writings, and often felt deeply the
burden of his calling, but his judgments were generally sound,
as is evidenced by the wide acceptance of his leadership and
writings.

Witness Through Suffering

The leadership of those like Menno Simons and Dirk Philips
was needed for the founding of the church, but thousands of
others demonstrated a heroic faith that was just as vital. They
were soldiers of the cross who fought with spiritual weapons
only. On this subject Menno wrote one of his best pamphlets,
The Cross of the Saints. The meaning of the cross became very
real to many of his followers in the Netherlands.

Church and state had been so closely linked in the medieval
period that the state considered it a part of its duty to enforce
the accepted belief of the established state church. If the church
declared someone a heretic, he was considered dangerous to the
state and removed from society. Anabaptists were considered
heretics. Their name, given to them by their opponents, was
chosen to point to an ancient heresy. In the Roman Empire
anyone who was baptized a second time was put to death. These
views continued to prevail in the sixteenth century, especially
also in the Netherlands, which were under the despotic rule of
Spain. Charles V had been more tolerant of Luther in Germany
because he needed the military and political support of the
German princes, but he was determined to stamp out the
Reformation in the Netherlands. Since the Anabaptists were the
major Reformation party there until 1555 when the Calvinists
gained in strength, they suffered severely. Studies of the

number of martyrs in Belgium and the Netherlands have shown that no less than 1,500 Anabaptists were killed, possibly as many as 2,500 from the early days of the movement to the death of the last martyr in 1574.

Typical of the spirit of the martyrs is that of Dirk Willems. He was pursued by a company of Anabaptist hunters when he escaped from prison in the midst of winter. He fled across the thin covering of ice on a river and seemed to have made good his escape when, looking back, he saw one of his pursuers break through the ice and cry for help. Dirk immediately turned back and managed to rescue him, but on orders of the burgomaster on the other side of the river, the man he saved arrested him on the spot. He was burned at the stake on May 16, 1569, paying for this deed of mercy with his life.

The treatment of prisoners was extremely cruel. They were broken on a torture device known as the rack to make them disclose the names of others, especially leaders. For those who remained steadfast, burning at the stake was the usual execution. Sometimes they were first strangled; sometimes a small sack of gunpowder was hung around their neck as an act of mercy since the quick fire and the smoke hastened the end. The men who renounced the Anabaptist faith were given the mercy of death by beheading, while the women were drowned. But some women were buried alive, and other women, as well as men, were hanged. An account of three brethren and a sister taken in 1536 tells of the steadfastness of most of the martyrs:

> They were then placed upon the rack, though contrary to their privilege, for they were mere citizens; however, they would not apostatize, though they were tortured so that the blood ran down their feet; but they trusted in and cried to God alone. After being tortured, they were brought up above again, where they comforted each other with the Word of God. 1 Thessalonians 4:18.

> Finally, on the fourth of September, they were sentenced to death. They were brought bound upon the scaffold, yet came forth boldly and humbly, as lambs of Christ, and finally knelt down, saying with Stephen: "Lord Jesus, receive our spirits into Thy hands." Acts 7:59. They were all then speedily beheaded, their bodies burned, and their heads placed upon stakes. Thus they offered up their sacrifices.[4]

Anabaptism flourished in Flanders, especially in the great trading centers of Ghent, Brugge, and Ypres, but after sixty years of bloody persecution the survivors moved north into Holland. Between 1535 and 1592 at least 110 Anabaptists were tortured and executed in **the castle at Ghent** alone. A display inside the castle shows a collection of **arm and leg irons** and a **canvas straightjacket.**

Persecution made believers learn to know their own faith early and well. Thomas van Imbroich, a printer's helper in Cologne, was put in prison in 1557. Two letters written to his wife have been preserved in the *Martyrs Mirror.* We also have a confession of faith from him which shows deep thought and conviction. In one of the letters to his wife and the brethren he wrote,

> Yea, if the Lord should count me worthy to testify with my blood to His name, how greatly would I thank Him, for I hope not only to bear these bonds with patience, but also to die for Christ's sake, that I may finish my course with joy; for I would rather be with the Lord, than live again in this abominable, wicked world; however, His divine will be done. Amen.[5]

Thomas did testify with his death, dying on March 5, 1558, at the age of twenty-five. So powerful was the Anabaptist witness at the time of execution, that they were increasingly carried on in secret, or the martyrs were gagged. Since some of them managed to free their tongues, however, a clamp was henceforth placed over their tongue and the tip burned so that it would not slip back through the vise.

Not everyone wanted to execute the Anabaptists. Joris Wippe was mayor of Meenen in Flanders but moved to Dordrecht when he became an Anabaptist. Friends and officials warned him to flee but he refused. Consequently he was caught, tried, and ordered to be executed, but the man who was to carry out the order wept because Wippe had fed his wife and children in a time of need. Finally another man was ordered to carry out the sentence.

The letters and testimonies of these martyrs are among the finest writings. Many have been collected and published in the *Martyrs Mirror.* They show that these believers looked upon their death by martyrdom as a seal of faith. God would not call them to such a fate if they were not given the grace to endure. So they gave thanks that they could witness to the truth in this way. Furthermore, they believed their sufferings to be a test that led to eternal life. They followed the way of the cross to final victory, believing fully that as they shared in the passion of Christ, they would also share in the joy of His final victory.

Chapter 7

Anabaptist-Mennonites in Northern Europe, 1550-1650

MENNO was a Frisian from the northern part of the Netherlands, but his labors were not restricted to that area. Indeed, most of his ministry as an Anabaptist was carried on outside of the Netherlands. His travels covered the territory where permanent churches were founded. It even seems that where the persecution was too intense or the group too small for a visit from Menno, there no permanent congregations came to exist.

The distinctions between countries were not nearly as sharp in sixteenth-century Europe as they are now, and movement across national borders was much easier. Only in late sixteenth century did the Dutch Mennonites become clearly defined as a fellowship, and even then congregations in Northwestern Germany and as far away as Danzig had close ties with the Dutch congregations. Still we can look at the geographic spread by areas within the whole of Northern Europe to understand the size and growth of the movement to mid-seventeenth century. In this chapter we will look first at Flanders, a province in Northwestern Belgium, then move across the channel to England and on to Northern Germany, as well as east to the Vistula Delta in what is now Poland. To conclude we will return to look more closely at the original center in the Netherlands.

Anabaptism in Belgium

The origins of Anabaptism in Belgium are very similar to those in the Netherlands. There, too, people had become weary with the medieval religious life and were ready for new ideas. The apostles of Melchior Hoffman also came to these areas and found a willing audience. Though their preaching was not confined to Flanders, the main impact of their message was felt in that area.

From 1530 to 1550 the major reform party in this area was Anabaptist. The first martyrs in 1523 had been Lutheran, but Lutheranism never gained a mass following. Likewise Calvinism had little influence before 1544 but increased in significance after 1550 with its greatest influence after 1560 during the war of independence from Spain. Later it was also driven out of Belgium but still constitutes the largest Protestant body in the Netherlands.

Anabaptism spread through the efforts of merchants and weavers who could move about with greater ease than many others. Persecution arose almost immediately with mandates being issued against them on October 10, 1535, January 24, 1539, and December 14, 1541. These mandates led to the death of many, but also to the flight of many more who followed the trade routes from Antwerp and other commercial centers. Flemish refugees are found very early in England and as far east as Danzig, where Flemish ships traveled for trade with the North German cities of the Hanseatic League.

The records show that the Anabaptists were very active, but the intense persecution prevented any one person from assuming prolonged leadership among them. The Flanders story, therefore, is primarily one of many faithful lay persons building, spreading, and upholding the church. We know, for example, of Jan Claeszen who in 1544 reported that he had 600 copies of the writings of Menno Simons printed in Antwerp. Not infrequently the witness of the death of the faithful was as effective as their living witness. The movement recorded steady growth from 1550 to 1576.

Some leadership help did come to these groups from the Netherlands. Gillis van Aken, a colleague of Menno and Dirk,

Holland's greatest poet, **Joost van den Vondel** (1587-1679), was a deacon in the Waterlander congregation in Amsterdam. **Jan Adriaensz Leeghwater** (1575-1650), a brilliant engineer, architect, and inventor, directed land reclamation projects for the Dutch, Danish, French, and Prussian governments. **Jeme (Johannes) Deknatel** (1698-1759) was instrumental in founding the Amsterdam Mennonite Seminary in 1735.

worked here until his arrest in 1555. His story has a sad ending. Though he recanted at the threat of death, his weakness only changed the form of execution from burning to beheading. At his execution on July 10, 1557, he reportedly said, "It is too much to lose both body and soul at the same time." The great missionary Leonard Bouwens also labored here. His diary records over 10,000 baptisms which he performed, giving the exact date and place of each. Of these, 592 seem to have been in the area which is now Belgium. So far as we know this constitutes a record for the entire Anabaptist movement for any one man. A letter from Menno Simons to Bouwens' wife has been preserved, in which he encourages her not to worry about the safety of her husband who is secure in the care of God Himself. She had apparently asked for a less dangerous assignment for him closer to home.

The period from 1576 to 1586 was one of relative freedom for Anabaptism. The tug of war between Calvinists seeking independence and Catholics loyal to Spain left the authorities little time for persecution of others, though neither group was actually willing to see Anabaptism flourish at all. But persecution began again in 1586 with the Spanish and, therefore, Roman Catholic victory over Calvinism in Belgium. With renewed pressure upon them, and the attraction of greater freedom in the Dutch provinces to the north, a gradual exodus of Anabaptists came under way again. Some moved to the larger cities in Belgium in order to hide better, but eventually even these were forced to flee. By 1640 there were few Anabaptists left in Belgium, martyrdom and emigration having decimated their ranks. Thus a promising start ended with little more than a trace of its life remaining in the homeland.

Anabaptists in England

To trace the Anabaptist movement in England is difficult but interesting. It is difficult because no separate church group can be identified as a direct result of Anabaptist efforts and because most of the records we now have come from those who opposed and persecuted them. It is interesting, however, because England differed considerably from the Germanic lands, the home for most of the Anabaptists, and because at least three major denominations show signs of influence from Anabaptism: the Congregationalists, the Baptists, and the Quakers.

As early as 1535-36 twenty-five Dutch Anabaptists were arrested and brought to trial in England. Anabaptist writings were known there even earlier. Most of these early refugees came to escape the wrath following the tragedy of Münster as, for example, Jan Matthijs of Middelburg (not to be confused with the Jan Matthijs who was at Münster). England was more tolerant later under Edward VI (1547-53) than under Henry VIII who preceded him and Mary who followed. Under Edward efforts at persuasion and some imprisonment constituted the extent of opposition to Anabaptism, as a result of which they soon worked more openly than before. Their greatest strength was in London and along the eastern coast where the refugees from Flanders landed first. The textile trade made it easy to move across the channel since it was a growing industry in England and continental weavers were much in demand.

Persecution increased under Mary (1553-58), but it is difficult to distinguish the Anabaptist martyrs from other Protestant martyrs, of whom there were many. It is significant, however, to note that the largest number of martyrs came from the areas where Anabaptism had been strongest. With Alva's "reign of terror" in Belgium from 1567 to 1573, thousands more sought safety in England, where Elizabeth was now queen. She issued an edict against them in 1560, and another in 1568, while also appointing a church commission to hunt out and bring to trial all Anabaptists in the land. The *Martyrs Mirror* has a long account of the arrest and persecution of Anabaptists in London in 1575.[1]

After 1580 a new era began for Anabaptists in England. Increased tolerance was won when other groups separated from the state church and began to organize themselves. Some of their central ideas are the same as, or similar to, those distinctive of Anabaptism, including the separation of church and state, the baptism of adult believers only, and the freedom of the local congregation from outside control. Again the leading centers for these groups were in those places where Anabaptists had been numerous earlier. A number of these new groups had close relations with the Dutch Mennonites, and some even migrated to the Netherlands in search of greater freedom. An example of this is in the case of John Smyth, who came to the Netherlands with his group in 1608. Two congregations were organized, one in Amsterdam under Smyth and another under John Robinson in Leiden. Of these congregations it has been said: "To the Smyth congregation, which accepted adult baptism as a result of contact with Dutch Mennonites, the General Baptists owe their origin.... A number of members from Robinson's church were among the Pilgrim Fathers when they sailed for the new world in 1620."[2] Anabaptist doctrine is reflected most clearly in the Quakers, who arose in 1644. George Fox and other Quakers traveled extensively among the Mennonites in the Netherlands and Germany in the seventeenth century.

In summary, it may be said that Anabaptism did not become a permanent church body in England, nor was their number ever very large. Their beliefs and practices, however, did influence the history of the Protestant church in England. The Anabaptist name was lost, but other groups accepted some of the principal points which were causing the Mennonites to remain separate in Germany, Switzerland, France, and the Netherlands at that time.

Mennonites in Northern Germany

In the previous chapter we told how Melchior Hoffman preached and baptized in Emden, in the province of East Friesland. The tolerance of the rulers, together with its crucial geographic location, made Emden a crossroads of northwestern Europe. Menno Simons spent much of his time from 1536 to 1544 in this area. Emden was, consequently, the site of several historic meetings of Mennonites. In 1547 Menno met there with six of his colleagues for a major discussion on the incarnation, infant baptism, and on avoidance, that is, whether a husband or wife should avoid his/her partner when the other partner was under discipline by the congregation. Usually such meetings included seven elders who had charge of the work in different areas. On January 17, 1568, the Waterlander Mennonites met at Emden and agreed on twenty-one points as a basis for working together. Still later, from February 25 to May 17, 1578, the Flemish Mennonites debated fourteen points of doctrine with the Reformed representatives in 124 sessions in Emden!

Mennonites could also be found in the late 1530s south of Emden along the lower Rhine, near the present Dutch border, but severe persecution destroyed the settlements eventually. Menno Simons worked there after 1544 for a time under the tolerance of Hermann von Wied, archbishop of Cologne, but when a radical Roman Catholic replaced the archbishop, all Reformation progress ceased in the area. Thomas van Imbroich, whom we met in the previous chapter, and others tried to continue the work.

Late in the sixteenth century Mennonites found refuge again in this area in the city of Krefeld. Here the history of the Mennonites has been tied closely with the history of the city itself to the present day. They contributed decisively to the economic, social, and cultural growth of the city, making it an important textile center. The Krefeld congregation was the only one in this area to survive later.

East from Emden, along the north German coast lies Schleswig-Holstein, where Mennonite refugees early settled on the estates of sympathetic noblemen. They knew the Mennonites to be sober and industrious people. The land was marshy, and as Dutchmen these refugees knew about dikes and the recovery of such land for farming. For these reasons they were not only tolerated but even received protection from the noblemen, who would warn them of hostile parties and other dangers. Congregations were founded near Hamburg and Lübeck, and eventually in Altona near Hamburg, where they are still strong today. Here they were legally tolerated after 1601 upon an annual payment of one Thaler tax for each Mennonite householder. By 1605 it is reported that 130 families lived in Altona.

Menno moved into this area for the last years of his life. He was in Wismar until he had to flee following the debate with Micron in 1554. He then settled on an estate of Bartholomäus von Ahlefeldt located between Lübeck and Hamburg, where he built a printshop and was active in writing. Here he also died on January 31, 1561, and was buried in his own garden. The estate was laid waste during the Thirty Years' War, 1618-48, and the Mennonite congregation scattered. Today a monument to Menno Simons, the house where his printshop was located, and a huge linden tree called *Mennolinde* mark the place.

The Vistula Delta Settlements

Mennonites found refuge in another area along the coast of the Baltic Sea. Here again they were welcomed because of their farming and irrigation skill, but there was also more religious tolerance in the free city of Danzig, and on the large estates of the nobility. Many of these estates were in Poland and, for a time, it seemed that there might be as much religious freedom there as in Strassburg. Because of this, and because it was easy to follow the trade routes by water from Amsterdam to Danzig, many Mennonites and other Dutchmen came to the Vistula Delta in the 1530s and after.

A Mennonite congregation was soon established and grew rapidly. Close ties were maintained with the churches in the Netherlands, as the many old letters still kept in Amsterdam show. Menno Simons visited the congregation in 1549 to aid in the solving of a church problem, and Dirk Philips actually lived in Schottland, a suburb of Danzig, approximately from 1561 to shortly before his death in 1568. Church centers were established around the cities of Danzig and Elbing, and further east near Koenigsberg. Mennonites were usually not allowed to settle in the cities themselves, and were constantly subjected to oppressive measures by leaders of the state church. Still, they remained a large and significant group until World War II. Most of the Mennonites who went to Russia in the eighteenth and nineteenth centuries came from these congregations.

A Fellowship Divided

Under the pressures of finding itself as a movement in the midst of persecution, internal problems also arose to trouble the Dutch Mennonites. To some these problems simply proved that the early vision had been lost, to others they were an un-

Gateway to the priory church of St. Bartholomew, Smithfield, London, outside which Anabaptists were burned at the stake in the reigns of both Queen Mary and Queen Elizabeth I. Nearby is a monument which honors the "noble army" of Protestant martyrs. The Anabaptist victims of Smithfield have no memorial.

fortunate but human and necessary part of growing up to Christian maturity as a fellowship. We have already seen how extreme positions arose with David Joris's belief in prophecy and Adam Pastor's tendency to unitarianism and how these movements were rejected by the main body under Menno's leadership. But where do you stop, when you begin to separate from those with whom you disagree? Much of the history of the Mennonites in the Netherlands from 1555 to 1650 shows that there was no clear and simple answer to this question.

In the disputes of this period some weaknesses became clear. The need to maintain purity in beliefs and practices, for example, is a demand which the church and the Christian ought to feel at all times. But how can this be prevented from becoming an unfair judgment of others who are also striving sincerely but find different answers? For some the church as an organization which demands complete agreement and purity overruled their love and concern for those who needed fellowship and support. There were also personal rivalries, though not immediately recognized as such. Even great leaders such as Menno, Dirk Philips, and Leonard Bouwens were not free of this weakness which led to tension and an unforgiving spirit.

A significant source of their difficulties arose from their refugee life and persecutions. As people moved, they took with them the customs of their native land, customs which sometimes became a source of friction in new surroundings. Thus, for example, the Flemish from Belgium were rather quick-tempered and emotional in expression; they enjoyed fine clothing and good food. The northern Frisians, into whose territory they came, were reserved and did not easily show their feelings; they were not as open in their anger, but when aroused did not easily forget it. They were less concerned about how they dressed, but had fine household goods and linens. These differences rubbed the wrong way despite the common Anabaptist faith which these people shared.

There were also differences in how the faith was to be lived. Some people wanted to try new ideas and practices; others wanted to hold to the tried and true ways of the past. Both groups undoubtedly loved the church, but these attitudes were sufficient cause for disagreements. It must be remembered that these people had, for the most part, suffered persecution and believed strongly in their doctrines. Those who were willing to face death for their faith were also often ready to break fellowship with a brother or sister if they thought them wrong. It was the heritage of an age in which religious convictions ran deep and tolerance was not a virtue.

The Waterlanders: The Mennonites of the Netherlands and North Germany today are unions of groups which were divided earlier. Such a division came about in the sixteenth century between the Waterlanders, who received their name from the lakes and rivers region in which they lived north of Amsterdam, and the followers of Menno Simons. The Waterlanders opposed the strict use of the ban and of shunning or avoidance. Menno himself would probably have worked with them, had it not been for pressure from Dirk Philips, and especially from the missionary Leonard Bouwens. Because the church must be kept "without spot or wrinkle" as the bride of Christ, the husband of Swaen Rutgers was banned about 1556 for a reason which has long since been forgotten. But she continued to live with her husband in spite of Bouwens' demand that she shun him. For this disobedience she was herself placed under the ban. In protest the more moderate believers among the Waterlanders left the movement to form their own group. Unfortunately, Bouwens immediately called them the "garbage wagon" because they no longer demanded a pure church. The Waterlander group nevertheless continued to grow, apparently representing the sentiments of a large number of Mennonites. Being opposed to Menno in this, though he was much more moderate than Bouwens, they obviously did not wish to be called Mennonites and were simply known as Waterlanders. They were the first group to hold church conferences with some regularity and with broad representation, beginning in 1568. Under the leadership of Hans de Ries and others, they actively sought unity among the various groups of Mennonites. Their own preferred name *Doopsgezinde*, meaning baptism-minded, is the name used by all Dutch Mennonites today.

The Frisian-Flemish division: Scarcely five years after the death of Menno Simons, a major division was developing among those who, during his lifetime, were united under his leadership. It was the most serious split among the Dutch Mennonites and took the longest to heal, though no major differences in belief were involved. Both parties later divided again but these divisions had less meaning for the Mennonites as a whole. The story of this split is tangled and the interpretation of events is not always clear. It may be, however, that a look at this situation can be of help in seeing how people who were probably right in principle acted wrongly and how difficult reconciliation becomes when divisions are allowed to continue.

A large number of Flemish Mennonites had come to Friesland, as indicated earlier, and placed much stress on local congregations. In 1560 the church councils in four cities—Harlingen, Franeker, Dokkum, and Leeuwarden—made an agreement to work together but, for some reason, kept the agreement a secret. Of the nineteen articles agreed upon, three dealt with the use of ministers in all four congregations, the support of the poor, and a procedure for settling disputes which could not be resolved locally. The Flemish, who had not been included, now wanted their minister included in the team with the others, but his service was called into question by the others because of the secret agreement. This disclosure of the agreement made the Flemish feel that they had been discriminated against. When the congregations were called upon to vote on the Flemish minister, the voting was not properly held and further difficulties resulted.

In this situation Jan Willems and Lubbert Gerrits of Hoorn were prevailed upon to come to Friesland to mediate, both parties having agreed to accept whatever decision they might arrive at. After a careful study, the issues seemed clear to them. They called a meeting of reconciliation on February 1, 1567, which was well attended, also by outside visitors. After a careful introduction the Frisians were asked to kneel and pray for forgiveness for their error. Then they arose and the Flemish were asked to do the same; when the Flemish wanted to arise from their knees, however, they were told that the Frisians would help them up since they, the Flemish, had the greater guilt.

Anyone who knew Flemish tempers should have guessed the result; some assented, but the majority were deeply indignant, and the split was far worse than before.

As the final hope, Dirk Philips came from Danzig to help, together with two other leaders from that area, but no peace could be achieved. The Frisian-Flemish division spread across Northern Europe, drawing other issues into it until few knew just how it had started. The disunity spread within each group as well as between them until there were "Old Flemish" and "Soft or Young Flemish," "Old Frisians" and "Young Frisians," and other smaller splits occurred again from these subdivisions. The tragic, and in a way almost comic, point was reached in Emden, where minister Jan van Ophoorn finally banned everyone in the congregation except himself and his wife!

When people take their convictions seriously and seek purity, they may be tempted to make high demands on others. They may fail to recognize to what degree they have personal weaknesses. Factors such as rivalries between older and younger generations, between leaders, and between groups who rally around some particular idea or practice become occasions for pride and bitterness. Many Mennonites were lost to the Calvinists in the sixteenth century because of their quarreling and splitting. It may be that Mennonites have not yet fully solved the problem of how to be earnestly seeking purity and hold strongly to deep convictions, without splitting over differences between equally sincere believers.

Hans de Ries and Unity

The picture of the church is not as dark as the history of these splits makes it appear to have been. Leaders of broader vision and greater spirit tried to rise above the disputes and restore unity. Lubbert Gerrits, who was unsuccessful in healing the Frisian-Flemish division, later made major efforts for unity, but only the story of Hans de Ries will be told in some detail here. He stands as a symbol of others who shared his spirit.

Hans de Ries was one of the refugees who came north from Belgium. He was born in Antwerp on December 13, 1553. He was a member of the Reformed Church. He was called to the ministry among them, but he objected to their use of arms, which they even brought into church to guard against an unexpected attack. The Mennonites he knew were too divided and rigid for him to join. Later he came north and met the Waterlanders. In 1575 or 1576 he was baptized by Simon Michels and joined that group. He returned to Belgium and was married there, but persecution, which included the burning of his close friend Hans Bret, caused him to flee again. He settled in Alkmaar but spent the years from 1578 to about 1600 in Emden and in traveling from that city. In a sermon shortly before his death in 1638, the octogenarian shared how the poor and suffering church of his youth had now become rich and socially acceptable but how much spiritual vigor had been lost in the process. It was out of this concern to remind children of the heritage of their martyr parents that he had already in 1615 published a history of martyrs which became the basis for the larger and more popular *Martyrs Mirror* by J. van Braght. He also produced a hymnal which went through six editions after the first printing in 1582.

In Alkmaar he helped draft the first-known Dutch Mennonite confession of faith and subsequently became instrumental in formulating additional confessional statements. Mennonites were opposed to confessions lest they replace the Bible as the only authority, but, nevertheless, many confessions did appear in the Dutch Mennonite congregations during this period. They were not intended to measure the orthodoxy of one another. Confessions explained Mennonite interpretations on points under dispute; groups used them to discuss differences and find unity; and congregations used them both for joining with other congregations in fellowship and as expressions of a common faith for admitting others into membership. The primary test, however, continued to be a life of discipleship rather than assent to a set of propositions.

In his unity efforts Hans de Ries stands out more for his kind spirit than for his achievements. Thus, for example, he succeeded in 1601 in uniting some groups into what they called the "Pacified [Reconciled] Brotherhood." Those who did not join formed the "Separated Brotherhood." From 1610 to 1615 he worked hard to make it possible for the Brownists to join the

In 1660 Mennonite minister Thieleman Jansz van Braght published the **Martyrs Mirror**. The book contains two parts: accounts of the Christian martyrs from the time of Christ to the 1500s, and a record of the Anabaptist martyrs until the date of publication. The **Martyrs Mirror** went through several editions and translations and is still in print today. An engraving from the second edition (1685) shows a **multiple execution of Anabaptists on Dam Square** in Amsterdam.

Waterlanders. The Brownists were a refugee group from England who had come to believe at many points as the Mennonites and asked for permission to join them. De Ries carried on a large correspondence in the interest of the church and was frequently called upon to mediate in difficulties as in Haarlem in 1608, Workum in 1618, and Amsterdam in 1626.

Hans de Ries, however, was not the only one working to bring unity to the Mennonites. As early as 1574 Jan Willems of Hoorn was able to get an agreement on the use of the ban which, many hoped, would make unity possible. The agreement was signed in the province of Groningen at Humsterland and was called the Humster Peace. But the Flemish elders would not accept it and attempts to make peace at Emden and Hoorn in 1578 failed. In 1591 the Concept of Cologne did lead to agreement among the High German and Frisian congregations. Later the Waterlanders also joined them. In 1632 a confession was drawn up at Dordrecht and further unified the groups. This Dordrecht Confession came to be widely accepted among conservative Mennonite groups, partly because of its emphasis on discipline and foot washing, two articles which are not found in some of the other confessions. The Palatinate and Alsatian churches adopted this confession in 1660, from where it was brought to North America.

Another step toward unity was taken in 1626, when four ministers of the Flemish branch in Amsterdam sent a letter to all churches in the Netherlands asking what the marks of a Christian church are, whether only the Flemish congregations had them, and whether peace was forbidden by the Scriptures. The answers were not too satisfactory; so on September 16, 1627, they drew up a letter to prepare for peace and sent it along with a confession of faith which they had written. The confession was called the Olive Branch, having been drafted as a sign of peace. Other steps were taken until on October 2-5, 1630, the Flemish and Frisian High German congregations joined them.

These various attempts at union did not bring all the Mennonites together. Two more centuries were to pass before that could happen, yet the forces were working for unity and overcoming the tendency to move apart. By mid-seventeenth century

Hans de Ries (1553-1638) an outstanding leader among the Waterlander Mennonites. Throughout his life he worked toward the unification of the various Mennonite groups.

the Dutch Mennonites were entering more fully into the total life of the country and no longer spending most of their energy on internal disputes. They entered upon a Golden Age, if one measures it in terms of achievements in commerce and culture. Not all of this Golden Age brought gain to the church, however, as Hans de Ries had also said.

The Golden Age

The last Dutch Mennonite martyr died in 1574. With the winning of Dutch independence from Roman Catholic Spain, Prince William of Orange established a policy of toleration which soon benefited the Mennonites. In the city of Middelburg the local authorities had closed all shops owned by the Mennonites and were attempting to force them into military service, but on January 26, 1577, Prince William wrote a letter ordering the authorities to leave the Mennonites in peace so long as they remained quiet and useful citizens. The Union of Utrecht in 1579 provided that each person should be allowed to remain free in his religion.

These actions did not mean that all oppression had stopped, but the Mennonites were no longer forced to go to prison or to the stake for their faith. The Reformed ministers continued to harass them considerably, even rudely interrupting their worship services to ridicule them, but the government increasingly came to their defense. Full freedom of worship, however, did not exist for them until the nineteenth century.

Mennonites nevertheless soon made a place for themselves in the life of the nation. The overseas trade with Greenland and whale and herring fishing were almost completely in Mennonite hands. Most of them did not engage in trade with the United East Indian Company because ships had to be armed with cannons or travel under armed escort to guard against pirates and Mennonites had still retained their nonresistant heritage. They did, however, carry on the less profitable, but still valuable Baltic Sea trade. They were also active in ship-building and in the lumber business. In Amsterdam and along the Zaan River they were leaders in the food industry, and in Drenthe they constituted the backbone of the textile industry.

For the most part, Mennonites were highly literate, partly from a desire to read the Bible and martyrologies, but also by way of overcoming their social disadvantage. In the seventeenth century a high percentage of the medical doctors in the Netherlands were Mennonite, this being one of the professions open to them. Since doctors were the best educated members in a congregation, they often served as pastors at the same time. As engineers, the Mennonites made significant contributions to the draining of swamps. Many also engaged in agriculture and became recognized leaders in that field.

In the fine arts Mennonites soon contributed a number of well-known names also. Carel van Mander was a poet and painter from the Old Flemish of Haarlem and lived from 1548 to 1606. Jan Luyken, who lived from 1649 to 1712, was also known for his work in both fields. The etchings for the second edition of the *Martyrs Mirror* were made by him. The one who ranks among the Dutch people as Shakespeare among the English was Joost van den Vondel, 1587-1679, whose parents fled from Antwerp because of their faith. He was a deacon among the Waterlanders, but left them to become a Roman Catholic about 1640. Other painters and etchers were Solomon van Ruysdael from 1602 to 1670, and Govert Flinck, at least in his youth, 1615-60. It is doubtful whether Rembrandt, 1606-69, was ever a member of a Mennonite congregation, but he had many close associations with them which no doubt affected the religious content of his paintings.

All this progress in material and cultural ways was not pure gain. A century or more after the Mennonites suffered deeply for their faith, they were tolerated and many were wealthy. Many no longer believed deeply in the things for which their fathers had died. Ease and luxury had done what persecution could not do. Galenus Abrahams, a leading minister in Amsterdam, proposed that the devil had found a clever way of dealing with the Mennonites; he stopped persecution and led them to become interested in the material things of the world. The words of Hans de Ries were clearly to the point when he said, "The goods are enriched but the soul is impoverished. Clothing has become precious but the internal decorations have perished. Love has cooled and diminished, and quarreling has increased."

In mid-seventeenth century the Dutch Mennonites had no serious threat to their life from without; leaders arose who tried to reverse the process of cooling off from within. They collected the stories of the martyrs, the writings of the heroes of faith, and wrote the history of their heritage in order to renew succeeding generations. They have left a rich treasure of works. All this, however, could not fully stem the tide of weariness from the quarrels within, and the persecution from without. The peak of membership and activity had passed, and the following century and a half were to witness a gradual, but continuing decline.

Chapter 8

A Summary of the Anabaptist Vision

"ZWINGLI brought me into this thing," Conrad Grebel is supposed to have said about the beginnings of his·reforming zeal, thereby acknowledging his dependence on the reformer. The Zurich Anabaptists made no bones about their indebtedness to others. Only when they became convinced that Zwingli was no longer willing to pay the price of obedience to his own best insights, did they let themselves be led into the creation of an independent movement. Therefore, as we try to identify and summarize those convictions which formed the center of what Harold S. Bender called "The Anabaptist Vision,"[1] we need to remember that it was not the intention of the Anabaptists to provide a full system of truth or an independent organization; they wanted only to correct the inadequacies of the other Reformation attempts which they saw around them.

Scripture Alone

Every branch of Protestantism was committed to letting the Bible be the final rule for faith and practice. For the "official" Reformation, however, it was still the responsibility of political authorities to determine what was to be done about the truth found in the Bible. Thus Zwingli accepted a delay of eighteen months in the abolition of the mass because the government was not ready to move. This was the issue on the afternoon of October 27, 1523, as referred to in Chapter 2. *Zwingli:* "Milords [the city council] will decide how to proceed henceforth with the mass." *Simon Stumpf:* "Master Ulrich, you have no authority to place the decision in the hands of Milords, for the decision is already made; the Spirit of God decides."

This exchange does not, as some scholars have thought, mark the clear and final break between Zwingli and his more radical disciples. It does, however, symbolize the insistence of the Anabaptists that the authority of Scripture takes precedence even over the authority of government. This conviction, as we shall see later, has implications for the government itself—it will lead to the rejection of persecution, war, the oath, and the death penalty—but its first importance is for the church. The organization, the worship, and the doctrine of the church are not the prerogative of government. Although this position is widely accepted today, it was then held only by the Anabaptists.

By the Power of the Spirit

If the Scriptures are to be the final guide for faith and practice, it is logical to ask how they are to be read, since every preacher and every scholar has his own interpretation. The answer of the Anabaptists was clear: in the gathered congregation. They believed that when Christians gather, the Word is preached, some listen, some prophesy, others weigh what is said (1 Corinthians 14:29), and then the Holy Spirit, who is promised to those who gather in the name of Christ, will lead them to be of one mind. It was this conviction about the way in which the Holy Spirit leads in the congregation, which led the Anabaptists to reject any final authority of theologians or princes in the church. Nor was this simply a confidence in the democratic processes of majority rule; the Spirit would overrule human weakness and allow the will of God to become known in their gathering.

This same vision of how the Spirit worked was also applied to problems and discussions in the larger fellowship. We recall from Chapter 3 how such a unifying work of the Spirit was actually experienced at the Schleitheim conference in 1527. The same method was used later in the reconciliation and unity meetings among the Dutch. Unity in the knowledge of the will of God was not to be reached by political or intellectual authorities, nor by religiously gifted leaders enforcing a correct creed, but by the working of the Holy Spirit within the fellowship gathered to study the Scriptures.

Following Christ in Life

Article six of the Schleitheim agreement states, "As Christ, our Head over us, is minded, so should we as members of His body be minded, that there may be no division in the body, by which it would be destroyed." Thus to follow Christ was not childish mimicry but necessary obedience in order that His body the church might be a unity in the world. It was the central argument of the Schleitheim agreement on the sword and the oath. This too had been learned from Zwingli who had said, "To be a Christian is not to talk about Christ, but to walk as He walked."[2] Better known is Hans Denk's motto, "No one may truly know Christ except he follows Him in life."

To see why "following Jesus" was a unique position we must be reminded of what the other churches were saying. The question of the sword is a good example. Whereas Jesus refused to bear the sword and so taught His disciples, Roman Catholics and Protestants alike were agreed that that was not a standard for the sixteenth century. Some appealed to the Old Testament warriors or to the example of honored Christian emperors like Theodosius or Justinian. Some argued that reason or even natural behavior and instinct in a Christian society shows that someone must guarantee peace and order and have the physical power to enforce it. Some again felt that the existing social order was instituted by God in such a way that if you were born a peasant God wanted you to remain a peasant, if you were born a prince God wanted you to be a good prince, and so on. The "vocation" or "station" in life has its own standards and, since it is established by God, must not be changed. Thus when the Anabaptists insisted on following strictly the words and example of Jesus, this was not easily understood nor accepted. Most could think of Jesus as a dying Savior, or as a future judge, but not as someone to follow earnestly in life. Such an attempt seemed not only impossible to begin with since Christ was the Son of God but seemed also to lead back to the Roman Catholic system of saving works by which salvation could be earned.

The call to "follow Christ in life" may seem self-evident today, but for the Anabaptists of the sixteenth century it was a rare and daring claim, and a costly one, for the path of Christ led to the cross.

Love

In the letter which Conrad Grebel and his friends wrote to Thomas Müntzer, referred to in Chapter 2, they said:

> The Gospel and its adherents are not to be protected by the sword, nor are they thus to protect themselves. . . . True Christian believers are sheep among wolves . . . they must reach the fatherland of eternal rest, not by killing their bodies, but by mortifying their spiritual enemies. Neither do they use worldly sword or war, since all killing has ceased with them.

To follow Jesus meant especially to bear the cross with Him, to love one's fellowmen absolutely, even at the cost of one's own life. This position has sometimes been called pacifism, but the term is inadequate because it places the focus on the political goals of peace rather than on the loving concern for persons and the refusal to harm them intentionally. Recently Mennonites in North America have spoken of nonresistance, a term which is also inadequate because it sounds passive and uninvolved instead of actively opposing evil. The traditional German Mennonite term *Wehrlosigkeit* (defenselessness) is a little better. The earliest Anabaptists seem to have had no term specifically for it; they spoke of surrenderedness *(Gelassenheit),* or of the cross, of "the faith and patience of the saints" (Revelation 13:10), or simply of discipleship. Today we might best speak of the way of the cross, of agape (self-giving love), or of suffering servanthood. Jesus called it perfect (i.e., undiscriminating) love. Conscientious objection to military service and to war taxes, and the rejection of litigation (1 Corinthians 6) have been its most obvious expressions in the past. A rejection of national, racial, and class selfishness and an active promotion of international and interracial reconciliation is the obvious modern extension of the disciple's love.

Believers Only

Baptism was not the first difference to emerge between the Anabaptists and the reformer Zwingli, nor the logically most basic one, but it somehow became the most offensive issue. It was the first issue to call down governmental persecution and the one which was to give the young movement its name. In the above-mentioned letter which Grebel and his friends wrote to Müntzer, they said:

> We have learned that even an adult should not be baptized without Christ's rule of binding and loosing. Scripture tells us concerning baptism, that it signifies that through faith and the blood of Christ (as the one baptized changes his attitude and believes therein before and after the baptism) his sins are washed away; that it signifies that one is and should be dead to sin and should walk in newness of life and the Spirit.

The accent does not lie on the emotions involved in the conversion experience, nor on a discussion of what kinds of sentiments a child can or cannot have. The accent is that baptism has a clear, positive meaning. It points to forgiveness but also to a change of attitude, a determination to lead a new kind of life, and a commitment to the fellowship in "Christ's rule of binding and loosing." That this commitment, which is required by the teaching and example of Jesus and the apostles, will not be made by infants need not be argued; it will not be made by all adults, either.

It follows that the church which is faithful cannot expect to be a large or powerful group. By no means could the true church be, like those churches supported by the state and practicing compulsory infant baptism, identical with the nation in membership. From this it follows further that the church must have its own distinct standards for organization, leadership, and membership. The church must be *free* in two meanings of the term—membership must be voluntary, and its organization must be independent. This was precisely what all of the reform-

Because the Anabaptists held that the church is a fellowship of believers rather than a building or an organization, they referred to their simple gathering place as a **meetinghouse** rather than a church. They noted the close relationship between **communion** and community and practiced **foot washing** as a symbol of servanthood.

ers, like the Catholics, feared. They felt this would make the state pagan, and the church would be in danger of collapse if the alliance between the two were broken.

Thus the unique and fundamental meaning of believer's baptism is not just what it says about believers—that faith must be their own; it says something about the church—that membership is free and voluntary and that her only loyalty is to Christ alone.

The Rule of Christ—Admonition

Article six of the Schleitheim agreement states: "In the law the sword is ordained over the wicked ... and the secular governments are ordained to use the same ... but in the perfection of Christ only the ban is used for the correction and exclusion of the one who has sinned." What the sword is to the compulsory community of the state, the discipline of admonition is to the voluntary community of the church. The earliest Anabaptists referred to this practice of taking moral responsibility one for another as "The Rule of Christ," referring to Jesus' words:[3]

> If your brother sins, go to him alone. . . .
> If he listens to you, you have won your brother. . . .
> If he refuses to listen to you, take with you two or three. . . .
> If he refuses to listen to them, tell the congregation. . . .

The normal outcome of this approach is repentance and reconciliation; only in extreme cases will the ban (exclusion from the fellowship) result. The Anabaptists believed that this person-to-person and case-by-case means of restoration and education was the major tool for reformation of the church: "Discipline with the Word and establish a Christian church with the help of Christ and His rule, as we find it instituted in Matthew 18 and applied in the epistles."[4] We have seen that the reason for not baptizing infants was that they cannot voluntarily submit themselves to the "Rule of Christ." Since this practice of voluntary submission provides the method by which all other principles are applied, it is the key to the reformation of the church and its continuing faithfulness.

Membership is made meaningful to the individual by the fact that members share with each other the responsibility for discipleship. Only in this way does membership become important. For the state church reformers *church* meant that organization which, led by princes and scholars, provided for correct preaching. It needed no membership of its own since all people were its responsibility, whether they agreed or not. For the Anabaptists the church was a visible fellowship, separate from the state and other powers in society because its membership is voluntary and because the gathering of such a distinct, visible, caring, and sharing fellowship is God's saving purpose in the world.

With the passing of time it was possible for this redemptive vision of the "Rule of Christ" to be lost. The ban could be applied woodenly, by a minister acting on his own without congregational approval, and on the basis of rules rather than in open reconciliation with the offender. The result would be an attitude of punishment rather than restoration. When this happened, particularly in the Netherlands as we have seen, both the meaning of discipline and the unity of the fellowship were lost. It was on this point that the Swiss and German Anabaptists rejected the rigor of these Dutch practices in 1557.

Never Alone

From the very beginning the Anabaptists spoke of the community of goods as a necessary part of the Christian life. By this they did not mean a common treasury for the whole congregation and its needs; nor did they ever mean what some feared, a revolution to abolish private property as a pattern for a whole society. They were clear, however, that Christians can not call their property their own. They are responsible for their stewardship, not only in some vague way to God, but also concretely to their brothers and sisters and to anyone in need. Where there is need they will give without hope of return. Thus when the common treasury was established in 1528, under the pressure of banishment from Nikolsburg, as seen in Chapter 4, this was no radical innovation but only a further step in the direction already established. The reasoning behind this general Anabaptist teaching on property followed several lines. Love for the brethren demands a willingness to share with them (1 John 3:17); the Lord's Supper itself expresses this sharing of worldly goods. Jesus' teaching on mammon (Matthew 6) and on the conditions of discipleship (Mark 10:21-31) makes it clear that our property is a major focus of our self-centeredness, search for security, and idolatry. If Christ is truly our Lord, our hold on possessions (or their hold on us) must be loosened. They also studied carefully the example of the early church as recorded in Acts 2:44 ff.; 4:34 ff., and, while not taking it as a legal command in every detail, came to see it as a powerful demonstration of the truth that economic sharing and vital apostolic obedience belong together.

Only a Beginning

The vision of the Anabaptists has been sketched here only as it appeared in the very earliest period of the mid-1520s. It was not meant to be a complete charter for the founding of a denomination. On many points, such as the deity of Christ, the authority of the Scriptures, atonement by the death of Christ, and others, the Anabaptists agreed with other Protestants. They wished only to complete the process of reformation and purification which the others had begun and failed to finish. In the mid-1520s they still hoped to win others to this vision. When the pressure of developments forced them unavoidably to the forming of a separate movement, other kinds of growth naturally followed. The scattering of the believers, the small groups which were inevitable and necessary, the different geographic and hence cultural environments added new insights to the movement and broadened the vision, as we have seen in the preceding chapters.

Any listing of how the original vision was filled out and tested in their experience over all Europe would include the pre-Reformation mysticism of Hans Denk with his stress on the importance of the living Word. It would include the arguments on such issues as freedom of the will and original sin in which he, together with Balthasar Hubmaier, furthered theological understanding. Such a listing would include the missionary zeal of

Hans Hut, together with his deepening of the meaning of suffering; it would include the concerns of Pilgram Marpeck, Menno Simons, and a host of others for the wholeness of the fellowship and the fullness of its witness.

At other points the passing of time helped to clarify the boundaries of the Anabaptist movement, showing what belonged in and what did not. The stiffened practice of the ban in the Netherlands, as also the legalism among some of the Swiss Brethren, muddied the waters for a time, but these were, nevertheless, signs of the love they had for the church. The peaceful and revolutionary Anabaptists were clearly and finally distinguished from one another with the collapse of Melchior Hoffman's separate movement and the tragedy of Münster, though their opponents seemed unable to distinguish between them. Similarly the claims of David Joris helped the main body to reject the temptations of "new revelation" in favor of careful biblical interpretation, while the straying of Adam Pastor into Unitarianism warned of the dangers of rationalism. Pilgram Marpeck's successful identification of the issues separating Anabaptism from Spiritualism and the way in which he pointed up the consequences of the doctrine that the true church must remain invisible strengthened the Anabaptist sense of purpose and mission in the world.

At still other points local adaptations were made without really changing the essence of the movement. This may be said of Hoffman's view of the incarnation, of the institution of formal community of goods in Moravia, and later of the use of confessions among the congregations in the Netherlands in which beliefs held in common with other Protestants were included.

It is significant, however, that through all of this broadening and deepening, the essentials of the original vision were retained and clarified. They stood the test of adaptation and of persecution without basically changing in nature. The central understanding of the church's way in the world, which was first hammered out in the mid-1520s survived.

Chapter 9

Mennonites in Europe, 1648-1815

UNDER THE IMPACT of martyrdom, internal divisions, and accommodation to their environment the strength of original Anabaptism had gradually been lost in the four generations from 1525 to 1650. New movements were arising, however, and capturing elements of their spirit. The Baptists emerged with a concern for believer's baptism and congregationalism and the Quakers with a strong peace emphasis. Pietism came to stress the importance of an inner relationship to God. These movements were not without influence upon the Mennonites, but rationalism also came and had a particular effect upon the congregations in the Netherlands. The Swiss and South German Mennonites were best able to preserve their traditional way of life during this period and, to some extent, also the congregations in Eastern Europe in Prussia.

The South

Switzerland: Though Zurich had been the first center of Anabaptism, only the groups in the *rural* cantons of Zurich and Bern remained in 1648. This decline in membership was due, in part, to the strong emphasis upon military preparedness among the Swiss and the consequent pressure upon· nonresistant Anabaptists. But the separateness of the congregations from the

rest of the people and their culture also made them appear un-
patriotic to the nationalistically minded Swiss population. The
resulting pressure to conform led many to give up their faith
and many others to emigration. But emigration itself was very
difficult. It became possible only after 1642 through the
intercession of the Dutch Mennonites with the Swiss authorities. Until 1661, most of these emigrants came to the
Palatinate from Zurich.

As a result of these developments only the Bern Mennonites
remained in Switzerland in the late seventeenth century. Efforts
to win them to the state church through persuasion and persecution continued. Innumerable mandates of suppression were
issued against them in the seventeenth and eighteenth
centuries. The persecutions of 1671, 1691, and 1711 were particularly tragic. A special commission was established to deal with
them from 1699 to 1743. While the death penalty was no longer
applied, other severe measures were taken against them. Many
were sent to the sea as galley slaves. Many were imprisoned.
They were frequently branded on the forehead to identify them
as undesirables. No one was allowed to give them board or room.
Those who reported them to the authorities received a reward.
Mennonite children were considered illegitimate and had no
rights before the law, not even the inheriting of their parents'
property. They could not be buried in the community
cemeteries. Thus it is clear that those who could, emigrated,
especially since they were welcome in Southern Germany and in
Prussia because of their agricultural skill.

Most of the Swiss Mennonites were farmers, though there
were some craftsmen, especially linen weavers, among them.
Because of the persecution few were able to secure an education,
and as a consequence very few writers arose among them. In
matters of faith they simply adhered to the 1527 articles of
Schleitheim, and in their worship the martyrologies of their
forebears, to which they added from time to time, were important. The *Ausbund* was their hymnal. Eventually they also
began to use a Reformed Church hymnal containing translations
of the psalms, but they usually tore out the front page to
eliminate the identity of the book. Use of the 1632 Dordrecht

Confession may have begun as early as 1691. Later, pietism influenced the congregations in the direction of a simple, emotional and inner piety, possibly through the reading of the devotional tract, *The Wandering Soul,* written by John Philip Schabaelje in 1635 and printed later in the German language.

Alsace: In 1648 the Treaty of Westphalia gave Alsace to France, except Mulhausen, which returned to the Swiss Confederacy. This political division also had its effect upon the Mennonite congregations, but they continued to meet as best they could. The record of a ministers' meeting held in 1660 shows the seriousness with which they worked at matters of faith. Names represented at the meeting were Egley, Frick, Habich, Husser, Muller, Ringer, Schmidt, and others. The Dordrecht Confession, which the Flemish Mennonites had prepared in 1632, was adopted for use by the Alsatian congregations. We note further from the record of the meeting that a vigorous discussion was held on the nature of the church, including baptism, swearing of oaths, the ban and avoidance, foot washing, and the nature of Christ. Foot washing, which had been neglected, was reinstated as a biblical ordinance. Questions about the nature of Christ were not fully resolved at this meeting. At issue, presumably, was the question about whether Christ had received His flesh from Mary or from heaven, a question which had been discussed vigorously among the Dutch Mennonite congregations during and following the ministry of Menno Simons.

Meanwhile Mennonite refugees continued to come into the region. Among them was Jacob Ammann (b. 1644), who soon became minister and elder of the congregation in Markirch. There he became troubled over the lack of church discipline in his and other Alsatian and Swiss congregations. Appealing to the Dordrecht Confession which the congregations had now adopted, he insisted that church discipline should include avoidance, i.e., that members have nothing whatever to do with transgressors who had been excommunicated. In its strictest form this meant that even family members must avoid them, making them eat, sleep, and live completely alone. The goal of this action was to force them to repentance. Ammann also insisted that all congregations should practice foot washing, that members wear simple clothing including beards for the men. Though he met with considerable opposition, particularly from elder Hans Reist in Switzerland, he traveled through the churches in Alsace and Switzerland to share his convictions, frequently banning those who disagreed with him. Numerous attempts were made at reconciliation, even Gerhard Roosen came from Hamburg for that purpose, but without success. Gradually this division became sharper among the churches with most of the Alsatian congregations following Ammann, and with most of the Swiss and South German congregations opposing his teaching. From this time (ca. 1700), his followers have generally been known as Amish Mennonites, or simply Amish.

Soon after this division the Amish were faced with an expulsion order from Alsace by the French authorities in 1712. Though they appealed the order they were told to leave. It is likely that the order was given to please Roman Catholics in the area who felt that the authorization of Lutheranism and Calvinism was going too far. Some did leave, but most of them managed to stay, though the instruction to leave was repeated in 1744, 1766, and 1780.

Three Amish conferences were held during this period, one at Steinseltz in 1752, and two in Essingen in 1759 and 1799. The leader among them during this period was Hans Nafziger, who was elected minister in 1731 and ordained as elder soon after. It is he who wrote the detailed statement of how an Amish congregation was to be organized and which has become the pattern for most of their congregations from that time to the present. The first Amish Mennonites probably came to Pennsylvania in 1720. Large migrations to America came later in the eighteenth and to mid-nineteenth century. Settlements were also established in Canada, as well as in Ohio and other Midwestern states.

The Palatinate: The Palatinate of South Germany seemed to be a veritable crossroads for Mennonites in the seventeenth and eighteenth centuries. During this period one finds Swiss Mennonites, Hutterian Brethren from Moravia, Dutch Mennonites, and refugees from other areas all together in this region. The estate owners apparently even welcomed heretics such as the Mennonites were considered to be, if they could work to restore the land after the devastation of the Thirty Years' War. An edict of toleration was issued in their behalf in 1664 by elector Karl Ludwig of the Palatinate. This allowed them to worship in their homes but not to baptize and required the payment of an annual tax for the privilege of toleration.

There is a story of how the elector was riding across his lands one day and come to a Mennonite farm. One of his aides whispered the rumor that the Mennonite was so wealthy because of his skill in making counterfeit money. When the elector confronted the Mennonite with this charge, the farmer simply showed him his blistered hands and said. "All the money I possess has come from this soil through the work of my hands under the blessing of God." According to the records there were twenty-seven congregations with a total of 618 families in this area by mid-eighteenth century. One of their number, David Moellinger (d. 1787), is known to this day as the "father of Palatine agriculture." The Mennonite name Detweiler likewise became synonymous with good farming at this time.

Here as in other congregations of Southern Germany, pietism came to have particular influence among the Mennonites. Leaders in this movement were Peter Weber (d. 1781) and Adam Krehbiel (d. 1804). The leading pietist, John Henry Jung-Stilling, was a personal friend of Moellinger. It was among these congregations also that the prayer book, *Ernsthafte Christenpflicht* (serious attention to Christian duty), was published in 1739, followed by other prayer books later. Of great significance for their congregational life was the publishing of the *Martyrs Mirror* in 1780 through the efforts of Weber and Hans Nafziger.

The North

The Netherlands: In the south the inner life of the Swiss congregations was less open to outside influences than that of those who left to settle in Alsace and the Palatinate. In the north, however, it was the mother congregations in the Netherlands who were influenced, rather than the colonies in Prussia which had sprung from them. Here Galenus Abrahamsz de

Haan (d. 1706) assumed leadership after the Thirty Years' War. He was known as "the last prophet among the Anabaptists." He was a medical doctor ordained to the ministry in the Flemish congregation known as *The Lamb* in Amsterdam. Through him the Mennonites soon came into contact with the English Quakers. In an account of a visit with Galenus the Quaker patriarch George Fox reported that the former asked Fox to take his eyes off him, for they bothered him! Through Galenus many Dutch Mennonites also had contact with the Collegiants, an unorganized lay movement concerned with deepening of the spiritual life. It was his openness to the Socinian brethren from Poland, however, who were anti-Trinitarians, which brought him into difficulties, though he did not agree with them about the nature of Christ.

In time a serious division arose among the Mennonites in Amsterdam. Those worshiping at *The Lamb* church, and led by Galenus, were inclined toward a more liberal interpretation of the authority of the old confessions and stressed the importance of right Christian living under the actual leadership of the Holy Spirit. Those worshiping at *The Sun* church, the conservative wing, with the same intentions as the others, stressed the importance of right doctrine, calling for adherence to the old confessions and traditions of the past. Galenus finally wrote a clarifying statement in 1699, in which he listed the differences between Mennonite doctrine and Reformed or other groups as consisting of (a) the supremacy of the New Testament over the Old Testament, (b) believer's baptism, (c) non-swearing of oaths, (d) nonresistance. The conservatives soon replied with their own statements and a history, written by Herman Schijn (d. 1727), which erroneously linked Anabaptism to the twelfth-century Waldensians.

In addition to these somewhat polemical writings a host of devotional and worship literature appeared among the Dutch Mennonites at this time. These included the *Wandering Soul* and *Martyrs Mirror* (already referred to), numerous hymnals, and a collection of writings from Menno Simons known as the *Little Menno*. These selections from Menno, which were chosen to stress the importance of conversion and discipleship, helped to shape the life and thought of European Mennonites for many years. They were edited by John Deknatel (d. 1759), a minister at *The Lamb* church who was also a close friend of the leading pietist Count von Zinzendorf of the Moravian (Herrnhuter) Brethren. A pietist emphasis soon came to be felt in a number of congregations.

The Dutch Mennonite congregations were also influenced by their economic experiences. Since they had earlier not been allowed to enter such professions as teaching, nor to hold any public offices, many had become traders, i.e., businessmen. By mid-seventeenth century many of them, having now long enjoyed toleration, became quite wealthy. This in turn led to social, cultural, and educational interests and influence. With many members becoming well educated, the demand for trained ministers arose. For a time members who were medical doctors were often ordained, since they had received the most training, though it was not theological training. By 1735, however, a seminary was founded in Amsterdam under the leadership of *The Lamb* congregation to provide leaders and to prevent the continuing loss of their young men who were seeking theological training in the Remonstrant Church seminary. Beautiful churches were built, including the one built in Rotterdam in 1773. With the new buildings came the desire for musical instruments. In 1765 the first organ was installed in Utrecht. Haarlem followed in 1771. Eventually organs were found in most Dutch Mennonite churches. Audible prayer also gradually replaced the traditional silent prayers of the congregation.

Out of the stress upon discipleship among the Dutch Mennonites arose a strong concern for mutual aid. Not only did they seek to meet the needs of unfortunate members among themselves, they also sent relief to the congregations in the Palatinate in 1696, as well as to Prussia and Poland in 1711 and 1713. The aid given to the Swiss has already been referred to. An administrative organization for relief abroad was established in 1725. A society was founded to aid the families of men lost at sea. Pieter Teyler van der Hulst, a Mennonite merchant, established a foundation in Haarlem in 1778 to support museums and scientific research. This foundation is still active. There was

Local, regional, and imperial mandates calling for the extermination of Anabaptist-Mennonite heretics were issued in great number. The city and canton of Bern alone issued 47 mandates between 1527 and 1743. The **mandate of 1711** calls for the compulsory emigration of all Anabaptists. Only a small number of Anabaptists reported for the exile, but on July 13, 1711, four boats sailed down **the Rhine.** Near Mannheim half the passengers escaped to settle in the Palatinate.

genuine concern to use their wealth responsibly as Christian disciples. Through these activities and resources Mennonite cultural, social, and even political influence in the Netherlands grew stronger than Mennonites have enjoyed anywhere else at any time.

In spite of these developments a decline set in among the congregations. Church discipline became lax, as did the observance of traditional ordinances such as foot washing. Mennonite traders and shipowners began to arm themselves, mounting guns onto their ships, because of pirates. When the privilege of nonresistance was withdrawn by the state in 1799, very little objection was heard from the Mennonites. Membership declined sharply, forcing congregations to join together to maintain their programs. Some left for social or economic reasons, some because their heritage no longer meant much to them, some because the Reformed Church seemed to offer much spiritual stimulation. And so, while there had been some 160,000 Mennonites in the Netherlands in 1700, in 1808 there were only 26,953. One hundred congregations became extinct in those 108 years. A gradual recovery was to set in, but was followed by another decline, leading to a baptized membership of 25,589 in 1978. The founding of an all-Mennonite conference known as the *Algemeene Doopsgezinde Societeit* (ADS) in 1811 became the first of many developments which helped to reverse the decline.

The Lower Rhine: The city of Krefeld was destined to become one of the key centers of Mennonite activity in the Lower Rhine region in the seventeenth century. Because it was under the sovereignty of the Dutch House of Orange many Dutchmen, including Mennonites, found their way to the city. Among these was Herman op den Graeff, a competent Mennonite businessman, who came there either in 1607 or 1608. He not only founded his business but established a Mennonite congregation in the city, with close spiritual ties to the Flemish Mennonites. In 1632 he signed the Dordrecht Confession on behalf of the congregation. Numerous new members were added in 1654 and the following years of that decade when Mennonites were expelled from the neighboring duchies of Juelich and Berg. Since these refugees were more High German than Flemish, they gradually turned the life of the congregation in the direction of north German Mennonitism. An open and tolerant attitude to matters of faith became a distinguishing mark of the Krefeld congregation from this time on. In 1693 they were allowed to build a fine church on one of the main streets of the city.

A period of intense prosperity began for Krefeld and the Mennonites when the city came under Prussian control in 1702. Most of the Mennonites in this area were linen weavers, though some, like the von der Leyen family, specialized in silk. In 1731 this family founded the Frederick and Henry von der Leyen company which came to be known internationally for its silk products. For a time the company employed over 3,000 workers, almost half of the population of the city. Special privileges were granted to the Mennonite congregation by Frederick William I of Prussia because of the von der Leyens and in 1721 and 1738 he visited their plant. Later Frederick the Great likewise visited them in 1751 and 1763, presenting them an oil painting of himself. In due course the family was knighted because of their achievements and became a part of the German nobility.

Meanwhile the life of the congregation also changed, particularly through the influence of other religious movements. From 1670 to 1683 the English Quakers worked in that area, influencing some and actually causing some to leave the Mennonite church. Eventually thirteen families followed the invitation of William Penn and settled in Pennsylvania in 1683 to become the first group of German settlers in America. From 1705 to 1725 some of the Mennonites came under the influence of the Dunkards, now known as the Church of the Brethren, who practiced immersion. The mysticism of the poet and hymn-writer Gerhard Tersteegen also influenced the congregation from 1735 to 1769. The Mennonite meetinghouse was one of the few places where he was allowed to preach. This mystic piety soon prepared the way for rationalism. Through the generosity of the von der Leyen family an organ was installed in the church in 1768, and from 1770 graduates of the Amsterdam Mennonite seminary were engaged as ministers. By late eighteenth century one Mennonite mansion after another was being built on Frederick Street, the most imposing one being the von der Leyen "castle" which today serves as the Krefeld city hall. To it Conrad von der Leyen would invite representatives of all confessions in the city for conversations in an effort to encourage tolerance and mutual understanding. A cluster of small congregations formed around Krefeld in the Duchy of Cleve, including one in Emmerich in 1676, Cleve itself in 1681, Rees in 1738, and others. Most of these groups received financial help and spiritual encouragement from the Amsterdam and Krefeld congregations.

South of Cologne, on the right bank of the Rhine, lay the Duchy of Wied. Following the destruction of the Thirty Years' War, Count Frederick (d. 1698) built a new capital on the Rhine in 1653, calling it Neuwied. To rehabilitate his lands he invited whoever would come to settle, including Mennonites, to whom he granted special privileges in 1680. His nephew, Count Alexander, who ruled from 1737 to 1793, caused the Mennonites to build a church near his castle in the same architectural style. Leader of this congregation during this period was Lorenz Friedenreich of Switzerland, a pietist who maintained intimate contact with like-minded brethren in Holland and the Palatinate. The German literary giant Goethe once visited the congregation and subsequently wrote about the "wonderful honesty and integrity" he had seen in the faces of the Mennonites.

East Friesland: In mid-sixteenth century East Friesland became a haven for Mennonites who fled the Netherlands to escape the tyranny of the Spanish occupation. Consequently there were Mennonites in this area throughout the seventeenth century, and several congregations continue to this day. During the early days numerous families had located in the villages of the Krumhorn west of Emden, but by mid-eighteenth century only four city congregations remained in East Friesland, namely, Leer, Emden, Norden, and Neustadt-Goedens. Among these Emden was the center of most activity. Though several graduates of the Amsterdam seminary served these congregations, the members were careful to resist outside influences. Menno Simons' understanding of the incarnation was not forgotten. Church discipline was taken seriously.

While the Mennonites were generally tolerated in this area,

Twice-uprooted Swiss families settled near **Wintersheim in the Palatinate** where they restored neglected fields to fruitful vineyards and abundant fields of grain. In 1770 the Mennonites were given reluctant permission to build a meetinghouse on **the Weierhof,** provided it looked like a farm structure and not like a church.

J.E.N saw This Church Aug 1984

every change of government required a renegotiation of their privileges and the paying of additional compensatory taxes. Nevertheless, these families prospered. As in Krefeld, so here most of them were also weavers, though some became quite wealthy in the whaling industry. Here too the Mennonites began to build beautiful church buildings, installing organs, and calling trained seminary graduates to serve them. One of these men, Hinderk Waerma (d. 1741), representing the old Flemish tradition, prepared a Dutch-French confession of faith in 1757 for use by his congregation. The Emden church experienced a division 1692-1732 over the issue of silent or audible prayer during the worship services. While the traditional form had been silent prayer, the progressive Waterlander Mennonites had shifted to audible prayer early in the seventeenth century under the influence of elder Hans de Ries (d. 1638). This influence was now asserting itself in Emden, itself a Waterlander congregation.

In 1720 Joachim Christian Jahring (d. 1729), a Lutheran pastor in the area, described the Mennonites as follows:

> As is generally known, their life and conduct is praised by many, and it is indeed true that they lead an honest and disciplined life. If differences occur with others over financial affairs, they seek private settlement rather than a decision of the courts. They are never heard to swear, nor do they have disputes and violence among themselves. They seek with all diligence to avoid immorality in every respect. So far as their economic life is concerned most of them are engaged in trade, which they carry on in as large a scale as opportunity provides. Because of this many are very wealthy, which is also enhanced by their frugal living. Some support themselves through farming, linen weaving, bakeries, etc.

Hamburg and Schleswig-Holstein: Anabaptists from the Netherlands and the Lower Rhine had been fleeing to Holstein as a sanctuary from the early days of the movement in the sixteenth century. In Fresenburg near Oldesloe, where Menno himself had spent his last days, a congregation flourished until 1656, in Luebeck until 1720. Particularly attractive were the lands under Danish sovereignty. Congregations arose at Glueckstadt on the Elbe, at Friedrichstadt on the Eider River, and in Altona near Hamburg.

Though Mennonites had received an invitation with special privileges from Duke Frederick in 1623 and settled in the Friedrichstadt area, the high point of their congregational life was reached only in early eighteenth century. Already in 1698 the Frisian, Flemish, and High German groups had united as one congregation. By 1708 they had their own meetinghouse with a cemetery. They also established two homes for orphans, widows, and others without income. Here, as elsewhere, they acquired an excellent reputation through quiet living and intense devotion to agriculture and other peaceful vocations. For a time the same issues confronting the Amsterdam congregations were faced here, but their decisions eventually favored the more conservative position of *The Sun* congregation rather than that held by de Haan. In mid-seventeenth century a serious problem also arose when the magistrates refused to give legal sanction to marriages performed by Mennonite ministers, making their children legally illegitimate, but toleration was finally won.

Mennonites were entrusted with public offices in this area sooner than almost anywhere else in Europe. As early as 1607-8 Jan Coodt Classen near Eiderstedt achieved public recognition in municipal affairs. In 1680 a Mennonite became a member of the city council, followed by others including Nicholas der Ovens who became mayor of Friedrichstadt in 1711. At the same time, however, serious reverses were being felt within the congregation itself. Many young people had apparently been marrying members of the Lutheran state church who thereupon also became Mennonites. In 1751, however, a royal mandate decreed that all marriage partners had to become members of the state church if not already so. This led to a rapid decline of Mennonite membership. Thus, while Friedrichstadt counted 178 members in 1703, they counted only 30 members in 1803, one hundred years later.

A large congregation also arose in Altona. With its adjoining city of Hamburg, Altona enjoyed free city status, both cities governing their own affairs. As traders Mennonites soon found their way to Hamburg-Altona. A special edict favoring them was issued in Altona in 1601 and four years later in Hamburg, as a result of which many Mennonites came to settle there. Though these groups belonged to different traditions, i.e., Frisian, Flemish, and High German, they soon merged into one congregation which located in Altona, while many of the members lived in Hamburg. Coming from the Lower Rhine and the Netherlands, these immigrants naturally brought with them the textile industry as also an interest in shipping and commerce. Some were engaged in whaling expeditions to the coast of Greenland and apparently did very well financially. The profits of the Mennonite whaling crews in 1675, in fact, enabled them to build and completely pay for a new church structure.

An insight may be gained into the life of the congregation through the experiences of two prominent families among them, the Roosen and van der Smissen families. The Roosens came to Altona in 1611 and for 300 years provided strong leadership in the congregation. Prominent among them was Gerhard Roosen (d. 1711), who firmly resisted the immersionist teachings of the Dunkers and the mystical piety of the Quakers around them. At the age of ninety he published a catechism for use in membership classes. This catechism went through many editions and was even translated into the English language. The tenor of this catechism, as of his other writings, was one of accommodation, however, it being Roosen's concern to make Mennonitism appear harmless and as nearly like other Protestant groups as possible. One might describe his catechism as Mennonitism in a minor key (Friedmann).

The van der Smissens came from a patrician family in Brussels and settled in Altona in 1632. Henry (d. 1737) brought fame to the family name through his involvements in the textile and bakery industries. He became so active in rebuilding the city following the Swedish-Danish War of 1712-13 that he was given the honorary title of cofounder of the city. The van der Smissens have been active in the Hamburg-Altona congregation since that time. The life of the congregation would, in fact, be almost unimaginable without the van der Smissen and Roosen families. In 1868 members of the General Conference Mennonite Church persuaded C. J. van der Smissen to come to America as director of the Wadsworth Institute (Ohio), the first Mennonite school for higher theological education in America.

The Mennonites in Prussia—Poland

West Prussia: In 1642 King Wladislaw IV of Poland issued an edict favoring Mennonite settlements in his lands. From the wording of this edict it becomes clear that they had won the respect of their government, and of their neighbors. This became true particularly through their work in draining the swamp lands bordering the Vistula and Nogat rivers, turning erstwhile useless lands into profitable pastures and wheat farms. The cost, however, was high and countless numbers died of swamp fever during the first generation, the estimate of deaths going as high as 80 percent of the settlers for a time. Toleration was the reward granted them for their labors.

This tolerant attitude can be seen, for example, from their experiences in the city of Elbing which belonged to the Hohenzollerns. As early as 1585 two Mennonites were given citizenship in the city, and five years later the congregation was allowed to build their own church. The city council in Danzig likewise was tolerantly disposed toward them but frequently forced to exert pressure upon them to retain favor with the guilds and others who were jealous of Mennonite prosperity. Because of these pressures Mennonites could not receive citizenship in the city of Danzig as late as 1800 and normally had to live on the outskirts of the city.

Persecution was particularly persistent in Danzig. During the Swedish-Polish War of 1655-60, and the Polish War of Succession, 1733-35, many of their houses were destroyed by the war and by those who resented them as a people. In 1660 they were charged by the city with having proselyted and baptized a Roman Catholic woman. Expulsion seemed imminent. The charge could not be proved, however, since the woman herself denied having been rebaptized at all. Similar problems arose again and again, usually initiated by those who were envious of their economic successes. Perhaps the Mennonites, on the other hand, failed to take time for their poorer, non-Mennonite neighbors and scorned them for their poverty. It was also unfortunate that anti-Trinitarianism was strong in that area and that Mennonites were sometimes confused with this movement. Repeated hearings were held to discover their theology, but no anti-Trinitarianism could be found in their doctrines and they stoutly denied it as well.

With the eighteenth century came greater tolerance. This immediately led to the building of churches in many places, though only simple sheds were permitted at first. Thus Thiensdorf built in 1728, Rosenort in 1754, and Fuerstenwerder, Heubuden, Ladekopp, and Tiegenhagen in 1768. In 1783 a second meetinghouse was built in the country, near Elbing. During this period also the congregations gradually shifted from the use of Dutch to German in their worship services. Of significance for the Mennonites was the transfer of sovereignty of this area from Poland to Prussia in 1772 and the subsequent edict of toleration issued by Frederick the Great in 1780. This and later edicts, nevertheless, did not long satisfy the Mennonite conscience, and by 1789 the great migration to Russia was under way.

East Prussia: In early eighteenth century the plague decimated the population of East Prussia. To revitalize his lands Frederick I invited any who would come, but especially also the Mennonites, to settle in that region. The first Mennonites arrived from Switzerland in 1711 but did not stay long. They were followed by others from West Prussia in 1713, who settled in the Memel region near Tilsit. By 1724, however, they were forced to leave again because they refused military service. This expulsion was revoked in 1740, and they returned to establish thriving agricultural communities in the Memel River valley. By 1765 there were 570 members in this region. Congregations had now been established in Königsberg, Brenkenhofswalde, Franztal, and other locations. It was here also that they came into close contact with the Moravian Brethren (Herrnhuter), from whom they learned the practice of child consecration but also acquired a new concern for missions and for the establishing of their own schools in order to preserve their heritage. Gerhard Wiebe (d. 1796) of West Prussia wrote a catechism which was used much in this area and which later found its way to America among the Amish congregations.

Poland: As a buffer state between Germany and Russia, Poland has experienced many boundary changes in its history. West and East Prussia, for example, were added to Poland in

1466. Thus when Mennonites from the Netherlands came to settle along the Vistula River after 1530, they settled in Polish territory. From that time onward until their flight-expulsion from the area in 1945, Mennonites seem to have fared better under the rule of the Polish nobility and kings than under the pressures of state church Lutheranism and Prussian militarism when the latter were in control of the area.

When lands in the Vistula delta and Danzig (Gdansk) area became crowded, or unavailable, the Mennonites moved south along the Vistula River into the interior of Poland, settling at Schwetz, Graudenz, and Culm and eventually near Warsaw at Kazun and Wymysle, as well as southeast to Michalin and into Volhynia. Mennonites and Amish from Switzerland, South Germany, and Alsace settled near Lemberg in Galicia in the eighteenth century, but most of the Swiss-Volhynian and Swiss-Galician settlers later joined the migration of the 1870's to America.

Summary: As we observe the Mennonites in Europe from 1648 to 1815 we note the following phenomena among them: (1) dispersion continues, but toleration is gradually achieved in most places; (2) general economic prosperity which makes them attractive to governments, but stirs envy in the hearts of their neighbors; (3) in the major cities some Mennonites achieve civic prominence and are honored as leading citizens; (4) there is a general numerical decline among them which, if it had continued, would have made them extinct in Europe today; (5) numerous outside influences help to shape their religious life in addition to their economic environment, notably pietism, Quakerism, and rationalism; (6) prominent leaders arise from time to time who, through their writing and active participation in the life of the congregations, give new vision to their people; (7) some of these leaders, and some of the outside movements, brought divisions into the life of the congregations, but by 1815 the impact of tolerance and enlightenment was making it possible for most of the Mennonites to overcome their earlier schisms; and (8) some of this new unity must also be attribed to the influence of pietism, which had led to a recovery of Bible study, prayer, and a sense of mission among them.

Chapter 10

The Mennonites in Russia (USSR*)

THE STORY of Mennonite life in Russia goes back to 1762-63 and the manifestos issued by Catherine II inviting Germans and other Europeans to settle on lands vacated by the Turks in Southern Russia. Catherine II was the German-born wife of Peter III and succeeded him as ruler of Russia in 1762. Within ten years her invitation had resulted in the establishment of about one hundred German colonies in Southern Russia, but the Mennonites were not to come until the 1780s. Even then they were not motivated so much by the attractive settlement opportunity as by the pressure of events at home in Prussia. Growing military preparations, in the face of a Europe made restless by the political upheaval in France, made the Mennonites apprehensive. Then, too, many were coming to be without land. The problem arose from the fact that both military and church taxes were based on land ownership, and Mennonites would pay neither for support of the military nor for support of the state church. The more land they owned, the more difficult it became to finance military and church activities in Prussia, and they already owned approximately 300,000 acres. Consequently,

---

*Union of Soviet Socialist Republics, a federation of republics established in 1917 on the territory of the former Russian Empire.

government controls prevented Mennonites from buying more land. But they had large families to support and what should young couples do for a living?

It is not surprising, therefore, that George Trappe, the special representative of Catherine II, found a very cordial reception among the Mennonites when he came to their Prussian communities in 1786. His reports of the settlement possibilities in the new Russian lands were enthusiastic, kindling a like response among those who heard him. At his urging some of the Mennonites appointed Jacob Hoeppner and Johann Bartsch to visit Russia and bring back a firsthand report. This they did, leaving on October 19, 1786, and returning just over a year later. They had many things to report—a visit with Catherine II herself, real travel difficulties, Hoeppner's broken leg—but most important of all, they reported very favorably about the lands they had visited and the agreement they had been able to make with governmental authorities in St. Petersburg.

The special charter of privileges granted to the Mennonites on March 3, 1788, and later reaffirmed by Tsar Paul I on September 8, 1800, did not vary significantly from the privileges granted to other immigrants. Russian colonial policy at that time aimed at a complete separation of all foreigners from the native population, with the result that colonies were quite independent in their affairs. This pattern appealed to the Mennonites, who cherished the right to control their own religious, educational, and civic affairs as they had been accustomed to doing it in Prussia. Among the privileges was the guarantee of complete religious freedom and exemption from military service for all time. There was also an interesting provision granting the Mennonites special permission to brew beer and vinegar and distill brandy, a trade for which they had already been famous in Danzig and Prussia. These special considerations were justified in the preamble to the charter as follows:

> Conceding to the petition of the Mennonites settled in the New Russian territory, whose excellent industry and morality may, according to the testimony of the authorities, be held up as a model to the other foreigners settled there and thereby deserve special consideration; now therefore with this Imperial Charter we most

graciously wish not only to confirm all their rights and privileges specified in the preliminary agreement concluded with them, but in order to stimulate their industry and concern in agriculture even more, to grant them also other advantages, as follows: (the listing followed).[1]

The First Colony at Chortitza

Under these favorable conditions the first eight families, totaling fifty souls and including Hoeppner, left Danzig (present-day Gdansk) by wagon train on March 22, 1788. It took the group five weeks to reach Riga, less than 300 miles away, where they rested their horses for a month. The next 300 miles took six weeks, bringing them to Dubrovna on July 24. Since Russia was again at war with Turkey, they were forced to spend the winter there. More immigrants joined them in the months following, until there were 228 families in the Dubrovna camp.

For some reason there was not a single ordained minister among all these people. Consequently four men were elected to read sermons they had brought with them, but this did not seem satisfactory to many. Soon there were also twelve couples wishing to get married. An offering was finally taken and sent back to Danzig with the request that it be used to send a minister to them. At the same time, however, the Danzig church had written that they should conduct their own elections for a minister. This was done and twelve names were submitted to Danzig, from which four were approved for ministry. One of them, Bernhard Penner, was later commissioned by letter to serve as elder.

Three weeks before Easter, 1789, six families broke camp and set out for their final destination by sleigh and wagon. Travel was extremely slow, however, and eventually the rest of the group caught up with them. The group had grown larger with other families coming direct from Danzig. Upon arrival at the land selected earlier by Bartsch and Hoeppner, they were advised to settle on the west side of the Dniepr River instead, the east side still being under military operations. A Russian settlement director, who turned out to be greedy and inefficient, was appointed to help them. The new colony, which by now consisted of 400 families, finally located on the banks of the Chortitza River which was a tributary of the Dniepr River. Eventually the

A **Mennonite home** on the outskirts of Millerowo, South Russia. In 1924 almost all the Mennonites of Millerowo migrated to Canada. The **Mennonite Hospital and School of Nursing** at Muntau on Krim Island was built in 1889. In 1927 the hospital was placed under communist control and the last Mennonite manager, Franz Wall, was exiled to Siberia.

entire settlement came to be known as the Chortitza Colony, or also Old Colony since it was the first of the Mennonite colonies in the Ukraine.

Pioneering difficulties were so many in these early years that most of the immigrants became quite dissatisfied. Disease and death took a heavy toll. Rains made the mud huts even muddier. Horses were stolen or lost for lack of fences. Wood for construction was slow in arriving and of inferior quality. The promised government assistance of 500 rubles per family was delayed, much of it arriving eight years later. The people were very poor; even elder Bernhard Penner had to wear homemade sandals to church instead of shoes. Nevertheless, by the turn of the century the 400 families had become established in fifteen villages and were farming approximately 89,100 acres of land.

The problems of pioneer life were made more difficult by a lack of unity among the settlers. In time the frustrations of a large number focused on Jacob Hoeppner, who was accused of withholding funds from the others and of using the knowledge gained on his exploration trip for selfish ends. He was excommunicated from the church and denounced to the Russian authorities, who imprisoned him and made plans to send him into exile in Siberia. He was eventually released, however, and joined the church which had been established by the immigrants of Frisian extraction, though he himself was of Flemish origin. His land had been sold while he was in prison, and he lived the remaining years of his life in silence at Kronsweide. Some years after his death a beautiful monument was erected in his honor on the island of Chortitza in the Dniepr River. The monument was brought to Canada and erected at the Mennonite Village Museum in Steinbach, Manitoba, in 1973.

Educational facilities and leadership were also totally inadequate in these early years. Primitive schools were established, but the children were frequently needed at home, and the teachers were appointed in a haphazard manner. The curriculum was limited and centered around the Bible and catechism. In most villages the same building was used for school and church meetings. These schools, as all affairs of the colony, were under the control of the Mennonites themselves, with little

After initial years of hardship and discouragement, the Mennonites in South Russia built up excellent farms and helped make the Ukraine "the bread basket of Europe." Their buildings were well-kept and orderly; here a Russian employee shows off a prize **Oldenburger stallion** on a Mennonite farm.

interference from the Russian authorities. To facilitate this control each village elected its mayor or *Schulze* with an *Oberschulze* governing the entire colony. Through the *Oberschulze* contact was also maintained with the Russian authorities in Odessa.

The Molotschna Settlement

In spite of these hardships and problems more Prussian Mennonites became interested in establishing new homes in the Ukraine. Economic and religious restrictions were increasing in Prussia, and the reports from Chortitza were not sufficiently negative to discourage others from coming. Elder Cornelius Warkentin of Rosenort in Prussia had visited the Chortitza settlement in 1798, and had discovered the availability of a large tract of land 100 miles southeast of Chortitza on the Molochnaya

River. With this news, others prepared to leave, and the first Molotschna group arrived in Chortitza in the fall of 1803. Their stay with these pioneers during the winter taught them many things which would make their own settlement less difficult. In the spring of 1804 they occupied their lands, soon to be joined by others, until 365 families had arrived from 1803 to 1806.

By now the Prussian authorities were becoming alarmed about the loss of some of their best citizens. The restrictions on land and taxes, which had been so troublesome to the Mennonites, were relaxed and a 10 percent tax was imposed on all immigrants leaving the country. These provisions, together with the Napoleonic War and Napoleon's march on Moscow in 1812, slowed down the movement but did not stop it altogether. By 1835 some 1,200 families had made their home in the Molotschna colony, settling in fifty-eight villages with an acreage of 324,000, thus constituting the largest settlement Mennonites were to establish in Russia. The villages of Halbstadt and Gnadenfeld served as administrative centers. Because this second movement included many teachers, ministers, and other aggressive community leaders, as well as being generally more prosperous than the 1788 movement, progress was rapid and the colony was soon thriving in every respect.

Am Trakt, 1853, and Alexandertal, 1859

Two other colonies were established in Russia before the flow of immigrants from Prussia stopped, the Am Trakt colony in 1853, and the Alexandertal colony in 1859. The Am Trakt settlement was located near the Volga River in the province of Samara, receiving its name from the *Salztrakt*, a road which was used primarily to haul salt and which ran near the settlement. The first nine families arrived in 1853, followed by others until 197 families had located in ten villages by 1872. The original settlement privileges were limited somewhat in that the immigrants had to make a deposit with the Russian embassy in Berlin against costs which the Russian government would have in their behalf. Exemption from military service was limited now to twenty years but available after that upon payment of a tax assessment.

Alexandertal, the last of the original Mennonite settlements to be established in Russia, was also located near the Volga River, not too far from the Trakt colony. It was named after Alexander II, who was ruling Russia at that time, and who showed considerable favor to the Mennonites. Settlement privileges were more limited, and the settlers had to buy their own land, but nevertheless by 1870, 106 families had come to the colony. Marketing problems, and some internal tensions due to the religious fanaticism of Claasz Epp, limited progress in both colonies for a time, but strong leadership helped to place them on a permanent basis by the 1880s. Among the outstanding leaders of the Am Trakt settlement were Johannes D. Dyck (d. 1898) and Johann Bergmann, the former being decorated three times by the Russian government for pioneering achievements. He had spent over a decade in the United States before settling in the Volga region.

With these settlements the Mennonite immigration to Russia came to a close. By this time the threatened loss of exemption from military service in Russia was to lead 18,000 to North America as will be seen in the following chapter. That some Mennonites were sufficiently attracted to come to Russia, while others were, at the same time, sufficiently threatened to leave, is an interesting commentary on Mennonite (and human) nature. In part it was a question of values. Sometimes spiritual values came first; sometimes material values seemed to dominate. Usually it was difficult to distinguish clearly between them.

It is interesting to note that at this very time another large Mennonite group in Prussia, possibly as many as 3,000 were considering settlement in Russia and were ready to forgo exemption from military service, provided they would be allowed special tax and settlement privileges.

In all four colonies the difficult pioneer years gradually gave way to years of remarkable prosperity. Whereas the settlers had originally occupied themselves primarily with small crafts and industries including silkworms, the development of Black Sea ports by Russia gave the Mennonites the possibility of grain production and export. The rich Ukrainian soil was ideally suited for the production of hard winter wheat, for which there was increasing demand all over Europe. With economic prosperity also came greater attention to educational, religious, and cultural affairs. Stronger leaders with better training began to emerge, and the economy was better able to support the increasing cultural and socio-religious activities.

Johann Cornies, 1789-1848

Among these emerging leaders none influenced the settlements more than Johann Cornies, who was appointed mediator between the Russian government and the Mennonites by the czar at the age of twenty-eight. In that capacity he became, in a sense, director of the growth and development of the Mennonite communities in their economic and educational activities, thereby also influencing their religious life.

Johann Cornies was born in Prussia in 1789 and accompanied his parents to the Molotschna settlement in 1804. After his preliminary grade school education he worked for a year as a laborer in a flour mill, than began marketing agricultural produce in nearby towns. Following his marriage in 1811, he settled on a farm in Ohrloff, a village of the Molotschna colony, but without intending to limit his activities to that location. Soon he was renting large tracts of government land for sheep and cattle grazing, including a 9,000-acre tract by 1830. Among his primary interests were the improvement of horses and livestock and the establishing of nurseries for trees and other horticulture. The government soon recognized his outstanding abilities and gave him almost unlimited authority to promote good agricultural practices among the Mennonites and beyond. In 1817 he was made permanent chairman of the Agricultural Association, which came to include all of the economic and cultural activities of the colonies.

Under the umbrella of this association Cornies founded a society for Christian education in 1818, an organization which was eventually to control all of the educational activities in the Mennonite colonies. Under its auspices the first secondary school was founded in Ohrloff in 1820. Through his efforts curriculum reform was undertaken, as was better teacher training, and the groundwork was laid for an excellent school system. Among his specific contributions was a major document on "General Rules Concerning Instruction and Treatment of School Children," containing much excellent counsel for teachers in relation to their school responsibilities.

With his knowledge, drive, and power of position Cornies influenced not only the Mennonites but also the Hutterites and various Russian ethnic groups including the Doukhobors and Molokans. Special instruction in agriculture was given to Russian boys and girls in the Cornies home where they were temporarily employed, and Cornies did need many workers. At the time of his death in 1848, he was farming about 25,000 acres and keeping some 500 horses, 8,000 sheep, and 200 other head of cattle.

Growth in Russia

The large number of children in most Mennonite families in Russia led to a very rapid increase in population and a consequent continuing need for more land since the vast majority gave little thought to any occupation other than farming. The original 10,000 settlers had grown to 34,500 by 1859 but had added very little land to the original acreage. There were, of course, men like Cornies who rented or purchased large estates wherever they could and farmed on a large scale. It is estimated that by 1900 there were as many as 384 such large estates, totaling approximately one million acres, but these estates were the exception. Government regulations stipulated that the original 176-acre plots of land for each family were not to be subdivided by the colonies.

The result of this policy was that many families were soon without land, and without land they became, in a sense, second-class citizens in the land-conscious Mennonite communities. These landless families were given a garden plot at the outskirts of the village and were, for that reason, known as *Anwohner* (marginal people). The landed farmers, on the other hand, were known as *Wirte* or landlords. While the former had no vote since the franchise was based on land ownership, they were obliged to pay taxes which were based on population. The situation became most acute in the Molotschna colony where there were 2,356 landless workers and 1,384 landed farmers in 1865.

The Molotschna landless appealed to St. Petersburg where they received a sympathetic hearing. With pressure from the government, the colony divided up the 64,500 acres of communal land which the landed farmers had been using thus far, into 88- and 40-acre tracts for the landless. But this was only a temporary solution.

With a vision they had not shown before, the two oldest colonies initiated a vigorous program of fund-raising among their established families for the purchase of large tracts of land in other areas of Russia. Here they established the landless and young people in what came to be known as "Daughter Colonies." The new settlers were given ten years to pay for their lands, the proceeds being used for the purchase of more land. While the first daughter colony to be established was Bergthal in 1835, more than forty-five had been added a century later in the Ukraine, Crimea, Caucasus, south central Asia, and in Siberia. In Siberia Mennonites from all of the four old settlements founded the large Slavgorod-Barnaul colony in 1908, with fifty-nine villages on 135,000 acres of land.

Religious Developments

The plight of the landless in mid-nineteenth century gave impetus to a growing restlessness within the church itself. In those years religious organization paralleled community organization; citizens of the community were almost certainly members of the church also.

As the *Oberschulze* (mayor) was in charge of civil affairs, so his counterpart the elder was in charge of the church and, therefore, a powerful figure. The elder was assisted by ministers and deacons who together constituted the *Lehrdienst* (teachers) and who, as preservers of the tradition of the fathers, frequently became defenders of the status quo. In describing the difficult pioneer era, one writer has said:

> Under these circumstances a slow stagnation crept into the intellectual and spiritual life of the group. When missionary David

> Schlatter visited the colonies in 1825, he reported that the church
> had lost its salt. But the spiritual life was to sink even lower during
> the next two decades. What impact could have come from the
> Russian culture was lost since the settlers did not know the
> Russian language.... By 1845 only one item had been printed by
> the Mennonites in Russia.... Continued intermarriage within the
> group led to a unique self and group consciousness. To be a Men-
> nonite meant not primarily religious but ethnic relations.[2]

The dissatisfaction of many with this low spiritual state was
increased by the failure of the church to champion the cause of
the poor, who were all members of the one Mennonite church.
The economic and educational progress made under Cornies'
leadership clashed increasingly with the spiritual traditionalism
of the church and finally stirred the people to action.

Kleine Gemeinde: As early as 1814 a break had occurred in
the unity of the Mennonites in Russia. Klaas Reimer, a young
minister who came to the Molotschna Colony in 1804 from
Danzig, was appalled at the low spiritual life that developed
among the immigrants, especially the lack of personal morality
and ethical concern. He also opposed Mennonite contributions to
the Russian government in the war against Napoleon. He was
particularly opposed to the use of corporal punishment by the
civic Mennonite leaders, believing that since all were church
members, only excommunication should be used to discipline offenders. In reaching these conclusions he was guided by a
serious study of the Scriptures and a diligent reading of the
Martyrs Mirror. This indicated that his central concern was the
restoration of authentic biblical-Anabaptist Christianity. Finding little response in the church, he began meeting separately
with like-minded members in 1812, and by 1814 they were organized as a separate group. The others mockingly called this
minority group the *Kleine Gemeinde* (small church), a name
which the group itself soon accepted fully as indeed indicating
the true nature of the faithful church in a hostile world. (The
group is today known as the Evangelical Mennonite Conference.)
In 1869 a group broke with the *Kleine Gemeinde* over the mode
of baptism and formed the Krimmer [Crimea] Mennonite
Brethren.

Mennonite Brethren Church: Another division which grew out of this restlessness, and eventually affected all of the Mennonite communities, was the organizing of the Mennonite Brethren Church on January 6, 1860. In 1834 Wilhelm Lange, a Mennonite elder in Germany and former Lutheran, had led a group to the Molotschna settlement to found the village of Gnadenfeld (field of grace). Through contact with Moravian pietism in Germany, these settlers had brought with them a strong spiritual concern and religious fervor, and in turn provided contact with other evangelicals traveling through the area. Among these latter travelers was Eduard Wüst, a German pietist, who was soon conducting a series of meetings among the Mennonites. His messages stressed repentance and conversion and called for a life consistent with Christian faith. His meetings led to Bible study and prayer cells. When these Brethren, as they called themselves, despaired of working renewal among the Mennonites, they organized their own fellowship in 1860, with eighteen charter members. Their story will be told·in Chapter 15.

Other signs of renewal: The invigorating forces which gave birth to the Mennonite Brethren Church did not bypass the other Mennonites known simply as *Kirchliche,* i.e., Church Mennonites, or Mennonite church. New spiritual concerns began to emerge among them also, undoubtedly stimulated by the challenge of the division. In 1883 all of these congregations united to form a conference in order to work together in the fields of education and charity. The conference took as its motto, "In essentials unity, in nonessentials liberty, in all things love." In addition to renewed attention to education, a concern also developed for missions and evangelism. Though the Mennonites were forbidden to proselyte among members of the Russian Orthodox Church, a significant outreach began among their neighbors, at times leading to imprisonment and even exile for Mennonite missionaries. Although the Mennonites in Russia had been supporting the Amsterdam Mennonite Missionary Society since 1854, no missionary had been sent by them until 1871, when Heinrich Dirks went to Sumatra. His return ten years later, and appointment as elder among the home congregations, added considerably to their sense of mission. Dirks was followed by at least twenty-eight workers to Java and Sumatra, and one to Egypt. The much smaller Mennonite Brethren Church was also active in mission work during this time, having sent twenty-two workers to India, and two to Africa by 1914.

This new vitality was sparked by the work of numerous members who felt deeply the inadequacies of their church but decided not to break with it. One of the foremost among them was Bernhard Harder (d. 1884). Harder had also been inspired by the preaching of Eduard Wüst and became a powerful evangelist among the congregations without stressing separation as a mark of renewal. He was roundly criticized by many in the Mennonite church for sounding too much like a Mennonite Brethren, and by the Mennonite Brethren for not joining them. But he coveted all the open doors he could find and had ready access to most Mennonite congregations of that time. Though he was a teacher by profession, he occasionally interrupted his teaching to pursue evangelism, being supported during those times by a special group of friends. He has been called the greatest evangelist and pulpit man to arise among the Mennonites in Russia. In the course of his ministry he wrote many poems and hymns, of which over 1,000 have been published.[3] On September 27, 1884, he returned ill from a series of meetings in which he had preached four times daily and died of pneumonia five days later.

Two other developments in the life of the church at this time were the flight into the wilderness of a group under the visionary Claasz Epp, Jr., in 1880, and the establishment of the Evangelical Mennonite Church, generally known as the *Allianz Gemeinde,* in an attempt to overcome the separatist spirit in the settlement, in 1905. Epp was an able leader and farmer who became captivated with the books of Daniel and the Revelation. Under pressure of the events which caused many to leave for America, Epp was led to believe that deliverance from the great tribulation of the last times would come in the East, not in the West. Thus to go to North America was to run away from the Lord. Consequently he led a small group deep into Asiatic Russia in search of the haven *(Bergungsort)* which the Lord had prepared for His people, the Mennonites. Another group, which had joined them from the Molotschna Colony, settled in Aulie-Ata in Turkestan, while Epp pressed on to Ak-Mechet in the Khanate of Khiva. After untold hardship and suffering some eventually found their way to North America anyway, but Epp died lonely and under excommunication in 1913, having climaxed his vision by proclaiming himself to be the Son of Christ and the fourth person of the Trinity.[4]

The *Allianz Gemeinde* arose in the villages of Lichtfelde and Altonau as a unity movement opposed to the increasing separatist tendencies among the Mennonite Brethren. Its founders were prominent leaders within the Mennonite Brethren Church. They advocated and practiced open communion of all true believers in Christ, accepted as members without rebaptism persons who clearly professed and evidenced faith, regardless of their mode of baptism, and broadened the authority base in the congregations by abolishing the one elder system in favor of a council of elders. The well-known historian P. M. Friesen (d. 1911) was a strong advocate of this unity movement, but not one of the original founders. Their bridge-building efforts of love were inspiring, but not too successful. In later migrations those in Canada joined the Mennonite Brethren, those in Paraguay remained separate, while those in Brazil joined the General Conference Mennonite Church.

Economic and Social Progress from 1850 to 1920

The high point of community development among the Mennonites of Russia was reached during this period from mid-nineteenth century to the Bolshevik Revolution. As indicated above, the establishment of daughter colonies continued rapidly under the pressure of a high birth rate. The most comprehensive statistics of Mennonite life in Russia were taken for the decade of the 1920s and constitute an invaluable study of the socio-economic conditions at that time. From them it appears that there were 120,000 Mennonites in Russia after World War I, of which 75,000 lived in the Ukraine and 45,000 in Siberia and other parts of Russia.[5] This does not, of course, include the 18,000 who emigrated to North America in the 1870s.

The agricultural development promoted by Johann Cornies

also made possible and necessary a limited industrial program. Mennonites concentrated on the production of agricultural machinery and the processing of their own agricultural products. Thus by early twentieth century they had seventy large steam-powered flour mills, factories whose combined output included 15,000 mowers and 10,000 plows annually, creameries, and other industrial projects. Six percent of the industrial production in Russia was carried on by the Mennonites. But the vast majority of them were farmers. It has been estimated that the industrial wealth, which accounted for 50 to 75 percent of total Mennonite assets, was in the hands of 2.8 percent of the people. Some of them were very wealthy.

This flourishing economy made possible civic and educational programs unmatched anywhere in the Mennonite world at that time. Mutual aid, homes for the aged, orphanages, hospitals, including a psychiatric hospital, a school for deaf-mutes, a girls' school, and a school of business for young men were only a part of the vast provisions the communities made for their people. By 1914 they had 400 elementary and thirteen secondary or high schools, two teachers' colleges, four trade schools, one Bible school, and negotiations were soon to be carried on with the government for permission to establish a seminary. In addition there were approximately 250 Mennonite students attending higher Russian educational institutions and some fifty in seminaries and universities abroad. It is clear that all of these institutions could not have been supported adequately except by congregations who were experiencing a recovery of their spiritual life and were willing to sacrifice for these causes. This willingness was verified further by their support of some 12,000 Mennonite young men in the forestry and medical corps during World War I which, in 1917 alone, cost the congregations three million rubles.

Developments to 1930

Meanwhile the Russian reform and nationalization program which had begun in 1866 was also affecting the Mennonites. The government-sponsored agricultural reforms led, for example, to a change in regional administrative boundaries. As a result

Mennonites began to find themselves a minority in a local
Russian administrative unit. Where they were in the majority
they were now forced to keep all records and official correspondence in the Russian language. They had also to
contribute to the tax support of local political, welfare, and
educational institutions, as well as support their own. The fact
that many of the landless now received the franchise, moreover,
threatened the traditional balance of power in the Mennonite
communities.

The biggest threat to the Mennonite way of life, however,
lay in the requirement that Russian be taught in all schools and
that Russian teachers would be provided where Mennonite
teachers were not qualified. Russian had been used in some
Mennonite schools as early as the 1830s, and many more used it
by the 1860s, but from 1881 the State Department of Instruction
kept close watch over the Mennonite schools, and in the 1890s all
instruction came to be in the Russian language, with the exception of Bible and German as a language. It is possible that this
development conditioned the Mennonites to see the German language as an essential part of the Mennonite faith itself. Elder
Leonhard Sudermann spoke for many in 1873 when he said,
"those of our young people who enter Russian high schools are
lost," but a Mennonite opponent of this view wrote in 1874:

> It has been shown that the dear, honorable, bishop was wrong. Our
> American brethren confess that it is much more difficult to keep
> their young people in the congregations than in Russia.... The
> number of those who have left the Mennonite faith while studying
> at Russian schools, or later ... is very small. More have been lost
> from those who did not attend Russian schools ... although these
> too have been few.[6]

Most of the Mennonites, nevertheless, had completely learned to
identify themselves in terms of their totally self-sufficient and
exclusive Mennonite communities. The changes which were
coming threatened to assimilate the Mennonites into the
Russian population. This seemed to many to forecast an end to
their historic faith as a people.

The climax of this development was reached with the

passage of the universal military service law of 1874. In antici-
pation of its passage the Mennonites sent five delegations to St.
Petersburg from 1871 to 1873 to plead for the old privileges. We
can appreciate the displeasure of the president of the Imperial
Council when he discovered that two of the leading elders could
not speak Russian even though they had lived in Russia all their
lives. Eventually the delegations were promised an acceptable
form of alternative service instead of military training, but even
this was more than some could tolerate. They asserted that they
did recognize government as necessary, they did obey it
whenever possible, and they did pray for it. They also cited the
official recognition given to them following the Crimean War of
1854-56, when they had made major medical and food contributions and had cared for 5,000 wounded which were brought to
their colonies from the nearby front. Section 157 of the law of
1874 did provide for alternative service by the Mennonites, but
those who felt this to be a violation of conscience, or an indication of further threats to their faith, emigrated to the United
States and Canada. This group totaled 18,000. Among those who
remained was a critic who charged that too many Mennonites
identified their faith with the German language, whereas in
Christ there should be neither Jew, nor Greek, nor Scythian, and
then he added:

> Thank God that they went. It was good for them, their children,
> and for America. They have calmed their conscience ... and
> America has received many good farm families to Kansas,
> Nebraska, Dakota, Minnesota, etc., who will make these states
> rich.... It was also good for us and for Russia; their stubborn
> piety could no longer be met with the concessions they demanded,
> the like of which are almost impossible to grant in a modern Eu-
> ropean nation.[7]

Meanwhile the involvement of the Mennonites with their
Russian environment increased. The Mennonite hospitals served
many non-Mennonites, business contacts with others increased,
and friendships developed as the Russian language ceased to be
a barrier. Thousands of Russians served the Mennonites as farm
laborers and household help and, in many cases, became very

fond of each other. Among Mennonite intellectuals were many who admired Russian literature and read deeply in Russian history to understand the soul of the nation. In the Russo-Japanese War of 1904-5, the families of Russian soldiers from Mennonite areas received very substantial monetary and food aid from the colonies. This involvement, however, was not sufficient to close the social, cultural, and economic gap that existed between the Mennonites and their neighbors. The peasants and many Russian officials were jealous of Mennonite achievements, piqued also no doubt by a certain Mennonite hauteur and condescension which they regarded as a feeling of superiority.

These attitudes, together with Mennonite wealth, brought great difficulty to the colonies with the coming of the Bolshevik Revolution in 1917. As German-speaking people the Mennonites were suspect as enemies of the state in its war against Germany; and as prosperous farmers and businessmen they were soon suspect as enemies of the revolution as well. For a time the struggle between the Red and White Russian armies centered in the Ukraine, the battle front having moved back and forth as many as twenty-three times in some Mennonite areas. With this devastation came pillaging by ruthless bands of robbers and opportunists. One of the most dangerous leaders was Nestor Machno, a political prisoner whom the revolution had released from Siberian exile and who was out to take his revenge on society. Machno knew the Mennonites well, having worked for them as a young man; and he even spoke the Low German language. In his opinion they had underpaid him and he was now collecting his wages with the help of thousands of peasants. As a result of this reign of terror hundreds of Mennonites were killed (240 alone in Zagradovka in November 1919) and countless villages completely destroyed.

During these dark hours most of the Mennonites sought to remain true to the principle of nonresistance and of love for the enemy. For a minority of young men, however, this was too difficult to accept in the face of murder, rape, and wholesale plunder. With earlier advice and some equipment from the German forces they organized what was known as the *Selbstschutz* (self-defense), and gave armed resistance to

Legally exempt from military service, Mennonite young men served as hospital orderlies or as **foresters** instead of serving in the army. To escape the terror of the Stalin era (1919-1953) tens of thousands of Russian Mennonites attempted to migrate to North and South America, but only a small percentage succeeded. **Railroad boxcars held 25 to 28 refugees each,** with meager personal belongings placed on shelves at each end of the boxcar.

Machno, particularly during the winter of 1918-19. Mennonite church conferences later condemned the *Selbstschutz* as both a tactical blunder and a violation of historic biblical nonresistance.

A terrible famine swept over the newly formed USSR from 1921 to 1923 in the aftermath of the revolution and thousands of people died. In desperation the Mennonites sent four brethren to North America to plead for help from the Mennonite churches. The Mennonite Central Committee, which was organized in 1920 in response to this request, sent immediate help and averted heavy casualties among the Mennonites in the USSR as well as aiding non-Mennonites wherever possible. Clayton Kratz, one of the relief workers from Pennsylvania, disappeared mysteriously late in 1920 and was never heard from again. It is estimated that no less than 2,200 Mennonites perished during these years as a result of war, famine, and the typhus epidemic which scourged the land. The four men who had been sent for help had, in the meantime, explored settlement possibilities in Canada and by 1923 a steady flow of immigrants was on their way to join those who had settled there in the 1870s.

Those remaining in the USSR began the difficult task of rebuilding their communities. An agricultural association was organized to coordinate their concerns and to speak unitedly in their behalf. It also became a channel for emigration which made it suspect in the eyes of the authorities. An office was established in Moscow to provide liaisonship with the new government. In 1925 this office began publishing *Der Praktische Landwirt* (The Practical Farmer) to encourage the Mennonites and keep in touch with them. Another publication, *Unser Blatt*, was begun the same year to speak to spiritual needs and issues. 1925 was also the year of the last large Mennonite church conference in the USSR.

With the initiation of the Soviet's first five-year plan on October 1, 1928, which included forced collectivization of their farms, new efforts were made by many to leave the USSR. In a desperate attempt to escape some 13,000 Mennonites made their way to Moscow in the fall and winter of 1929, but only 5,677 managed to get to Germany, due in large measure to the heroic work of a former Russian Mennonite Benjamin H. Unruh of Karlsruhe, Germany. From Germany they were sent to Canada and South America. More might have been allowed to leave if Germany and Canada had been quicker to grant visas, but these nations were having unemployment and other problems of their own as a result of the depression. A few were able to leave in 1930 before all emigration was stopped, bringing to 20,201 the number who had come to Canada from the time the movement began in 1923. Approximately 600 made their escape eastward across the Amur River into China from where they later went to Paraguay and the United States.

The 8,000 Mennonites who had gone to Moscow but had been unable to leave returned to their homes. But many did not arrive there, being sent on to prison or exile and hard labor in the forests of the north. These were followed by countless others who were considered obstacles to the complete collectivization of Soviet agriculture. Many of the exiled never returned. Meanwhile the terrors of collectivization were followed by another famine in 1932-33, in which from five to eight million Russians died, including over 100,000 German-speaking people. The world Mennonite fellowship was again able to send some help to the Mennonites in the USSR.

From 1930 to the Present

Spiritual poverty followed close on the heels of physical suffering. In the new society Christian concepts of right and wrong, property, marriage, education, responsibility, and freedom were changed. Revolutionary rights replaced human and civil rights. It became a time of great suffering. Many wives whose husbands had been deported had all they could do to provide daily bread for their children. The children grew up without proper parental attention and without Christian training. By 1935 a majority of the churches were closed and the buildings used as clubhouses, stables, theaters, or granaries. Membership in these congregations had declined rapidly because of the antireligious propaganda and other threats to the faith. Many strong leaders had escaped to Canada, and those who remained were soon in exile. Non-Mennonites settling in Mennonite villages contributed further to the cultural disintegration of their communities. Some Mennonites also participated actively in the new social revolution. The purges of 1937-38, which victimized over seven million Soviet citizens, also affected the Mennonites. Many of the remaining leaders and ministers were sent into exile. While the exact number may never be known, we do know that in those two years the Chortitza settlement alone lost 800 men. The stories of many of these have been told in a two-volume *Martyrs Mirror.*[8]

With the coming of World War II in 1939, the complete dissolution of the Mennonite communities was only a matter of time. Many were evacuated into Asiatic Russia in 1941, to escape the German front. For those remaining, the German occupation gave a brief period of relative freedom. While Russians suffered miserably at the hands of the Nazis, German-speaking peoples enjoyed numerous privileges; churches were reopened and religious instruction introduced into the schools. Soon, however, the rigors of war and occupation made the German rule almost equally oppressive. With the German retreat following the battle of Stalingrad in the winter of 1942-43, many ethnic Germans including some 35,000 Mennonites were evacuated westward by the retreating German armies. This retreat soon turned into a mass disorganized flight characterized by panic and terror. Hundreds of refugees died, while scores of families were separated. In the closing days of the war and its aftermath thousands were also forcefully repatriated into the USSR and only some 12,000 Mennonites were later found in the western zones of Germany. Most of these subsequently migrated to South America and to Canada.

Little was known about the Mennonites in the USSR immediately after World War II ended in 1945, except that there was continued suffering during the fourth five-year plan, 1946-50. Following the death of Joseph Stalin in 1953, internal relaxation and amnesties were granted to the inmates of many of the labor camps in 1953, 1955, and 1957. Although they were not permitted to return to their former homeland in the Ukraine and the Volga region, they were at liberty to establish new homes. Many of them moved to the USSR of Kazakhstan in central Asiatic Russia, frequently worshiping with Baptist congregations. An additional concentration of Mennonite families occurred in southwest Siberia. A few were allowed to join their families in Canada, and some families were reunited when those living in Canada returned to the USSR.

Meanwhile contacts had also been established between the Baptists in the USSR and the Mennonites in North America. Beginning in 1956 official exchange visits began to take place with Baptist delegations, frequently including Mennonites, visiting North America and North American Mennonite delegations visiting the USSR. These contacts confirmed that Mennonites were losing some of their traditional doctrinal distinctives, as well as their former ethnic identity, but that strong spiritual vitality was evident among many of the estimated 55,000 members scattered across the nation. Many worked intimately with the All-Union Council of Evangelical Christians-Baptists (AUCECB), but others considered these too cooperative with the state and made common cause with the protesting "Reform Baptists," the Council of Churches of Evangelical Christians-Baptists (CCECB) since 1961. The Russian language had almost completely replaced the German among them, and Mennonite young people were attending universities, as well as entering the various professions.

The Mennonite presence in the USSR had by no means come to an end, though their existence had changed radically since the first settlers had come 200 years earlier. By 1980 over 10,000 Mennonites had been able to leave the USSR for West Germany and Canada, but most of those remaining had settled down to being faithful disciples in the context of socialism and in spite of totalitarianism. In many congregations and house churches women were carrying primary leadership responsibility, though none had been ordained. Baptisms, communion, and weddings continued to be performed by itinerant male ministers. New congregations were being formed and some officially recognized. But some continued to suffer imprisonment and exile— ostensibly because they had violated the laws of the land, but laws which seemed to them to demand compromises they were unable to make.

Chapter 11

The Mennonites Come to North America

MENNONITES came to North America after their sixteenth-century persecution had ended in Europe. They came to escape the continuing oppression, discrimination, and intolerance they were experiencing, especially the pressure of rising militarism. They came to seek economic opportunity and adventure. Like the Puritans, who came to Massachusetts Bay by mid-seventeenth century to plant a new Eden in the wilderness, the Mennonites came to preserve the faith, to plant the seeds of a true New Testament church, and to fulfill the vision for which their fathers and mothers had suffered so much. God was giving them another refuge.

Those who came were part of two broadly related yet culturally unique streams, the Swiss-South German and the Dutch-Prussian-Russian, with the latter coming first but the former soon dominating the scene until well into the nineteenth century. There are references to Dutch *Menists* being in Manhattan (New York) as early as 1644, and on Long Island (New York) in 1657. In 1663 Pieter Cornelisz Plockhoy, a Mennonite Collegiant from Amsterdam and London, established a communitarian settlement of 41 persons, including Mennonites, at Horekill on the Delaware River. But the colony was destroyed a year later by British troops.

On October 6, 1683, a group of thirty-four Mennonites and Quakers from Krefeld, Germany, arrived in America after a 10½-week journey and settled in Germantown, just north of Philadelphia. It was from this group that the first formal protest against the slavery system in America was issued in 1688. By 1705 the Germantown settlers had been joined by others from the Lower Rhine area until they totaled approximately 200. A log meetinghouse was erected in 1708. It was replaced in 1770 by a stone building which is still in use.

From these early beginnings until 1824 European Mennonites settled primarily in the United States. First among these were some 4,000 Swiss and South German Mennonites and about 200 Amish. All went to eastern Pennsylvania. The Seven Years' War (1756-63) between England and France ended further immigration. Continuing unrest in Europe prevented renewed movements until after the Napoleonic wars were over in 1815. From that time on some 3,000 Amish Mennonites came from Alsace-Lorraine and South Germany to Pennsylvania. They also moved further west to Ohio, Illinois, and Indiana. By the time of the Civil War in 1860 a group of at least 500 Mennonites and Amish Mennonites had come to Ohio and Indiana directly from Switzerland.

Meanwhile some Mennonites had also begun moving north to Canada after the Revolutionary War of 1776. By 1800 a considerable group had left Pennsylvania for the Niagara area in Ontario. In 1807 Benjamin Eby founded Ebytown, now Kitchener. These were joined later by Amish groups coming directly from Alsace-Lorraine and Bavaria, as well as additional Mennonites and Amish from Pennsylvania. The need for more land and a desire to remain loyal to the British crown were the primary reasons for the northward movement.

The total number of South-German, Swiss, and Alsatian Mennonites and Amish immigrants to the United States and Canada probably did not exceed 8,000. This includes a small group which came after 1865, and to the present.

In contrast to this the number of Dutch-Prussian-Russian immigrants were far more numerous. But most of them entered North America only about a century ago, except for the initial small group mentioned earlier. From 1873-1884 approximately 18,000 immigrants came from Russia to the Midwest. Nearly 8,000 of these included the more conservative groups, who settled in Manitoba, Minnesota, South Dakota, Nebraska, and Kansas. Some 300 immigrants from Prussia and about 400 from Polish lands also arrived in Kansas and South Dakota. Fifty years later, in the decade of the 1920s, these were followed by an even larger number of immigrants. Some 21,000 from the Soviet Union entered Canada. A small group went to California via China. The number coming to Canada since the end of World War II in 1945, directly from the Soviet Union via Western Europe or indirectly via South America, has exceeded 15,000 and is continuing. Thus the total number of immigrants in this ethnic-cultural tradition stands at well over 55,000. When added to the earlier Swiss-South German figures, some additional Prussian Mennonites, and Hutterites, the immigrant total of all groups from the beginning to the present stands between 65,000 and 70,000.

The Environment of the Early Settlers

The Mennonites came to America at the invitation of William Penn who granted 18,000 acres to six men of the 1683 group on condition that they establish a colony. On their arrival they soon met Francis Daniel Pastorius (d. 1720), who had himself bought 25,000 acres from Penn and served as land agent for the Frankfurt Land Company. He helped to further Mennonite immigration. Through his efforts and the enthusiastic letters of the settlers, other German minority groups found their way to America and became the neighbors of the Mennonites. These included the Dunkers (Church of the Brethren) in 1719, the Moravians in 1735, and the Schwenckfelders in 1734.

These groups, and especially the Mennonites, soon almost covered what is now Lancaster County and continued to branch out. They had many things in common religiously, especially the moral earnestness and Bible-centered emphasis of both Anabaptism and pietism, yet they tended to keep to themselves. At first the Mennonites and Quakers shared a common meetinghouse for worship, but by 1705 the Quakers built their own, as did the

William Penn, an English Quaker, received land in America from King Charles II in payment of a debt. Penn extended a cordial invitation to the Quakers, Mennonites, and other oppressed minorities to join him in his noble experiment of a peaceful society. In the same spirit, Penn worked out a **treaty with the Indians** already living in the area.

Mennonites three years later. At first the Mennonites also shared in the duties of governing Germantown but soon left it to the Quakers who, in turn, were to leave it to the Presbyterians and Anglicans. Germantown had been incorporated in 1691 but lost its charter in 1707, during its Mennonite-Quaker period, because not enough members could be found who were willing to hold office.

While Mennonites preferred isolation and tried to preserve it through geographic and language boundaries, they could not escape the influence of their environment. Without realizing it or wanting it, they were becoming part of the North American social, political, and economic scene. Mennonite history cannot be rightly understood without understanding this context.

Long before the Mennonites came, earlier settlers had begun to occupy huge tracts of Indian lands, pushing the natives westward slowly but surely until, in the course of time, those who remained could be relocated onto reservation lands which the white man did not want. Most Mennonites tried to befriend the Indian and some suffered greatly because they would not resort to violence. But they did enjoy farming the good land and were probably unaware of what they were doing to the culture and future of the Indian nations. It is estimated that there may have been some 900,000 Indians in what is now the United States and 400,000 in what is now Canada when Columbus landed in 1492. But instead of increasing in number three fourths of them had been killed by 1800 until there were fewer than 250,000 in the USA and fewer than 95,000 in Canada. Spanish and French Roman Catholic missionaries were active among the Indians from the beginning. A few Protestants, including especially John Eliot, the Mayhew family, and the Moravians were also at work, but the Mennonites did not begin organized evangelistic outreach among the Indians until the late nineteenth century.

Negative feelings of Mennonites toward native Americans were undoubtedly stirred by unfortunate incidents like the following, resulting from the inevitable clash of interests on the frontier. A settlement of thirty-nine Mennonite families in Page County, Virginia, experienced an Indian raid in 1758, followed by a second raid in 1764. In this second raid the Indians were led by a white man on a bloody rampage which was to cost many lives. Preacher John Rhodes was killed in the doorway of his home and his wife and son in their yard. A son who climbed a tree to see what was happening was shot in the tree and killed. Still another son was shot and killed as he tried to swim across a river. Later they killed two daughters and another son whom they had taken as captives. A fourth captive was later released by treaty. The most remarkable escape was made by a daughter Elizabeth, who seized her baby sister and ran into the barn, barricading it against a pursuing Indian. While he ran away, presumably to get fire to burn down the barn, Elizabeth escaped through a hemp field with her sister, and fled twelve miles to a married brother's home.

An attitude of unconcern and of overcoming obstacles to pioneering was dominant along the frontier and naturally in-

The first permanent Mennonite settlement in North America was established in 1683 at Germantown, Pennsylvania. The log meetinghouse which served the pioneers was replaced in 1770 by this fieldstone building, the **oldest Mennonite meetinghouse** in continuous use in North America.

fluenced the Mennonites. This was true not only of the "American" Mennonites, but also of the later immigrants from Russia, as the "Metis incident," which occurred near present-day Winnipeg on July 1, 1873, illustrates. During their travel in what is now Manitoba the delegates sent from Russia to explore settlement possibilities in North America were set upon by an angry mob of natives who rightly sensed that their future was at stake. The delegates might never have lived to return home had it not been for the gun of their guide and the quick arrival of a contingent of troops. But this did not deter the delegates from recommending the area as a place of settlement. The incident was apparently considered to be the kind of problem pioneers ought to be prepared to expect. Violation of the rights of others—as we see it from the perspective of the 1980s—was not a central issue for them. The issue was the suitability of the location and the guarantees of the crown.

The story of the black minority experience in America is also part of the context for the Mennonite experience. In 1619 the Dutch ship *Jesus* arrived at Jamestown, Virginia, from the West Indies and landed twenty black Africans. These were to serve from three to seven years as "indentured servants" to pay for their passage. Then they would be free. Indeed one of them, Anthony H. Johnson, later himself became one of the largest holders of servants in the colony, both black and white. But only too soon the tobacco and cotton economy, requiring cheap labor, brought about the slavery system. By 1710 there were some 50,000 slaves in the USA, by 1776 some 500,000, and by 1860 some 4,000,000.

The petition of 1688 had placed Mennonites on record as opposed to slavery. So far as we know this attitude governed Mennonite conduct during the entire Colonial Period. The Quaker John Woolman (d. 1772) told of a Mennonite who traveled a great distance to visit a friend, but when he saw that he owned slaves he refused his hospitality and slept in the forest. So also the later Burkholder Confession of 1837 (Virginia) stated that "as all are free in Christ, they must take no part in slaveholding or in trafficking with them in any wise."

These were not isolated Mennonite statements or actions of that time; they were becoming increasingly conscious and concerned about racism. But often by quietly acquiesing in the racism of their surrounding culture they also participated in it. It is encouraging to note that what is now the Allegheny Mennonite Conference passed a strong resolution against the Ku Klux Klan in 1924 because it discriminated against "Jews, Catholics, and Negroes." In that same year, however, another district conference encouraged the establishing of separate congregations for blacks and cautioned against "close social relations" or intermarriage. It was only after World War II that Mennonites, as part of the Civil Rights Movement in America, began to speak and act courageously here and there against the sin of racism and began to help solve some of the enormous social problems with which racism had saddled the nation.

An early leader among the Germantown Mennonites was William Rittenhouse, who also became the first papermaker in North America. **The Rittenhouse home** still stands along the creek, but the mill was not rebuilt after floods washed it away the second time.

The Mennonites and Amish Spread Out

Surrounding the Mennonites during the Colonial Period, up to the Revolutionary War in 1776, were a growing number of other church and nonchurch people. While the Mennonites did have large families, the descendants of the original 4,000 immigrants were still a very small part of the total population of the United States, estimated at three million in 1776. Of these only about one in twenty was a church member. The size of the denominations in 1774 were approximately as follows: Anglican 480 congregations, Presbyterian 543, Congregationalists 658, Baptists 498, Quakers 295 "meetings," Dutch Reformed 251, Lutheran 151, and Roman Catholics with ca. 24,500 members in 50 parishes. The sum total might have been approximately 3,000 congregations, which would theoretically have meant at least 1,000 members in each—except for the one in 20 problem.

Yet most Mennonites remained largely to themselves, fearing rather than seeking contact in that vast sea of secularism. The desire to escape these contacts, the need for more land, and other factors led to their rapid spread across the land. In the 1760s and 1770s Mennonites and Amish settled in southwestern Pennsylvania and in Maryland to form what has been known since 1954 as the Allegheny Conference. As early as 1735, Lancaster Mennonite families located in Franklin County, and by the time of the Revolutionary War also in adjoining Washington County, Maryland. In approximately 1810-1830 they formed the Washington-Franklin Conference.

The movement to *Ontario,* referred to earlier, was not without its problems. A few families had moved there as early as 1786. By 1800 about sixty persons had settled at Vineland, and a settlement was begun that year in Waterloo County. It was in the latter county where the Mennonites bought land only to discover that it had a $20,000 mortgage on it. This was more than they could pay, so two men returned to Lancaster County for help, which they received. In the 1820s these groups were joined by Amish Mennonite immigrants from Europe, who formed the Ontario Amish Mennonite Conference a century later, in 1922. In 1959 they joined the Mennonite General Conference and in 1963 changed their name to Western Ontario Mennonite Conference. From these groups settlers began moving westward in the 1890s to Alberta and Saskatchewan. The Alberta-Saskatchewan Conference was organized in 1907.

Another problem facing the immigrants to Canada was the Militia Act of 1793, which stipulated that all persons between the ages of sixteen and fifty were required to pay a militia tax of twenty shillings per year in time of peace and five pounds per year in time of war. But even more threatening to the Mennonites was the fact that many of their young men did not join the church until some time after age sixteen and would, therefore, be eligible for the draft. A petition of 1810 to the Crown relieved them of this latter problem, but the militia tax remained in effect until 1849 when a bill was passed abolishing

The **Pioneer Tower** near Kitchener, Ontario, marks the spot where the first Pennsylvania Mennonites settled along the Grand River in the spring of 1800. The **Clemens family mirror** survived the trip from Montgomery County, Pennsylvania, to Waterloo County, Ontario, in a Conestoga wagon.

the possibility of paying a tax or a fine in lieu of military service and exempting the Mennonites from military service requirements. Meanwhile, however, they had encountered war first-hand when the British demanded their horses, wagons, and supplies in repelling the American invasion of 1812-14.

While the Ontario movement was under way, others moved west to *Ohio, Illinois*, and *Indiana*. Both Mennonites and Amish settled in *Ohio*, with the first families arriving in 1799. While the Old Order Amish formed no conferences and worshiped in homes, the Amish Mennonites gradually adopted the English language, Sunday schools, and church buildings. In the years 1916-27 they merged with what is now the Mennonite Church. Oak Grove in Wayne County became one of its major congregations.

As in Ohio, both Mennonites and Amish Mennonites settled in *Illinois*, largely in the 1830s and 1840s. The Amish Mennonites arrived first, coming from Alsace-Lorraine, Hesse, the Palatinate, Bavaria, and Switzerland, with the greatest number from Alsace. The first congregation to emerge was Partridge, which is represented today in the large Metamora church. One of the strongest leaders in the history of the Illinois Amish Mennonites was Joseph Stuckey (d. 1902), often called "Father Stuckey." In the course of time he found himself somewhat out of step with the other leaders of the Midwest and ultimately withdrew from the Amish Mennonites to form the Central Conference Mennonite Church (name adopted in 1914). In 1946 this group affiliated with the General Conference Mennonite Church. A second leader among the Amish Mennonites was John Smith (d. 1906), whose son C. Henry Smith (d. 1948) has been called the "dean" of American Mennonite historians.

Mennonites and Amish also came to *Indiana* in the 1840s. A few settlements had been established in 1838, when Swiss immigrants from the Jura in the canton of Bern began to settle in Wells and Adams counties. The Adams County Swiss Mennonites are now well known through the large Berne congregation with over 1,300 members. This congregation affiliated with the General Conference Mennonite Church in 1872. A strong leader in the Berne church was S. F. Sprunger (d. 1923). A few families from Lancaster County and the Shenandoah Valley began to settle near Arcadia, between Kokomo and Indianapolis, in 1838 but the congregation remained weak and died out by 1900.

The strongest settlement of Mennonites in Indiana was made west of Goshen in Elkhart County, beginning about 1840. Two early major leaders in this area were John F. Funk (d. 1930), who came to Elkhart from Chicago in 1867, and the outstanding evangelist, John S. Coffman (d. 1899). In 1853-54 a number of conservative Frisian families came from the Netherlands to settle in Elkhart County also. Amish families began moving into Indiana in 1841, settling primarily in Elkhart and Lagrange counties.

By 1839 the westward migration of the Mennonites and Amish reached *Iowa* with the arrival of John C. Krehbiel from the Palatinate in Germany. The first church was to be organized in Lee County in 1845, but was postponed to 1849 because of the murder of their minister. The movement to *Missouri* came about the time of the Civil War, and to Kansas early in the 1870s. By 1900 the descendants of the colonial Mennonites, and those coming directly to the west from Europe, had reached the Dakotas, Montana, Colorado, Washington, and Oregon, as well as Oklahoma, Arkansas, Texas, Florida, and California. By the mid-1960s few states remained where descendants of the early immigrants from Switzerland and Germany had not established thriving communities and congregations. In Canada, Quebec had been added as the fourth province in which congregations were established.

During this century or more of frontier experience the Mennonite self-image as the faithful remnant amid growing denominational proliferation remained relatively strong. The transition from Pennsylvania German to English was slow in the church and family, the Dordrecht Confession of 1632 served as guide in doctrine, church discipline was generally mild and loving, and discipleship was taken seriously in a tradition where little new biblical or historical study was being carried on.

The Revolutionary War of 1776, and the Civil War of 1861 were a time of testing for the Mennonites, but also strengthened their identity. Since about one third of the population in the United States was loyalist in 1776, and about one third indifferent to the issues, it was not difficult for the Mennonites to affirm loyalty to King George III, as well as to affirm their nonresistance. Here and there public feeling ran high against them, but already in 1775 the Continental Congress passed a resolution assuring nonresistant persons of their right not to bear arms, while encouraging them to be active in the meeting of human need caused by war. This did not prevent some from leaving for Canada, as we have seen.

The Civil War of 1861-65 brought into sharp focus that the Mennonites had grown lax in their teaching of nonresistance. Some hired substitutes to serve in their place, but the church soon discouraged this practice of paying someone to do what one's own conscience forbade. In the North most Mennonites ended up paying a $300 fee and in the South $500 in lieu of military service. Most Mennonites considered this a legitimate government-imposed tax, in contrast to the Quakers who mostly refused to pay it. The shock of the war and its pressure upon the Mennonites became a major factor leading to new spiritual life among them, but many potential members from among their own families were lost to the church in this period.

The Coming of the Mennonites from Russia

We have seen in Chapter 10 how and why the Mennonites went to Russia from Prussia beginning in 1789 and continuing to the mid-nineteenth century. By the time the last immigrants had arrived in Alexandertal in 1870, the first contingents were ready to move on to America. One of the major events in North American Mennonite history in the years from 1873 to 1950 was the coming of over 50,000 Mennonites from Russia to the central provinces and states as mentioned above. While their coming added significantly to Mennonite life in the United States, the locating of 36,000 of them in central Canada actually began an entirely new chapter in their own religious life, as well as in the life of their new homeland. Most of these immigrants eventually affiliated either with the General Conference Mennonite Church or the Mennonite Brethren Church, though some remained inde-

A massive migration of Russian Mennonites to the Canadian and American West began in 1874. They soon established new homes and farms, schools and industries. **The mill at Steinbach, Manitoba,** reveals a three-century accumulation of Dutch, North German, and South Russian innovations in its design.

pendent or belonged to the *Kleine Gemeinde*—now the Evangelical Mennonite Conference.

From 1873 to 1884: During this period approximately 18,000 Mennonites came to the central states and provinces from Russia, of whom 8,000 settled in Manitoba, 5,000 in Kansas, 1, 800 each in Minnesota and the Dakota territory, and the rest in Nebraska with a few in Iowa. They came because a new military law which became effective in 1874 seemed to threaten their exemption from military service. Section 157 of that law actually provided for alternative service in forestry or medical work. But they were not accustomed to alternative service and were afraid this was simply the beginning of an end to their coveted religious freedom. Other motives were also involved in their leaving: the increasing pressure upon minority groups to assimilate with the Russian population, land hunger resulting from the high Mennonite birth rate, and an unwillingness or inability to deal creatively with the problems of a changing society.

The way to North America had been prepared by twelve deputies who had been sent to spy out the land. These men were very much encouraged by the friendly attitudes of the American Mennonites and by favorable settlement opportunities. Their return in September 1873 marked the beginning of the emigration. While Canada had gone further in guaranteeing religious freedom than the United States because each state had to pass its own legislation, more settled south of the 49th parallel in order to escape the isolation and harsh winters they anticipated in Manitoba. At least one of the deputies would be extremely surprised if he saw Manitoba today, for he wrote very negatively about his impressions. Winnipeg, he said, "is only a small town," and as he traveled across the lands reserved for them, his diary reports:

> The people are lazy farmers of mixed Indian blood.... The land does not seem bad.... The wheat stand was small but looked fresh and healthy. One could also see considerable unthreshed wheat left from the previous year.... We continued our journey through many muddy and marshy places.... The roads were very bad.... We came to a house where only the wife was at home.... They had been living in Canada for two years.... She praised the country, very likely because she wanted neighbors.... This region seemed more subject to drouth.... The mosquitoes were so bad that one could hardly defend himself.[1]

His inspection report concluded with the remark, "To most of us Manitoba country was not to our liking, but seven of the brethren liked it." Since there were only twelve deputies, the majority actually preferred Manitoba. On his return trip through the Dakotas the deputy wrote that they saw some grasshoppers, "but not as many as in Manitoba." In strong contrast to this pessimism is the report of the Governor General Lord Dufferin after a visit to the Mennonite settlements in Manitoba in 1877, only a few years after their arrival:

Although I have witnessed many sights to cause me pleasure during my various progresses through the Dominion, seldom have I beheld any spectacle more pregnant with prophecy, more fraught with promise of a successful future than the Mennonite settlement. When I visited these interesting people they had been only two years in the province, and yet in a long ride I took across many miles of prairie, which but yesterday was absolutely bare, desolate, untenanted, the home of the wolf, the badger, and the eagle, I passed village after village, homestead after homestead, furnished with all the conveniences and incidents of European comfort, and of a scientific agriculture; while on either side of the road, cornfields ripe for harvest, and pastures populous with herds of cattle stretched away to the horizon. Even on this continent—the peculiar theater of rapid change and progress—there has nowhere, I imagine, taken place so marvelous a transformation.[2]

Reports from the other settlements in the United States were equally glowing. In 1883 one Kansas writer said that "the sight of their [Mennonite] fields and orchards, their trim buildings hedged in with mulberry, is like a glimpse of some fair new land of promise." A few years later *The Daily Record* of Lawrence, Kansas, reported:

After sixteen years those Mennonites are with us still. They abided and toiled in Marion, McPherson, and Harvey counties ... went on tilling their 100,000 acres of land ... and every fall, no matter what the season, wheat has been brought to the Newton market in untold quantities from that settlement.... The Mennonite says nothing, but goes on marketing his fat cattle, his corn and wheat....[3]

The wheat was the new, hard winter wheat which they had brought with them from Russia, and for which they were to become modestly famous.

The Mennonites of Ontario and in the United States had given real encouragement to the immigrants, having raised over $100,000 for their transportation and settlement costs. In 1873 they had set up a Board of Guardians to administer this aid in the United States and a similar committee in Ontario. John F. Funk, the publisher-editor in Elkhart, Indiana, who had been a most vigorous and able champion of the immigration, began a new paper called *Die Mennonitische Rundschau* in 1880 for the

Mennonites from Russia. It was hoped that this paper would help to overcome the geographical separation of the immigrants from each other and from the American Mennonite communities. The new settlements continued to prosper and congregations arose quickly. In 1882 they founded a school for higher education, which was to become Bethel College of Newton, Kansas. Several years later a deaconess hospital was established in the same city. Another school, which was to become the Mennonite Collegiate Institute, was founded in Gretna, Manitoba, in 1889. Soon the new immigrants seemed to be not only fully at home in the North American environment, but also surpassing the economic, social, and spiritual levels of their former home.

From 1922 to 1930: Meanwhile events in Russia were leading to the second major Mennonite exodus, bringing an additional 21,000 persons to Canada and some 4,000 to South America. It must be remembered that 70 percent of them had not emigrated in the first movement. Some had stayed because they were too comfortable to leave, some because they did not sense a threat to their freedom in the way those who left did, and some stayed because they felt that to be the will of God. Among these last were those who believed that God had called the Mennonites to Russia for a purpose and that leaving would be running away from God. One elder wrote, "Some consider it a matter of conscience to go; I consider it a matter of conscience to stay.... We are to be the salt of the earth, and salt is needed here as much as anywhere else." He added that the Mennonite witness had opened the door to religious freedom in Russia, and who could tell what God would yet do in that land because of this.

Even the most sturdy became concerned, however, with the bitter civil war and the establishment of a communist government in Russia after World War I. They sensed immediately that more would be at stake than the loss of exemption from military service, an exemption which was, in fact, maintained until the late 1920s by the new government; at stake would soon be the right to an undisturbed church life, the right to have their own church institutions to care for the sick, handicapped, and aged, the right to nurture their children in the Christian faith, and other rights which they considered essential to their identity and survival as a Mennonite people. Consequently a commission of four men was sent to North America by the Mennonite congregations and made arrangements for their coming to Canada. Others, however, still hoped to stay and carried on difficult negotiations with the young government. A petition in 1925, for example, pleaded, "Give us our children, give us freedom to train and educate them in accord with the commands of our conscience," but their hopes were not to be fulfilled in the new emerging social order. Thus they began to leave the land they had grown to love, at first reluctantly and in small groups, selling their lands to other Mennonites eager to extend their holdings; but soon reluctance turned to haste, and haste to panic until all emigration was stopped in 1930.

The life of those settling in South America will be told in Chapter 17. Those coming to North America all settled in Canada except perhaps 100 who were allowed to enter the United States for special reasons. The Canadian Board of Colonization, which had been organized under the chairmanship of David Toews to raise the necessary funds for travel, made valiant efforts in settling the newcomers on prairie farms. With the depression and drought years of the early 1930s, however, many relocated in Ontario and British Columbia. In keeping with their life in Russia, they again established schools, homes for the aged, and hospitals together with their constantly increasing congregations from the Pacific Ocean to the Great Lakes. An increasing number of their children acquired advanced training as teachers, doctors, social workers, and in other professions, but they remained essentially a rural people until World War II. With few exceptions, they were only moderately successful financially during the first two decades, but a strong spiritual life was apparent in many of their congregations. During this period most of their worship services were conducted in the German language, with lay ministers carrying primary responsibility.

From 1946 to 1954: Approximately 35,000 Mennonites in Russia were evacuated to Poland and Western Europe by the retreating German army following the Battle of Stalingrad in

1943. Of these, some 23,000 were later forcibly returned to Russia by the Russian and Allied troops, but approximately 12,000 remained in the west. Most of these wished to join their relatives in Canada, but health and other reasons prevented many from going. Rather than stay in Europe, they chose to settle in South America and nearly 5,000 located in Paraguay, Uruguay, and Argentina. Over 7,000, however, did come to Canada and were soon scattered across the land with friends and relatives, most of them preferring to live in cities where work could be found. With hard work and high postwar wages most of them were soon financially independent. Since few of them had settled in closed communities, they did not build their own churches but joined the Mennonite churches around them. Because of their urban living, acculturation was extremely rapid among them as they settled down to become Canadians in the full sense of the word.

For Conscience' Sake

All of these migrations, both to North America and within its boundaries, show the Mennonites to have been a people on the move. A study of their history reflects an endless pilgrimage from one corner of the earth to the other. We have seen, for example, how the first immigrants were ready to leave Russia for America by the time the last had come to Russia from Prussia. Similarly, the immigrants to Canada in the 1920s and again in the 1940s came just in time to buy up the farms of those Mennonites leaving for Paraguay and Mexico. From their sixteenth-century European origins the Anabaptist-Mennonites have spread to Asia, North America, South America, and even Australia. Africa was seriously considered at one time. Until recently the Mennonite self-image which has emerged because of these migrations has been that of pilgrims and strangers in a hostile world, the church in the wilderness seeking to remain pure for the coming of the Bridegroom, Christ. Harold S. Bender once wrote:

> It is not that Mennonites do not love the soil or have no sense of home and homeland. Nor is it that they have not loved the men and

women of the lands in which they have lived, or that they were unwilling to stay and carry on even after difficult circumstances. It was the hostile world around them which would not tolerate them, which forced them to go, which was unwilling to let them stay and maintain a faith and a spirit which was a challenge to its own system.[4]

It is clear that freedom of conscience was central to these migrations, particularly if conscience is defined to include the economic, social, and other conditioning factors which shaped their life together as much as pure religious convictions. And conscience worked differently with different people, urging some to leave for the sake of their faith and some to stay for the same reason. How can it be shown that those who left a country first were more faithful to God than those who stayed the longest and often perished for their faith? The faith and beauty but also the agony and pathos of those who were forced to make a decision one way or another are reflected in the words of a young colonist in Mexico:

Great-grandfather migrated with his family from Prussia to South Russia via the wheelbarrow route. He lies buried there. Grandfather with married sons and daughters came to Canada in 1873. He sleeps beneath the soil in Manitoba. Now father, an old man has brought his family to Mexico where he is starting all over again.[5]

Chapter 12

The Mennonite Church

EXCEPT for a few Dutch and North German families who settled at Germantown and from there spread out into Franconia north of Philadelphia, the original members of the Mennonite Church were almost pure Swiss in origin. We have seen earlier that the first members in Switzerland were called *Täufer* (Baptizers) or Anabaptists but that they preferred to be known simply as Swiss Brethren. In Germany and the Netherlands the Anabaptists were also known as *Wiedertäufer* (re-baptizers), or *Taufgesinnten, Doopsgezinden* (baptism-minded). After 1545 the Dutch Anabaptists, and eventually the Germans, came to be called *Mennists* or *Mennonists* after Menno Simons. Since Menno Simons had nothing to do with the Swiss Brethren, however, how would they be known after they came to America? The question was complicated by the fact that the very first Anabaptist descendants to settle in America were from the Dutch wing at Krefeld, hence Mennonites.

One of the earliest Mennonite documents in America is the 1724 deed for the land on which the first Germantown meetinghouse had been built in 1708. In it the land is described as belonging to the "Meeting of the people called Mennonist (alias Menisten)"—which means that the congregation was known as Mennonists or as Mennists. The 1738 Alms Book of the Skippack congregation refers to the members of the church as *Taufs-gesinden*, which is a variant spelling for *Tauffsgesinnten*. When the children of Bishop Henry Funck published his book on how Christ fulfilled the Old Testament, 1763, they described their late father as a "Minister [*Lehrer*] of the New and Old Testaments of the Church of the Believers on Jesus Christ which are nicknamed *Wiedertäuffer* or Mennonists." A common name for the church in Pennsylvania deeds of the 1700s was Mennonist Society. Mennonites did not like the German word *Kirche* for their fellowship, so in English they used the Quaker term *society* rather than *church*, which to Mennonites meant state church.

Finally, perhaps before 1800, the Mennonites of Pennsylvania began to call themselves Old Mennonites (*Alt-Mennoniten* in German). The later schismatic groups, such as the Herrites in Lancaster County, or the larger Oberholtzer body in Franconia, were then dubbed the New Mennonites. The main body actually became fond of the name, Old Mennonites. They used it on cornerstones of meetinghouses, on tombstones of ministers, and in common speech. The word was acceptable until various bodies of Mennonites who withdrew from the Old Mennonites from 1872 to 1901, because they rejected the Sunday school and other changes as the result of the "Great Awakening," came to be called Old Order Mennonites. Then some Old Mennonite leaders became sensitive about the word "Old," fearing, no doubt, that it would confuse the larger mother body with the Old Order children who opposed the Sunday school. Leaders like Bishop Daniel Kauffman, editor of the church paper, often wrote the name *Old* in parentheses, thus: (Old) Mennonite Church. Harold S. Bender, a more recent leader in the group, did not want the word *Old* in any shape or form; so he insisted that *The Mennonite Encyclopedia* refer to the group as the Mennonite Church (MC). In 1971 the Mennonite General Conference, which had existed since 1898, became the Mennonite General Assembly, with a new constitution which specifies that the official name of the group shall be the *Mennonite Church*.

Original Settlements

The oldest conference of the Mennonite Church, Franconia,

began in 1683 and became the Germantown congregation north of Philadelphia. From there a daughter congregation, Skippack, was started in 1702. In the next few decades the other congregations of the Franconia Conference were established. Most of these were located in what are now Montgomery and Bucks counties. Settlements were also made in neighboring counties, such as Chester, Berks, Lehigh, and Northampton. But the bulk of the Mennonites of the Franconia Conference live within a fifteen-mile radius of Souderton, a town within Montgomery County but near the Bucks County line.

In 1710, just eight years after the Germantown Mennonites started the Skippack settlement, Swiss and Palatine families settled near the present town of Strasburg in what is now Lancaster County. Here the Willow Street or "Brick" congregation developed. Other congregations soon emerged. New groups also formed in York, Adams, and Lebanon counties.

Within two decades after settling in Lancaster County, Pennsylvania, some enterprising Mennonites had found their way to Page County, Virginia. The early settlements in Page, Shenandoah, and Frederick counties died out, while the congregations in Rockingham and Augusta flourished. The scattered congregations of the Allegheny Conference, largely in southwestern Pennsylvania, were founded for the most part around the time of the Revolutionary War (1775-83) and the following years. The Mennonite churches of the Washington County, Maryland, and Franklin County, Pennsylvania, Conference were established for the most part a little before 1800. Although scattered Mennonite families were in Franklin County by 1735, the main migration to the area did not take place until the 1790s. The Ohio congregations of Mennonites began to spring up in the early years of the 1800s, and the Amish followed the Mennonites into Ohio as early as 1808. The Amish settled in Illinois in the 1830s and the Mennonites in the 1840s. Mennonites began to locate in Indiana in 1838, and the Amish followed in 1841. Mennonites reached Missouri in the 1850s, Kansas in the 1870s, and Oregon in the 1890s as discussed in Chapter 11.

The distribution of the Mennonite Church membership in North America is as follows:

Conference or District	Membership	Congregations
1. Allegheny	3,578	36
2. Atlantic Coast	4,060	40
3. Church Communities	83	19
4. Conservative	7,503	92
5. Conservative (York & Adams Co.)	233	7
6. Conservative Fellowship	496	10
7. Council of Mennonite Churches in New York City*		
8. Cumberland Valley	340	6
9. Eastern Pennsylvania	2,430	49
10. Fellowship Churches	1,019	25
11. Franconia	6,017	45
12. Franklin	948	11
13. Gulf States	379	9
14. Illinois	4,088	37
15. Indiana-Michigan	12,131	102
16. Iowa-Nebraska	4,767	41
17. Lancaster	16,466	192
18. Mennonite Christian Brotherhood	302	9
19. Mid-Atlantic Fellowship	558	7
20. Mid-West Fellowship	841	15
21. New York State Fellowship	563	5
22. North Central	529	14
23. Northern Light	249	21
24. Northwest	795	13
25. Ohio	11,404	81
26. Ontario	4,944	39
27. Pacific Coast	1,874	21
28. Rocky Mountain	1,428	21
29. South Central	3,939	49
30. Southeast	1,588	21
31. Southeastern	726	16
32. Southwest	985	16
33. Unaffiliated	4,567	79
34. Virginia	5,321	65
35. Washington-Franklin	836	10
36. Western Conservative	298	9
37. Western Ontario	2,993	15

*Congregations hold membership in Atlantic Coast or Lancaster Conferences. Total membership is 424 in 13 congregations.

Summary: Total baptized membership in Canada, 9,767; in the United States 99,511 for a combined total of 109,278. (*Mennonite Yearbook*, 1981, p. 147).

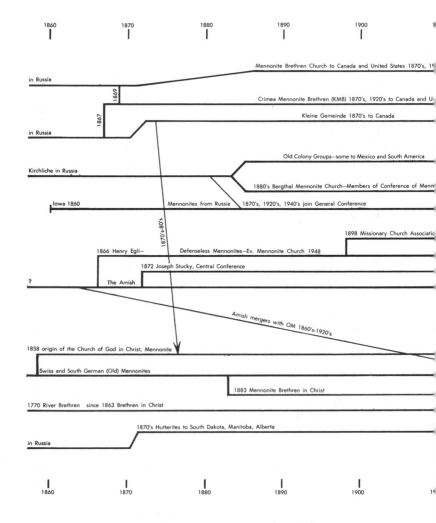

1860   1870   1880   1890   1900

Mennonite Brethren Church to Canada and United States 1870's, 1

in Russia

1869

Crimea Mennonite Brethren (KMB) 1870's, 1920's to Canada and U

1867

Kleine Gemeinde 1870's to Canada

in Russia

Old Colony Groups—some to Mexico and South America

Kirchliche in Russia

1880's Bergthal Mennonite Church—Members of Conference of Menn

Iowa 1860   Mennonites from Russia   1870's, 1920's, 1940's join General Conference

1870's-80's

1898 Missionary Church Associatio

1866 Henry Egli—   Defenseless Mennonites—Ev. Mennonite Church 1948

1872 Joseph Stucky, Central Conference

?   The Amish

Amish mergers with OM 1860's-1920's

1858 origin of the Church of God in Christ, Mennonite

Swiss and South German (Old) Mennonites

1883 Mennonite Brethren in Christ

1770 River Brethren   since 1863 Brethren in Christ

1870's Hutterites to South Dakota, Manitoba, Alberta

in Russia

1860   1870   1880   1890   1900   1

1920	1930	1940	1950	1960	1970

1960

Since 1959 Evangelical Mennonite Conference

Ev. Menn. Mission Conference

1936-37

joins GC 1946

Old Order Amish

1910 Conservative Amish Mennonite Conference

NONITE FAMILY TREE IN NORTH AMERICA

since 1947 United Missionary Church

Church Government

When the Mennonites began to come to America prior to 1700 and in the following years until the middle 1700s, there were no district conferences in Europe. The first American Mennonites were congregationalists in church government. Occasional ministers' meetings had been held in Europe to discuss issues, however, and the same was soon true in Pennsylvania. In the year 1725, for example, sixteen ministers from five congregations or settlements in southeastern Pennsylvania held a ministers' meeting and adopted the Dutch Mennonite Dordrecht Confession of Faith (1632) as their doctrinal standard. They wrote a quaint endorsement of this Confession of Faith: "We the hereunder written Servants [that is, Ministers] of the Word of God, and Elders in the Congregation of the People, called MENNONISTS, in the Province of Pennsilvania [sic!], do acknowledge, and herewith make known, that we do own the aforegoing CONFESSION, APPENDIX, AND MENNO'S Excusation, to be according to our Opinion; and also, have took the same to be wholly ours. In Testimony whereof, and that we believe the same to be good, we have here unto Subscribed our Names." Then follow the names of five Lancaster ("Conestoga") bishops, two Franconia bishops, and nine Franconia preachers.

Other ministers' meetings were held, both in the Franconia and Lancaster settlements. In the course of time these meetings were held regularly, each spring and fall, both in Franconia and Lancaster. Sooner or later, perhaps from the very beginning, the oldest bishop in terms of service presided. The first man to sign the above mentioned confession in 1725, was the first man to serve as an American Mennonite bishop, Jacob Gottshalk (d. 1763), who began to baptize and administer the Lord's Supper in 1708 at Germantown. There was no prepared program of addresses at these ministers' meetings, no written agenda, no constitution, no secretary, and no minutes, indeed, no officers of any sort. In a general way the bishops served as leaders, with the senior bishop presiding. What are now spoken of as the semiannual meetings of conference were therefore at first unofficial and informal ministers' meetings to discuss the life and welfare of the congregations of the area. In the course of the decades, however, these ministers' meetings grew in prestige and influence and eventually became church synods or district conferences which increasingly set the disciplinary standards for the congregations of the regions involved. For a century and a half, or longer, no disciplinary standards were printed and adopted. Lancaster adopted its first *Rules and Discipline* in 1881 and Franconia followed a few decades later.

The Mennonite Church, therefore, has a form of church government which is difficult to name. It is neither purely episcopal, synodal, nor congregational, but a combination of all three. The district conferences now set the basic disciplinary standards for the congregations. The bishops or pastors, assisted by the deacons or the congregational elders, attempt to carry out these standards in the congregations of their charge. Major matters of policy are, however, subject to congregational discussion and decision. This type of church discipline involves an intricate system of checks and balances, with some variations in different parts of the church. Some conferences put more weight on the authority of the bishops and on the decisions of the conference; others are more inclined to stress congregational government.

Organization

The organizational structure of the Mennonite Church has changed over the years with the changing needs of the congregations and their mission. In 1720 there were no Mennonite organizations in North America other than the several dozen congregations. By 1820 the older district conferences, such as Franconia, Lancaster, Washington-Franklin, and possibly Ontario, had emerged, and Virginia and Ohio soon followed. Between 1875 and 1895 three boards were organized: Publication, 1875; Missions, 1882; and Education, 1895. These, in turn, became the Mennonite Publication Board in 1908, the Mennonite Board of Missions and Charities in 1906, and the Mennonite Board of Education, also in 1906. In their earliest forms these three boards, therefore, antedated the Mennonite General Conference, which was organized in 1898.

As the church grew in its identity and sense of mission, these forms again seemed inadequate. There was need for

Directory of Mennonite
Church Organizations*

The churchwide mission of the Mennonite Church is carried out through the Boards listed below. These are supported by contributions from the membership, with exception that the program of the Mennonite Mutual Aid Board is supported by enrollment in their services and the program of the Mennonite Publication Board is supported by purchases of books, curriculum materials, and periodicals.

CONGREGATIONS

REGION—DISTRICT—CONFERENCE

GENERAL ASSEMBLY

Officers
Nominating Committee
Council on Faith, Life, and Strategy

GENERAL BOARD

Coordinating Council
Historical Committee
Convention Planning Committee
Interboard Committees
Minority Affairs Committee
Latin Caucus
Black Caucus

Mennonite Board of Congregation Ministries
Audiovisual Library
Congregational Education (English and Spanish)
Congregational Evangelism
Congregational Family Life Education
Congregational Leadership Training
Congregational Peace and Social Concerns
Congregational Program Planning
Congregational Stewardship
Congregational Youth Ministries
Cross-Cultural Experiences
Ministerial Information Center
Women's Missionary and Service Commission

Mennonite Publication Board
Mennonite Publishing House
Book Publishing (Herald Press)
Periodicals
Provident Bookstores
Congregational Literature

Mennonite Board of Missions
Child Welfare
Choice Books
Deaf Ministries
Developmentally Disabled
Home Bible Studies
Home Missions
Hospitals
Media Ministries
Minority Ministries
Nursing Homes
Out-Spokin' Bike Hiking
Overseas Missions
Retirement Communities
Student Services
Voluntary Service
Young Adult Services
Youth Services

Mennonite Mutual Aid Board
Menn. Mutual Aid, Inc.
Menn. Mutual Aid Assn.
Menn. Automobile Aid
Menn. Church Bldgs.
Menn. Retirement Trust
Menn. Foundation
Menn. Insurance Service.

Mennonite Board of Education
Subcommittees of the Board
Boards of Overseers
Colleges
Seminaries
High Schools
Elementary Schools

—From *Mennonite Yearbook*, 1981

greater freedom on the part of the congregations to do their work but, at the same time, an increasing need for conferences and boards and committees which could serve the congregations in fulfilling their mission. The old General Conference, which not all the district conferences had joined anyway, lacked the flexibility and openness for growth in the 1970s and beyond. Consequently the Mennonite General Conference was succeeded by the General Assembly in 1971, and with it a new commitment to doing God's will in church and world. The directory of organizations on the facing page, beginning with the congregations at the top, presents a simple but comprehensive picture of the channels set up for being and doing the work of the kingdom.

Four Major Leaders

John Fretz Funk, 1835-1930: The most important figure in the life of the Mennonite Church in the nineteenth century was John F. Funk. Born in Bucks County, Pennsylvania, he took summer courses in the Mennonite school, Freeland Seminary (now Ursinus College), and taught school three years. In 1857 he moved to Chicago and entered the lumber business, working first with his brother-in-law, Jacob Beidler, and soon going into business for himself but with a partner. Converted in 1858 under Presbyterian influence, he returned to his home church, Line Lexington in Bucks County, and was baptized a year later. In 1864 he started the first successful church periodical of the Mennonite Church, the English *Herald of Truth*, and its German twin, the *Herold der Wahrheit*. That same year, 1864, he also married his second cousin, Salome Kratz (d. 1917), one of his former pupils. They had six children, four of whom died in childhood. In 1865 Funk was attending the services of a small Mennonite congregation in a schoolhouse near Gardner in Grundy

---

*Additional Mennonite Church statistics include: (1) number of ordained persons in North America, 3,012; (2) regular places of worship, 1,247; (3) schools—88 elementary, 17 secondary, 1 junior college, 3 liberal arts colleges, 1 Bible institute, and 2 seminaries; (4) total giving in 1979 for all causes, $40,494,488; and (5) membership of overseas churches and programs related to the Mennonite Church—33,129 members in 610 congregations.

County, Illinois. There John M. Brenneman ordained him to the ministry. Two years later Funk, then thirty-two, sold out his lumber business in Chicago and established his home and a printing business in Elkhart, Indiana. Here he lived the remaining sixty-two years of his life, dying in his ninety-fifth year.

Funk started the publication work of the Mennonite Church, first as an individual, then in partnership with his brother Abraham, and finally as the Mennonite Publishing Company in 1875. In 1908 he sold his periodicals to the young Mennonite Publication Board which had its publishing house at Scottdale, Pennsylvania.

Funk also had a vision for building up the spiritual life of the church through Sunday schools. He had been an ardent Sunday school worker for D. L. Moody in Chicago and knew the value of the Sunday school. Indeed, he had regularly attended three Sunday schools in Chicago: as a pupil in one, as a teacher in a second, and as the superintendent of a third! By personal urging and by public appeals through his *Herald of Truth,* Funk was a leading figure in helping the Mennonite Church to establish Sunday schools throughout his church from east to west, largely in the period 1865-95.

As early as 1882 Funk led the Indiana Conference to set up an Evangelizing Fund to send preachers to neglected communities and members. This fund was administered by an Evangelizing Committee which ultimately developed into the general mission board of the Mennonite Church, the Mennonite Board of Missions and Charities.

Funk also felt that it would be a help to the unity of the Mennonite Church to create a General Conference. Consequently he mailed from his Publishing Company office a letter to the ministers of the church asking for their reaction to the plan of setting up a General Conference. The response was favorable and a number of district conferences appointed representatives to do the initial planning. After a number of committee meetings were held, a preliminary meeting was held at the Pike meetinghouse, Elida, Ohio, in 1897. The first regular session of the Mennonite General Conference was held in 1898. Funk preached the conference sermon.

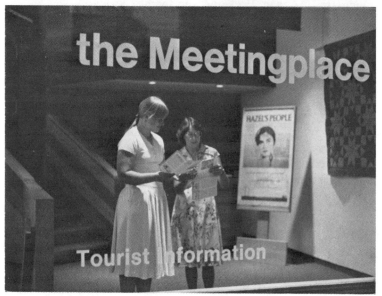

John L. Ruth—author, filmmaker, and storyteller—answers questions at an Anabaptist Heritage Seminar. Architect **Leroy Troyer** favors community participation in shaping our meetinghouses and educational facilities. **Mennonite Information Centers,** museums, and heritage centers help to share the story of our spiritual pilgrimage with interested outsiders.

No one can estimate the influence of John Fretz Funk on the Mennonite Church. He was more than any one leader the founder of the publication and mission work of the Mennonite Church and the strongest promoter of the Sunday school. He and Daniel Brenneman also held the first series of evangelistic meetings (then called Protracted Meetings) in the Mennonite Church: Masontown, Fayette County, Pennsylvania, 1872. He also served a vigorous ten-year period as a bishop in the Indiana Conference, 1892-1902. His biography was published in 1964 and was entitled *Bless the Lord, O My Soul.*

John S. Coffman, 1848-1899: One of Funk's most effective colleagues was John S. Coffman of the Shenandoah Valley, Virginia. Born in Rockingham County, Coffman early became a successful schoolteacher and an effective preacher. Funk urged him to locate in Elkhart and help in his publication work. Coffman made the move in 1879 and for twenty years he was an influential teammate of Funk, promoting all good causes in the church, serving as assistant editor of the *Herald of Truth,* and writing Sunday school lesson helps.

But Coffman's greatest contributions came in still other lines of Christian service. Daniel Brenneman had promoted an emotional type of piety and evangelism through which he eventually lost the confidence of many of his fellow ministers. He was expelled in 1874 for his unwillingness to accept direction from them. Coffman knew this history very well, yet he became convinced that the church had to engage in evangelistic work or perish. He therefore fasted and prayed for the Lord to open the door for the desired "Protracted Meetings." And open it did! In 1881, just two years after he came to Elkhart, the small Bowne congregation in Michigan invited him to hold a series of meetings. This he did, and with good success. Other churches heard of this pioneer evangelist, and they too called for Coffman to come and hold meetings. A handsome, well-built man with an open countenance, clear gray eyes, and a pleasant personality, Coffman was also a man of much prayer. Sometimes he prayed all through the night instead of sleeping. And yet he was also a man with a keen sense of humor with which he held and delighted his audiences. Thus he was a man of unusual effectiveness in the pulpit—undoubtedly the most effective preacher in the Mennonite Church in the last quarter of the nineteenth century. He gathered hundreds of fine young people, many already married, into the church. And just as significant, he helped to create a new image of a Mennonite. For he was friendly, progressive, intelligent, well-dressed, and favorable to higher education.

It was in the field of education that Coffman made his final contribution. A Mennonite physician, Dr. Henry A. Mumaw (d. 1908), had founded a small school in 1894, with the rather pompous title, Elkhart Institute of Art, Science, and Industry in Elkhart, Indiana. A year later he turned it over to a self-perpetuating board of trustees known as the Elkhart Institute Association. In 1896 Coffman became the president of this board and guided the school with a firm and able hand until his death three years later. This service on the part of Coffman cost him much, for some of his former friends and supporters turned away from him when he became the open champion of higher education in the church. Coffman's address on the occasion of the dedication of the Elkhart Institute building in 1896 was entitled "The Spirit of Progress," and it testifies effectively to the power and strength of the vision which possessed him.

In many ways Coffman served as a balance wheel to his employer and fellow minister, John F. Funk. Funk's junior by thirteen years, Coffman possessed in a remarkable degree a number of the gentler virtues which Funk may have lacked. Perhaps the word which would best characterize Coffman was "gracious" or "winsome," while Funk gave the impression of an iron will, although accompanied by a large heart, to be sure.

Daniel Kauffman, 1865-1944: The third major figure in the molding of the Mennonite Church was one of the many converts won by John S. Coffman, Daniel Kauffman. He was a native of Juniata County, Pennsylvania, and the son of David D. Kauffman and Elizabeth Winey Kauffman. In 1866 David Kauffman and family moved to Elkhart County, Indiana, and three years later to Morgan County, Missouri. There David served as a preacher and bishop. Son Daniel attended the Missouri State University and earned the degree Principal of Pedagogics. From the ages of eighteen to thirty-two Daniel Kauffman was a schoolteacher in Missouri, serving part of this time as county superintendent of schools. For a time he conducted a private business college at Garden City, Missouri. In 1887 Kauffman married Ota J. Bowlin who bore two children, a son and a daughter. She passed away in 1890. That same year he was converted, standing to accept Christ with his sleeping son James in his arms. In 1892 he was ordained to the ministry, having given up his planned political career soon after his conversion. He also remarried in 1892, to Mary C. Shank who bore six children. In 1896 he was ordained a bishop in the church and served in that capacity for forty-eight years. He served as editor, first of the *Gospel Witness*, which was published at Scottdale from 1905 to 1908, and then of the merged *Gospel Herald*, after the purchase of Funk's *Herald of Truth*.

In the long span, 1905-43, more than any other man, "D. K.," as his friends knew him, served as the chief leader and the major voice of the Mennonite Church. A man of great poise and dignity, a quiet man by nature, he was nevertheless, a most effective team worker. At one point he is said to have been a member of twenty-two committees and boards. He was four times moderator of Mennonite General Conference, including the first official sessions in 1898, and three times he was called upon to preach the conference sermon. He was also the author of twenty-two books and pamphlets. More than any man had ever been, he was the spokesman of his denomination. Among his books may be mentioned: *Manual of Bible Doctrine*, 1898; *A Talk with Church Members*, 1900; coauthor, *Mennonite Church History*, 1905; *Bible Doctrines Briefly Stated*, 1908; editor, *Bible Doctrine*, 1914; *The Conservative Viewpoint*, 1918; *The Mennonite Church and Current Issues*, 1923; *Doctrines of the Bible*, 1928; *My Vision of the Future* (a booklet setting forth his nonmillennial position), 1938; *Fifty Years in the Mennonite Church*, 1941; and *The Devotional Side of Life*, 1942.

Daniel Kauffman was a true church statesman. He saw more clearly than most people the basic spiritual issues which the church was facing, and he quietly took a courageous stand for what he believed was right. He loved people, and was a good arbiter in cases of tension and misunderstanding, a true peacemaker. He was basically conservative, yet he would gladly make concessions in religious practice in order to maintain the unity of the church. His delivery in speaking before an audience was unhurried, thoughtful, and forceful. Like all humans, he could make mistakes—and one of his "slips of the lip" was made at his home congregation at Scottdale: "We must," he urged his audience, "press on with fresh veal and zigor!"

John F. Funk was the great organizer of the church, founding its publication work, and its mission outreach, as well as the Sunday school movement of the Mennonite Church. John S. Coffman was the pioneer evangelist and man of prayer, and the chief promoter of the Elkhart Institute, which in 1903 was moved to Goshen, Indiana, and renamed as Goshen College. Daniel Kauffman was the statesman of the church who labored to consolidate the gains of the "Great Awakening," which came to the church in the latter decades of the nineteenth century, to clarify the doctrinal position of the church, and to maintain its unity. Who would be the fourth spiritual giant to lead and bless the group?

Harold S. Bender, 1897-1962: The fourth leader was to be Harold S. Bender. Born in Elkhart, Indiana, when Funk was sixty-two, when Coffman was forty-eight, and when Kauffman was thirty-two, Harold was a brilliant and gifted boy. At the early age of twelve he accepted Christ as his personal Saviour and was received by baptism into the membership of the Prairie Street Mennonite Church. He graduated from Elkhart High School in 1914, and from Goshen College in 1918, in spite of taking out a year to teach in the Thorntown (Indiana) high school, 1916-17. In August 1922, he received the Bachelor of Divinity degree from Garrett Biblical Institute; in May 1923, the Master of Theology degree from Princeton Theological Seminary; in June 1923, the Master of Arts degree from Princeton University; and the Doctor of Theology degree from Heidelberg University, Germany, in 1935. In 1923 he married Elizabeth Horsch, daughter of the Mennonite historian, John Horsch of Scottdale, Pennsylvania. They became the parents of two daughters.

Harold Bender was first of all an outstanding teacher, at Hesston from 1918 to 1920 and at Goshen from 1924 to his death.

He had the art of mastering his field of study so thoroughly that he was not bound to the textbook or to the outline of anyone. He came to class with a clear grasp of what he wished to share with his students, and he was able to do so effectively. As a teacher he was a competent lecturer, rather than a teacher who "discussed" the field with his students. Yet he stimulated interest and learning. He taught in many fields but excelled in Bible and church history.

Second, Harold Bender was also an able college administrator. When Dean Noah Oyer died in 1931, Harold Bender was placed in his chair, in which position he came to be known far and wide as Dean Bender. During his years in office the college received accreditment from the North Central Association.

Third, Dean Bender inaugurated at Goshen College in 1933, a theological course four years in length and leading to the ThB degree. Gradually this course was strengthened until a college degree was required for admission, the BD degree was offered, and the name of the Bible School was changed to the Biblical Seminary. The Seminary also achieved accreditment from the American Association of Theological Schools.

Fourth, Dean Bender put his hand to the writer's and editor's pens. His most outstanding book was his definitive biography of the chief founder of Swiss Anabaptism, Conrad Grebel, written in German in 1935, and published in English in 1950. But we must go back to 1924 for the founding of the Mennonite Historical Society at Goshen College, and to 1927 for the establishment of the leading journal in its field, *The Mennonite Quarterly Review*. Dean Bender served until his death as president of the society and editor of the *Review*. He was also the longtime chairman of the Historical and Research Committee of Mennonite General Conference. But his really huge contribution was as primary editor of the four-volume *Mennonite Encyclopedia*, published 1955-59.

Fifth, Dean Bender was an ecumenical Mennonite leader. He was assistant secretary and executive committee member of the Mennonite Central Committee (MCC) from 1931 until his death in 1962. In 1939 he became secretary of the Mennonite Central Peace Committee; and in 1942 chairman of the MCC

Active participation in **congregational life** locally, or active involvment in study and service opportunities elsewhere, are assumed as part of committed, voluntary, and adult membership. The ideals of being peacemakers in a broken world, and servants to one another, help Mennonites to seek **constructive work** in a world of destruction, to minister to the needs of the most disadvantaged.

Peace Section, and he retained that position until his death. In 1944 he was ordained to the ministry in his "Mennonite Church (MC)," as he preferred to call it, and at about that point he entered the most strongly ecumenical phase of his ministry. Beginning in 1945 he made annual trips to Europe for shorter or longer visits, largely devoted to MCC and Mennonite World Conference concerns. Indeed he was president of the 1952, 1957, and 1962 sessions of the World Conference. In 1948 he helped launch the German Mennonite periodical, *Der Mennonit* (The Mennonite). In 1949 he became chairman of the International Mennonite Peace Committee. His 1943 presidential address at the American Society of Church History was entitled, "The Anabaptist Vision," which soon became internationally known as a magnificent statement of what Anabaptism really was. Perhaps the cause dearest to his heart was the Biblical Seminary at Goshen College, and when its deanship was separated from the office of the college dean in 1946, he elected to go with the seminary, rather than to stay with the college. He was also delighted with the leading of the Lord when the Goshen College Biblical Seminary and the Mennonite Biblical Seminary of the General Conference Mennonite Church became the Associated Mennonite Biblical Seminaries in 1958.

Sixth, Dean Bender was a man of action. In addition to all his other projects he still found time to be the major figure in the establishment of Bethany Christian High School, by the High School Board of the Indiana-Michigan Conference, serving also on its board of control, from its beginning until his death.

He had his critics, of course, for how could a man be as active as he was without arousing criticism? Students were sometimes annoyed that he seemed so certain of what courses they ought to take, or what positions they should accept, and someone half-humorously one day dubbed him with the label, "The pope," which title was well known on the campus, beloved as he was at the same time.

And so Harold S. Bender was the outstanding scholar-leader of the Mennonite Church, the one who really led the intellectuals of the church to drink at the refreshing fountain of Anabaptism; he was the ecumenical Mennonite, who was per-

Passing on the story to the present and the coming generations has always been of vital importance to Mennonites—witness the *Martyrs Mirror,* the *Hutterite Chronicles,* and the *Mennonite Quarterly Review.* The **Historical Committee** of the Mennonite Church founded in 1911 meets twice yearly to report on an active program of research, teaching, and publishing. Shown here are Jan Gleysteen, Gerald Studer, Leonard Gross, John S. Oyer, Hubert L. Brown, James Mininger, Theron Schlabach, John A. Hostetler, and Lorna Bergey.

sonally a staunch (Old) Mennonite, and who was able at the same time to put a warm arm of love around all the Mennonites of all lands. He told the huge throng at the Seventh Mennonite World Conference at Kitchener a few weeks before his death that he was sometimes accused of being a "Mennonite Ecumaniac," and if loving all the brethren made him that, he added, then he would plead guilty!

Who is or will be the successor of Dean Bender? It is unlikely that there will be any one person as outstanding in the life of the Mennonite Church, as were the four leaders just described. The leadership of the church is becoming much more diffused, which is really a wholesome development. The church is growing larger, there are more able leaders, and as the institutions of the church grow, fewer and fewer leaders have the time, energy, or inclination to immerse themselves in so broad a spectrum of activities as did Funk, Coffman, Kauffman, and Bender.

Group Characteristics

Members of the Mennonite Church have a strong historical consciousness. They are keenly aware that their spiritual forefathers suffered and died for the faith and fled from one land to another in search of religious liberty. Many public prayers make fervent mention of and give thanks for the fact that we in this land may worship God according to the dictates of our conscience and with no fear of being harmed or molested.

They also have a strong sense of mission. They believe in the doctrines of the Scripture as understood historically, and they want to bring people of all lands and cultures to this same nonresistant Christian faith. Prior to 1940 three foreign missions were established, one before 1900, and one each in the next two twenty-year spans. Since 1940, however, work is being carried on in about forty countries. No cause appeals to Mennonite giving as much as missions. Because of this a high premium is also put on higher education. Many parents will borrow money, even mortgage their house or farm, in order to assist their children to get university degrees. Large numbers of young people are entering such service professions as the ministry, medicine, social work, and teaching. With other Mennonites the Mennonite Church emphasizes the simplicity of the gospel, reading the Bible in faith and obedience. They have a simple hermeneutic, that is, taking the Bible at face value. And so if it commands foot washing or anointing with oil, they practice these rites as a church.

The Mennonite Church has also developed a deep social concern. Members are distressed that anyone should be made to suffer for creed or color. They are eager to see all citizens everywhere enjoy the full benefits of citizenship. Many are increasingly concerned for social and economic justice stimulated, in part, by the growing number of black and Hispanic members among them. In the 1980s many are wrestling seriously with questions of ecology, nuclear power and armaments issues, poverty, the paying of taxes for war—and the implications of all these issues for Christian life style and witness. Inter-Mennonite agencies like MCC and Mennonite World Conference receive strong moral and financial support.

Mennonite Church people find deep satisfaction in their simple worship services. The entire congregation joins in the singing of four-part music, usually sung a cappella. The pulpit is placed in the center of the platform symbolizing the centrality of God's Word as it is read and expounded. Historically, everyone knelt for prayer, but this has changed since 1950 to standing in most congregations. Traditionally, the worship service was held every two weeks, but this too has changed to regular Sunday morning services and, in many congregations, evening services as well. Midweek Bible study meetings in church have become fewer, but members are increasingly meeting in homes for small-group sharing, study, and prayer. A number of house church fellowships emerged during the 1960s and 70s, as well as informally organized assemblies, bringing together numerous house group meetings. The influence of the charismatic movement was felt for good throughout the church in terms of new freedom to witness and a loosening of the remnants of legalism. Being a member of the church increasingly meant not only discipleship and hard work, but also a simple, unashamed joy in the Lord.

Chapter 13

The Amish and the Hutterian Brethren

The Amish

THE AMISH-MENNONITES or Amish, as they have come to be known, originated from the only major division among the Swiss Brethren in Europe. The Dutch Mennonites had experienced many divisions during the sixteenth and seventeenth centuries, frequently over issues of church discipline. They may have inadvertently helped to precipitate the Amish division through the article on discipline in the (Dutch) Dordrecht Confession of 1632, which demanded shunning or avoidance *(Meidung)* of a transgressing member of the fellowship. Such a member was to be expelled from the fellowship, but also "according to the doctrine of Christ and his apostles, be shunned and avoided by all members of the church ... whether it be in eating or drinking, or other like social matters."

The Confession itself had not been formally adopted by the Swiss Brethren, but was frequently referred to by them as a guide to faith. It was precisely on the subject of discipline that the Swiss had held discussions with the Dutch Mennonites, including Menno Simons, and urged them to moderation. In late seventeenth century, however, a young Swiss Brethren elder by the name of Jacob Ammann, became deeply concerned over their laxity of discipline when a woman who admitted speaking a falsehood was not shunned. He also identified as wrong the belief that sincere people (*treuherzige*) who were sympathetic to the Swiss Brethren doctrines but did not join the group would be saved.

In due course Ammann began traveling from his home near Berne, Switzerland, to visit all the congregations in the Swiss, South German, and Alsace areas to find support for his concern. He also criticized an older fellow elder, Hans Reist, for not disciplining the woman and other evidences of undue tolerance. Reist undoubtedly underestimated Ammann's zeal when he told others "not to consider seriously the teaching and ordinances of youths." Meanwhile Ammann's concerns grew to include other issues. Though the Swiss had never practiced foot washing, article XI of the *Dordrecht Confession* did teach it, and so Ammann did also. He saw worldliness coming into the fellowship in the clothes being worn and urged both simplicity and uniformity. Men should not trim their beards since this was an obvious sign of pride. To attend the services of the state church was also grounds for discipline. Communion service was to be observed twice annually, not once, Ammann insisted, and began the actual schism by observing it "out of order" in the summer of 1693. Eventually Ammann excommunicated all ministers who did not agree with him, including Reist, as well as many individual members. He found his strongest support in Alsace. Many attempts at reconciliation were made, even by North German Mennonites, but without success. While Ammann did apologize later and admit acting too quickly, he did not retreat from the substance of his position. The 1693 division seemed to be final by 1697. It was a reform attempt to recover doctrines which Ammann thought were being neglected, but it also included personality conflicts and the struggle for power. Sectarian divisions normally occur most frequently at the conservative end of the theological continuum.

The earliest records of Amish coming to North America are for 1727, but no congregation was organized until 1749 when Jacob Hertzler (d. 1786) came to Berks County, Pennsylvania, followed later by many others to Lancaster and Chester counties. Others continued coming directly from other parts of

Europe, including Hesse in Germany, and moving inland to Ohio and Indiana. By 1812 a large settlement was developing in Holmes County, Ohio, and by the 1840s in Lagrange and other counties in Indiana. The westward movement continued to Illinois, Oregon, and Kansas, but also including the Dakotas, Iowa, Nebraska, and other states. The largest settlements in the twentieth century, however, continued to be in Lancaster, Holmes, and Lagrange counties.

The Amish came to Ontario through the initiative of Christian Nafziger, a poor farmer in Bavaria, Germany. Mennonites in Amsterdam provided him with travel funds to New Orleans, from where he went to Pennsylvania in 1821. There, however, he discovered that land was too expensive for him to buy, but his Amish and Mennonite friends told him of ample, cheap land in Canada and provided the necessary travel funds for him. By 1822 he had indeed been able to make favorable land purchase arrangements in Waterloo County. He apparently negotiated directly with the governor of Upper Canada and on his return journey succeeded in having an audience with King George IV in London, who confirmed the reliability of the governor's offer. While Nafziger himself could not come immediately, the good news he brought put many on the way from Europe to Ontario and, eventually, even some from Pennsylvania.

Old Order Amish: From 1850 to 1880 the process of accommodation to the surrounding culture became the cause for a division among the Amish themselves. As those labeled Progressives began to modify the strict Amish disciplines on dress, on the use of modern inventions, and on other daily life issues, as well as on beginning the use of English in worship and on building church buildings, a rift became inevitable. In contrast to those now known as the Old Order, the Progressives came to be called Amish Mennonites and eventually did join the Mennonite Church in the twentieth century. In 1981 there were approximately 1,000 members in the Old Order Amish group in Canada and 33,000 in the United States. A few had also emigrated to Paraguay.

Most Old Order Amish communities meet in homes, that is in a large house, shed, or barn for worship every other Sunday.

Families with adequate facilities take turns inviting the group. Services last from three to four hours with several ministers speaking without notes. The language used is Pennsylvania "Dutch", sometimes sprinkled liberally with English words and some *Schrift-deutsch* (Bible German). An Old Order congregation or district consists of from forty to fifty-five families and is divided when it becomes larger. A bishop, two ministers, and a deacon preside over each district.

It is not correct to say, as some do, that the Amish believe in salvation by works instead of by grace, but it is correct that obedience to Jesus Christ is for them the real test of faith (James 2), and that the will of God is known to the believer both through the Scriptures as well as through the present living body of the church and the faithful church of all time, i.e., the tradition. The four questions of the Amish baptismal vow are as follows (with slight variation from place to place):

1. Are you able to confess with the Ethiopian eunuch that you believe that Jesus Christ is God's Son? (Answer: Yes, I believe that Jesus Christ is God's Son.)
2. Do you confess that you are uniting with the true church of the Lord? (Yes.)
3. Do you renounce the devil and the world with all its wicked ways, and also your own flesh and blood, and commit yourself to serve Jesus Christ alone who died for you on the cross? (Yes.)
4. Do you promise to keep the ordinances (*Ordnung*) of the Lord and the church, to faithfully observe and to help administer them, and never to depart from them so long as you shall live? (Yes.)[1]

It is also not correct, as many think, that the Amish do not believe in education. It is true that they hold a certain amount of education to be sufficient for their rural community needs, but within these limits the total emphasis is upon an integration of life and learning to equip the student to become a faithful member of the church and a useful member of society. As one former Amishman writes: "Where public schools emphasize competition and pride of achievement, the Amish stress cooperation and humility (not exactly unbiblical themes)."[2] This, it has been noted, requires qualified rather than "certified"

234 An Introduction to Mennonite History

teachers, i.e., the church rather than the state determines the qualifications:

> Although the Amish school is separated from "the world" outside, it is not separated from Amish life. The school supports the family and the traditions and economy of the Amish community and enables the child to learn both the facts and the roles he needs to function as an Amish person in twentieth-century America.[3]

It may well be argued that the Amish, despite weaknesses which can be found in any group, have much to teach society in the last decades of the twentieth century about the wise use of energy, near self-sufficiency together, and mutual aid, integrity, simplicity, and not least about love of the soil and its care. They have been the subject of many sociological studies. Those who seem to understand them best identify faith in God and a commitment to obey His will as they understand it, as the primary foundation of their existence.

Unfortunately, most Amish communities experienced a time of stress and division during the latter half of the nineteenth century. From 1865-75 the "Egli Amish," known as the Defenseless Mennonite Church until 1948 and then as the Evangelical Mennonite Church (Chapter 15), separated from the Old Order Amish in the Berne, Indiana, area after Egli experienced a new regeneration. In Michigan a group seeking reform of Old Order life and thought, but not in the way the so-called Progressives were going, came to be known as the Conservative Amish Mennonite Conference in 1910. They have since dropped the "Amish" from their name and are loosely affiliated with the Mennonite Church. Their membership in 1981 was 7,510, with 92 congregations, who support an active education and mission program.

Beachy Amish Mennonite: The record seems to indicate that this was more a development of separation by mutual consent than a schism. When Moses M. Beachy (d. 1946) became bishop in southwestern Pennsylvania, he could not find it within himself to shun all members of the Old Order who left for Mennonite churches as his predecessor had done. After a decade of struggle over the issue the retired bishop and about one half of

The largest concentrations of **Old Order Amish** are found in Pennsylvania, Ohio, Indiana, Iowa, and Kansas. They live a simple life, retain their German dialect, and resist large-scale mechanization. Their farming methods combine family effort and animal power.

the congregation began meeting separately for worship in 1927, but for the next twenty-six years both groups used the same meetinghouse, on alternate Sundays, though the Beachy group had introduced Sunday school and other innovations. The condoning of the use of automobiles by the Beachy group, however, created more serious tension. Other groups in Pennsylvania, Ohio, and Indiana merged with the Beachy Amish, bringing their membership to 4,920 in 77 congregations by 1977. Some congregations still use the German language. Most have Sunday school and midweek prayer meetings. Mutual aid is important: "... a religion that works is encouraged." Something of the spirit of the group is captured in the following words written by a member in 1978.

> Doctrinally the church emphasizes repentance, conversion, blood atonement, the new birth, believer's baptism, justification by faith, practical discipleship, and progressive sanctification. Eight Christian ordinances are practiced: baptism, communion, foot washing, woman's veiling, the holy kiss, anointing with oil, laying on of hands, and marriage.

> In spite of the differences, we love the Lord and we love one another. "For he that loveth not his brother whom he hath seen, how can he love God whom he hath not seen?" (1 John 4:20). We do sense a dire need for more spiritual growth, that we might love God and our fellow brethren enough that we might be one! Jesus is coming soon.[4]

The Hutterian Brethren

The sixteenth-century origins of the Hutterian Brethren were described briefly in Chapter 4. Persecution decimated their ranks in the seventeenth century and ultimately destroyed the communities in Moravia, though cultural remnants (Habaner) remained until World War II. Many, however, had continued their westward migration into Slovakia and Transylvania but the entire movement was on the verge of extinction when a Russian general invited a small remnant of 123 to settle in the Ukraine in 1770. Fifty-six of these were Lutherans who converted to the Hutterites and gave new life to the movement.

This was to be their home for 100 years. Some measure of

The Hutterites, established in Moravia around 1533, arrived in North America in 1874 after a three-century odyssey through Eastern Europe. These limestone buildings of the **Bon Homme** Colony near Yankton, South Dakota, were their first American home. Most of the Hutterite colonies are located in the Canadian and American West.

prosperity returned to them, but internal tensions led to a giving up of their historic communal lifestyle from 1819 to 1859. At this point a spiritual revival led to a new commitment to community life, but it was of short duration. The growing emancipation of the Russian serfs led to an egalitarianism which seemed to threaten the cherished privileges of the Hutterites, Mennonites, and other foreign colonies. The threat of a military conscription law passed in 1872 convinced the Hutterites, and many Mennonites, that it was time to leave even though the law provided for alternative service for conscientious objectors to war. In 1873 a twelve-man delegation was sent to North America to explore the possibilities for resettlement. Two of the delegates were Hutterites. Paul Tschetter, the older of the two, kept a most informative diary of the journey. Their recommendation was to settle in the Dakota territory. By July 1874 the first group had arrived and by 1877 all of them, numbering between 700-800 persons, were on the selected sites.

The original communities in the Dakotas consisted of three groups in addition to those who wished to live alone on their own properties. The first group came to be known as the *Schmied-leut*—the blacksmith people—after their leader Michael Waldner, who was a blacksmith. The second group was called the *Dariusleut* after their elder Darius Walther. The third group was called the *Lehrleut*—teacher's people—after their elder Jacob Wipf, who was a teacher. The first group located near the Missouri River at what is still known as the Bon Homme colony, the second near the James River, a tributary of the Missouri, while the third settled north of Wolf Creek as the (Old) Elm-spring colony.

The three communities now entered a period of rapid growth and economic success. Their population doubled during the next forty years and their settlements increased to seventeen. The near isolation of their communities from the surrounding culture was undoubtedly what they had been longing for and now experienced with gratitude.

This changed, however, with the coming of World War I in 1914. People looked with suspicion upon German-speaking conscientious objectors. Their refusal to buy Liberty Bonds was resented severely, even though they made donations to the Red Cross and other relief agencies. Acts of violence against the settlements increased. A group of angry patriots came to the Jamesville colony and drove off a herd of 100 steers and 1,000 sheep, ostensibly to sell them in order to purchase bonds, but they did this without censure from law enforcement agencies. Ugly rumors were circulated against the colonies.

The most suffering, however, was endured by the young men who were drafted for military service and taken to army camps, but refused to put on uniforms or follow the orders of their commanders. There were no provisions for alternative service at that time. The case of the three Hofer brothers, Joseph, David, and Michael, and Jacob Wipf shook the commu-

These **Hutterite girls** are members of the Milltown Colony near Elie, Manitoba, the oldest colony in Canada.

nities particularly. After two months in the military guardhouse they were sentenced to thirty-seven years in prison. They were taken to Alcatraz, handcuffed by day and chained by night. Here they were placed in wet dungeons in solitary confinement, wearing only their thin underwear, since they refused to put on the uniform which hung in the cell. For five days and nights they stood, sat, and slept on the wet floor without a blanket or other comfort. They received half a glass of water daily, but no food. Then their situation was eased somewhat.

Four months later they were transferred to Fort Leavenworth, Kansas. After four days and five nights of misery in travel they were marched on the run from the station to the camp, then made to strip their outer clothing and stand in the winter dripping with sweat. Two hours later they were issued prison clothing, but forced to stand outside in the cold. By morning Joseph and Michael Hofer collapsed and were taken to a hospital. The other two were placed in solitary confinement and issued a starvation diet. For nine hours each day they stood with their hands tied to an overhead beam and their feet barely touching the ground. Somehow Wipf had managed to send a telegram to the wives of the two hospitalized men. When they arrived they found their husbands near death. By next morning Joseph had died, but his wife, Maria, was not allowed to see the body. After much pleading she was taken to the coffin where she discovered that the uniform he had refused to wear in life had been put on him after he was dead. Michael died two days later. The other two were eventually released.[5]

Meanwhile negotiations in Washington, including discussions with the Secretary of war and a petition to President Woodrow Wilson, had not received a significant response. Consequently, the Hutterites saw no alternative but to emigrate to Canada where religious freedom was promised to them. The move began almost immediately and included all of the settlements except the oldest one at Bon Homme. The *Schmiedleut* settled in Manitoba, the *Dariusleut* and *Lehrleut* in Alberta. Within a few years sentiment, and eventually legislation, in the Dakotas began to change. By the time of the depression in the mid-1930s there was actual encouragement for them to return, largely for economic reasons, and many did until most of the earlier colonies were once more under cultivation. The Canadian settlements continued to serve the needs of the rapidly growing communities.

The Land Problem: The need for more land has gone hand in hand with Hutterite growth and prosperity. In contrast to the Amish, the Hutterites use the most modern machinery available for their farming, shops, and other production needs. The founding of a new community required a large tract of land, often 5,000 acres or more, and Hutterite economic strength made it possible to "buy out" smaller farmers. Settlements gradually became a threat to farming communities and to small towns who saw their markets disappear through Hutterite self-sufficiency and bulk buying at larger, more distant urban centers. As a result restrictive legislation was enacted in Alberta, but later modified to the present liaison office where Hutterite and provincial representatives agree upon new land purchases before they are made. Restrictive legislation was also proposed but never enacted in Manitoba and Saskatchewan, as well as in Montana and Minnesota.[6] Hutterite sensitivity to community feelings in areas of proposed purchases, as well as their reputation of being both good farmers and good neighbors, has seemed to resolve this problem. However, it continues to remain a source of concern to all parties potentially involved. For a time people believed that as a religious community the Hutterites did not pay any taxes. They do indeed pay, but as a colony rather than individuals, obviously. Today Hutterite baptized membership is 6,574 in Canada and 3,684 in the United States, with a total membership of 10,258.

The Society of Brothers: A fourth group known as the *Arnoldleut* was added to the Hutterite community in 1930. Eberhard Arnold (1883-1935), a German writer and teacher, became attracted to the sixteenth-century Anabaptist-Hutterite model and founded a community in Germany in 1920. In 1930 he visited the Hutterian communities in North America, having first heard of them in 1928, and was accepted, as well as ordained, by them before his return. Difficulties arose among the group soon after Arnold died. Under the pressures of World War II they were forced to leave Germany and settled in England, but after encountering considerable hostility there also because they were Germans, and nonresistant, they eventually migrated to Paraguay, locating near the Mennonite colony of Friesland east of the Paraguay River. The peak of *Primavera* (spring) colony life came in the early 1950s with a membership of around 650, of whom approximately one half were children. They were noted particularly for their thorough educational system, which was trilingual (Spanish, German, English), the diversity of membership background, with some ninety family names represented, and their hospital which became known far and wide for its excellence and compassion. A decline of spirit and then membership began to erode the community by the mid-1950s and eventually led to its dissolution. Some members joined a reconstituted community (Woodcrest) under the leadership of Heini Arnold, son of the founder, at Rifton, New York. This group is now known as the *Arnoldsleut* again, officially the Hutterian Society of Brothers, and is again in full membership with the Hutterian Brethren since 1974. An attempt to reestablish a community near the original site in Germany had to be abandoned about 1961-62.

Colony Life: Hutterite life is much more than sharing a common treasury and living together in a given communal setting. It is a total way of life with regulated lines of authority and responsibility and a specific place for every member. The time and abilities of the members is no more their own than money is. It is clear that order becomes a very central concept if many people are to work together harmoniously all their life. This order is rooted in God's orderly creation and influences the Hutterite understanding of order in space, in time, and in society. Buildings and living arrangements for families are not arranged haphazardly in the colony. Daily time schedules are precise, so also are the grouping of ages according to time (years) in terms of work, respect, and trust. There is social ordering ranging from education to young people's activities, marriage, male-female relationships, and the role of the elderly.

The ordering of all of these relationships does require authority, and there is a hierarchy of responsibility, but it is servant-oriented for the good of all. Within the larger colony community the church is the primary authority, with a spiritual leader or minister at its head. He in turn seeks the counsel of the other ministers and the total church. A council of from five to seven men chosen by the church, always including two ministers, the field manager, and the householder, is responsible for the daily running of the colony and making routine decisions. All major decisions are made by the church, in which only baptized males may vote. Church discipline includes excommunication and possible expulsion from the community.

Like the Amish, the Hutterites run their own schools whenever possible, with certified teachers, but supervision by the larger area school board or superintendent. Some of their young people do attend college in order to return to the colony as teachers. Filmstrips and other visual aids are normally not used. Television sets are not found in the colonies. Most children attend school through grades eight or nine. This is considered sufficient to help them adjust to the religious and social life in the colony and to cope with their place in the larger society and the world. The daily devotional services also serve an important role in furthering spiritual growth.

The *Baptismal Vow* normally used by the Hutterites today for admission to membership is as follows. They amount indeed to a total commitment. Questions asked of the applicants before the prayer:

1. Do you acknowledge the doctrines, which have hitherto been taught to you, as being the truth and right foundation for salvation?
2. Do you also believe in and agree with the twelve articles of our Christian faith which comprise: "We believe in God the Almighty ... " [Each repeats the Apostles' Creed]
3. Do you also desire the prayer of intercession of the pious that God may forgive and remit the sins committed by you in ignorance?
4. Do you desire to consecrate, give and sacrifice yourself to the Lord in the covenant of Christian baptism?

Here follows the prayer.

[After this prayer, while kneeling, follow these six questions:]

1. Do you now sufficiently understand the word of God and acknowledge it as the only path to life eternal?
2. Do you also truly and heartily repent of the sins which you have in ignorance committed against God and do you desire henceforth to fear God, nevermore to sin against God, and rather to suffer death than ever again to sin willfully against God?
3. Do you also believe that your sins have been forgiven and remitted through Christ and the prayer of intercession of His people?
4. Is it also your desire to accept brotherly punishment [discipline] and admonition and also to apply the same to others when it is needful?
5. Do you desire thus to consecrate, give and sacrifice yourself with soul and body and all your possessions to the Lord in heaven, and to be obedient unto Christ and His church?
6. Do you desire thus to establish a covenant with God and all His people and to be baptized upon your confessed belief?

[Note: All of these questions must be answered with a "yes." The minister, laying on his hands and sprinkling with water, speaks the following words:]

> On thy confessed belief I baptize thee, in the name of the Father, the Son, and the Holy Ghost. God Almighty in heaven who has given you grace and mercy through the death of Christ and the prayer of His Saints, may clothe you with fortitude from on high and inscribe your name into the book of eternal life, to preserve thee in piety and faith until death. This is my wish to thee through Jesus Christ. Amen."[7]

The age of baptism is normally between nineteen and twenty for girls and from twenty to twenty-six for boys. Individuals wishing to be baptized need to ask for it from the ministers. An instruction period of from six to eight weeks precedes baptism itself. The rite itself, as seen in the questions, promises unqualified obedience to Christ and to His church, i.e., the Hutterite church.

In the sixteenth century the Hutterites carried on itinerant missionary activity long after the other Anabaptist groups had withdrawn to sheltered places for survival. This is not their pattern of witness today, but a powerful witness is being given by their very existence and by a lifestyle so different from that of the surrounding culture. One of their leaders has written: "Some [Hutterites] say that the mission field is in their daily work and way of life. When researchers come and go and when the press reports about the Hutterian way of life, that is mission outreach. It is annoying to some that so much is published about Hutterites and that so many busloads of tourists come almost daily to the colonies."[8] The Hutterites have also themselves facilitated publications about their life and faith, which might be identified as witness through literature.

In connection with Hutterite missionary activity it is of interest to note that a Hutterite agricultural community was begun in Japan in 1971, and by 1978 had a membership of 22. The founder and spiritual leader of the group is Isomi Izeki, who has visited the Alberta Hutterite communities several times, and was ordained by them in 1977. He first learned about Hutterite history and life through two books about them published by Ian Sakakibara, a committed Anabaptist coordinating the establishment of an Anabaptist study center in Tokyo.

One keen observer of the Hutterian way of life has written: "Hutterites are rarely alone and seldom lonely."[9]

Chapter 14

The General Conference
Mennonite Church

MILITARY CONFLICTS sharply limited the flow of European immigrants to North America during the second half of the eighteenth century. There was first the Seven Years' War of 1756-63, between England and France over control of New World lands, particularly Canada. This was followed by continuing Indian skirmishes encouraged by the two European powers. Then came the American Revolution of 1775-83, the French Revolution of 1789-99, and the Napoleonic Wars, which finally ended in 1815. A renewed flare-up of hostilities across the 49th parallel between Canada and the United States had led to the War of 1812, but by 1815 tensions had subsided—until the American Civil War, 1861-65—and immigration again came into full swing.

Among the new waves of immigrants were also some 3,000 Mennonites from Alsace, Bavaria, and Hesse, who settled in Ontario, Ohio, and further west in Indiana, Illinois, and Iowa. While they carried the same names as those who had come to Pennsylvania a century earlier, and many came from the same communities in Europe, they were different because of different experiences. While those who came in the eighteenth century lived in relatively closed, self-sufficient Mennonite settlements, those who came after 1830 had experienced the spiritual and intellectual freedom which had arisen in Europe. They were beginning to be citizens of this world while still being pilgrims on their way to the world beyond. This new mood is reflected in the gentle but perceptive comment of Jacob Krehbiel, a minister from the Palatinate who settled in New York state but associated with the Franconia Conference. He wrote in a letter to his friends in Germany in 1841, ten years after his arrival in America:

> I do not wish to deny that in some American Mennonite congregations too much emphasis is placed on outward forms and at times, therefore, some points seem exaggerated. But this is admitted by most of the preachers here themselves, and I would not want to say that there is no good intention at heart. Rather it is the case with a good many that they possess only to a small degree the gift of differentiating between the greater and the less, wherefore nonessentials are made to be essentials and consequently too much strictness is laid upon these matters, forgetting that Paul laid the first emphasis on a "new creature in Christ...."[1]

Some of the immigrants who had come to Illinois settled near Summerfield, across the Mississippi River from St. Louis. In 1851 a group settled in Lee County, in Southeast Iowa. True to their Mennonite tradition they began to organize churches as soon as they arrived. One congregation was organized at West Point, Iowa, in 1849, with two men chosen as ministers. A small log cabin church seating thirty people was built four miles from town. Because it was located on the edge of a wooded area the congregation was often referred to as the *Busch Gemeinde*, i.e., bush church. Another congregation, called Zion, was organized nine miles from the first, in Franklin Township, in 1852. They were allowed to use a German Lutheran church building on alternate Sundays until their own building was completed in 1855. A third congregation was organized at Summerfield in 1858. Krehbiels were among the leading men in all three congregations. There were other Mennonites and Amish in these communities also, families who had moved west from Pennsylvania and Ohio, but because of their different background and experiences these German immigrants did not seem to have much contact with them.

Because fellowship is necessary for Christian growth the three congregations at West Point and Summerfield tried hard to overcome their geographical and spiritual isolation. In 1853 the West Point and Franklin Township congregations united to form the *German Evangelical Mennonite congregation* with a total of 181 members. Since the two churches were nine miles apart, they continued to meet separately but had annual conferences together. By 1859 they felt a strong urge to do something concrete in home and foreign missions. They had become alert to the need for missions through the work of an itinerant British Baptist who had visited their communities while they were still in Europe,[2] and especially through the impact of pietism in their home communities. They became convinced that they needed to be united in order to undertake such work. Three resolutions were adopted at the conference that year: first, to take an offering for missions on the first Sunday of every month; second to take offerings for the support of a minister who could be asked to visit the scattered Mennonites in the Middle West; and third, to appoint a business committee to take care of these affairs and to "correspond with other Mennonite churches and invite them to join this union." When minister Jacob Krehbiel I sent these resolutions to be published in the Mennonite paper, *Das Christliche Volksblatt,* he added a letter saying:

> May the Lord lend His blessing to this small beginning, that eventually a common bond of brotherhood bind all our Mennonite communities to work unitedly that the brethren living in isolation may receive the pure Gospel, and thereby the scattered sheep be held for our church.[3]

Almost unknown to these congregations was the fact that four years earlier, in 1855, a similar unity had been achieved by the congregation in Wadsworth, Ohio, with several Mennonite congregations in Ontario. The minister of the Wadsworth congregation was Ephraim Hunsberger, a real frontier preacher who felt Mennonites were too slow in spreading the Gospel. The leader of the participating Ontario congregations was Daniel Hoch, a zealous evangelist who disturbed many Mennonites with his emphasis upon prayer meetings, freedom of expression in church meetings, and holiness. Here too missions and unity received primary attention. Hoch himself was commissioned an itinerant evangelist and union negotiations were begun with the East Pennsylvania Conference. At the third meeting of this group, which was known as the Canada-Ohio Conference, approval was given to a proposal which had appeared earlier in *Das Christliche Volksblatt*. The proposal began with the words, "Let all ministers of the various branches of the denomination cultivate a fraternal confidence toward each other and abandon all prejudice." It further urged the preparation of a confession of faith and added that "all those who will accept this confession and unite upon it shall be considered the real Mennonite denomination." The desire for unity among Mennonites, which was to become a major concern of the General Conference Mennonite Church, was already present.

John H. Oberholtzer, 1809-95

There was another group involved in unity negotiations. This group was under the leadership of John H. Oberholtzer, minister of the Swamp Mennonite Church near Quakertown, Pennsylvania. It is interesting to note that while this group was deeply interested in *union* with other Mennonites, their own little East Pennsylvania Conference had originated in 1847 after a *break* with the older and larger Franconia Conference.

Oberholtzer was born on January 10, 1809, in Berks County, Pennsylvania. His great-grandfather Jacob Oberholtzer had come to Philadelphia from Switzerland in 1732. Young John received the best education a farm boy could acquire during the winter months in the German church school. By the time he was sixteen years of age he was himself employed as a teacher every winter until he was ordained as a minister in 1842. But this teaching had its own problems. For a time his classroom was the second floor of a hog barn on the farm of John Ritter. It seems that the older boys enjoyed asking for permission to leave the room and then used the occasion to stir the swill barrel downstairs until the hungry pigs were in a real uproar waiting to be fed. Classes naturally had to be dismissed for the remainder of the period because of the noise and dust. This practice became such a nuisance that the school had to be discontinued at that location. Since the school year was short and the salary small, young John also learned the locksmithing trade, later establishing his own shop near Milford Square. This skill became his main financial support for thirty years.

His call to the ministry came through the lot. Since the minister of the Swamp church was over eighty years old, the congregation nominated fifteen members of the church as possible ministers, John among them. Though he had real misgivings about calling ministers by the lot, there was really nothing he could do about it since that was the way tradition demanded. When the fifteen candidates were together, each was given a Bible, but only one had the lot in it. This was a slip of paper on which the words of Proverbs 16:33 were usually written: "The lot is cast into the lap, but the decision is wholly from the Lord." John drew the lot.

One Sunday morning about six weeks later John was told, upon arriving at the church, that he was to preach his first sermon that morning. Silently he called upon God for help and chose as his text Ephesians 2:8, "For by grace you have been saved, through faith." After the service he overheard the remark, "That was a scholarly sermon," and since scholarship was seen as a sign of pride the remark probably meant that it had been a bad sermon. Yet he himself shared later that he had experienced real divine help in this hour, having claimed the promises of Joshua 1:5 and Hebrews 13:5.

Nevertheless, he continued in his ministry but felt increasing opposition to his thinking. He was an able preacher and administrator, with many new ideas which he believed to be biblical. He was young and possibly somewhat impatient with the old forms of worship and community life. More and more he found himself distinguishing between practices which were followed from force of habit only, without clear biblical precedent, and those which he found in the life of the early church according to Acts and the epistles. Why, he asked, should ministers wear different coats than laymen, why should no minutes be kept of church meetings, why is a church constitution sin, and why could Mennonite ministers not have Christian fellowship with other ministers except Quakers? There were other lesser things which troubled him, and personality clashes must have been inevitable. He could not get used to the authority of bishops, believing rather that the entire congregations should decide all major issues in the church. And slowly the fellowship was broken, though several attempts were made at reconciliation. Like Oberholtzer, Christians have often believed so strongly that they have been more willing to break fellowship with each other than to give up what they considered to be biblical and right. God does expect His children to be faithful, but He never expects them to stop loving each other.

This had indeed been a difficult time for the Mennonites in Pennsylvania. Being both hard-working and frugal, they had become quite wealthy. Religious freedom meant for them the freedom not to change their old customs. In describing this time one writer says, "From 1683 to the ordination of John H. Oberholtzer, almost 160 years later, no significant changes were made, and no one intended to make any. The Bible had not changed; why should anyone introduce any innovations?"[4] The War of Independence had cut them off from stimulating contacts with their European brethren, and the democratic American environment seemed foreign to them. Missions were not undertaken, education was suspect, and prayer meetings were frowned upon. Members were forbidden many things that seemed harmless, such as picnics or celebrations, farm exhibitions and poultry shows.

But all this must not be taken as a lack of spiritual interest. There was, on the contrary, very strong Christian conviction, but it was not nourished by fresh Bible study and prayer and fellowship with other believers. The unfamiliar constituted a threat to the faith because they were so conscious of a heritage to preserve. And so the faith was seen as a timeless deposit to be guarded zealously from the world, rather than as a living power meant precisely for the world in its lostness. The consequent stress upon external forms and customs left too little freedom for the renewing work of the Holy Spirit.

A particular problem among the two groups was the constitution Oberholtzer had written for adoption by the conference. Known as the *Ordnung*, it not only gave full authority to the entire congregation instead of to the bishop but also proposed the keeping of minutes, regular elections, and a modification of the use of the lot in choosing ministers. It urged a greater openness to other Christians, also suggesting that Mennonites might marry outside of their church so long as it was "in the Lord." It was clear that the *Ordnung* would lead to less separation from the world and greater adaptation to their American environment. With this, it seemed, would come a loss of the heritage of faith through outside influence. By 1847 the rupture was complete and the representatives of fourteen congregations met to form a new organization which they called the East Pennsylvania Conference of the Mennonite Church. Soon this group became known as the *New* Mennonites to distinguish them from the *Old* Mennonites, though neither group really considered the other to be true disciples of Menno any longer.

In addition to leading the affairs of the new conference and ministering to his own congregation, Oberholtzer now worked tirelessly for spiritual renewal. He was to establish one of the first American Mennonite Sunday schools. He ordered Mennonite literature and catechism materials from Europe to teach young people the meaning of their faith, and he carried on a vigorous correspondence with Mennonites scattered throughout the Middle West. Particularly important was his founding of a newspaper, *Der Religiöser Botschafter*, in 1852 by which it became possible to reach the most scattered believers with greetings and spiritual help. Four years later the name was changed to *Das Christliche Volksblatt* and continued successfully under the editorship of Oberholtzer.

A General Conference Is Born

The initiative toward union came from the two congregations at West Point, Iowa, with the editorial support of Oberholtzer. Having themselves united in 1853, they published the minutes of their 1859 conference which invited others to join them and announced the next meeting for "the second day of Pentecost in 1860 at West Point." Neither the Canada-Ohio

Conference nor the East Pennsylvania Conference took much notice of his invitation. Shortly before it was to meet, however, the latter group adopted a motion stating that "Since the Iowa conference has come to notice, it is agreed that ministers who wish may attend voluntarily." At the last minute friends raised enough money for Oberholtzer to go to the conference.

When the conference convened, only the two sponsoring churches and four visitors, including Oberholtzer, were present. Five sermons were preached before they turned to the agenda of four points. These were the organization of a missionary society, the establishment of a training school for Christian workers, the formation of a historical society, and the publication of tracts. During the conference a committee of five was appointed to draw up a plan of union by the following morning. This they did and the resulting plan, with six points, was adopted without much change. Its provisions were to make it possible to work together on all important matters without violating the congregational freedom of the churches. Uniformity in all things was not considered necessary for cooperation. It was agreed to work earnestly in home and foreign missions and establish a school for the training of Christian workers just as soon as possible. It was also agreed to meet again the following year at Wadsworth, Ohio. John H. Oberholtzer was elected chairman of the new conference.

A significant decision of the 1861 conference was the appointing of Daniel Hege as *Reiseprediger*, i.e., a traveling minister for the conference. It was to be his duty to travel through the Mennonite communities to promote unity, evangelism, and the need for a stronger educational program. In speaking of this need before the conference he said:

If we Mennonites are not to increase our guilt by longer neglecting the duty of missions as commanded by our Lord ... we must, not singly, but as a denomination, make missions the work of the Lord by our people. If we would undertake our mission duty, we first need Christian educational institutions. But to found and carry on institutions ... demands not only active interest, but also much money, and for that, churchwide participation and unremitting sacrifice is required as well as unity.[5]

Because of the Civil War Hege was unable to begin his journey immediately, but in May 1862 he set out to visit the churches in the Middle West, the East, and in Ontario. He normally conducted at least four preaching services each week and as many as fifty and sixty house calls. In every home he challenged them to give to missions and education, sharing with them his vision of a united Mennonite church forgetting its differences in the work of the kingdom. He was very well received in most places after he had presented his case, though questions and criticism were often leveled at him before they discovered his fine Christian spirit. In November he returned home to Summerfield, planning to finish the work in Iowa by the end of the year, but he took seriously ill and died of typhoid fever on November 30. His itinerant ministry had made a deep impression upon the churches, however, so forceful that Oberholtzer wrote, "If the aims of the general conference of Iowa and Ohio are ever accomplished, then Brother Hege stands forever as one of the first men who helped break through the opposition." In a way Hege represented in himself the vision of the young, emerging conference at that time with his interest in missions, education, and unity.

We have seen earlier that the initial membership in the conference consisted of two kinds of groups: South German and Alsatian immigrants coming after 1815, and the American Mennonites of the East Pennsylvania Conference originating in 1847. The conference founded in 1860 was thus not a split from the so-called (Old) Mennonites of that time, but, at its founding, drew in the Oberholtzer group as one of its participants. It was, in fact, only after the *Reiseprediger* Daniel Hege visited the Oberholtzer group in 1862 that they developed some enthusiasm for the union. Ten years after its founding the General Conference thus consisted of some twenty congregations with approximately 1,500 members. To these were later added as a third group, the congregations in Ohio, Indiana, and Missouri which had come directly from Switzerland between 1817 and 1854. It was from the Swiss congregation at Berne, Indiana, that S. F. Sprunger (d. 1923) was to come. Known as Sammy to most people, he had a great influence upon the conference through his deep spiritual concern and evangelical power.

The fourth and by far the largest group to join the conference were the Mennonites from Russia. The history of their experiences has been told in Chapters 10 and 11. Leaving Russia to escape the military draft and the threat of gradual assimilation into the surrounding culture, the first groups arrived in the United States and Canada in 1873. During the ten following years a total of 18,000 were to come, 10,000 settling on the frontier lands west of the Mississippi in Dakota, Nebraska, and Kansas, and 8,000 locating in Manitoba. A large number of these soon joined the General Conference. The coming of these immigrants has been described in detail by C. Henry Smith in *The Coming of the Russian Mennonites* (1927).

It has sometimes been asked why these 1870s immigrants joined the General Conference rather than the American or (Old) Mennonites who had given them so much moral and financial help. The answer lies partly in the fact that the latter had not unified as a conference at that time which they could have joined, but even more in two other factors: The immigrants felt a greater cultural affinity for the more Germanic element in the General Conference, in terms of language, social attitudes, convictions about education. Second, they did bring with them a mission concern which identified them with the young conference, and which they did not find among the others. When they asked John F. Funk about this, he referred them to the Dutch Mennonite missionary program in Indonesia.

The Conference of Mennonites in Canada

The immigrants of the 1870s had found the Manitoba frontier congenial and progressed rapidly. An additional 21,000 persons from Russia joined them during the 1920s and, after World War II, more than 7,000 others came also. While the first group of the 1870s stayed mostly in Manitoba, until the later migrations of some of them to Latin America, those of the 1920s located primarily in Saskatchewan and Alberta, though some stayed in Ontario. Since the depression and its crop failures came soon after their arrival many experienced extremely difficult pioneering years. In time, large numbers left their prairie farms for the fruitlands of British Columbia and Ontario. By the close of World War II farming had become so mechanized that few immigrants of the last mentioned group could afford to buy land or machinery. Consequently they located in urban areas. This, in part, accounts for the large Mennonite congregations in the cities of Canada in direct contrast to the pattern in the United States, a fact that was to add to unique social dynamics in General Conference relationships. By 1978 two thirds of the General Conference was of Russian Mennonite background and 40 percent of its membership was in Canada: 24,000 members in Canada and 36,397 in the United States for a total of 60,397 in 321 congregations, not adding the 3,044 members in Paraguay, 524 in Uruguay, and 550 in Brazil, who also belonged to the Conference.

The coming of the Mennonites to Canada is described in Frank H. Epp's, *Mennonite Exodus* (1962), and their history in Canada in his volumes I (1974) and II (1981), *Mennonites in Canada.* A sociological analysis of some of them has been provided by E. K. Francis, *In Search of Utopia* (1955). Each of these movements called forth men of vision who were willing and able to direct them and who frequently risked a great deal to bring them to pass. Prominent in the movement of the 1870s was Cornelius Janzen (d. 1894), a man of courage and ability who was exiled from Russia for encouraging the Mennonites to leave and who himself settled in Beatrice, Nebraska.

Central to the movement of the 1920s to Canada was the life and work of David Toews (d. 1947), who came to Kansas from Russia via Asia at the age of fourteen, moved to Canada as a young man to teach school, and came to be known as the Moses of the Mennonites before he died. Traveling far and wide from his modest home in Rosthern, Saskatchewan, in the interests of the emigration he soon had many friends and helpers, even in Ottawa. When he borrowed nearly $400,000 in the name of the Mennonites to make the coming of these immigrants possible, he also had numerous opponents among his own people. Total borrowings and interest were to grow to 1.9 million dollars before all was repaid in 1946, one year before his death. Central to the immigration of the 1940s were B. B. Janz (d. 1964) and C. F.

Klassen (d. 1954), both members of the Mennonite Brethren Church. The work of the Canadian Board of Colonization which had been established by Toews was of particular significance. The human drama of these migrations was filled with pathos, faith, but also humor, and is gradually finding expression in biographies and novels.

The Conference of Mennonites in Canada had its origin in the concerns of two multi-congregational groups, the Bergthal group near Winnipeg in Manitoba and the Rosenort group north of Saskatoon in Saskatchewan. The former had come from Russia as an entire colony group in the 1870s, the latter included immigrants from Russia and from Prussia both. Since Bergthal members continued to move west they were encouraged to affiliate with the Rosenort group. Eventually a meeting to regularize pastoral concerns and discuss closer cooperation between the two groups was held in Elder Peter Regier's garden near Laird in 1902. The following year the Conference of Mennonites in Middle Canada was organized at Hochstadt, Manitoba. The name was later changed to what it is today.

Numerical growth has been steady in the Conference of Mennonites in Canada through natural increase and immigration but, in recent years also through evangelism. Conference activities have proliferated enormously in education, relief, mission, native ministries, camping, and other programs. It must be remembered that each of the five Western provinces have their own conference structures and also carry on ministries in these and other areas. When the General Conference is added as a third layer of organization and activities the problems of duplication, jurisdiction, and bureaucracy increase at times to significant levels of frustration. To this situation must yet be added the activities of the Mennonite Central Committee at the provincial, national, and North American levels. Alternate ways of relating meaningfully in issues of faith and action, while at the same time simplifying existing structures, continue to be explored.

The strong interest in education in the Conference is seen in the support given to the following institutions: Canadian Mennonite Bible College, Winnipeg, Manitoba; Columbia Bible Institute, Clearbrook, British Columbia (inter-Mennonite); Conrad Grebel College, Waterloo, Ontario (inter-Mennonite); Mennonite Collegiate Institute, Gretna, Manitoba; Rosthern Junior College, Rosthern, Saskatchewan; Swift Current Bible Institute, Swift Current, Saskatchewan; United Mennonite Education Institute, Leamington, Ontario; Westgate Mennonite Collegiate, Winnipeg, Manitoba; and Elim Bible Institute, Altona, Manitoba. With $324 the Conference ranked first among all General Conference regions in per member giving in 1977.

Other Groups in the General Conference

Other smaller groups also joined the General Conference in addition to those already mentioned. There was immigration from Prussia to both Canada and the United States in small numbers from the 1870s to the 1940s. In 1946 the Central Conference with 3,211 members primarily of Amish background joined. Later some 3,000 Prussian and Russian Mennonites, who had settled in Uruguay, Paraguay, and Brazil were received into the conference. Approximately one half of the Bergthal congregations decided to join more recently, bringing the totals to the numbers indicated above. Of particular interest is the growing tendency for congregations to have dual membership by joining the given conference of the Mennonite Church also. In North America the heaviest concentration of General Conference membership was in the Middle West, stretching from the Prairie Provinces in Canada through the Dakotas and Nebraska to Kansas and Oklahoma.

United to Serve

"From the very beginning of the General Conference," wrote J. W. Kliewer, chairman of the Mission Board for twenty-five years, "missionary interest has been the cement that has held this structure together." As has been seen, missions, unity, and education were indeed the primary motives leading to union. The wide variety of ethnic and cultural backgrounds of the groups joining the conference indicated that something stronger than family relationships was drawing them together. Nor were they uniting simply for the sake of unity, as their minimal organizational machinery verifies. They did not adopt a formal constitution for thirty-six years. They united in order to do together that which none of them could do alone. A constant theme of their early correspondence and conferences was that they needed each other to carry on the work of the Lord.

American Christians were long familiar with the idea of missions, but the Mennonites were too isolated by their own cultural patterns to be inspired by them and the mission zeal of the sixteenth-century Anabaptists had long been lost. The Dutch Mennonites, however, being more open to the influence of others, had organized a missionary society in 1847, and sent their first missionary Pieter Jansz (d. 1904) to Java in 1851. The Mennonites in Germany and Russia soon supported this work. The immigrants coming from South Germany to West Point and Summerfield in mid-century brought an interest in missions with them. In 1853 Oberholtzer published an article about Methodist mission work, the first of many on this subject. At the 1858 meeting of the East Pennsylvania Conference he was asked to write to the European Mennonites for information about their missionary activities. Their response was an invitation to join in the work with the Dutch, German, Austrian, and Russian Mennonites who were already supporting it. The following year the Ontario Mennonites organized the "Home and Foreign Mission Society of the Mennonites," and in 1866 the Pennsylvania Mennonite Mission Society with seventy-two charter members was organized in Oberholtzer's church. Nevertheless, it was to take until 1872 before the first missionary candidate was available.

The founding of an educational institution was seen as part of their interest in, and preparation for, missions. For a time this absorbed all the energies of the new conference. Mennonites had generally been opposed to higher education. They believed that much learning made people proud and prevented them from seeing simple spiritual truths. The persecutors of the sixteenth-century Anabaptists had, for the most part, been learned men. Faith, the Mennonites had come to believe, was not so much independent study and intellectual understanding, but a matter of the heart and of obedience to the requirements of the church. The new conference, however, saw education as inseparable from missions; those chosen for this work should be well prepared. The institution they wanted to establish was to be a missionary training school, missions meaning not only bringing the gospel to distant lands, but working with the unevangelized at home, and even gathering indifferent and scattered Mennonites.

At the conference sessions of 1863 a report was received from the committee which had been appointed to study the school question. This report called for the school to be built at Wadsworth, Ohio, as soon as possible and to be named the "Christian Educational Institution of the Mennonite Denomination." Funds were immediately solicited and the building was finished in time to be dedicated at the next conference session in 1866. Classes began in 1868 with twenty-four students and six teachers. That same year Carl J. van der Smissen was called from a pastorate in northern Germany to be principal. The curriculum was divided into three departments—theology, German, and English. Under the latter department were included most of the subjects normally taught in academies and colleges at that time. That the field of education was indeed new to the Mennonites in North America, became clear when the school had to be closed in 1878, after eleven years of operation, because of financial and internal problems. But this first attempt was not without result. A total of 209 students had come under its influence, including the first missionaries to be sent out and many others who were to assume leadership in the conference. The school taught the people to give of their money and to think in terms of missions. Consequently the same session which closed the school in 1878, authorized the Mission Board to establish another school at a more favorable location but no immediate steps were taken.

With the coming of the Mennonites from Russia in 1874-83, many new congregations were added to the conference together with fresh enthusiasm for missions and education. Because they had conducted their own schools in Russia for over one hundred years, they were familiar with school problems and procedures. By 1877 a committee had been appointed to study the possibility of founding a school for higher education in Kansas. That school

Mennonite settlers in Kansas, Minnesota, and Manitoba built homes in their accustomed styles out of available materials. This **adobe house** still stands in Hillsboro, Kansas; the **adobe brick molds** now rest in a Mennonite museum at Freeman, South Dakota. The newly constructed transcontinental railroads actively invited immigrants to settle along their lines. The Santa Fe brought the Russian Mennonites and their wheat to **Newton, Kansas.** Bernard Warkentin built his mill alongside the main line.

opened its doors in 1882, and eventually became known as Bethel College. They also brought an interest in mission with them, stimulated in Russia by German pietism and by the work of the Dutch Mennonites. In 1868 Henry Dirks, the first Mennonite missionary from Russia, had gone to the Java field. The financial help which they received from their American brethren upon arrival in the Middle West accustomed the latter further to sacrificial giving, which directly benefited the mission cause a few years later. All of these factors caused the Pennsylvania minister N. B. Grubb to write that "It was not until the Russian brethren had come to America and united with the General Conference that the cause of missions took definite action and the spirit of missions became fact."[6]

Judged by modern standards the beginning was slow and painful. The mission societies of 1859 and 1866 had confined their activities primarily to fund raising and the publishing of articles about mission. Now, in 1872, S. S. Haury, a former student of the Wadsworth school, declared his intention to become a missionary and to prepare for this by further studies in Barmen, Germany. The conference thereupon promptly established a Mission Board of five members to work with him, also agreeing to support him financially during his studies. Following his return in 1875, he was ordained and commissioned to find a suitable field. Since the Mission Board preferred to begin their own work rather than lend him to the Dutch for work in Java, he spent five difficult years in this search. When the door seemed to close for work among the American Indians, he made a 9,000-mile trip to Alaska, but since the Presbyterians were already locating there, he returned to explore the Indian territory further. Finally, in 1880, the way opened for him to locate at Darlington, Oklahoma, to work among the Arapahoes. There were many hardships. A fire claimed four lives, including his own child, and destroyed the new mission building. But the work prospered and by Christmas, 1882, fourteen workers were on the field.

Overseas work began in 1899 when famine relief was sent to India, followed by mission workers in 1901. In 1911 the Central Conference, which later merged with the General Conference, began work in the African Congo (Zaire). In 1914 the work begun earlier in China by private persons was taken over by the Mission Board. Soon after World War II, work was begun in Colombia, Japan, and Taiwan. Later work was extended to Paraguay, Uruguay, and Brazil in a cooperative arrangement with Latin-American Mennonites. In the 1970s work was also begun in Bolivia and Costa Rica. The 1979 mission budget was three million dollars of which some seventy-five percent went for overseas projects. The number of North American workers serving abroad in 1979 was 142, with national churches rapidly filling the remaining needs. The era of mission was by no means over, but a new chapter was being written in how this witness was to be carried out in the post-colonial, late twentieth century.[7]

With the increase in conference activities came the need for a clear understanding of responsibilities such as a constitution helps to provide. The first formal constitution was consequently written and accepted in 1896, providing for the boards of Home Missions, Foreign Missions, Publication, and a Business Committee. In order to preserve the congregationl autonomy so dear to General Conference people the constitution provided that the conference could *advise* but not *legislate*, with the final authority remaining in the hands of the congregations. After continuing revision to meet new situations, the constitution established the commission for overseas ministries (COM), home ministries (CHM), and education (COE), as well as a board of directors for Mennonite Biblical Seminary, which worked together with Goshen Biblical Seminary as the Associated Mennonite Biblical Seminaries at Elkhart, Indiana. Staff offices were located in Winnipeg, Manitoba, and Newton, Kansas, with a General Board responsible for overall guidance in cooperation with an annual Council of Commissions meeting. In addition to the Conferences of Mennonites in Canada and the South American Conference, five district conferences carried on regional work in the Central, Eastern, Northern, Pacific, and Western districts of the United States. The Conference as a whole met in plenary session every three years. Its official papers are *The Mennonite* and *Der Bote*.

Faith and Life

At a centennial study conference in 1960 the following statement of goals was adopted as expressing the hopes and vision of the people of the General Conference:

> As we of the General Conference stand at the threshold of our second century, we look back to the work of those who walked before us, faithful in the cause of Christ and His church. We also look up in gratitude to our heavenly Father for His merciful guidance in the century now closing; and we look forward humbly to the century ahead, aware of the far-reaching warfare we may be called upon to wage against unprecedented demonic power.
>
> So we stand at the threshold, seeking inspiration from the past and praying for God's strengthening in the present and the future as we surrender ourselves in deeper discipleship to Him who is our Saviour and Lord, dedicating ourselves to

WITNESS

to the saving power of Jesus Christ our Lord
to the unity of all believers in Christ
to the Gospel of peace and reconciliation through Jesus Christ
to the priesthood of all believers

to the growing multitudes in our cities
to all who have not heard the Gospel
to each succeeding generation

against the spirit of materialism of this age
against the spirit of exclusivism in our fellowship
against the spirit of division in the Christian Church
against the rising tide of moral laxity

through personal evangelism
through the witness of the printed page
through our institutions of higher learning and all conference
    institutions
through the efforts of the conference in the area of Christian
    service
by reaffirming our faith in the inspiration and authority of the
    Scriptures
by dedicating ourselves anew as disciples of Christ
by living a life of dedicated stewardship
by keeping open our hearts to the regenerative and sanctifying
    work of the Holy Spirit.

by strengthening the Christian family
by manifesting concern over social evils of our culture
by a prophetic witness to state and society.

These goals represented dedication to greater faithfulness. A spirit of repentance and hope was evident at the study conference which adopted them. A sign of this repentance was the adoption of a statement asking forgiveness of the Mennonite Brethren Church for wrongs forefathers of the General Conference had committed in Russia during the painful experience of division, and the sending of a representative to bring this message to the Mennonite Brethren Conference in session. Repentance has been the first requirement for renewal in every age.

Study conferences and commissions became a significant vehicle for the continuing search for greater unity and faithfulness. The Believers' Church Study Conference in 1955, identified nine suggestions for recovering biblical fellowship within and among congregations, and in a letter to the churches said:

> It [the church] is composed of those who have voluntarily accepted Jesus Christ as Savior and Lord and have committed their lives to Him.... It is a fellowship of brotherly love and discipline controlled by the Holy Spirit.... Its authority lies in the Scripture seen particularly in the revelation of God and Jesus Christ.... It reveals itself as a missionary church with each believer as active witness.[8]

The Study Conference on Evangelism in 1958, located responsibility for outreach and witness squarely in each congregation and its members when it said: "Even as the crucial link in the church of Christ is the local fellowship, so the crucial link in effective evangelism is the lordship of the living Christ in the local fellowship."[9] It made a particular point of stressing the unity of word and deed when it said: "Teaching, preaching, Christian nurture, as well as the ministry to human need through healing rehabilitation, and relief are but different phases of the total task of the church."[10] This same concern was underscored even more forcefully in the Church and Society Study Conference of 1961, the findings of which included the following words:

We often deny the Incarnation by the very methods of evangelism which we employ. Should our ministers act in the same way in which Christ did, and seek out the town drunk in the local saloon, they would most likely receive from their congregations the same condemnations that were heaped upon Christ Himself. What we plead for is not evangelism on the one hand and social service on the other, but a getting through to human beings in their total need with the one Gospel to the whole man.[11]

A particularly important *Study Conference on the Church, the Gospel and War* was held in 1953. World War II (1939-45), had shown that the teaching of biblical nonresistance had been neglected by the churches, in that one half of the young men of draft age rejected that position. Part of this response may have been due to the usual nationalist pressures of wartime society, but part of it was also the heritage of the Modernist-Fundamentalist controversy in the Conference during the 1930s and 40s. As a progressive body the Conference was open to liberal theology and scientific modernism, though the spokesmen for this position were actually few, and often misunderstood. Social concern was not, for example, as some opponents insisted, a sign of modernism. There had been the inevitable clash of personalities. Beyond this, numerous good men and women who no longer felt accepted in their respective Mennonite affiliations joined the General Conference, which did not help its image with other Mennonites. In any case, considerable segments of the Conference came increasingly under the influence of Fundamentalism which, at that time, meant the end of any thought of nonresistance. Romans 13:1-7, often misinterpreted, rather than the Sermon on the Mount and the life of Jesus, became the guide in citizenship decisions. The conference of 1953 became a turning point back to nonresistance. It closed with the following moving appeal to the congregations:

Therefore, we call upon you, to help reexamine and strengthen our peace position. We believe that by making an unqualified commitment of allegiance to Christ, a genuine searching of the Scriptures, an early training of our children, the building of churches as consecrated brotherhoods who love their Christ, the development of Christian communities with spiritual patterns of living, the move toward redemptive Church discipline, and a mighty thrust of

Mennonites of Russian origin also came to **Mountain Lake,** Minnesota, on the Chicago and North Western Railroad. The Mountain Lake train depot in the top photo was built in 1873, one year before the arrival of the Mennonites. The bottom photo shows the town in the mid-1920s.

preaching, teaching and healing, that these will help to revive the doctrine of love and nonresistance in our fellowship. May God lead and bless us in this endeavor, is our prayer.[12]

In addition to these and other study conferences, study commissions worked at specific issues at the heart of General Conference concerns. These included church discipline, the inspiration of Scripture, race relations, the Christian and nuclear power, capital punishment, inter-Mennonite cooperation and unity, evangelism, nationalism, poverty and world hunger, and church renewal. Statements were adopted for discussion and printed on most of these issues. In 1979 a special mid-triennial session of the General Conference was called in Minneapolis to deal with the question of paying taxes for war in view of nuclear proliferation, the growing worldwide arms race, and the seeming helplessness of nonresistant Christians in the face of this course of potential global genocide.

There were other signs of spiritual vigor. The Canadian schools referred to, as well as Freeman, Bluffton, and Bethel colleges, were receiving strong student and financial support. The inter-Mennonite seminary program at Elkhart, Indiana, received gratifying encouragement and support. In the decade from 1967-76 the Conference experienced a 10 percent membership increase, of which a proportionately larger share occurred in Canada because of immigration, but also through the adding of new members, including at least two Chinese-speaking congregations. Meanwhile in the United States over 11 percent of the members had parents of non-Mennonite background. A particularly strong concern for native ministries was evident in Canada. Small groups were being formed in most congregations for sharing, confession, and mutual support. New intentional communities, convenanting house fellowships, and persons in the charismatic movement brought new vitality and joy in many places without the threatening divisions of earlier history. Sacrificial giving of time and money was being practiced by many, even as they struggled with how to simplify their lifestyle in the North American environment.

There were, of course, also continuing concerns. The earlier shortage of pastoral and other church workers continued throughout the 1970s. Women were ministering increasingly in new ways in the church, but traditional roles were slow to change. Only two women were ordained as pastors in the Conference in the 70s. Members from minority groups were not being added to the Conference in significant numbers. Midweek Bible study and prayer meetings had all but disappeared, Sunday evening services received modest support, and adult interest in Sunday school studies seemed to be declining, but family clusters and other alternate activities were arising, too. Problems of divorce and remarriage were baffling congregations who had not coped with these issues before. Nonresistance continued to grow, but troubling questions about taxes, nuclear power, the meaning of good citizenship, and other ethical issues were part of the continuing conference dialogue.

In the midst of these developments many members were experiencing increasing affluence; the gap between rich and poor was widening locally, as well as globally. A 1975 study asked for a response to the following statement: "For the most part, people are poor because they lack discipline and don't put forth the effort needed to rise above poverty." Fifty percent of the General Conference persons sampled disagreed with this statement, placing them highest among the Mennonite groups polled in sensitivity to poverty,[13] but it still reflected the fact that the power of social and economic forces in a capitalist society were not being recognized. The question of simplifying structures between the Canadian and United States parts of the Conference was not finding an easy solution. The continuing Conference desire for more unity with other Mennonite groups, particularly with the Mennonite Church, was a frequent agenda item, but some were impatient with what they considered a lack of progress.

Nevertheless, these concerns were not unusual for persons deeply concerned for faithfulness and obedience even while they lived in contemporary urban, mobile, and secular society. The recognition of these problems, and the openness with which they were being faced, were an encouraging sign of the power of the Holy Spirit at work among the churches.

Chapter 15

The Mennonite Brethren Church

ALTHOUGH spiritual life was at a low ebb in the Mennonite colonies of South Russia, there were also strong influences for renewal. The sermons of Ludwig Hofacker were read by many ministers in private as well as in public meetings. These sermons were not spectacular in style but stressed the need for repentance and forgiveness. Tobias Voth, the first teacher of the Ohrloff high school, manifested strong pietistic leanings also and organized evening services, mission fellowships, and youth meetings.

The village of Gnadenfeld, which had been influenced by Moravian pietism in Germany, began observing harvest-thanksgiving Sundays annually at which particular emphasis was given to the subject of missions. Preachers from surrounding non-Mennonite churches were sometimes invited to speak at these occasions, among them Eduard Wüst, a Lutheran pietist serving a nearby separatist Lutheran church. Wüst was a dynamic speaker, with strong convictions, stressing free grace and holy living. His style and message presented a sharp contrast to the more unassuming, conventional preaching of the Mennonite ministry. He led many Mennonites to a conversion experience, following which they witnessed to their faith in a free and open manner.

Under the influence of these brethren, lay evangelism was introduced into the villages from Gnadenfeld. House visitations were made and meetings held in homes to which unbelievers could be invited. Larger prayer and Bible study meetings were initiated on Saturday afternoons in order not to conflict with the regular Sunday worship services. Pastor Wüst was present at many of these meetings, usually assuming responsibility for preaching and teaching.

Many of the elders in the church appreciated Wüst's message. Even August Lenzmann, an influential elder at Gnadenfeld, expressed his willingness to cooperate with Wüst. When criticism was expressed over the extreme emotionalism in the group meetings, Lenzmann defended Wüst by attributing the deviations to a misunderstanding of the nature of free grace. This criticism was, however, confirmed by P. M. Friesen when he wrote that "Sanctification, to which he [Wüst] referred and which he earnestly practiced, was not preached in a systematic way nor was it in proper relationship to his joyful and evangelical sermons of grace."

Wüst died in 1859, but his conventicle groups continued to meet. Since they addressed each other as Brother, they came to be known as the Brethren. Increasingly they became discouraged with the opposition of many of the leaders in the church and charged them with unspirituality. This, in turn, led to estrangement and separation, which prevented the new spirit from working its way into the church as a whole. With the growing separation, the new group felt drawn more closely to each other. This encouraged them to observe the Lord's Supper together late in 1859 under the leadership of Abraham Cornelsen, a schoolteacher. Since none of the church elders were present, though they had been invited, this procedure was considered highly irregular. As a result, calls for discipline were heard. Elder Lenzmann consequently invited the offenders to a hearing, at which six of the brethren promised to refrain from further irregularities, pledging obedience to all things not contrary to their conscience and the Word of God.

Elder Lenzmann and other ministers in Gnadenfeld were, however, deeply concerned for reconciliation and worked to this end. Their efforts were thwarted by the demands of the church majority that private communion services must be discontinued, while the Brethren insisted they could no longer have fellowship with the entire membership of the large church. On January 6, 1860, the Brethren met in a private home to discuss the possibility of organizing a separate fellowship of believers. A document, addressed to the elders of the church, had been drawn up by Abraham Cornelsen and was considered carefully. Attention was called to the persecution which might follow formal separation. A prayer session followed. Finally, toward evening, the document was laid on the table and signed by eighteen of those present with several of those present refraining. However, nine of these added their signatures two days later.

The document accused the church of being in a state of growing corruption and its leaders of tolerating this condition of spiritual decay. There seemed to be little quarrel over doctrine. The primary concern centered around moral and ethical laxity among church members. While the charges brought against the ministers may have been too sweeping and severe, they were not without basis in fact. The statement consciously stood for historic Anabaptism-Mennonitism in its discussion of baptism, communion, foot washing, election of ministers, church discipline, and other issues. In addition to the signatures, the document named a committee of three who had been appointed as spokesmen for the new group.

The signers of the document could hardly have anticipated the results which would follow immediately. Since the elders either refused to admit the moral and spiritual decay charged to the church, or were defensive about it, the document was considered a serious attack against them and the establishment. Consequently, at a meeting of elders on January 18, a statement was drafted which placed the entire matter into the hands of the civil authority in the colony, the *Gebietsamt*, i.e., the state. This statement was signed by five elders, several others saying they needed "more light on the matter." It was clear that the five wanted the new group to be disciplined by force in order, as the statement said, "to bring them back from the error of their ways."

In thus turning a religious issue into a state, *viz.*, colony matter, the elders did what the Anabaptists had experienced so harshly at the hands of the establishment in the sixteenth century, they identified the cause of the church with that of the state. But this violated a very basic conviction of the Anabaptists, who rejected the jurisdiction of the state in matters of faith. Not all of the elders were in agreement with the action of the five. Even before the January 18 meeting, the Ohrloff-Halbstadt church council had pleaded for tolerance and urged that efforts should not be directed against the new group but against the evils they were criticizing. Many were troubled by the issue but seemed unable to do anything about it. Little was known about the entire problem in the two colonies on the Volga River.

Meanwhile the colony administration accepted the responsibility given to it by the elders and asked the Brethren for an explanation. In their response of January 23, they declared that they would gladly have remained in the church, but since the ministers were not obedient to the Word of God, they felt compelled to leave. They also declared their intention to remain Mennonites. The colony administration, however, invoked Article 362 of the Penal Code of 1857, which dealt with secret societies, against the Brethren. Religious meetings not sponsored by the established church were forbidden. Physical suffering followed. P. M. Friesen speaks of "continuous examinations, threats, imprisonments, sentences to hard labor, and starvation." Abraham Cornelsen, the father of a large family, was banished from the colony and spent a long time among one of the surrounding nomadic tribes. Others were ruined economically. Since legal travel documents were denied them, the Brethren were unable to leave the colony, yet staying became uubearable.

The revival which began in the Molotschna Colony had its counterpart in the Chortitza Colony, though the two movements were not related at first. Unfortunately the Chortitza movement, centering in the village of Kronsweide, embodied emotional excesses which led to a false freedom and to immorality which, of course, brought further disrepute upon the movement.

In the village of Einlage, however, sanity prevailed and the renewal group there disassociated itself from the others. It appears that the Einlage group was influenced by the German Baptists through periodicals which they had been receiving from them. In spite of these distinctions, the Brethren in Chortiza had as hard a time of it as those in the other colony. Wilhelm Janzen was given ten lashes and jailed in an unheated room, while his overcoat was taken from him.

Early Organization and Recognition

One of the first problems which faced the Brethren was a lack of strong leadership. On May 30, 1860, an election of ministers was held by the Molotschna group. Three of them immediately disqualified themselves for office, though they had seemed likely candidates, because they had earlier given a promise to the Inspector of Colonies not to organize a church without official permission. Consequently Heinrich Huebert and Jacob Becker were elected and ordained three days later. While there are no official records of the ordination itself, unofficial reports indicate that the oldest member of the group, Franz Klassen, upon the request of the others, laid his hands on the two candidates and, with earnest prayer, dedicated them to the ministry of the church. Though the elders had been invited to the ordination service, none were present. The historian P. M. Friesen considered this election and ordination to constitute the official organization of the Mennonite Brethren Church.

Now began a long struggle for official government recognition of the new group, which would force the Mennonites to also recognize them. Failing this, they stood in danger of losing all of their special privileges as Mennonites. Repeated trips to St. Petersburg showed the government to be both friendly and helpful, and contact was also made with the Baptists. The colonies, on the other hand, tried to prevent the government from granting the desired recognition and identified them as no longer being Mennonites but "a new sect." At home the Molotschna colony administrator asked the elders to choose between two options for the new group: expulsion from the colony or recognition, apparently hoping thereby to prepare the way for the first option

An **M. B. evening Bible school class** in Wohldemfürst, Kuban, South Russia (ca. 1925). Johann J. Toews (1878-1933), seated near the middle, was a highly gifted itinerant teacher. **Four of the leading M. B. preachers** visited the Kuban region in 1913: Peter Koehn from Waldheim, Molotschna; Kornelius Wiens, an elder of the Kuban church; Jakob Reimer from Rückenau, Molotschna; and Johann Fast of Alexanderfeld, Kuban.

to be implemented. Meanwhile the Brethren had also presented a petition to the czar in the spring of 1862.

A break came in the tense situation through the leadership of the well-known teacher and minister Johann Harder. In a letter of November 12, 1862, to the colony administration he wrote:

> Following the general conference held on the 11th of October, 1862, in the colony administration building, in which the administrator proposed that the Mennonites which had left the corrupt churches be either banished from the colony or recognized as a congregation with equal rights; our congregation, having had the matter presented to them, declared that since the former is not scriptural, it is willing to accept the latter on the condition that their confession of faith, should they be asked for the same, be in accordance, essentially, with ours.
>
> As a result of our request the seceders have declared in writing that the *Confession of Faith of the So-Called United Flemish, Frisian, and High German Anabaptist Mennonite Church* published by the congregation of Rudnerweide, South Russia, was their own. Consequently, nothing hinders the Ohrloff-Halbstadt congregation from recognizing the Mennonites in question as an independent congregation of which I now, according to our verbal agreement, wish to inform the colony administration.

This recognition was a direct challenge to the five elders who had signed the objection, and they drafted a lengthy reply. In it they accused the Brethren of acting without the sanction of ordained leadership, particularly in observing communion. The reply further referred to improper conduct in the meetings of the Brethren and to the practice of rebaptizing persons who had already been baptized in the Mennonite church. A last attempt to suppress the movement was made by the administration of the colony late in 1863, by ordering village officials not to recognize marriages performed by the Brethren, and to record the children of such marriages under the mother's name as in the case of illegitimate births. This instruction roused the Brethren to send a petition to the government, which was answered on March 5, 1864, with the coveted official government recognition that they were still considered Mennonites in the full sense of the word.

The period of litigation had come to an end, but the division remained. Bitterness and strife continued for a time, but gradually church leaders of both groups again began working together in matters of common interest to them all.

Doctrine and Church Government

Baptism: The question of the mode of baptism was not an issue for the first group of Brethren; the original document had simply stressed the importance of believer's baptism. Jacob Reimer, one of the signers, had, however, come to question sprinkling or pouring as a biblical mode already in 1837. As an eighteen-year-old, before his baptism, he had read the biography of Anna Judson and had expressed the desire to be baptized by immersion. When he asked whether there were still people who baptized by immersion, his father answered that he had known such people in Prussia.

The first baptism by immersion occurred in the Molotschna Colony in September 1860. The memoirs of Jacob Becker, one of two baptized at that time, throws some light onto the developments which led to the introduction of the practice of immersion in the Mennonite Brethren Church. He writes:

> We knew nothing of immersion until the first Sunday in September, 1860, when two sisters who had not been baptized in the Mennonite Church applied for baptism. After the church had examined them, I received the charge to baptize them. Then brother Johann Claassen came to me and asked me: "According to which form do you intend to baptize?" He went on to say: "The way the church baptizes is not scriptual." These were strange words to me.

Claassen then gave Becker a pamphlet on baptism which he studied carefully and gave to his neighbor, Heinrich Bartel. From it both received the conviction that they themselves would need to be baptized before they could baptize others. Fearful lest the elders would interpret this as proof that they were indeed introducing a new religious fellowship, they read the works of Menno Simons to see whether he confessed baptism in water. Becker found a reference in which Menno stated that although the mode of baptism had changed several times since the apostolic age, it had originally been in running water. [Jesus was, of course, baptized in the Jordan River. The second century *Didache* makes specific reference to running water.] From this the Brethren concluded that they were in agreement with Menno and that they now had good historical backing for immersion, while still remaining Mennonites.

When Becker brought his convictions to the attention of the Brethren, many agreed with him, and it was decided that he should baptize the women by immersion. He himself, however, felt that he would first need to be immersed, before he could so baptize others. Consequently he writes:

> On a day of the second week of September, a wagon load of Brethren drove to the water. First, we knelt by the water in prayer. Then we stepped into the water. Jacob Becker baptized brother Bartel, and then Bartel baptized Becker. The latter then baptized three sisters by immersing them backwards three times.

The early Brethren did not make immersion obligatory for those who had already been baptized by sprinkling or pouring in the Mennonite church. Heinrich Huebert, one of the eighteen and later the first minister and elder of the church, was rebaptized in May 1861, the year following his election as a minister. Johann Claassen, who was always highly recognized among the Brethren, was not baptized until June 30, 1862.

Early Mennonite Brethren historians note the fact that the conviction to baptize by immersion came to them independent of direct Baptist influence from the outside. However, since Johann Claassen had been in fellowship with the Baptists in St. Petersburg, it is quite possible that they influenced him in his understanding of the Scriptures at this point. In the Chortitza Colony the question of baptism emerged later, after Abraham Unger, a leader among the Brethren, had corresponded with a German Baptist minister in Hamburg. Eventually the insistence upon immersion as a prerequisite for membership also came from Chortitza, where the Einlage group made immersion a requirement for participation in communion. The churches in the Molotschna Colony were more tolerant on this issue, and until

The noted Mennonite Brethren minister, educator, and historian, **Peter Martin Friesen** (1849-1914), shown here with his wife, Susanna. Friesen served the Zentralschule at Halbstadt as teacher and principal, and formulated the M. B. Confession of Faith in 1902. He was a strong promoter of Allianz (see page 282).

1863, it was still possible for non-immersed persons to fellowship with the church. However, the advocates of immersion as a prerequisite for membership and the proponents of close communion were finally successful in establishing these practices in the church.

Extremism Is Overcome. Meanwhile the emotional excesses referred to earlier were leading to a crisis in the young movement. Members involved in this overenthusiasm, which came to be known as the *fröhliche Richtung* (joyous movement), called themselves the "happy" ones, and "strong" ones. Several of the leading men were drawn into this circle, though Elder Heinrich Huebert was a staunch opponent and declared it unbiblical. The moderates, however, were unable to stem the tide of emotionalism and soon leadership fell to the radicals both in Chortitza and Molotschna. Those who did not participate in the movement were excommunicated. All social contacts were forbidden to the elect, and even the greeting of a relative on the street was considered to be fellowship with the world.

Johann Claassen, who was in St. Petersburg at this time, wrote strong and pleading letters to these new leaders, but without effect. By spring, 1862, their excesses reached tragic proportions. The doctrine of "liberty in Christ" was interpreted to mean that all usual proprieties between men and women could now be disregarded. The saved, after all, were free from the flesh. This attitude led one of the radicals to engage in sexual immorality. He was excommunicated by his own group, and the case served as a deterrent to the entire radical movement among the Brethren.

In June, 1865, five brotherhood meetings were held and a sixth one on August 4. One meeting, begun on Saturday morning, lasted throughout the night. The following day, Sunday, was observed as a day of repentance and prayer. Letters of repentance were written to church and government leaders. And so ended a most unfortunate chapter in the early development of the Mennonite Brethren Church.

Baptist influence: During these early years the inexperienced Brethren often turned to their Baptist contacts for help and counsel. Those in the Chortitza Colony were particularly open to them. It was natural, therefore, that Abraham Unger should write to Hamburg for counsel in connection with the extremist problem, from where the Baptist August Liebig arrived to help them in the spring of 1866. Finding the Chortitza Brethren somewhat bewildered and disorganized, he began to preach and to organize brotherhood meetings to bring order into the movement.

Many of the Brethren were opposed to formal organization of any kind, lest it hinder the free work of the Holy Spirit. But Liebig served as chairman of the meetings and took the opportunity to show them parliamentary procedure. Minutes were also kept at his request. After two weeks' stay, however, the authorities arrested him and deported him back to Germany, but even in that brief time he had given invaluable aid and counsel to the Brethren. Unger stayed in touch with him by letter, and in 1869 the Baptists sent J. G. Oncken to South Russia to organize the scattered Baptist groups. A special meeting was called for October 18, 1869, at which meeting Oncken ordained Unger as elder, Aron Lepp as minister, and two men as deacons. The Molotschna Brethren also desired Oncken's services, but the aging minister was anxious to return to Germany before the rigors of winter set in.

Oncken's visit proved to be a mixed blessing. He stimulated the Brethren spiritually, and helped to organize them further. But he smoked, and his influence inspired several of the Brethren to follow his example. Also, since he was a Baptist, many considered those who had been ordained by him to be Baptists as well. Furthermore, he seems to have had a negative influence upon the traditionally Mennonite belief in biblical nonresistance. The anti-Oncken group finally won, and the ordained men were considered still to be Mennonites. The brethren who smoked were excommunicated. The Brethren continued to cherish fellowship with the Baptists but favored organizational separation from them. They had chosen to remain Mennonites and were not to be deterred from this decision.

Allianz Gemeinde: Very little genuine fellowship existed between the Mennonite Brethren and other Mennonites. With the growing convictions about immersion and close communion an increasing rigidity led to exclusivism and consequently isolation. After the crisis of emotionalism had passed, Johann Claassen and Jacob Reimer ceased to be very influential, and a new set of leaders emerged. Many of them were limited in their theological understanding and carried the pure church concept to such extremities that fellowship with other Christians was impossible. A reaction came to this in the *Allianz* or alliance movement.

There were other Brethren in addition to Claassen and Reimer who favored wider contacts than the new leadership wanted. One of them was Christian Schmidt, an evangelist sometimes called "the Wüst of the Mennonite Brethren." Schmidt worked toward fellowship with all true believers, irrespective of their church affiliation. At one of the annual conferences of the Brethren several of these ecumenically minded persons announced their intention to practice open communion, and the service was held in 1899. The repercussions were almost immediate. The congregation of which the evangelist Jacob W. Reimer was a member was asked to discipline him by the others. But the congregation loved Reimer and refused to do so.

As this spirit of tolerance spread, a group of the Brethren met on May 16, 1905, to organize the "Molotschna Evangelical Mennonite Brethren Church," a fellowship dedicated to serve all Mennonite believers, regardless of the mode of baptism practiced by them. The group soon came to be known as the *Allianz Gemeinde*, i.e., alliance or unifying church. Its single requirement for membership was the new birth, and this also meant open communion. Immersion was practiced, but members who had been baptized by another mode were not required to submit to immersion. The office of elder was abolished. In one way this group represented another division, but in another it served as a wholesome corrective to Mennonite Brethren exclusiveness. It constituted a bridge between the Mennonite Brethren and the other Mennonite churches.

Krimmer [Crimea] Mennonite Brethren: Another group born in the midst of revival and closely related to the Mennonite Brethren Church in thought and practice was the Krimmer

An outstanding leader in helping Mennonites move out of Stalin's Russia to Canada in the 1920s was **B. B. Janz.** He himself settled near Coaldale, Alberta.

[Crimea] Mennonite Brethren Church (KMB). The village of Annafeld in the Crimea experienced a revival, and Jacob A. Wiebe was converted. A potential leader, Wiebe became a dominant figure in the new movement. He had had previous contacts with the *Kleine Gemeinde* (see Chapter 10), and had been impressed by their peity. He invited Elder Johann Friesen to visit Annafeld and to organize the new group into a *Kleine Gemeinde* congregation. This was done in 1867, with Wiebe as its first minister.

Since many of the members had been baptized before

experiencing a conversion, the question of rebaptism was raised. Elder Friesen would not condone a second baptism; so the group commissioned one of its own brethren to baptize Wiebe, who in turn baptized eighteen others, on September 21, 1869. The group chose the name *Brudergemeinde* (Brethren Church) and, to distinguish it from the other Mennonite Brethren, added the geographical designation *Krimmer*, i.e., from the Crimea. The contacts with those other Mennonite Brethren, however, were few, though they agreed doctrinally except on immersion. The new group practiced kneeling and immersing forwards. Rigorous austerity in dress and life, coupled with strict church discipline, marked the KMB's even more than the Mennonite Brethren.

Mennonite Brethren in North and South America

With the immigrants of the 1870s, who have been described earlier, were also numerous Mennonite Brethren and KMB families. One of the first of these was Peter Eckert, a Mennonite Brethren elder who arrived in Kansas in 1875, bringing a number of families with him. The group was of Lutheran background and had become Mennonite through the early revivals and evangelistic efforts which followed 1860. Eckert was a tolerant and open-minded Christian and, therefore, made an attempt to form one group with the KMB families who had located nearby in the village of Gnadenau. They lived fourteen miles northwest of Peabody, in Marion County, but preferred to remain separate.

In 1876 some seventy-five additional families arrived from Russia. Although the majority were from the Volga area, a number had also come from the Kuban and Chortitza colonies. Those from the Volga and the Kuban settlements immediately joined Eckert's group, but the Chortitza families remained separate. The reason for this seems to have been the close feelings not shared by the others. From 1874 to 1880 a total of approximately 200 Mennonite Brethren families came to the Middle West, including Elder Abraham Schellenberg of the Molotschna, who exerted a stabilizing influence in the new settlements.

The Mennonite Brethren own two publishing houses: the **Mennonite Brethren Publishing House** in Hillsboro, Kansas, and the Christian Press in Winnipeg, Manitoba. The **M. B. Seminary** in Fresno, California, is located on the campus of Pacific College.

After these congregations had become established, a general desire was expressed for the organization of a conference of local churches. The first meeting for this purpose was called by Peter Regier and eleven delegates representing the churches in Kansas and Nebraska came to it. Because of inadequate representation and decisions made which later conferences could not approve, this meeting has not been accepted as an official conference. The first official conference was held in Henderson, Nebraska, in 1879. From that time on they were held annually until 1909, and triennially thereafter.

The Mennonite Brethren church in Canada began through the missionary activities of David Dyck of Kansas and Heinrich Voth of Minnesota in 1884. The first converts coming from this work were baptized near Winkler, Manitoba in 1886. Later, there were also Mennonite Brethren families among the 8,000 immigrants who settled in Manitoba in the 1870s migration, as well as *Kleine Gemeinde* and KMB's. Four years after the first Mennonite Brethren conference in 1879, Heinrich Voth of Minnesota was sent to Manitoba to evangelize among these Mennonites, with the help of David Dyck, one of the immigrants. The first converts coming from this work were baptized near Winkler in 1886. Later, Gerhard Wiebe, an immigrant of 1888, was supported by the conference in an evangelistic ministry. The first congregation was organized at Burwalde, with smaller congregations organized at Plum Coulee in 1897 and Kronsgart in 1898. From these centers workers were sent to Saskatchewan, where congregations were established in Rosthern and Herbert.

By 1900 membership in the Mennonite Brethren churches in North America was a little over 2,000. Annual conferences made it possible for them to carry on projects in missions, evangelism, and literature. In 1903, the conference delegates were asked to consider the possibility of dividing the total constituency into district conferences which could convene annually, and to have the entire conference meet every three years. No agreement was reached, however, and the question was tabled. Meanwhile a constitution was written, and accepted in 1908. The following year the projected division was carried out with the establishing of the Southern, Central, and Northern District conferences. At the 1911 conference in Rosedale, California, the Pacific District was added as a fourth conference.

The migration of the 1920s brought many additional Mennonite Brethren families to Canada and, from 1930 on, also to Paraguay and Brazil in South America. Those settling in Canada soon established strong congregations in the Prairie Provinces. After the depression many were forced to move to British Columbia and Ontario, where conferences were also established. On the prairies, Winnipeg emerged as the largest urban concentration of Mennonites, including the Mennonite Brethren. Many became leaders in business and a wide variety of the professions.

On June 9, 1930, a group of fifty-five brethren met in the village of Gnadenheim, Fernheim Colony, Paraguay, to organize the Mennonite Brethren Church in that country. Leaders in this movement were Heinrich Pauls and Gerhard Giesbrecht. The newly organized group adopted the constitution they had brought along from Russia. With the founding of Friesland Colony in Paraguay in 1937, active Mennonite Brethren congregations were established in that area also, under the leadership of Kornelius Voth. When more settlers arrived after World War II, the Volendam Mennonite Brethren Church was organized in 1947 and the one at Neuland Colony in 1948.

The first Mennonites to settle in Brazil arrived in January, 1930. An intimate relationship was maintained among the Mennonite Brethren, Evangelical Mennonite Brethren, and Mennonite churches. However, efforts to organize a united Mennonite church failed and the Mennonite Brethren Church was officially organized in the Krauel Valley under the leadership of Elder Jakob Huebert.

Several Mennonite Brethren churches were then organized in other districts. The district around Curitiba had attracted many Mennonite settlers from the Krauel, and the Boqueirao Mennonite Brethren Church was organized, with Peter Hamm as its leader. Later, the churches at Guarituba and Neu-Witmarsum were established; also, the churches of Vila Guaira and Xaxim. One of the larger Mennonite Brethren churches in Brazil is the Bage church, founded in 1949 in the province of Rio

Grande do Sul. Smaller congregations now exist at Blumenau, Saltobach, and Sao Paulo.

Several Mennonite Brethren churches have been established in Uruguay as well. The first church was organized in 1950 by the immigrants coming there directly from the Danzig and Prussian settlements which had been abandoned. Congregations were later also established at Gartental and Montevideo.

According to the official statistics for 1981, the total number of members in North America were 21,428 in Canada and 16,728 in the United States, for a total of 38,156. However, the Mennonite Brethren Church has more members outside of North America than any other Mennonite group. In 1978 there were: 250 members in Austria and 575 in Germany; 1,020 in the Brazil Convention and 1,340 in the German Association in Brazil; 725 in Colombia; 30 in Mexico; 700 in Panama; 500 Spanish, 2,000 Indian, and 1,000 German members (estimated) in Paraguay; 600 in Peru; 154 in Uruguay; ca. 25,000 in India; 868 in Japan; 19,586 in Zaire; and an estimated 22,000 in the USSR, for a worldwide total of 112,053.[1] The work among the Indians in Paraguay was carried on by an inter-Mennonite agency "Light to the Indians" (*Licht den Indianern*) and the members, therefore, belonged to all conferences of the agency, but for many years the leading workers were Mennonite Brethren.

Distinctive Characteristics

The Mennonite Brethren Church stands fully in the Anabaptist tradition together with the other Mennonite groups. Though Baptist and pietist influences were evident in their early history, as other influences were clear in other Mennonite groups, the intention has been and remains to be true to the sixteenth-century heritage of biblical Anabaptism. This has been restated clearly in the following:

(1) The early Mennonite Brethren were definite in their desire to remain Anabaptist in their confessions. Every attempt was made to declare themselves in harmony with the basic tenets as set forth by Menno Simons.
(2) The radical advances toward affiliations with the Baptists were

made by isolated individuals who failed to receive the support of the brotherhood.

(3) It seems rather clear that the Mennonite Brethren revival was meant to be a return to the Anabaptist vision, rather than a deviation from it. The desire to build a community of believers who had personally committed themselves to follow Jesus Christ, and who were willing to live a separated life of holiness, was certainly in keeping with what the Anabaptist forefathers felt was the New Testament pattern for a believers' church. [2]

Baptist influence on the mode of baptism by immersion is clear. The influence of pietism on the nature of Christian experience expected is also clear. Wüst has been called the "second reformer" of Mennonitism after Menno. Because of his influence, some of which continued later in American revivalism, the Mennonite Brethren Church has been described as "Mennonite in doctrine, pietistic in spirit."

This statement confirms that what are sometimes called *distinctives* in a group, here particularly the Mennonite Brethren Church, are often more a matter of style and emphasis than doctrinal difference. The following points may be accepted as normally central to "MB faith," without implying that other Mennonite groups do not also hold to these affirmations. [3]

Practical Biblicism. Frequent Bible study sessions give direction to members for faith and life. The stress upon the practical affirms that faith is more than a set of theological propositions, and that the Scriptures are given for daily spiritual nurture and guidance. The temptation has occasionally arisen to stress the *letter* rather than the *spirit*, to consider "proof-texts" as being the biblical approach, but the centering of all faith in the Bible and to make it the test of tradition has been healthy.

Experiential Faith. Emphasis upon a definite conversion experience has been central to Mennonite Brethren doctrine from the beginning. This represents a different course than entry into the church through mastery of the catechism. The convert is normally expected to be able to state time, place, and specific insight into God's Word as the spiritual turning point. This has sometimes led to the "dated" conversion experience, or to being conditioned to think and say what is expected. Christian nurture has sometimes been neglected in favor of the subjective experience [cf: the comment of Philip Jakob Spener, German pietist (d. 1705), that he had learned more in one dramatic night with God than in all his years at the university], but ideally both experience and nurture-growth are expected.

Christian Discipleship. Practical holiness was not a new teaching for the nineteenth-century Mennonites in Russia. But there was laxity in emphasizing actual, loving, corrective discipline. Yet new life is to be seen in a new direction taken under the leading of the Holy Spirit. Frequently this concern has taken the personal route of not smoking, drinking, dancing without a concomitant concern for the social evils of poverty, injustice, racism. The old doctrine of separation from the world would require a new definition in the present age of social, economic, and political acculturation-assimilation. Frequently nonresistance has become a casualty of this accommodation, though it remains the official doctrine of the church today.

Brotherhood Emphasis. Early use of the term *Brethren* indicated their intention for the nature of the church in 1860. Much of this spirit has been retained to this day, but in North America considerable individualism is also evident. This is not surprising as a legacy of pietism and within the context of a capitalistic economy. The church becomes less important, admonition, the congregational functions of binding and loosing, tend to disappear. The M. B. *Confession of Faith* lists the characteristics of the true church as including: "fervent brotherly love, fellowship and submission among themselves and love of their neighbors . . ."[5] The powerful unity which the Spirit brings has been evident in numerous decisions of the Mennonite Brethren Church in recent years.

In his definitive *History of the Mennonite Brethren Church* the late John A. Toews identifies Fundamentalism and dispensationalism as two major influences on Mennonite Brethren theology in the twentieth century. He finds a primary reason for this in the opposition these movements represented to modernism, which most Mennonites also rejected, and especially in the high view of Scripture the former advocated. But Fundamentalism "concentrated on Christian dogmatics, rather than

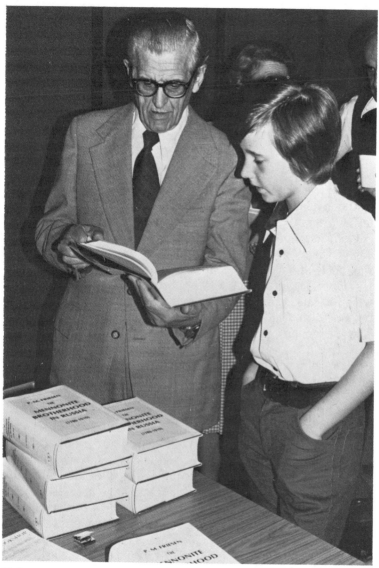

M. B. historian **J. B. Toews** and a young student browse through the English translation of P. M. Friesen's voluminous *History of the Mennonite Brotherhood in Russia, 1789-1910.*

on Christian ethics and ... has weakened the historic evangelical Anabaptist foundations of Mennonite Brethren faith and
practice."[6] On dispensationalism Toews wrote as follows:

> Although Mennonite Brethren, like the earlier Anabaptists, have
> consistently held to the view of a progressive revelation in Scrip-
> ture and to the finality of the New Testament, they have at the
> same time accepted the significance and relevance of the whole Bi-
> ble for the faith and work of the church. The artificial and arbi-
> trary division of Scripture found in dispensationalism is foreign to
> historic Mennonite Brethren theology.[7]

Freedom of Spiritual Expression. An open sharing in the
warmth of Christian fellowship is encouraged in expressions of
testimony, prayer, aspirations, calls for intercession, and new
insights from God's Word. There is a closeness of clergy and
laity. When it became apparent in Russia by 1900 that the elders
among them tended to defend the status quo, the office of elder
was abolished with the comment, "The system is sick, that is
why our men get sick." Lay ministers continue to be elected
from the congregations, though many receive formal theological
training also. One writer stated: "It is hardly possible to see the
New Testament church without a multipastoral system. The
ministry in the early Christian church was a shared ministry.
Paul appointed elders for the new churches, always in the
plural. There was a uniqueness in sharing the ministry."[8]

The Present Witness

In the first decades, the Mennonite Brethren of Russia participated with Baptists in a missionary program in India.
Similar cooperation with other agencies has continued through
the years, including relief related activities with the Mennonite
Central Committee. Zaire and Indonesia have been added to a
number of other areas in which missionary cooperation is practiced. In North America the Mennonite Brethren are associated
with the Evangelical Foreign Missions Association (EFMA) and
with the National Association of Evangelicals (NAE). In local
areas, churches associate themselves with evangelicals of
similar doctrinal positions in social concerns, service, outreach,
and witness.

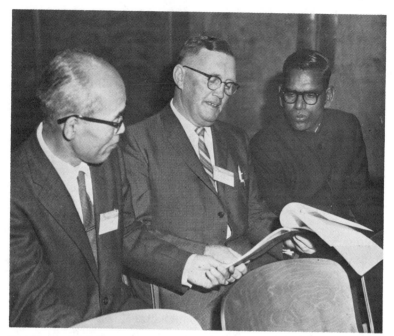

The Centennial Conference of the Mennonite Brethren, 1860-1960, in Reedley, California, brought together M. B.s from far and wide—in this case from Japan, Paraguay, and India.

Publication activities began in 1884, when the conference elected a committee of three to arrange for the editing and printing of a church paper, the *Zionsbote*. This paper was published in German until January 1, 1965, when it was discontinued. *The Christian Leader* was first published in English as a monthly periodical (1936-48) and since 1948 twice a month. In Canada the German family paper, *Die Mennonitische Rundschau*, originally founded by John F. Funk, as we saw in Chapter 10, is published by the Christian Press of Winnipeg, a publication house owned by the Canadian area conference. *The Mennonite Brethren Herald* is the English language Canadian periodical. Two publishing houses serve the Mennonite Brethren: the Mennonite Brethren Publishing House in Hillsboro, Kansas, and the Christian Press in Winnipeg, Manitoba. The Mennonite Brethren of South America cooperate in the publishing of the *Menno-Blatt.*

Mennonite Brethren have a history of strong interest in education. At one time or another, for varying numbers of years, five Bible schools were or are operating in the United States and twelve in Canada, including Columbia Bible Institute, Clearbrook, British Columbia, which has been operated jointly with the General Conference Mennonites since 1970. Five high schools were also established in Canada. Two four-year liberal arts colleges are also maintained, Tabor College in Hillsboro, Kansas (1908), and Pacific College in Fresno, California (1944). The Mennonite Brethren Biblical Seminary began operations in Fresno in 1955. The Mennonite Brethren Bible College was founded in Winnipeg, Manitoba, in 1944. During the mid-1970s the seminary and the colleges at Hillsboro and Winnipeg founded a joint Center for Mennonite Brethren Studies to serve as archival center, heritage research and promotion center, as well as being a resource for local congregations. One of the first major achievements of the Center has been the translation and publication of P. M. Friesen's monumental (1,065 pages) history of *The Mennonite Brotherhood in Russia (1789-1910)* in 1978.

In discussing the relevance of the Anabaptist heritage for Mennonite Brethren today one writer stated, "To be Anabaptist-New Testament we must be willing to become a Jesus movement once again ... we must be willing to become a believers' church movement once again ... To be Anabaptist necessitates the rejection of ethnicity as in any way determining Christian faith and faithfulness. He continues:

> Anabaptism is not identical with contemporary Mennonite Brethrenism. In many ways it is in serious conflict with it. Therefore, for us to flesh out the New Testament heritage means we must make a choice. We can face the difference between the New Testament vision and present Mennonite Brethren reality and conclude that out of faithlessness to the vision we are no longer Anabaptist-New Testament Christians. Or we can repent and be renewed. That will mean recommitting ourselves to the New Testament vision of faith and church, being judged by it and thereby being justified by it.[9]

Chapter 16

The Smaller Mennonite and Related Groups in North America

IN ADDITION to the three larger Mennonite groups, the Amish, and the Hutterian Brethren, which have been discussed in the preceding chapters, there are other branches of the Anabaptist-Mennonite family tree. For a proper understanding of the legacy of sixteenth-century Anabaptism in our day, these branches should be discussed. The total baptized *membership* of these smaller Mennonite groups in North America is approximately 47,000, not including 38,146 *persons* of Germanic ethnic background in Mexico and 3,555 in Belize. The two Mennonite-related groups discussed in this chapter had a combined membership of 40,000 in 1978.

The uniqueness of these smaller groups will be seen in the following brief discussion of their historical development and present emphasis. Often the specific emphasis of a group arose in response to the particular cultural and geographical environment in which it found itself, rather than in a negative response to what other Mennonites were saying. Other differences emerged from the variety of ways in which congregations in the same environment responded to the same challenge because they were independent and free to act as they thought best. Different leaders also had different visions for the church, and obedience meant different things to them depending on their background, character, and use of the Scriptures. To some obedience meant the establishing of communities which were isolated from the world either by geographical location or by language and other cultural barriers. In time this isolation obviously had its effect on their life and thought. To other groups obedience meant going into the world with the good news, and the ensuing influence of their environment often changed them radically, some even leaving the Mennonites in their desire to be faithful to the heavenly vision.

We cannot conclude from these reasons for the differences among them, however, that the Mennonites were not interested in unity. Rather, they gave a higher priority to obedience as they saw it. It may be that the heritage of suffering and persecution influenced them more than they suspected. Or that their stress upon the importance of love as a doctrine made it easier to forget it in practice as they labored to establish the disciplined and faithful church. If spiritual unity is considered a primary goal of the church, most of the Mennonites were far more united than might appear from an organizational chart. It was, in fact, their very oneness which accented the image of their diversity.

Groups of Swiss Ethnic Origin

Reformed Mennonite Church: John Herr of Lancaster County, Pennsylvania, founded the Reformed Mennonite Church in 1812. His father, Francis, had been excommunicated from the Mennonite church earlier for reasons which are not entirely clear. They seem to have centered around his conviction that the Mennonites had forsaken the faith of Menno Simons, especially in their lax discipline of erring members. Francis had subsequently met in homes with his followers until his death in 1810, after which his son John continued as leader. In 1812 the group elected him minister and bishop, though he was unbaptized. One of the members subsequently baptized him even as the Swiss Brethren had done in 1525. The group was variously spoken of locally as "New" Mennonites, or *Herrites*, but eventually came to be known as the Reformed Mennonites.

In doctrine the Reformed Mennonites seek to return to what they believe was taught by Menno Simons, whom they regard very highly. Their basic position is spelled out in the *Restitution,* a book which indicates clearly where they believe the church needs restoring. It seems to them that the rest of the Mennonites have left the true faith because most of them vote, some take part in local political issues, all have fun and tell stories, and some neglect the biblical requirements of foot washing, the kiss of peace, and strict discipline, including shunning. The church has no Sunday school work, no youth work or mission activities, concentrating its efforts primarily in the Sunday morning worship service. Young people are active participants in the normal life of their community until they join the church. Then a radical transformation in attitudes, dress, and social relations is expected. This may be one reason why many find it difficult to join the church of their parents. As a result, there has been a steady decline in membership in the twentieth century, until only some 600 remain. Of these, about 200 are located in Ontario, and most of the rest in Pennsylvania, with a few scattered families in Ohio, Indiana, Illinois, Michigan, and New York. A church paper, *Good Tidings,* was published from 1922 to 1932.

Church of God in Christ, Mennonite: Originating in Wayne County, Ohio, in 1859, this group is also known as the *Holdeman Mennonites* after the founder John Holdeman (d. 1900). Like the preceding group it protested against the seemingly low level of spiritual life in the church. Unlike the former, its central thrust arose from a deep religious experience rather than from a concern over discipline. John Holdeman had a deep religious experience at the age of twelve. At twenty-one he was baptized and reconsecrated himself to the work of God would have for him. He felt a strong calling to preach; but the church had not, and might never call him to the ministry. At the same time, he was appalled at the traditionalism he found as he entered into the life of the congregation as a new member. His concerns were not shared by the leaders, however, and he soon faced the necessity of either giving up his vision of what the New Testament church should be like or breaking the fellowship.

After much prayer and inner struggle he chose the latter course, calling separate meetings in homes for those of like concern. Because he wanted to see his church directly in line with the New Testament church, he called it the Church of God in Christ. To avoid being confused with other churches of God, and to show that they cherished the Anabaptist heritage, the name "Mennonite" was added later. The Dordrecht Confession of 1632 was adopted as spiritual guide. Added to this was a particular emphasis on nonconformity to the world in dress and all of life, one of the more obvious marks being the wearing of beards by all male church members. Strong stress was placed on the actual study of Menno, to the point where some even shared his understanding of the incarnation. The strong Anabaptist emphasis on discipleship has led to a warm fellowship among the Church of God in Christ, Mennonite congregations and a gentleness in human relations which makes visitors feel unusually welcome among them.

The spiritual concern of John Holdeman led to missionary activities from the beginning. After a slow start in 1859, the church won numerous members from other Mennonite churches, especially the *Kleine Gemeinde*, now the Evangelical Mennonite Conference, in Manitoba and Kansas soon after their arrival from Russia in the 1870s. An energetic mission program, including a hospital and several schools, was begun in Mexico in 1927, and more recently in Haiti and Nigeria. In 1965-66 a delegation was sent around the world to pursue contacts arising from radio and Bible lessons, and to explore the possibility of new mission programs in Egypt, India, and other countries. Out of this grew the Gospel Tract and Bible Society which carries on a Christian literature program in forty-nine countries. This work is seen as preparing the soil for missionary work.

During the 1970s many church schools were established to achieve greater nonconformity to the world. "The church seeks to maintain the 'stranger-pilgrim' stance" in society. Because the *Holdeman* consider themselves to be in the true spiritual lineage of the apostolic church, the impression is sometimes conveyed that they consider themselves to be the only true church. This doctrine of apostolic succession is a variant of early Anabaptism's appeal to the New Testament church as norm. An emphasis on conversion, proper baptism, excommunication and avoidance, and the careful calling of ministers are considered important in achieving the ideal pure church "without spot or wrinkle" (Ephesians 5:27). The church participates in the work of the Mennonite Central Committee in relief and peace programs, but is also careful to cite a favored text from Amos 3:3, "Can two walk together except they be agreed?"

The administrative offices of the church are located in Moundridge, Kansas. A hospital and printing press are also located there, with *The Messenger of Truth* being the official church periodical. Nursing homes and a child care facility are also maintained. In 1981 the membership of the church was 9,527, of whom 2,268 lived in Canada and 7,259 in the United States.

Evangelical Mennonite Church: The impetus leading to the founding of this group in 1864 was again a personal experience of deep spiritual significance, this time on the part of Henry Egly, an Amishman near Berne, Indiana. Because of his leadership they were frequently known as the "Egly Amish" but called themselves the Defenseless Mennonite Church of North America until 1948 when they adopted the present name. This use of the name *Defenseless* was probably the most accurate translation of the German *wehrlos*, which is today translated as nonresistant. As in the case of John Holdeman, so Egly charged the church with indifference in things spiritual, especially in forsaking the genuine inheritance of the Mennonite fathers. Among these important essentials was the new birth. Soon those who felt as he did, and who had experienced conversion themselves, joined him in separate meetings which led to their formal organization as a group.

A strong conservatism prevailed in dress and doctrine during the early years, but gradually the distinctive external masks of faith were discarded, including bonnets and beards. The practice of the holy kiss was largely abandoned, musical instruments were introduced into the worship services, and English replaced the German language. The early zeal, however, continued. Several preaching services were held every Sunday, Sunday schools were organized in the 1870s, and regular evangelistic meetings were held once or twice annually. Missionary work was begun in what is now Zaire in 1896. Out of this program the Africa Inter-Mennonite Mission, formerly known as the Congo Inland Mission, was organized in 1912, in cooperation with the Central Conference of Mennonites, now part of the General Conference. Since 1949 mission activities have been carried on in the Dominican Republic and, more recently, in other countries also.

The first annual conference of the Defenseless Mennonites was held in 1883, but formal organization was not completed until 1908. Publication of the first conference paper began with the *Heils-Bote* in 1897, but the name was later changed to *Zion's Tidings* and is now called *The Evangelical Mennonite.* In 1978 the total membership was 3,507 located especially near Berne, Indiana, Archbold, Ohio, and Gridley, Illinois.

Old Order Mennonites: The groups in the Old Order Mennonite story trace their origins to two schisms—the Stauffer schism from the Lancaster Mennonite Conference in 1845 over excessive social involvement, and the Wisler schism of 1872 in Indiana over Jacob Wisler's refusal to sanction Sundays schools and other innovations. Both groups have numerous autonomous congregations in their lineage, with some variations in emphasis on a variety of issues.

The Stauffer Mennonites are also called Pike Mennonites because the old meetinghouse near Hinkletown, Pennsylvania, was close to a pike, i.e., road. Nonconformity is outlined in eleven articles ranging from a rejection of secular office holding, jury duty, voting, insurance, lawsuits, and lightning rods to modesty in dress, housing, and a stress on the need for shunning of excommunicated persons. Automobiles are not permitted. Of the eleven groups in this lineage the largest is found mostly in the Ephrata, Pennsylvania, area with some 450 members in 1978. Movements have begun from Pennsylvania to Maryland and Missouri.

The Wisler schism in 1872 soon spread to Ohio, Ontario, Pennsylvania, and Virginia. Two major lines emerged—the English churches open to more accommodation to their environment, and the German churches with less openness. The former have also been known as Black Bumper Mennonites and the latter, who do not drive cars, as Team (horse and buggy) Men-

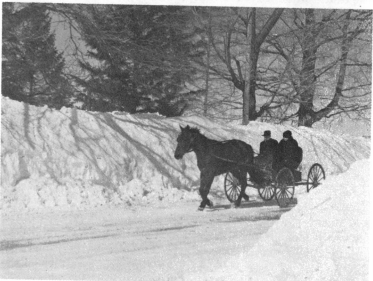

An **Old Order Mennonite meetinghouse** at Churchtown, Lancaster County, Pennsylvania. The largest concentration of Old Order Mennonites is around St. Jacobs and Elmira, Ontario. During the winter months they use both **buggies and sleighs** for their transportation.

nonites. In Pennsylvania the progressive Wisler group is also known as the Weaverland Conference or Horning group and the German group as the Groffdale or Wenger Mennonites. Because of the need for more land these groups have spread out also to Missouri, as well as to Ohio, Kentucky, Wisconsin, and other states during the 1970s. In 1978 there were a total of 12,801 members in the Old Order, of which 4,810 were in Ontario and about 8,000 in the United States.

In doctrine they affirm the Dordrecht Confession of Faith of 1632. Simplicity in all areas of living is emphasized. *Gemeinschaft*, meaning fellowship, mutual interdependence, and love is most important in all groups. Since there have been as many as fifteen separate groups or movements among them, they have seemed unduly divisive and unloving to many outsiders. Some of these groups, however, are not the result of schism, but simply groups meeting separately and named after the leading bishop. The issues which have led to separation, or perhaps it should be called *swarming*, like bees forming a new group, were not usually doctrinal but the practical application of the faith, especially in the area of nonconformity to society, which involved cars, telephones, electricity, amusements, clothing, homes, and total lifestyle. All of the groups are *restitutionist* in spirit, that is, wanting to return to the original Anabaptist and New Testament church in spirit and in form. They differ on how this might best be achieved, but are one in their desire to be faithful to Christ, the Scriptures, and to the heritage received.[1]

Groups of Dutch Ethnic Origin

Old Colony Mennonites: Many of the immigrants coming to Manitoba in the migration of the 1870s were from the Chortitza settlement which was also known as the Old Colony, since it was the oldest Mennonite settlement in Russia. They were joined by immigrants from the two daughter colonies of Chortitza, Bergthal and Fürstenland. The Bergthal group settled on the East Reserve, about sixty kilometers south of Winnipeg, and came to be known as Bergthal Mennonite Church. The Chortitza and Fürstenland groups settled on the West Reserve, west of the Red River, and came to be known as Reinland Mennonite Church after the municipality of Reinland, in which many of them lived.

A decade later, in the 1880s, about one half of the Bergthal settlers moved into the West Reserve areas occupied by their people from the other two groups. Problems soon developed because of the progressive spirit of many of the Bergthal members who were willing to abandon the old pattern of settling in villages in favor of the individual farm pattern prevalent in Manitoba. Many of the Chortitza and Fürstenland leaders saw a real danger to the faith in the scattered farm life. As early as 1880 the Reinland Mennonite Church had made willingness to live in closed villages a test of membership, causing many to join the Bergthal Church. Some of the progressive Bergthal members constituted an additional threat in their attitudes to education. Instead of being content with the simple seven-month school led by untrained teachers under the supervision of the elder, they desired teachers who could pass government inspection and were not opposed to receiving tax support.

By 1890 a major regrouping of loyalties occurred among all of them, including the Bergthal Church. Bergthal members living in the West Reserve and opposed to the new progressive movement came to be known as the *Sommerfeld Church*, after their elder who lived in the village of Sommerfeld. Bergthal members living in the East Reserve and sharing the same fear of progress came to be known as the *Chortitza Mennonite Church*, after their elder who lived in the village of Chortitza. The progressives in both Reserves retained the name of *Bergthal Mennonite Church*, while the largest and most conservative group of all came increasingly to be referred to as the *Old Colony Mennonites*.

Following this regrouping, the Bergthal Mennonite Church moved foward rapidly. Local schools were improved and a high school, later to be known as the Mennonite Collegiate Institute, was established in Gretna in 1891 with H. H. Ewert (d. 1934), a government inspector of all Mennonite schools in Manitoba. In 1903 he became one of the founders of the Conference of Mennonites in Canada, now affiliated with the General Conference Mennonite Church, together with Peter Regier of the Rosenort church in Saskatchewan and David Toews, the "father" of the

Mennonites in Canada. In 1929 a Bible school was begun in Gretna and relocated to Altona in 1940, where it is known as the Elim Bible School. In 1967 the Bergthal Church voted itself out of existence by granting local autonomy to each congregation. All of them joined the Conference of Mennonites in Canada. About half have also joined the General Conference.

In the meantime many Old Colony families had moved to Saskatchewan, settling in the Rosthern and Swift Current areas. The coming of World War I in 1914, however, revived their concern over education. Schools failing to meet government standards were to be subjected to official control, and English was to be the language of instruction in all subjects except religion. It was clear that most of their schools would not meet minimal government standards. When numerous petitions to the provincial authorities in Manitoba failed to bring any promise of relief in this threatened area of the faith, a delegation left for South America on July 15, 1919, to explore the possibility of settlement in those lands. Neither Brazil, Uruguay, nor Argentina seemed willing to grant the desired privileges, however, and the search continued. By 1921 it was clear that Mexico was to be the new haven of refuge to which these people could escape and by 1926 some 4,500 moved to that land, the first trainload leaving Canada on March 1, 1922. Nevertheless, the continuing pressures in Canada led to further search, and in 1926 the first contingent left for Paraguay, where good settlement possibilities seemed to exist. This will be discussed in the following chapter.

According to statistics available in 1981 there were approximately 955 Old Colony Mennonites in Manitoba, 3,650 Sommerfelder, 2,000 Chortitzer, 800 Reinlander, and other groups totaling 2,310 for a combined total of 9,715 members. This does not include the 38,146 persons (members and children) who migrated to Mexico, as mentioned earlier, nor those who went to Belize, Bolivia, and Paraguay as will be seen later. As with the divisions among the Old Order Mennonites, so these migrations were caused by concern about separation from the evils of society and conformity to the will of God. However, there seemed to be less reliance upon Scripture than among the Old Order and a greater reliance upon tradition and the authority of the elders. Both the Old Order and the Old Colony Mennonite movements were attempts to be the faithful remnants in an unfaithful church as they understood it, but sociologically many other elements would be added to understand the extreme right of the progressive-conservative continuum.[2]

Evangelical Mennonite Mission Conference: In the preceding paragraphs we have seen the Old Colony Mennonites as the most conservative and the Bergthal Church as the most progressive of the immigrants of the 1870s, with the Sommerfeld and Chortitza groups somewhere between these two on questions of change. In 1936-37 a split occurred in the Sommerfeld Church as a result of the evangelistic work of I. P. Friesen of Rosthern, Saskatchewan. Under the impact of his three-year ministry people were changed and became willing to break with the traditionalism of the past. Their church, however, remained intransigent until the new believers eventually formed a separate group called *Rudnerweide Mennonite Church*, after the village of Rudnerweide in Manitoba, Russia, and Prussia. In 1961 the name was changed to the Evangelical Mennonite Mission Conference (EMMC).

In contrast to the mother church, the new group immediately carried a strong missionary concern, as also interest in education and discipleship. It appeared to be a genuine recovery of the vision of the sixteenth-century Anabaptists at many points. The EMMC became particularly active in working with the brethren they had left in the old church and eventually also established churches among them in Saskatchewan. In 1978 the EMMC included approximately 2,240 members in twenty-seven congregations and twenty missionaries in Belize, Bolivia, and Mexico ministering both to Old Colony Mennonites and nationals. A strong concern for members of the old church continued, evidenced in Low German radio programs and other mission activities. A Bible school has been established at Aylmer, Ontario.

Evangelical Mennonite Brethren: Another of the groups arising to work for renewal among the immigrants of the 1870s, the Evangelical Mennonite Brethren founded their own church at Mountain Lake, Minnesota, in 1889 under a slightly different name, changed it later, and in 1937 adopted their present name. For a time they were also known as the Brudertaler Church. Reasons given for the initial break were insufficient emphasis upon the new births in their old church, too much conformity to the world, and the lack of scriptural church discipline. The form of baptism has remained optional, either by immersion or by pouring.

With the break came a strong emphasis on education and missions, though most of their missionaries served under other boards. The A. F. Wienses were among the first Mennonites to work in urban areas when they located in Chicago in 1906. In addition the conference cooperated in the support of numerous Bible schools, including those at Dalmeny, Saskatchewan, Steinbach, Manitoba, Meade, Kansas, and a College of the Bible at Omaha, Nebraska. Its congregations were scattered through the entire Middle West, from Manitoba to Kansas, with some also in the Pacific Northwest. In 1953 a loose federation was entered into with the Evangelical Mennonite Church, which was rescinded a few years later, primarily because of the distances separating the congregations of the two groups. The conference paper is the *Gospel Tidings*. Membership in the church numbered ca. 4,000 in 1981 in thirty-two congregations, and a giving budget of nearly $2,000,000 in 1976.

Evangelical Mennonite Conference: The origin of the Conference was in the same kind of spiritual restlessness we have seen in most of the preceding groups. Klaas Reimer, ordained to the ministry of the Word in Prussia in 1801, emigrated to Russia four years later. He was appalled at the lack of spiritual concern and the ethical laxity he found in the Molotschna Colony. Soon others felt drawn to his deep faith commitment, and in 1813 eighteen families formed their own renewal group, which was derisively referred to as the *Kleine Gemeinde* (the little church) by others. In addition to the Bible, Reimer had found particular inspiration in reading the *Martyrs Mirror* accounts of how early Christians and later sixteenth-century Anabaptists had been willing to die for their faith.

In 1874 most of the group emigrated to North America, with sixty families settling in Manitoba and thirty-six at Janzen, Nebraska. In 1881-82 one third of the Manitoba group joined the Holdeman group from Ohio (Church of God in Christ, Mennonite). The Nebraska group, meanwhile, had migrated to Meade, Kansas, where they soon dissolved as a group. Some joined other groups, but others formed a new congregation, the Emmanuel Mennonite Church, in 1943, which remains unaffiliated. In 1948-49 about 400 members emigrated to Mexico from Manitoba to avoid the pressures of acculturation. In 1952 the group adopted the name Evangelical Mennonite Church, changed to Evangelical Mennonite Conference in 1960. Membership in 1981 was 4,974 in forty-six congregations.

The Conference has continued to promote serious intentional commitment to Christ in keeping with Klaas Reimer's early concern. Because of this tensions have arisen in the area of public school education from time to time. The Steinbach Bible Institute has provided a partial answer to this concern. Graduates are encouraged to attend the colleges of other Mennonite groups. The early concern for nonconformity also remains but, instead of stressing the evil of certain externals, emphasis is placed upon regenerate attitudes and behavior. A strong missionary program is also being carried on. Whereas many groups have been sending fewer missionaries abroad in recent years, the Conference had over 100 serving in some twenty countries in 1978. Official publications of the Conference are *The Messenger* and *Familien Freund* (Family Friend).

Groups Related to the Mennonites

The Missionary Church: The United Missionary Church and the Missionary Church Association merged in 1969 to form the Missionary Church with a 1978 membership of 26,690, of which 5,129 were in Canada and 21,561 in the United States. Average Sunday attendance at Missionary churches is 38,254.

Historically, the United Missionary Church was known by that name from 1947 to 1969. Before that it was the Mennonite Brethren in Christ Church, which in turn had originated in 1883 through the merger of the Evangelical United Mennonites with a

Brethren in Christ group in Ohio known as the Swankites. The Evangelical United Mennonites had, in turn, originated from earlier divisions and mergers.

The Missionary Church Association originated in Berne, Indiana, in 1898, when several members of the group now known as the Evangelical Mennonite Church were excommunicated. The reason for this discipline was their belief in the necessity of baptism with the Holy Spirit after regeneration as a separate work of grace. They had also stressed the importance of divine healing, immersion as the only valid form of baptism, and had developed new insights into the second coming of Christ. Several ministers of the General Conference Mennonite Church were also influenced by these questions and joined the movement in its early years. One historian has aptly described the process of division and union among small renewal groups as follows:

> In the case of each division the cause was somewhat the same—a large body desiring to cling to the established methods, with a smaller body wishing to adopt a more aggressive, evangelistic type of work. This in each case eventually led to an estrangement resulting in division. It should not be thought that insignificant trifles produced these ruptures. There was generally a pronounced difference of spirit that only showed itself in little things that then became the occasion of difficulty.[3]

Much of the impetus for the new spiritual vigor of the Mennonite Brethren in Christ Church came from contacts with Wesleyan piety and church organization, together with an emphasis upon holiness prevalent among some Methodist churches. Under this influence the Anabaptist ingredient of the faith grew less with the passing of time, and few contacts were sought with the Mennonites. The Pennsylvania Conference withdrew from the United Missionary Church in 1952 and adopted the name Bible Fellowship Church in 1959.

In addition to the usually accepted evangelical doctrines, a strong emphasis is placed on sanctification as a second work of grace following regeneration. The spirit of the Missionary Church might be described as the search for a religion of the heart, for a faith that makes a difference in all of life. Baptism by immersion continued after the merger. Annual camp meetings have become important for the renewal of members and the winning of new converts. The emphasis in these meetings is upon both salvation and sanctification. These camp meetings also form an integral part of a vigorous missionary program around the world. Both Fort Wayne Bible College in Indiana and Bethel College in Mishawaka, Indiana, serve to train workers for this global ministry. The latter is an accredited four-year liberal arts college. The official periodical of the Missionary Church is called *Emphasis.*

Brethren in Christ: The beginnings of the Brethren in Christ movement go back to about 1780, when a revival movement spread through the Lutheran, Baptist, and Mennonite communities in Lancaster County, Pennsylvania. They preferred simply to be called *Brethren,* but were soon known as the *River Brethren* after one of their groups which met near the Susquehanna River, and because they wished to stress their nonresistance during the Civil War, they called themselves Brethren in Christ. In Canada they became known as *Tunkers* because of their baptism by immersion.

One of the men involved in the Lancaster County revival were Philip Otterbein, a pietist, and Martin Boehm, who had been excommunicated from the Mennonite church for participating in the revival work. They eventually founded the United Brethren in Christ but their greatest significance lies in the way they combined Anabaptism and pietism. From the former came a stress on simple living as "the plain people," from the latter an emphasis on the need for a crisis conversion experience and belief in divine healing. From both traditions came an emphasis on discipline according to Matthew 18, which in the Brethren in Christ Church was called "keeping house." Nonconformity also came from both roots, including nonresistance, non-swearing of oaths, rejection of public office holding, reluctance in using modern technology, and in all things a sharp distinction between church and world.

From about 1880 to 1910 many changes were introduced, including Sunday schools, home and foreign missions, protracted (extended) meetings, a church school, and a church paper. The change that made for the greatest denominational uniqueness, however, was that of Wesleyan holiness. It encountered considerable resistance, but eventually won general acceptance. This included an emphasis on sanctification, and eventually, a second work of grace after conversion. In contrast to Mennonites, greater emphasis was placed upon emotion and feeling, and on perfection. The "camp meeting" became an important part of Brethren in Christ life, a week or more of intense preaching and counseling to achieve conversion, sanctification, and spiritual growth. This proved to be an effective missionary tool also and made the group less ethnic as well as more individualistic than the Mennonites, who had a stronger doctrine of the church.

The period from 1910 to 1950 was one of stress but also consolidation and expansion in Brethren in Christ history. The impact of American Protestantism was eroding some of the historic convictions about nonconformity, nonresistance, and discipleship, leaving more and more issues to personal rather than group decision. In an attempt to stem this trend a series of rules for dress and conduct were drawn up during the 1930s, but it led to the loss of a significant number of young people. Fresh life came when this legalism was ended in the 1940s and when new associations were formed—with the MCC in 1942, and both the National Association of Evangelicals (NAE) and the Christian Holiness Association (NHA) a few years later. A new organization divided the church into six regional conferences, one of them in Canada, each served by a full-time bishop. Each congregation received representation at the annual regional and biennial General Conference sessions. A new sense of unity was felt by 1950, and with it new support for education and missions. By 1981 the total membership stood at 15,096, with 2,173 in Canada and 12,923 in the United States.

Social and missionary concern increased by mid-century. To the earlier work in Zambia, Zimbabwe, and India were added teams of workers in Cuba, Japan, and Nicaragua, but also a significant new interest in church extension in North America itself. While there had been a continuing concern for racial justice, the discovery in 1970 of a segregated Brethren cemetery led to a rigorous challenge to racism throughout the conference. The implications of world hunger became an increasing concern among members. In 1976 the General Conference agreed to have a man spend at least one year among the congregations stressing "the stewardship of possessions, the simple life, and the underlying causes and unjust structures which contribute to widespread poverty and hunger in the world."[4] While the first woman delegate to conference was elected only in 1964, by the late 1970s women were members of the major boards and exercising influence at regional levels. The diverse early roots in Anabaptism and pietism continued to find echoes in vigorous discussions about the relationship between discipleship and holiness, social action and revivalism and other related issues, but there was conference-wide commitment to the authority of the Bible, the importance of the congregation of believers, and the need for a strong witness to the power of Christ in the words and deeds of every conference member.

Chapter 17

Mennonite Churches in Latin America

NORTH AMERICANS have generally been so busy with themselves that they have remained largely unaware of the vast lands south of the Rio Grande River, yet in this region live over 300,000,000 people who are also American. This region is generally known as Latin America, comprising Central and South America, but it also includes the West Indies (or Greater and Lesser Antilles) with the islands of Cuba, Haiti-Dominican Republic, Jamaica, and various United States possessions, including Puerto Rico, the Virgin Islands, and others. Sometimes Trinidad and Tobago are added to this group. The states of Central America are Belize, Costa Rica, El Salvador, Guatemala, Honduras, Nicaragua, and Panama. North of these is the closest neighbor, Mexico, while South America includes Argentina, Bolivia, Brazil, Chile, Colombia, Ecuador, French Guiana, Guyana, Paraguay, Peru, Surinam, Uruguay, and Venezuela. The name Latin America is a cultural term derived from the fact that the two primary languages used there, Spanish and Portuguese, as well as French, are *Latin* in origin. All together these states make up a land area almost as large as Europe and the United States combined.

In this vast region climate and topography have played a decisive role. Latin America is 25 percent mountainous, almost 25 percent swampy, and about 10 percent desert land. The gigantic Andean mountain range on the West Coast, the steaming jungles in Brazil, and the four great rivers—Amazon, Magdalena, Orinoco, and La Plata—have determined the flow of population, economic development, and political boundaries. Agriculture is still the dominant activity of many people, but most farms are very small. Some farms, on the other hand, are gigantic in size, given to ranching or parceled out in small plots to peasant farmers. Some 90 percent of the land is still owned by about 10 percent of the people; land reform or redistribution has been difficult to achieve. In recent years great emphasis has been placed on industrialization as a means to economic prosperity. Latin America is rich in natural resources. But industrialization has only encouraged the movement of peasants to the cities, where many live in extreme poverty. A small, but growing, middle class is arising in most of the states.

The economic problems of Latin America are accentuated by a birth rate ranging between 2 and 3 percent in the various states. This means that the population nearly doubles every twenty-five years. Of these people over one half live in urban areas, and over one half are under twenty years of age. Poverty, a high rate of infant mortality, and a short life expectancy encourage large families, but the social and economic services cannot keep pace with this growth. Schools continue to be completely inadequate for vast numbers of children even at the elementary level, though the universities of Peru, Mexico, and the Dominican Republic are the oldest in the Western Hemisphere. In many areas health facilities reach only a relatively small number of people with preventive or even emergency care. Welfare burdens likewise break down under excessive demand and wrong political-social priorities.

Politics become volatile when people are hungry, unemployed, and only partially literate. For those who are disillusioned and have nothing to lose, Marxism is often seen as the only alternative, though it does not shy from violence when necessary. Its defenders argue that the violence of oppression is worse than the violence of possible liberation by revolution. These attitudes have led to large expenditures for military equipment by many governments as well as to the suppression of civil liberties. A social revolution of major proportions is under way everywhere in Latin America. It is peaceful in some areas, but violent or potentially violent in others.

Most Latin Americans consider themselves Roman Catholics, but for the majority this is little more than a cultural tradition. The number of active communicant members ranges from a low of ten percent to a high of thirty percent of the population. There is an acute shortage of priests and many who do serve in Latin America have been brought from Europe. As in North America secularism is the dominant orientation of the majority of the people, though the cultural aspects of Roman Catholicism—laws, social institutions, language—permeate their life and thought. While Roman Catholics themselves referred to this situation as tragic not many years ago, there are signs that renewal has come to many aspects of church life and work. The impact of Vatican Council II (1962-65) and the visits of two popes to the continent since then, the use of lay people in the work of the church, and the prophetic voices and actions of many clergy and bishops are having a profound influence on educational, social, and economic problems. A total ministry to body, mind, and spirit is under way in many places.

Protestantism was slow in coming to Latin America, but is now growing rapidly. At the International Mission Conference in Madras, India, in 1938 Protestant missionaries saw the possible loss of their fields in Asia because of Japanese military exploits on the eve of World War II (1939-45), and looked for other areas in which to work. Many turned to Latin America, where some Protestants were already working since the nineteenth century. Vigorous activity followed, particularly after 1945, but the mainline denominations were soon surpassed in vigor by the Pentecostal groups, who constitute a new "third force" besides Roman Catholics and Protestants, and who make up over one half of the more than ten million Protestants.

Mennonites Move to Latin America
An interesting account written in Spanish by a traveler in Argentina in 1877 reports the existence of three thriving Men-

nonite villages on the banks of Nievas Creek and in the Olavarria Valley. They had apparently arrived from Russia recently and harvested two excellent crops of wheat. They were part of a larger settlement of Germans from Russia. Unfortunately, this is the only knowledge we have of such a group. The story of their migration and what eventually became of them awaits further research.

Apart from this mystery, the first Mennonite settlers to come to Latin America, as far as we know, were Old Colony and Sommerfelder groups from Manitoba and Saskatchewan. Both groups felt threatened by a new law passed by the Manitoba legislature in 1915 providing for provincial control of education and the use of the English language in all schools. They considered this law to be a violation of the promises given to their fathers when they first came from Russia in 1874. The loss of German meant to them the gradual loss of their Mennonite faith and culture through assimilation into the Canadian environment. The Manitoba government had no desire to undermine the faith of any of her settlers but, in contrast to the multiculturalism now being promoted, desired to create greater national unity through standardization of education and less emphasis on the ethnic uniqueness of minority groups.

Mexico: With this apparent threat before them, the Mennonites sent out commissioners to find a new land of greater freedom. Numerous locations were considered, including North Africa and Australia. A team of six explored settlement possibilities in several of the South American countries including Paraguay, but finally returned with the recommendation to settle in Mexico. Mexico could be reached with little difficulty from Canada. Even more important was the fact that its president Alvaro Obregon had personally guaranteed to them all the rights and privileges they requested, including freedom of religion and full control of their own school program.

From 1922 to 1926 several thousand Old Colony and Sommerfelder Mennonites left Canada for Mexico, most of them settling in the state of Chihuahua. Others followed in a continuing stream, some settling south of the earlier colonies in the state of Durango. In 1948 a major movement, including 100 families of the *Kleine Gemeinde* (Evangelical Mennonite Conference) who were troubled by the progressive thinking of some of their leaders, likewise left for Mexico. All of these migrations, together with the high birth rate since the settlements began, brought the total number of Mennonites in Mexico to approximately 16,000 by 1950 and to 26,124 by 1978, of which approximately 13,800 were members of the church.

Most of these settlers were and remain farmers. Members who leave the colonies for the cities are not in good standing with the church. The village pattern of settlement which had prevailed in Russia and Canada was also followed in Mexico. Each village consists of from ten to thirty farms of approximately 160 acres and sufficient grazing lands for the village cattle. Corn, beans, and a variety of other crops are grown, but the climate is not suited to wheat production. Some modern machinery is used. The buildings are usually of adobe brick with a tin roof. Particular attention is given to the raising of cattle and horses. Cheese factories are scattered throughout the colonies.

All colony life is under the control of the church. Because of the geographical and cultural isolation, the ban is a much feared form of discipline since the delinquent has nowhere to go when he is excommunicated except into the strange and unknown outside world. Each village has its own school, but the teacher is selected at random and has little special training. A simple reader, the Bible, catechism, and hymnary are the basic study materials. Emphasis is placed upon memorization rather than upon independent thought. Sunday morning worship services are usually two or more hours long with silent prayer, the reading of an ancient sermon, and exhortation to obedience by the ministers and elder.

A General Conference Mennonite fellowship was organized in the city of Cuauhtemoc by Mennonites from Russia who were unable to go to Canada and came to Mexico in 1929-30. Some of the men who felt uncomfortable in the colonies have moved to the city and joined this fellowship. Membership of the group was 315 in 1978. Five families of the Church of God in Christ, Mennonite (Holdeman) moved to Mexico from Oklahoma in 1927 to

witness to the Mennonite settlers but soon shifted their attention to work with the native Mexican population. Extensive
medical, educational, and agricultural assistance programs have
been carried on by the Mennonite Central Committee for many
years. In 1957 this work was transferred to the General
Conference Mennonite Church.

Many of the settlers do not believe Mexico to be their
permanent home and confidently wait for God to lead them on.
During a prolonged drought in 1954 several hundred returned to
Canada. Others began to settle in *Belize* in 1958 until more than
3,000 persons had moved there from Mexico, settling at Spanish
Lookout, Orange Walk Colony, and the Blue Creek Colony.
While Orange Walk was by far the largest settlement and pros-
pering, as Spanish Lookout also did, the future of Blue Creek
Colony remained uncertain with many of the Old Colony
families moving to Bolivia. Mennonite Central Committee
transferred responsibility for the Belize settlements to the
Eastern Board of Missions and Charities (Salunga) in 1963.

Paraguay: In contrast to the negative report which a delegation had brought back from Paraguay in 1920, six delegates who
left Manitoba on February 11, 1921, brought back a very favorable description of Paraguay and many became eager to leave.
Through the help of a New York banker, Samuel McRoberts, the
Paraguayan government was asked to provide guarantees of full
religious and educational freedom to the Mennonites if they
should settle in Paraguay. This request was generously met by
the Paraguayan Congress in its passing of Law No. 514 on July
26, 1921, the provisions of which are commonly referred to as the
Privilegium by the Mennonites of Paraguay. With the passing of
this legislation came a most cordial invitation to the Mennonites
to make Paraguay their home. Economic conditions in Canada,
however, delayed emigration until 1926, though large numbers
did go to Mexico.

In the meantime banker McRoberts formed two land holding companies, the Inter-Continental Company in Winnipeg to
buy the land of the emigrants in Canada, and the *Corporación
Paraguaya* in Paraguay to sell them lands there in return. The
first land purchased by the Mennonites consisted of 137,920

acres in the Chaco, approximately 155 miles west of the river
landing at Puerto Casado, which in turn lay some two days and
two nights by boat up the Paraguay River from Asunción, the
capital city. The first group of fifty-one families (309 persons)
left Altona, Manitoba, on November 23, 1926, followed by other
groups totaling 279 families or 1,767 persons by 1930. Though
they received a cordial presidential welcome in Asunción, the
immigrants were soon to experience great suffering. Upon arrival at Puerto Casado they discovered that few preparations
had been made for their coming. Worst of all, their land had not
been surveyed by the *Corporación Paraguaya*. Sixteen weary
months were to elapse before they could move to their farm locations in April, 1928. During this difficult period many became
discouraged and returned to Canada, while 147 died of a typhoid
epidemic. The majority remained, however, to establish Menno
Colony with thirteen villages and learned to wrest a simple living from the region which had been known as the "Green Hell"
prior to their coming. By 1978 the colony had grown to *ca.* 6,100
inhabitants in eighty villages, owning nearly a million acres of
land used in agriculture and ranching. Forty-five primary
schools, a secondary school, churches, and other social organizations had become well established, bringing to mind the words of
Isaiah 35:1, 2: ". . . the desert shall rejoice and blossom; like the
crocus it shall blossom abundantly."

A second colony known as *Fernheim* was established in the
Chaco in 1930 by Mennonites from Russia. They had fled to
Germany from their lands in 1929 in the hope of finding a new
home in North America, but neither Canada nor the United
States was willing to receive them at that time and they could
not remain in Germany. Through the Mennonite Central Committee arrangements were finally made to have them settle in
the Paraguayan Chaco. The government was willing to include
this group also under the privileges of Law No. 514, and *Corporación Paraguaya* had sufficient land available. Consequently
a total of 1,853 persons in 374 families made their new home in
the Chaco in 1930. Though they were aided by the Menno Colony
people pioneering hardships again took their toll, including
sixty-five persons who died of another typhoid epidemic. Drink-

ing water was so scarce from their only good well during the early months that a boy was at times stationed at the bottom of the well to dip the trickling water with a cup and gradually fill the bucket. Many of the immigrants were extremely frustrated with their location and economic potential, but few had sufficient resources to leave. In 1937 a group of 140 families relocated in East Paraguay in the hope of achieving greater economic success, founding what became known as colony *Friesland.* Through great sacrifice and unrelenting toil both colonies gradually became moderately well established. In 1978 Fernheim counted *ca.* 3,000 persons and Friesland just under 1,000.

A third group of immigrants came to Paraguay from Russia after World War II, establishing colony *Neuland* in the Chaco and colony *Volendam* near Friesland in East Paraguay. Having fled westward before the advancing Russian armies, thousands of Mennonites from Russia had been crowded into Berlin and West German refugee camps awaiting resettlement. When emigration to North America seemed impossible, large numbers of them decided to go to Latin America. Consequently 2,314 persons in 641 family units, of which 253 were without father or husband, came to establish *Neuland* Colony between 1947 and 1950. During the same period 1,810 persons in 441 families founded the *Volendam* Colony, so named after the Dutch ship which brought them to the New World. Though the help of the previous immigrants made life much more bearable for the later groups than they themselves had experienced, many of the *Neuland* and *Volendam* settlers left at the first opportunity, some going on to Canada and others returning to Germany. Consequently the number of persons in *Neuland* was ca. 1,000 in 1978 while *Volendam* counted approximately 600.

There was a fourth group of Mennonite immigrants to Paraguay. Like the first settlers, these came from Manitoba and Saskatchewan for the same reason as in 1926, *viz.,* to preserve their spiritual heritage through isolation from the corrosive influence of modern society and its effects upon their children. Nearly 1,700 persons left the prairie provinces in 1948 to settle on 27,500 acres of primitive forest land in Eastern Paraguay some 100 kilometers east of Villarica. They came with substantial financial resources which made possible the purchase of modern farming equipment, but the agricultural patterns as well as the climate were so different from what they had been accustomed to that approximately one third of the immigrants returned to Canada. The remainder were able to establish themselves in two colonies, *Bergthal* and *Sommerfeld*, some twenty-five kilometers from each other.

All of these colonies—*Menno, Fernheim, Friesland, Neuland, Volendam, Bergthal,* and *Sommerfeld*—are predominantly agricultural communities with only sufficient industrial equipment to meet their own agricultural needs. With hard work and frugal living most of the colonists can claim to have their daily bread and modest comforts. In an attempt to help meet their economic needs North American Mennonite businessmen formed a Mennonite Economic Development Association (MEDA) and have achieved significant results in partnership with the settlers. In the Chaco the primary cash crops are cotton, peanuts (oil), and kafir corn. In East Paraguay the acreage is much smaller but peanuts, sugarcane, and other crops provide some cash income, as does the sale of timber. In recent years the experimental farm in the Chaco has successfully developed a strain of wheat suited to the climate of East Paraguay to the great joy of the people who had not forgotten the white loaves of bread they took for granted on the steppes of Russia. This has led to a significant strengthening of the economic base in both Volendam and Friesland. Manioc has replaced the potatoes of Europe and Canada. Fresh vegetables are strictly seasonal in the Chaco, but citrus fruits are available in abundance. Meat is the staple food of most major meals.

The educational program of all classes is completely under the control of the colonies themselves and is conducted in both the Spanish and German languages by their own teachers. As with the Mennonites in Mexico, only a few years of schooling are offered in the *Bergthal* and *Sommerfeld* colonies. A more adequate basic education is being achieved in the *Menno* Colony, though trained teachers are limited. In the other colonies the European system of six years' elementary and four years' secon-

Since the late 1920s successive waves of Mennonite immigrants from Russia and Germany have moved to Paraguay to establish **colonies in the Chaco** and in the forests of Eastern Paraguay. Mennonite Economic Development Associates (MEDA), now an organization with a worldwide mission, was originally set up to improve the economic situation of the **Paraguayan Mennonite farmers** through loans, donated equipment, and professional counsel.

dary training is followed by a two-year teacher-training course available to those who desire it. A cooperative Bible school is conducted in Filadelfia, the center of Chaco activities, during part of the year. Together with Mennonites in other lands in Latin America, a Bible Institute is operated in Brazil and a seminary and Bible school in Asuncion. For advanced studies students travel to Europe or North America, though several Mennonite medical doctors have received their degrees from the University of Paraguay.

Church activities continue to remain central to the social and community life in the colonies, with regular worship services held in many places. With the exception of Bergthal and Sommerfeld, an active Sunday school, prayer meeting, and mid-week Bible studies program is carried on. The Bergthal and Sommerfeld communities have not formed an official conference, but work together among themselves and maintain close relationships with their co-religionists in Canada. In 1978 the Bergthal membership was 435 and the Sommerfeld membership 600. The Mennonite Brethren membership was 952, the Evangelical Mennonite Brethren Church 322, and General Conference membership 3,044. Reference will be made later to members of Indian and Spanish-speaking congregations. A strong spirit of fellowship among the churches has strengthened their ministry and witness. Coordinating committees serve to unite church and mission activities. The biweekly paper *Menno Blatt* keeps the scattered settlers in touch with each other, as does a radio station established by North Americans in Filadelfia in the 1970s.

From the time of their arrival in the Chaco in 1930, the Fernheim group, and those who came later, as well as the Menno Colony churches more recently, have been keenly aware of their mission responsibility, and numerous programs have been undertaken. A radio ministry was carried on in Asunción originally, and now also operates in the Chaco. Bookstores have been established, and evangelism outposts were founded initially in Asunción, Itacurubí, Villa Hayes, and Cambyreta, and now there are outposts in many other locations. A medical and gospel ministry is also being carried on among Paraguayans suffering from Hansen's disease (leprosy). This was undertaken together with the Mennonite Central Committee in gratitude to Paraguay for admitting the Mennonites when no other nation seemed to want them.

Brazil: Among the Mennonites who left Russia for Germany in 1929 were about 280 families totaling 1,300 persons who chose to settle in Brazil instead of Fernheim in the Chaco of Paraguay. This became possible for them through the efforts of the German government and substantial help from the Dutch Mennonites. Land was secured for them in Santa Catarina, a state with a large German population in Southern Brazil, and the first Mennonites arrived there on February 10, 1930. Two settlements were laid out. Witmarsum in the Krauel River Valley and Auhagen on Stoltz Plateau, but neither seemed to prosper economically, though the forests, hills, and valleys afforded very beautiful scenery. The Auhagen settlers soon moved to the outskirts of Curitiba city and took up dairying on such a large scale that they eventually supplied over half of the milk required by the one quarter million inhabitants of that city. The Witmarsum Colony also relocated, some establishing themselves 100 kilometers northwest of Curitiba in New Witmarsum and some near the Uruguayan border in Colonia Nova at Bagé. Some also found employment in the cities, particularly in Sao Paulo. Through these relocation efforts most of the immigrants were soon able to achieve economic independence. In 1978 the ethnic German Mennonite community totaled some 4,100 persons but was scattered over much of south and central Brazil with primary concentrations at Curitiba, Bagé, and New Witmarsum. Of these 1,227 were members of Mennonite Brethren congregations and 550 of General Conference members. A biweekly paper *Bibel und Pflug* kept them in touch with each other and served to strengthen their spiritual life.

As in Paraguay, church and school activities are patterned after the traditional forms developed in the Mennonite settlements in Russia. Since all education is state controlled, however, the Mennonites have sought to preserve their values by having their teachers receive state training and certification and by bringing their own schools to meet certification requirements.

In this way several excellent schools have been developed, including the elementary and high school *Erasto Gaertner* in Curitiba, and many non-Mennonites are being taught together with their own students. A Bible Institute has been established in Curitiba by the Mennonite Brethren churches of South America and in 1963 had fourteen students enrolled. An orphanage in the same city, likewise sponsored by the Mennonite Brethren churches, cares for approximately seventy children between the ages of four and seventeen.

Church activities are carried on in both the German and Portuguese languages. The pressures to acculturation are much greater than in Paraguay and young Mennonites consider themselves more Brazilian than German. Fortunately, there is a growing cooperation with the larger evangelical Protestant community in Brazil, which helps to make their faith indigenous rather than extraneous to their culture. Difficulties have been encountered in securing conscientious objector classification for Mennonite men of draft age, due in part perhaps to the lack of conviction of some of the men themselves on this issue. For a time internal tensions among the churches prevented serious devotion to their teaching and witnessing ministries, but these problems have been overcome and a strong evangelical concern is evident among the congregations.

Uruguay: The settlement of Mennonites in Uruguay began in 1948 with the coming of 750 immigrants from the Vistula Delta. Together with all of their coreligionists they had been forced to leave these homelands in the closing days of World War II in 1945. Upon arriving in Uruguay they immediately found employment and by 1950 were able to purchase *El Ombu,* a 2,900-acre ranch northwest of Montevideo, with the help of the MCC. In October 1951, a second group of 431 came to join them, locating on an even larger ranch near Tres Bocas, and which they named *Gartental.* A third colony was established in 1955 on 3,600 acres some ninety kilometers northwest of Montevideo and named *Delta* after their Vistula Delta homeland in Prussia. All three of the colonies are primarily agricultural, growing wheat, peanuts, corn, potatoes, and other crops, as well as raising cattle and operating a successful dairy industry. Except for help in

Thirty-three Mennonite families from Russia settled in Brazil in 1930, followed shortly by numerous additional arrivals including a group of thirty-four families from Harbin, China. All of them located in Santa Catarina State where they established the villages of Witmarsum and Auhagen. Because of economic hardships and adverse climate these villages were later abandoned. The majority of the settlers moved on to **Curitiba,** capital of Parana State. The Mennonites in and around Curitiba are engaged in dairying and in the plywood and furniture industries. The ninth Mennonite World Conference was held in Curitiba in 1972.

purchasing land, most of the settlers were self-supporting from the beginning due to their energetic spirit and the rich economy of the country. National economic and political difficulties led many to return to Germany, leaving the total census at just under 1,000 in 1978. Of these 140 were members of Mennonite Brethren and 524 of General Conference congregations.

As in Brazil the schools are subject to state supervision and must meet national certification requirements. In 1956 Montevideo was chosen as the location for a seminary sponsored by the Mennonite Church and General Conference Mennonite churches of North and South America. It was known as the *Seminario Evangélico Menonita de Teología* and offered a three-year course of instruction to some thirty-five to forty students annually. Theological, economic, and other factors led to its closing early in the 1970s and reopening on a small scale in Asunción, Paraguay, several years later, where workers were once again being trained for congregational and missionary tasks.

This, then, is the picture of the ethnic German Mennonite groups in Latin America. Statistics about total Mennonite population figures and about baptized membership have been difficult to obtain. Part of this difficulty is due to the constant migration process which, however, is again compensated for by large families among the Old Colony groups. While there have been many migrations from Mexico, the figure of 26,124 persons is believed accurate. Paraguay would rank next with ca. 16,000 including the large Old Colony settlements in East Paraguay. Bolivia has received over 7,000 thus far, and the total in Belize may be listed at 3,555. Brazil may be listed with 4,100 and Uruguay with ca. 1,000. No fewer than 500 live in Argentina, primarily in the greater Buenos Aires area, where a congregation is active. This would place the totals at somewhere between 58,000 and 60,000 persons, of which it is estimated approximately one half to three fifths may be baptized members.[1]

"New Mennonites" in Latin America

With a task force of this size it might be assumed that a great believers' church witness is being given by these heirs of sixteenth-century Anabaptism. This is indeed true in some areas. In others, ethnic Latin Mennonites are the primary agents of witness. In still other areas North American mission boards are in the first stages of church planting, and in many places two or all three of these groups combine in a joint program. There seems to be hardly a country in Latin America where Mennonites are not actively witnessing, with the possible exception of Chile, Guyana, Surinam, French Guiana, and some of the islands of the Caribbean.

In assessing the witness of the early settlers it should be remembered that many came to their new lands as refugees and were for a time completely submerged in their struggle for existence and relative economic security. Others, like the first groups of the 1920s, had not yet caught a vision for mission. Nevertheless, some form of witness, like the work with the Indians of the Paraguayan Chaco, was begun almost the day of the arrival of the Fernheim group in 1930. In the eyes of most Latin Americans, however, the ethnic German Mennonites have until recently been seen primarily as good farmers and hardy pioneers, not as evangelicals with a faith to proclaim. And they were often content to remain "the quiet of the land."

Long before the first immigrants came to Paraguay, North American Mennonites were interested in Latin America as a mission field. One of the first missionaries described this interest as follows:

> During the 13 years, 1904 to 1917, the movement developed that gave birth to the Argentine Mennonite Mission. Mennonite youth in Goshen College studied about the neglected South American continent. Churches and wide-awake individuals contributed to a fund for South American missions. The Mennonite Board of Missions and Charities in 1911 sent J. W. Shank as its representative on a six months' tour of investigation in Peru, Bolivia, Chile, Argentina, and Uruguay. Then followed a general solicitation campaign that brought over $20,000 for the new mission. By the late summer of 1917 the four missionaries under appointment, the T. K. Hersheys and J. W. Shanks, sailed to Buenos Aires, arriving on September 11.[2]

After language study and careful survey of possible loca-

tions the first work was begun in a semi-rural town called
Pehuajó, some 300 kilometers west of Buenos Aires, in 1919.
After ten years seven growing young churches, with outstations
and Sunday schools, were in existence. In 1942 work was begun
among the Toba Indians of the Argentine Chaco, and a little
later, in Buenos Aires itself. In 1978 these efforts had multiplied
the congregations to twenty-eight, with a total membership of 1,
230 in what is known as the Argentine Evangelical Mennonite
Church. The work among the Toba Indians has led to a completely autonomous, non-Mennonite group known as the Evangelical United Church. North American mission personnel relate
to them as needed in Bible translation, literature production,
and other ways as fraternal Christians.

An equally dynamic program was launched in *Colombia* by
the General Conference Mennonites in 1943 and the Mennonite
Brethren Church in 1946. Both groups established schools and
orphanages, the General Conference Mennonites giving
particular attention to the care of children of parents suffering
from Hansen's disease (leprosy) near Cachipay. A second and
third school were added later as were medical clinics. A Bible
school is operated by the Mennonite Brethren Church. Almost
from the beginning both missionary groups experienced strong
opposition from authorities, at times even persecution. A 1959
report of the Evangelical Confederation of Colombia listed 115
Protestant Christians martyred, sixty-six churches destroyed,
as well as robbery and vandalism almost without government
intervention during the decade of severest persecution following
1945. During this period the government closed over two
hundred Protestant schools, though 43 percent of the population
was illiterate. Yet during this same period more believers were
added to the Protestant churches than during the preceding
ninety years.

The spirit and decrees of Vatican Council II (1962-65)
marked a turning point in Roman Catholic-Protestant relationships. Tolerance and even cooperation became increasingly
common and with it mutual benefits. While continuing to relate
to the General Conference in North America, the Evangelical
Mennonite Church also relates in new ways to Mennonites in

In the mid-1950s Old Colony Mennonites from northern Mexico began to settle in Belize. At the same time MCC, the Eastern Mennonite Board of Missions, MEDA, and our colleges established mission, medical, and economic assistance programs in the country. Today Mennonites produce most of the food needed in the country. The **papaya processing plant** operates in Shipyard Colony. The Virginia Conference began mission work in Jamaica in 1954. Today there are a dozen Mennonite churches on the island, including the **Calvary Mennonite Church** near Retreat on the north coast.

Latin America. The membership in 1981 was 484, but with a much larger participating community. The Conference of the Mennonite Brethren of Colombia was likewise autonomous, with a membership of 840 in twenty-four congregations. Colombian Christians were themselves reaching out to their neighbors in Christian witness in word and deed, including schools, retirement homes, children's homes, a rice-processing plant (with the help of MEDA), and in many other ways.

Different circumstances led to the beginning of Mennonite work in *Puerto Rico* in 1943. Mennonite conscientious objectors, who were not permitted to serve abroad in relief ministries, were invited to do so in Puerto Rico. Initially their program included medical, recreational, educational, and agricultural services at La Plata and surrounding regions. Two years later the Mennonite Board of Missions began work on the island, establishing a church at La Plata in 1947. In 1958 both the service and evangelism programs were united under this board, including the administration of a 32-bed hospital in Aibonito. Meanwhile the Conference of Mennonite Evangelical Churches had been established and began taking responsibility for its own life and work. By 1978 its membership had risen to 1,034 in eighteen congregations.

In 1950 a radio program *Luz y Verdad* (Light and Truth) was begun by Mennonite Broadcasts, Inc., to which a woman's program *Corazón a Corazón* (Heart to Heart) was added in 1965. This work has now grown to be a major outreach program of ten Mennonite conferences in as many countries, sponsored by the conferences themselves, and including television spots as well as a large Bible correspondence school. It is commonly referred to as JELAM (Junta Ejecutivo Latinamericano de Audiciones Menonitas). The headquarters of JELAM is in Aibonito. Since 1953 the Mennonite Brethren Church has helped to support with funds and personnel German language and other broadcasts transmitted over the powerful, nondenominational Christian radio station HCJB at Quito, Ecuador.

Among the earlier Mennonite missionary programs in Latin America was also the work in *Paraguay*. As mentioned above, the immigrants of 1930 began an informal witness program to the Chaco Indians almost as soon as they arrived. Little did those early pioneers envision the scope these early beginnings would lead to by 1980. After years of work with the Lengua tribe people, it seemed best to locate them away from the colony center in Filadelfia and a separate settlement was formed at Yalve Sanga. The first congregation was founded in 1946, after many years of loving, but seemingly fruitless ministry. By 1981, however, there were thirteen places of worship, with 2,350 baptized members and a total community of 5,210 persons. Similarly the witness to the Chulupi tribe people, which had begun in 1958, led to fourteen places of worship and 1,080 members by 1981, with a total community of 3,350. In 1958 Cornelius Isaak was speared to death as he attempted contact with the fierce Moro tribe people, but by 1978 many of these had also been won to Christ and His church. Major attempts were being made by the Mennonite colonies, together with the MCC, to resettle into self-supporting agricultural communities these thousands of people who streamed to the Mennonite communities in search of work. Health services were established, as also cooperatives, schools, crafts and light industry in a total missionary effort probably exceeding in scope that of any other effort by Mennonite missions anywhere.[3]

The Mennonite settlers also reached out to the national population of Paraguay, at first through two city missionaries in Asunción and a Bible school program. In 1959 the first congregation was formed in Asunción, but by 1962 active work was also being carried on in the Chaco and numerous other locations. By 1981 there were seven meeting places with a total membership of 410 and a relating community of 800. The conference was known as the Evangelical Convention of Mennonite Brethren. The work at Kilometer 81 (Itacurubí) with persons suffering from Hansen's disease was also having a profound Christian witness impact upon many across the nation, including state and Catholic church officials, but also upon the Mennonites themselves, who supported it with gifts and services.

A veritable explosion of Mennonite missionary activity began in Latin America about 1950. In Central America, for example, we see the following: the Eastern Board of Missions and Charities began work in *Honduras* in 1950 and by 1978 an independent Honduras Mennonite Church reported a membership of 1,200 in forty-eight places of worship, with a total community of 4,500. The Eastern Board took over work from MCC in *Belize* in 1961, forming the first Spanish-speaking congregation in 1965, and reaching a membership of 194 by 1981. In 1971 the same board began work in *Guatemala*, reaching a membership of 320 by 1981, meeting in nine congregations. In 1961 the Mennonite Brethren Board of Missions and Services began work in *Panama*, reaching a membership of 700 by 1981 in an autonomous community of ca. 1,000 persons. The first Brethren in Christ congregation was organized in *Nicaragua* in 1965, reaching a membership of 402 by 1981 and in 1970 the Fraternity of Evangelical Mennonite Churches of Nicaragua formed its first congregation, growing to a membership of 180 by 1981, autonomous, but with fraternal help from the Evangelical Mennonite Conference. Meanwhile the Nicaragua Mennonite Conference had been formed with a membership of 211 in nine congregations. Work was begun in *Costa Rica* by the Conservative Mennonite Board of Missions and Charities in 1961, leading to a membership of 450 by 1981. This left only *El Salvador* without a Mennonite or Brethren in Christ witness in Central America.

The same intense activity was also being pursued in the area we identified as the West Indies. The Brethren in Christ and the Mennonite Church both began work in *Cuba* but were forced to leave after the revolution. The Church of Christ did not leave, however, nor did the Mennonite and Brethren in Christ congregations fade away. One of the active pastors in a congregation of twenty-one (1976) was a woman. The Virginia Board of Missions began work in *Jamaica* in 1954 and by 1981 the Jamaica Mennonite Church counted 453 members. The Church of God in Christ, Mennonite is at work in *Haiti*, and the Evangelical Mennonite Church began work in the *Dominican Republic* in 1949, reaching a membership of 975 and a total community of 3,000 by 1981. The Virginia board was also at work in *Trinidad*.

Reference has already been made to the work in *Argentina*, *Colombia*, and *Paraguay* and the absence of work in Chile, Guyana, Surinam, and French Guiana. A vital Mennonite presence is being established among the national people of the other countries in South America, except for *Peru*, where only one couple is on loan to the Wycliffe Bible Translators. The earlier work of the Krimmer Mennonite Brethren begun with the Choco Indians and nationals seems not to have survived. In *Brazil* the Mennonite Board of Missions began work in 1954 at Campinas, Sao Paulo, and other places. Eventually a ministry to plantation workers developed, as did a number of bookstores including one in the new capital city Brasilia. An additional outreach was also established at Araguacema on the Araguaia River, south of the Amazon. The first congregation was founded in 1958 under the name Evangelical Mennonite Association. A similar witness has been carried on by the Mennonite Brethren Church leading to a membership of 1,050 in 1978. The language, of course, is Portuguese.

The ethnic German Mennonite settlers in *Bolivia* have, thus far, not shown much concern for evangelism beyond their own, but a small beginning has been made by workers from Argentina and North America. Both the Mennonite Church and General Conference Mennonite Church mission boards facilitated the forming of the Uruguayan Mennonite Conference in 1956, including 138 members in 1981. A Spanish-speaking Mennonite Brethren church was formed in Uruguay in 1948 with a membership of 126 in 1981. In both of the latter groups, as in the congregations in Brazil mentioned here, immigrant Mennonites (and their descendants) worship together with nationals in the same congregations, though the strictly German language congregations are also continuing. The Eastern Board began work in *Venezuela* in 1978, in Caracas, and in July of 1979 the Evangelical Mennonite Church of Venezuela was formed with the baptism of the first five believers.

Finally, with reference to *Mexico*, we remember that both the General Conference and Mennonite Brethren mission boards began work there in 1950. While the former concentrated their primary efforts, though not exclusively, on the Mennonite settlements, the latter established four areas of evangelistic outreach, combining education, medical, and gospel ministries. Major attention was given to literature distribution. The Franconia Conference began work in Mexico City in 1958 and in 1978 reported 118 baptized members with a total community of ca. 250 in six locations. The group became known as the Evangelical Mennonite Church of the Central Plateau of Mexico. The Pacific Coast Mission Board began work in Mexico in 1959, working in three locations with Sunday and Bible school programs and community service activities.

Some of these pages can be read as little more than dates and statistics, but they can also be read as individual biographies of persons coming to faith in Christ and into fellowship with other believers in the church of Christ. The number of those we called "New Mennonites" totaled approximately 13,000 members in 1978, persons who made a deliberate choice, often with dire social consequences, and who are sharing their faith in nearly every part of Latin America. If we add to this one-half or more of the total of 60,000 ethnic German Mennonites as members, i.e., 30,000—which is a conservative percentage, we have a total of at least 43,000-45,000 members in the believers' church, or Evangelical Church (Evangélicos), as they are known in Latin America to distinguish them from Catholicism, living and speaking for their faith.

The significance of these developments lies not only in the statistics, but much more in the spirit which prevails in the churches, in the quick maturity and autonomy new congregations and conferences have developed—and mission boards have been willing to let happen—and in the usually strong partnership between North and South in carrying on the missionary task. Also significant is the fact that in many instances these witnesses have been able to work not only with Protestant denominations but with Roman Catholics in a common front against the forces of social evil and spiritual darkness. In this struggle the believers' church conviction that *word and deed must be kept together* is often sorely tried.

Chapter 18

Mennonite Churches in Asia

THE PEOPLE of Asia are justifiably proud of their ancient cultural heritage. Thousands of years before the American continents were known, great civilizations flourished in India, China, and the large peninsula between them. Any good museum with an Oriental section will quickly convince one of this. India's literary tradition goes back at least 500 years before the Old Testament and the Homeric epics. The Chinese were using movable type in printing books about 700 years before printing was invented in Europe and have a national literature equal to anything in the Western world. The architectural wonders of Burma, Thailand, and Indonesia are accessible to us all through art books and encyclopedia.

Moreover the peoples of Asia have been as zealously religious as any people in the world. Hinduism and Buddhism, the main religions, are both much older than Christianity and have much in them that is both worthy and admirable. With the emergence of national independence for most of the Asian countries, these ancient religions are experiencing a revival, so that today Buddhists in Asia are sending missionaries to North America! Islam, the youngest of the great world religions, is also again allying itself with nationalism and experiencing resurgence and growth.

The change of the Asian nations from colonialism to political independence hastened the process of change from mission to church in the whole of the Christian missionary enterprise. While there was some sentiment in the 1960s and 1970s for the withdrawal of Western missionaries from Asia, the wiser course has been recognized to be a partnership relationship, missionaries and national leaders working together as equals. Furthermore, the organizational structure of the newer churches in Asia has become Western-oriented, making it irresponsible for the Western church to expect the younger churches to carry alone an institutional structure too big for their meager resources. Throughout Asia, therefore, we have today independent Mennonite churches, themselves assuming responsibility for mission work in their own countries, and gradually developing structures suited to their needs and tasks.

Indonesia: For over a century there have been Mennonites in the world who were not white, German speaking descendants of European ancestors. On March 16, 1854, Pieter Jansz, a Dutch Mennonite missionary, baptized five persons near Japara on the Indonesian island of Java. It was the beginning of the first "younger" Mennonite church. Soon there were to be others in India, Africa, and elsewhere for a total of forty-four countries by 1978.

In July 1851, Pieter Jansz and his young wife sailed quietly from Holland without a farewell. Although they knew they were going to Java, they had no idea where they would settle down. After traveling about the island, Jansz decided on the Muria Mountain area in the north central part as a suitable place for his work. Progress was difficult and very slow. Gradually Jansz developed a novel strategy which was put into practice about 1890 by his son. The Javanese who became Christians were settled in a colony because, argued missionary Jansz, it was very difficult for new Christians to live in a hostile Muslim environment. They could better grow as Christians if they lived and worked together. Actually anyone was free to join but all had to adhere to the Chritian rules of the colony. The church developed slowly with help from Mennonites in Holland, Germany, Switzerland, and Russia both in missionaries and in money. By 1940,

Dutch Mennonites started mission work on the island of Java in 1851. By 1980 the two conferences of Indonesian Mennonites totaled 53,000 members. **An informal gathering of students** turns into a sing-along on the porch of the seminary at Pati. Recently the Java Mennonites began a relocation and mission program resulting in the construction of **new Mennonite meetinghouses** in the fishing villages of Sumatra. The smaller of the two Indonesian conferences was once known as the Chinese church because of the ethnic origin of the majority of its members. The **church at Jepara** belongs to this conference.

nearly a century after the beginning of the church, there were twelve congregations and about 1,200 members.

In addition to the Javanese Mennonite Church, a church developed among the Chinese in the neighborhood as well, primarily through the vision of a layman, Tee Siem Tat, who was a printer by profession. He began his work in 1918 and in 1927 a separate Chinese conference was organized. Except that Tee and others were baptized by a white missionary, this Chinese Mennonite Church was begun and is being continued without any missionary help.

The Javanese Mennonite Church became completely independent from the European church in 1940, although developments toward independence began in 1928. Almost immediately the new church faced severe tests. The Japanese invaded Java in 1942 and in the attending unrest Christians were cruelly persecuted by Muslims and much church property was destroyed. Japanese, Muslims, and Dutch all suspected the Christians of collaborating with the enemy. But the time of testing strengthened the church, and after peace finally came to Indonesia in 1949, a period of growth and expansion set in. Schools and churches were built, and medical service was again established with the help of the MCC.

In 1965 a communist attempt to win control of the nation failed. In the aftermath of the coup over 100,000 people were killed. The army issued a decree that anyone not belonging to an approved religious group would be considered a communist and either jailed or executed. This both helped the church and became a problem for it because people came to join, Mennonite churches also, with very mixed motives. The need for teachers and other church workers for these new converts became very great. But many new converts also came from Islam, which was an approved religion, partly because they could not understand the *Koran,* which must always be in Arabic, and partly because they sensed among the Mennonites a spiritual depth and caring which they longed for.

Two experiences have forced the Indonesian Mennonites to clarify for themselves their identity and their mission. First, the difficulties of independence as a church and the strain of the war

An **Indonesian Mennonite teacher** instructs children from the village of Jemeluk in reading and arithmetic. **Young people from West Kalimantan** travel by canoe to share the gospel.

years raised seriously the question about the justification for continued existence as a Mennonite church. The Reformed Church in Java urged the Mennonites to join them, but at a conference in 1942 they overwhelmingly decided to remain Mennonites. A statement of faith drawn up at that time said: "We believe that God has helped us during all these difficulties, and that our church will now be used by God to do the part of the task He has given to the church in Indonesia."[1]

The second experience was that of living and working as the church of Jesus Christ in the new Republic of Indonesia. One of the principles of Indonesia's "guided democracy" is belief in one great God. All religious groups including the Christian church are called upon to participate actively in the construction of Indonesia, especially in the intellectual and religious area. The churches, including the Mennonite church, are given certain privileges by the government in return, as it were, for their contribution to the life of Indonesia. The Mennonites share in the excitement of playing a meaningful part in the building of a new nation. This represents both an unparalleled opportunity and a subtle danger. It can mean the increased possibility of rendering the educational and humanitarian services so much needed today. It can also mean an identification with Indonesian nationalism which will prevent them from being truly the church which knows no national boundaries.

In recent years the Mennonite churches of Indonesia have worked closely with the government in relocating landless families from overcrowded Java to the island of Sumatra. Although Java is a small island about two thirds of the population of Indonesia which is nearly 150 million people live there while many islands lie idle. By 1978 some 645 Mennonite families had been relocated in South Sumatra on land of their own. The Indonesian Mennonite church, with some help from the MCC, supplemented government aid as possible, including pastors and teachers. In a new region different agricultural practices must be developed. The families are happy and the church is growing there too. One man, who had been a Muslim, was asked why he was happy and he replied: "Because I know Jesus. Because I and my family are healthy. Because I can be a part of the church. Because I own all this land (five acres). Because I have a draft ox (a gift from MCC). Because my house keeps the rain out even though it is a poor man's house."[2]

There are two Mennonite conferences in Indonesia, the Evangelical Church of Java with a membership of 47,711 in 1981, and the United Muria Indonesia Christian Church with 5,369 but a total community of ca. 20,000. The latter have sometimes been known as the "Chinese" church because of their ethnic origin but they are now as Indonesian as the others. Neither of the groups use the term Mennonite. Elementary and secondary schools are maintained and particular attention is given to leadership training at a seminary in Pati, sponsored by both conferences. Women play a significant role in the churches, including some who are ordained. Clinics, a hospital, and an orphanage are being supported. The conferences are also constituent members of a Christian university in Salatiga. The Indonesian churches are among the fastest-growing Mennonite churches in the world. In 1978 one of their leaders, Charles Christano, was elected president of Mennonite World Conference.

Japan: The growth of the Christian church in Japan has always been slow. The Jesuit mission of the sixteenth century won many converts, but the young church was soon destroyed by persecution. When Protestant mission work began in Japan in the 1860s, becoming a Christian was a crime punishable by death. This law seems not to have been enforced, however, and was soon removed. In 1978 fewer than one percent of the 110 million population of Japan were Christian. With a land mass approximately the size of California, but of which only about 20 percent is arable, Japan ranks among the most densely populated areas of the world.[3]

Mennonite missionaries followed close on the heels of the conquering American army, and reconciliation was indeed needed after the war ended with the atomic destruction of Hiroshima and Nagasaki. A specific peace and reconciliation ministry was begun in Hiroshima by Mennonites in the late 1970s. In 1949 the Mennonite Church began work on Hokkaido Island. In 1950 the General Conference Mennonite Church began on Kyushu Island and the Mennonite Brethren on Honshu Island. In 1953 the Brethren in Christ likewise located on Honshu. From the beginning the Mennonite Church, General Conference Mennonite Church, and the Brethren in Christ have worked together in Tokyo in evangelism, peace witness, literature production, and young people's work. In the 1970s an Anabaptist study center was being developed in the city.

Though the Mennonite missionaries wished to work also in rural areas, their success has been limited. This is due, in part, to the drift of young people to urban centers, and in part to the strong social ties of the rural *buraku* (a group of households or families). The *buraku* is a voluntary association for dealing with common concerns like festivals, road repair, seeding and harvesting, funerals, but it is also concerned for religious affairs. Disagreement with a decision within the group can lead to social ostracism. The *buraku* is said to be collapsing due to rapid changes in agricultural techniques and family structure, but it still remains a major obstacle to the personal acceptance of the Christian faith in rural areas.

The high literacy and advanced technology of Japan also help to determine the manner of church growth. Missionaries do not normally engage in medical and education work as in Africa and other parts of Asia, these services being adequately provided for by the government. Consequently there is a strong emphasis on personal evangelism along with radio evangelism and literature distribution on a personal basis, through the mails, and by operating bookstores. During the early years effective work was done through kindergartens operated by missionaries, frequently leading to the formation of Sunday schools and contacts with the whole family. Work among high school and university students, often through the medium of English instruction offered by the missionaries, has shown itself to be both rewarding and challenging.

The Mennonite church in Japan will continue to be a cooperative work, with Japanese and North American Christians working side by side for some time to come. Though it is an independent church, it receives some support from North America, primarily to uphold the unique roles of missionaries and their expense. If, however, it should become necessary for

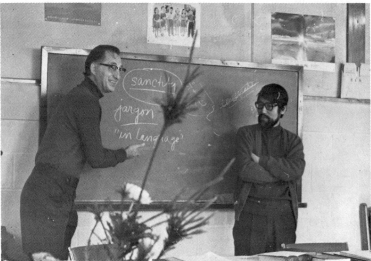

Mennonite missionaries arrived in Japan in 1949. By 1980 there were fifty-eight congregations with a combined membership of over 2,000. The **congregation at Obihiro** on the island of Hokkaido is one of the older ones. Visiting professor **C. Norman Kraus and native pastor Takio Tanase** conduct a seminar with the Kushiro churches on the theme "What is church?"

the missionaries to leave, the work of the Mennonite churches would continue, for they are fortunate to have the leadership of trained and dedicated young men and women. In 1981 the Japan Mennonite Church Conference had a membership of 327 in a total community of 950, the Japan Mennonite Christian Church Conference numbered 610 members in a total community of 715, the Japan Mennonite Brethren Conference listed 1,102 members and a community of 2,020, the Yamaguchi Prefectural Conference of Brethren in Christ had 47 members in a community of 221, and the Tokyo Area Evangelical Mennonite Cooperative Conference had 125 members for a total of about 2,000 members. The Japan Mennonite Fellowship, an inter-Mennonite successor to the MCC, is alert to needs in and beyond Japan, e.g., in Vietnam and other areas.

China: Although it is almost completely cut off from its sister churches elsewhere in the world, a Mennonite fellowship continues to exist in the People's Republic of China. That fellowship began in 1905 when H. C. Bartel, a member of the Krimmer Mennonite Brethren Church, began independent work in Ts'aohuen, Shantung province, in the hope of attracting Mennonite support. This work was adopted and supported by the China Mennonite Mission Society, an organization in which several Mennonite bodies participated. In 1909 and 1912 the General Conference and Mennonite Brethren began work with J. J. Brown and F. J. Wiens in Hopei and Fukien provinces respectively.

In all areas of Mennonite work, expansion was rapid during the first few decades, with considerable numbers of converts being baptized. The main methods of church extension were evangelism, medical work, distribution of literature, and education work at the primary and secondary levels. Immediate assumption of missionary responsibility by the Chinese themselves characterized the Chinese Mennonite Church, and the move to independence began early.

All of this subsequently proved to be of great importance since China has had a troubled history in this century. Serious political unrest nurtured by antiforeign feeling disturbed China in 1926 and 1927. In the early 1930s civil war, involving the developing communist power, ravaged a number of provinces. Added to this was the undeclared war between China and Japan which began in 1931, and which became a war of Japanese conquest in 1937. This unrest brought the work of the Mennonite Brethren to an almost complete stop. Then came World War II. In 1940 a number of missionaries were evacuated only to be interned by the Japanese. Others remained and moved into Western China where Chiang Kai-shek ruled over what was called Free China. During this time the Chinese Mennonite churches continued their work of preaching and living the gospel under very difficult conditions. When the war ended in 1945, many of the missionaries returned to their old places of work. But the trouble was not yet over, for throughout the years of unrest since the early 1930's the communists had been establishing control over larger and larger areas of China. This provoked the civil war lasting from 1946 to 1950. Thus prompted, the Mennonite missionaries moved westward again to establish new work in Kansu and Czechwan provinces.

In 1948, just when the tide of the civil war turned to favor the communists, the Mennonite Church entered China with a mission at Hochwan in Czechwan province. But the days of the missionaries in China were numbered. Conditions became more and more difficult and missionaries began to go home or to other fields, leaving the Chinese Mennonite churches to carry on the "ministry of reconciliation" in a war-weary and exhausted land. The last Mennonite missionary to leave was H. C. Bartel, the founder of Mennonite work in China. That was in 1952. There were at that time over 5,000 Mennonite Christians in China.

One missionary, Loyal Bartel, remained in China. In more recent years word of his death from natural causes was received in North America. In the spring of 1979 MCC and several former missionaries received letters from former friends in China expressing joy and confidence: "... We are living a happy life." "... The Hengyang and Pooyang Mennonites are all fine." The former location had been the site of an MCC orphanage, the latter of a high school operated by the General Conference. In 1980-81 a teacher-student exchange program became possible between China and Goshen College, Goshen, Indiana. News of strong small Christian fellowships was also being received. Further developments were being awaited eagerly by Mennonites in North America.

Taiwan: When the communist regime consolidated its control over mainland China in 1948 and 1949, the nationalists, under the leadership of Chiang Kai-shek, fled to Taiwan and soon established control of the island. Christianity had been brought to the island by the Dutch in the seventeenth century, but they were driven out in 1661. It remained for British and Canadian Presbyterians to begin work there in 1865. Mennonite work in Taiwan began in 1948 when MCC workers were forced to leave mainland China. Many mission agencies did the same. In 1978 there were over 500 Protestant missionaries, representing over sixty groups, in Taiwan.

Political and cultural tensions exist in Taiwan over its history, identity, and future. Mainland China considers it as one of its provinces and seeks its return to their control. The Taiwanese, who numbered about thirteen million in 1978, and who are the descendants of immigrants from the mainland in the seventeenth century, consider themselves a separate nation at present under the occupation of some three million mainland nationalist Chinese. Nine aboriginal tribes are also on the island.

MCC work concentrated first on mobile clinics and a small hospital at Hualien on the east coast. In 1954 this work was transferred to the General Conference Mennonite Church. By 1978 the hospital had been enlarged to over 100 beds, and a strong evangelism program had been undertaken mostly by Taiwanese Mennonites. In that year membership stood at 907, with a total community of 1,900 in sixteen congregations. These congregations had organized the Fellowship of Mennonite Churches in Taiwan (FOMCIT) as fully independent churches carrying on a variety of ministries in cooperation with each other and North American workers. Particular attention was being given to the training of theological leadership by sending students to schools in Taiwan and in North America. A newspaper called *Manna* served as an important communication link between the widely scattered congregations.

Vietnam: Christianity first came to Vietnam in 1533 with

MCC workers forced to leave mainland China in 1948 relocated on Taiwan. By 1980 there were nearly a thousand Taiwanese Mennonites in sixteen congregations. Members of **the Po-Ai Mennonite Church** are seen here enjoying an outdoor service.

the Portuguese. The Jesuits opened a mission in Danang in 1615. In due time Roman Catholicism became a dominant Christian faith, competing with Buddhism, as well as ancestor worship, Caodaism, and other forms of religion. The first Protestant missionaries seem to have been sent by the newly founded (1887) Christian and Missionary Alliance Church in North America in 1893, but their work really began only in 1911. Numerous other missions followed during the French colonial occupation until 1954, and after.

The Evangelical Mennonite Church of Vietnam began with the coming of MCC in 1954. Three years later the Eastern Board of the Mennonite Church initiated work in Saigon. Because of the ravages of war and political unrest, progress in building Christian fellowships was slow, but relief and educational services were given, including help with the leprosarium at Banmethuot. By 1961 the building of a hospital in Nhatrang had been completed with the help of MCC. Later MCC also gave leadership to Vietnam Christian Service, which included Church World Service and Lutheran World Relief.

By the end of the war in 1975 most North Americans, including Mennonites, had left the country. MCC had given heroic service during the long and tragic years of the war. Daniel Gerber, a Mennonite, was one of a number of relief workers who perished there. Several MCC workers continued their work for a time after 1975. Their return was not encouraged, but the Evangelical Mennonite Church continued its witness. Membership had grown to 150 by 1978, meeting in two congregations. Hope continued for the return of fraternal relations with North American Mennonites.

Philippines: The Mennonite congregations of the Philippines had their origin in the vision and commitment of Felonito A. Sacapaño, an executive of International Nutrition Products, Inc. Together with another Christian they used their available time and resources to initiate weekend Bible studies among the mountain tribes of Abra, near Luzon, beginning in 1950. A unique part of their ministry was a deep concern for the economic and social problems of the people they were teaching. Small cottage industries were started, carpentry was encouraged, fishing, rice processing, and other income-producing activities soon flourished. This gave necessary income to impoverished families and from their tithe they helped to begin similar projects in other areas.

Nine churches had been started in this way by the time Eastern Board representatives of the Mennonite Church came in contact with them in 1972. With their help and some small loans from MEDA these efforts could be extended to the lowlands and markets could be developed for their products, both at home and abroad. A strong mutual concern permeates the congregations in which helping each other with difficult or unexpected problems is taken for granted, whether the needed help is economic, spiritual, or social in nature. By 1978 there were ca. 2,000 believers in twenty-two congregations in what has come to be known as *Missions Now, Inc. (Mennonite),* headquartered in Manila.

Felonito Sacapaño, a businessman with a vision, is the leader of the twenty-two Philippine Mennonite churches. Modern-day Anabaptists, the Philippine Mennonites combine a vigorous evangelistic effort with a practical approach to social issues. A class at the **Philippine Mennonite Biblical Institute** studies Christian stewardship.

Eight of these congregations are among the very poor of Filipino society, while the members of the other congregations come from all social and economic levels, with 75 percent having a farming base.

Central to the work of all of these congregations is the task of evangelism. Sessions on how to win people to Christ are a regular part of worship experience. It appears to take about three years for a new congregation to be founded in a new area. Particular emphasis is placed upon using the skills (gifts) of lay people, but in 1978 alone forty-eight students were also being supported in secondary school and college studies. Plans are underway for a Bible school. In all activities the early church of the Book of Acts is taken as a model. In addition to sharing as needed, an experiment in community of goods has been initiated in one location. The unique blending of message and method has shown evangelistic power which is attracting the attention of other mission and church groups. Meanwhile Felonito A. Sacapaño states: "There are 7,000 islands in the Philippines. We are only on five yet. . . . "[4]

Australia: In 1952 Foppe Brouwer, a young Mennonite from the Netherlands, arrived in Australia as an immigrant. He knew of no Mennonites in the country and occasionally attended a Presbyterian church because the preaching was in Dutch. Four years later he met and married Alice, an immigrant from Friesland. While visiting their families in the Netherlands in 1964 they received catechism instruction and were baptized in the home church in Friesland.

On their return to "down under," as Australia is sometimes referred to, they placed a notice in the Dutch Sydney paper inviting other Mennonites to write to them. When nine persons responded the Brouwers mimeographed a news sheet and called it *De Mennist.* By 1978 they were mailing out 200 copies of each issue, many of them abroad. They estimate that there may be from 2,000-5,000 ethnic Dutch Mennonites in the land, of which no fewer than 500 might be baptized members of some Mennonite church in the Netherlands or elsewhere. A few families also live in New Zealand.

A turning point to the Brouwers' life came in 1975, begin-

For the past two decades **Foppe Brouwer** of Fennell Bay, New South Wales, Australia, has attempted to forge a tie between the widely scattered Mennonites of Australia and New Zealand through personal correspondence, lending of books by mail, and publication of a Dutch/English periodical called **De Mennist.**

ning with Alice's involvement in a small charismatic group in a Methodist church. Before long Foppe too had experienced new Holy Spirit power at a conference in Brisbane and later their children and relatives. Neighbors were won to Christ through their new life and witness. The Brouwers do not consider themselves charismatic but simply new, joyful disciples of Jesus. Without their realizing it a church of Jesus Christ was being born in their midst.

In 1977 Ian Duckham of Australia, who had studied at the Eastern Mennonite Seminary of the Mennonite Church, was ordained and, with his wife, commissioned to work in Australia.

They located in Perth on the west coast. Meanwhile, Foppe Brouwer continued his planning for a Mennonite church. He hoped this might include a retreat center where Mennonites could vacation, meet, fellowship together. "The Mennonite Church in Australia has a future," he wrote. "The peace doctrine, believer's baptism, and the separation of church and state appeal to the youth. The time has come for Mennonites to plant a church in Australia."[5] In July 1979 the first congregation was indeed organized at Fennel-Bay, on the east coast (where the Brouwers live), and Ian Duckham installed Foppe Brouwer as pastor. While most immigrant Mennonites in Australia live in the Melbourne, Sydney, and Brisbane areas, the initial membership of the church is made up of "New Mennonites" coming from all walks of life.

It may be noted that a group of Mennonites from Russia settled in Palestine about 1870, expecting the imminent return of Christ. They became known as the *Templers*. During World War II many of them and their descendants were deported to Australia as German aliens. Others followed later. Considerable growth in membership has been reported. There may be as many as 2,000 "Templer-Mennonites" of Russian Mennonite background in the Victoria and New South Wales states.[6]

India: When we speak of the Mennonite church in India we actually also include the United Missionary Church and the Brethren in Christ Church, all of whom together numbered approximately 35,000 members in 1981. Together with the four Mennonite groups they share a commitment to the Anabaptist vision of faith and church life, and all six groups are members of the "MCSFI Family" (Mennonite Christian Service Fellowship of India), a service agency created by them in 1964.

The first Mennonites to come to India as missionaries were the Abraham Friesens from the Mennonite Brethren Church in Russia, who came in 1889 and worked with the American Baptists. Two years later the Mennonite Brethren Church was officially organized in India. The first Mennonites from North America came in response to the famine of 1898-1900, bringing wheat and other relief supplies sent by the Mennonite Brethren, Mennonite Church, General Conference Mennonite Church, and

North American Mennonites arrived in India just before the turn of the century in response to the spiritual and physical needs of the subcontinent. As a result, practical programs have always occupied a central part in the work of the church in India. **Lab technicians** received their training and employment in Mennonite hospitals, and **nurses** graduated from Mennonite schools of nursing.

others. They spent the first few years in the physically and spiritually exhausting work of trying to feed too many people with not enough food. Many children orphaned by the famine became their complete responsibility. A number of these eventually became strong leaders in the churches.

The Mennonite Brethren churches are located in Andhra Pradesh, and have been unusually effective in winning others to Christ, totaling 25,142 members in 1981. In identifying the methods used intensive evangelism is listed first, followed by mass movements including sociological or other factors, and third, the transfer of members from missions terminating their work in a given area. With this "... automatically came hundreds and thousands of baptized believers. Suddenly, they were all Mennonite Brethren."[7] The Mennonite Church work centered in Madhya Pradesh (1,900 members), and later on a second field in Bihar (552 members), while the General Conference workers also located in Madhya Pradesh (4,246 members). The India United Missionary Church located first in West Bengal (1,800 members) and the Brethren in Christ in Bihar (1,480 members). In each case work began at one initial station and then branched out in all directions into the many villages of India.

The primary methods of church extension in India have been personal and preaching evangelism, medical work, and education. Medical work soon occupied a central place, with hospitals and clinics being built, and mobile clinics put into operation. Nursing schools were begun to provide the necessary help for these institutions, and to bring health care into the villages. Special efforts were made early to help those suffering from Hansen's disease (leprosy). At first it was simply a matter of providing food and shelter, but treatment programs soon followed. With the advance of modern medicine, many could experience the arresting of their disease and return to meaningful living. Several missionaries received the Kaisar-i-Hind medal from the Viceroy of India for distinguished service to patients.

It is no accident that literacy is high among Indian Christians since the church in India has always considered education

A group of Mennonite young people meet for **an evening of music.** The educational program of the church in India includes secondary schools, reading rooms, adult literacy projects, and Bible correspondence courses. **Teacher Kesho Rao** checks on the work of one of his high school students.

to be one of its first responsibilities. Primary and secondary schools came into existence in large numbers on the mission stations, as well as in the villages. Industrial schools were also begun to teach agriculture to the boys, and homemaking to the girls. All six groups send students to, and support Union Biblical Seminary at Yavatmal, which is to be relocated at Pune. The production of literature for use in school and church programs has also been carried on jointly by these groups. They likewise cooperated in sponsoring the first Asia Mennonite Conference at Dhamtari in 1971, and later in refugee and relief aid to Bangladesh.

Because of the devoted work of missionaries and national leaders, and because of the strong educational program, responsibility for the gospel ministry has been assumed fully by the churches in India. Today we can truly speak of these churches as independent in every way. Mennonite missions in India continue, but as the joint work of foreign and national missionaries. Occasional governmental pressure upon foreigners in the 1970s made their continuing stay tenuous, but this was not much different from other times and places of mission.

The 1960s and 1970s brought significant changes in the areas of the Mennonite churches in Madhya Pradesh. Dhamtari, the first station of Mennonite Church activity, was suddenly near a center of steel production because of the presence of iron ore. Korba, the location of one of the first General Conference stations, became an electric power center because of large deposits of high-quality coal in the area. It attracted a large fertilizer plant and a technical institute. Suddenly a quiet rural area became an industrial center. This created new opportunities, as well as new problems for the church.

A large number of technicians and workers from all over India came to Korba. They spoke different languages. Among them were Christians from various denominations. The language used in the Mennonite church is Hindi which many of the newcomers did not know. How was the church to minister to these people? These new situations demanded the development of new methods. In 1958 a "church-in-the-house" was begun partly to deal with the language barrier, partly to overcome transportation difficulties. Soon numerous house churches employing different languages were meeting regularly for worship and study. Each one had a leader but members participated freely. Because of the high literacy rate of the newcomers, the Dhamtari and Korba churches have established reading rooms and bookstores to provide Christian literature. Graduates of Yavatmal Seminary are in charge of this work, seeking to meet the educated on their own level.

The Christian church in India is not keeping up with the population growth numerically, but its witness is creative and effective: evangelism, relief ministry to the poor, schools including a seminary and Bible schools, a Bible correspondence school with offices in Calcutta has over 100,000 students enrolled, radio broadcasts even in Sri Lanka and Manila, clinics and hospitals which also practice preventive medicine and train nurses and midwives, youth work and voluntary service programs, prayer fellowships and many other forms of witness. P. J. Malagar, a leader in the Mennonite Church has written:

> Our opportunities are great in this day and age. For a numerically small church, the area is too big; the opportunities are too many for planting churches and gathering in the harvest. "Laborers are few." Our stewardship of the gospel and means are inadequate.

> But our hopes and challenges for the future are thrilling and exciting. By the grace of God the roots of the church are firmly set. We are true both to the gospel and to our Anabaptist-Mennonite heritage in this land.[8]

Nepal: Mennonites have been in Nepal since 1954, working in cooperation with the United Mission to Nepal, an interdenominational agency, in clinics and other health services, in education, and agricultural and technical development projects. These are being carried on jointly by the Mennonite Board of Missions and the MCC. Some persons have been won to faith in Christ, but this has also led to suffering and persecution.

Other areas: There continues to be a Mennonite presence in other areas of Asia—in Bangladesh through the work of MCC, in Hong Kong through mission agencies, and until recently in South Korea and Laos through MCC. There are, however, no plans presently to follow up this presence with church planting activities. But we have seen that Asian Mennonite Christians, numbering at least 76,000 members in 1978, are reaching out in constantly new forms of witness and service in partnership with each other and other Mennonites. In 1974 Asia Mennonite Services was established to coordinate and pioneer in ministry to the needy in word and deed. Takashi Yamada, a Japanese Mennonite leader, has said: "The world of Asians is still largely an unsecularized one, and the people keep a sense of respect for the holy." This respect for the holy is generally rooted in one of the ancient Asian religions, which are experiencing new vitality. The opportunities for Christians in Asia to share and live their faith continued to be enormous on every hand.

Chapter 19

Mennonite Churches in Africa

FROM ASIA we move across the Indian Ocean to the continent of Africa. Christianity is old in Africa, having existed there in some form since apostolic times. Four of the greatest church leaders after the apostles, Tertullian, Origen, Cyprian, and Augustine, were all North Africans. Much of our theology today is indebted to their work. However, Christianity was limited to the area bordering the Mediterranean and Red seas and did not penetrate into the interior of the continent until David Livingstone took it there between 1850 and 1870. Since then, it has been as busy a place for Christian witness as any in the world.

Africa, too, has a rich cultural history. The great civilization of ancient Egypt is well known to most people, but beyond that Africa was often called the "Dark Continent" by whites who saw black as bad and knew little about African history except some awareness of the slave trade. Artifacts from Ethiopia and the Sudan indicate an early and dynamic culture. Tirhakah, the king of Ethiopia (2 Kings 19:9), called himself "the Emperor of the world." North Africa, the Nile Valley, and West Africa all developed together before climatic changes displaced fertile land with what we know today as the Sahara Desert. After that West Africa became particularly noted for its culture, centering in the kingdoms of Ghana, Mali, and Songhay in the areas of the Senegal and Niger rivers. By AD 800 Ghana was a powerful trading state, succeeded eventually by Mali. Under King Mansa Musa (d. 1332) the Egyptian scholar As-Saheli became the master architect for the city of Timbuktu which by late fifteenth century had a population of about 100,000, a banking and credit (card?) system, poetry and chess clubs, and a good medical school at Sankore University, which reportedly even performed cornea transplants. Islam, luxury, and European penetration led to the disintegration of the Songhay dynasty, which was overthrown by the Sultan of Morocco, who had guns, in 1585. Gradually Africa came under European domination, beginning with King John II of Portugal, who settled the Gold Coast region in 1482. In most areas of Africa colonialism only began to disappear in mid-twentieth century.

The Republic of Zaire: The Mennonite church began in what was then known as the Belgian Congo in 1911 when a missionary couple was sent to find a suitable site for a mission location. The area chosen is located west of the Kasai River, a large tributary of the Congo, and about 400 kilometers southeast of Kinshasa. It was chosen, in part, because of the influence of Alma Doering, who was not a Mennonite, but who had spent a mission term in the Congo and who played a major role in bringing Mennonites to this undertaking.[1] Mennonites had been in the Congo since 1890. In the year 1912, the Congo Inland Mission (CIM—since 1972 the Africa Inter-Mennonite Mission AIMM), was organized as the joint enterprise of the Defenseless Mennonite Conference (now the Evangelical Mennonite Church) and the Central Illinois Mennonite Conference (now part of the General Conference).

Initial progress was slow, with only twelve converts by 1916, but soon membership increases exceeded all expectations. By 1981 membership stood at about 62,000 with a total community double that number. In the course of time other Mennonite groups became involved in the work, either through the sending of workers or through membership in AIMM, including the Mennonite Church, the Evangelical Mennonite Conference, and others. This has been one of the best examples of inter-Mennonite cooperation, including a fruitful relationship with MCC.

Mennonite mission work in the Belgian Congo, now Zaire, started in 1911. By 1981, with a combined membership of nearly 62,000, the Zairean Mennonites form the largest Mennonite presence in any country outside North America. A Mennonite village parsonage serves as the backdrop for this pose of **Zairean sisters and their children.** At the medical center in Tshikaji **student nurses** learn operating room procedures.

Since 1943 independent work has been carried on by the Mennonite Brethren Church to the west of AIMM related congregations. Their membership in 1981 was 22,000.

The twentieth century saw many denominational missions in Zaire, including particularly Roman Catholicism which tended to be favored by the Belgians. It may be significant for the context of our discussion of church life in Zaire to take note of a major renewal movement, *Kimbanguism,* which began in 1921. By 1980 it had a membership of ca. three million in Zaire, making it in effect *the* non-Catholic national church. Known officially as *The Church of Jesus Christ by Simon Kimbangu,* it began through a spiritual revival Simon Kimbangu, a Baptist catechist, experienced while reading the Sermon on the Mount. He came to believe it was meant for now, for himself and all Christians, including nonresistance. When he began preaching this it seemed so revolutionary to the Belgian authorities that he was sentenced to death, a sentence eventually commuted to life imprisonment. From his lowly work in the prison kitchen radiated such faith and joy that the movement grew rapidly. Following his death his two sons continued in leadership unhindered. Aside from several schools of high caliber few institutions are supported by the Kimbanguists. It is in every sense an African church, having arisen without the help of a single missionary dollar. North American Mennonite individuals have been relating to them, at the request of the church, to facilitate biblical-theological studies. In addition they have also developed a working relationship with the Reformed (Calvinist) church in Europe. As a quasi-nonresistant church, potentially the largest in the world, North American Mennonites have had a particular interest in Kimbanguism.

The move to political independence of Zaire in 1960 brought serious problems to all the churches. For some years prior to that time there had been progress among the Mennonites toward an independent, self-supporting, self-governing church. In February of 1960 a meeting took place in Charlesville at which the national Mennonite leaders were invited by the mission to assume full leadership responsibility, with the missionaries remaining as counselors. The invitation was accepted with the knowledge of its importance and awareness of the weight of responsibility involved, and *The Mennonite Community of Zaire* came into existence.

Although there was a definite connection between this move and the forthcoming political independence, no one could have guessed in February how important this action would turn out to be in July and August of that year. When the Belgians left, law and order crumbled rapidly, and missionaries were forced to leave. The responsibility for the church in Zaire had been accepted by the Africans in February. In July it was forced on them in extremely dangerous and uncertain circumstances. But the responsibility was shouldered; the work of the church continued, and when the missionaries returned later in the year they found the church of Christ a living, active reality. This was followed by a very determined attempt at communist take-over; missionaries left and returned a second time.

The missionaries survived the revolution following independence, but many members of the church did not. Their suffering was accentuated by tribal rivalry between the Luluas and the Balubas, both of which had Mennonite members. Eventually the Balubas were forced to flee eastward to their early tribal homeland, including some of the most capable leaders in the church. There they organized a new conference in their ancestral location, *The Mennonite Evangelical Community of Zaire,* which in 1981 counted 3,705 members. Deep gratitude was felt some years later when full reconciliation was able to take place between the divided groups, but the conferences remained separate.

The Mennonites had long been known in Zaire for their extensive literature program, including a large printing press at Kinshasa, as well as for their educational, medical, and evangelistic programs. Since 1970 they have cooperated with other Protestants in supporting and staffing a theological school in Kinshasa. Perhaps their most innovative program, however, was the combining of all of these concerns, together with the economic, into the Service for Development of Agriculture (SEDA) in the mid-sixties. Teams of two young men, one from North America and one from Zaire, worked from village to village in teaching agricultural techniques, with significant success. Out of these developed New Life for All weekend seminars conducted in village after village, with the team including an agriculturist, evangelist, public health nurse, bookseller, woman's worker, and a youth folk-singing group.[2] Never had word and deed been combined more effectively.

Before 1960 the Mennonite churches in Zaire were a rapidly growing fellowship, working with the missionaries but also heavily dependent on them. In the wake of the revolution they truly became the suffering church, but then also the victorious church with faith and optimism. They were entering the decade of the 1980s fully autonomous, working in close partnership with ca. seventy-five missionaries who continued to serve in Zaire. Meanwhile AIMM had also sent workers into Lesotho, Botswana, and Upper Volta.

Eastern Africa: Three Mennonite churches have emerged in eastern Africa since 1934—Tanzania, 1934, Ethiopia, 1948, and Somalia, 1953. Events have moved fast, for in only thirty years the church in *Tanzania* is a free, self-governing sister church of other Mennonite churches throughout the world. Perhaps this particular Mennonite church stands out as one that has grown rapidly through the impetus of a revival which began in those regions in 1942 and which had a profound influence upon the church. Through confession of sin and the resulting establishment of mutual trust, confidence, and love, the maturity and strength of the church was greatly increased. Its transnational and transcultural concern could put to shame many churches of the traditionally Christian West. The rapid growth of this church has brought with it the problem of keeping up a high standard of Christian instruction for all the inquirers and the need for a sufficient number of qualified teachers. Yet this has not kept the church from healthy growth to 10,045 members in 1978.

The Mennonite church in *Ethiopia* faces a different situation altogether. The Ethiopian Orthodox Church, which is a daughter church of the Coptic Church of Egypt, has existed there in unbroken succession since the fourth century. This gives it a Christian background which no other country in Africa, ex-

The **Bukiroba Mennonite Church,** Musoma, Tanzania, is considered the center of the 10,000-member Tanzania Mennonite Church. A group of **Tanzanian church leaders' wives** exchange ideas after a church fellowship meal.

cept Egypt, can claim and the latter has been predominantly Muslim since the seventh century. In 1948 Emperor Haile Selassie made a special concession to the Mennonites to begin missionary work because he had been impressed with the work of MCC, but on condition that they not interfere with the Orthodox Church. By 1950 Eastern Board representatives had begun to operate a number of schools and clinics. The *Meserete Kristos Church* was founded in 1959 and early distinguished itself with the maturity of relationships to the missionaries, working autonomously yet cooperatively. The church has never been granted formal government recognition.

In 1974 a revolution replaced the traditional monarchy with a socialist government. Together with the continuing civil war against the Eritrean guerrillas in the north, this became a time of troubles for the nation and the church, including the Mennonite church though few of its members advocate nonresistance. Since the new regime assumed responsibility for education and welfare, most of the Mennonite institutions ceased to be the responsibility of the church. At the same time an awakening spread among its ranks. Members began giving time and funds in totally new proportions with the result that membership increased rapidly to about 5,000 in 1981. Since membership had been around 500 when the missionaries left, "more than 4,500 come from other evangelical groups having been attracted through the efforts of our own evangelists." Many of these evangelists are young people. In 1979 a delegation of six members visited the Mennonites and Baptists in the USSR and identified particularly with the Baptists, whose roots in the USSR are also in an Orthodox Church claiming apostolic succession. Consideration was being given to sending students to the seminary which the Baptists hope to open soon in Moscow— to study the Scriptures, to learn how to live and witness in a socialist country and, perhaps, to avoid the unsettling affluence they might encounter in North America or Europe.

Somalia: Somalia is a predominantly Muslim country. It is also one of the poorest and driest countries in the world. Missions to Muslims have usually been extremely difficult because of the nature of Islam and its traditional hostility to Chris-

The twenty-year-old Meserete Kristos Church grew eightfold after the missionaries were forced to leave Ethiopia in 1974. To accommodate all the worshipers, four services are conducted each Sunday in **the meetinghouse at Addis Ababa,** capital of Ethiopia.

tianity. USSR influence ended in Somalia in the 1970s but a border war with its long-standing enemy, Ethiopia, left the country exhausted.

In 1950 two Mennonite Church missionaries from Tanzania entered Somalia, then an Italian-UN trusteeship, to investigate the possibility of establishing a Christian witness. In spite of official warnings of the danger involved, and the difficulties of working in a Muslim area, they recommended to the Mennonite Board of Missions that mission work be started. The recommendation was accepted and the Mennonite Church became the first Protestant body to establish work in that land. Two groups had begun earlier but had withdrawn. Work began in 1953 and slowly expanded into six stations, including, primarily, educational and medical services.

The warnings of the dangers involved became tragically real in 1962, when a fanatical Muslim attacked missionaries Merlin and Dorothy Grove, killing the former and seriously wounding the latter.[4] Despite this setback and a government curb on evangelism, work continued and a handful of deeply committed believers began meeting regularly and unobtrusively for fellowship and prayer. The educational opportunities provided by the schools were deeply appreciated by many students. Nevertheless, all missionaries were ordered to leave in 1976. Some contact with the believers, of which there may be as many as 100, continued through congregations in Kenya.

Kenya: The *Tanzania Mennonite Church* is the parent body of the congregations in Kenya. Its origin seems to have been with the Luo people of Kenya who settled in Tanzania in the 1930s and were won to the faith, but returned to Kenya again in the 1960s. Congregations, including 1,200 members and a total community of about 5,000, are located in South and Central Nyanza, along the Tanzanian-Kenya route, as well as in Nairobi. Some of the workers formerly in Somalia have given particular attention to work with Muslims. Nairobi has also served as an administrative center for East African Mennonite missions. The first congregation was organized in 1963 and a national conference in 1977. In 1978 there were twenty-five regular places of worship and some believed that the church would continue to grow at the rate of 20 percent annually. Methods of witness centered primarily around personal evangelism and small-group Bible studies rather than an institutional approach through schools and hospitals. A great need for Bible training schools was, however, being expressed.[5]

Ghana and Nigeria: The Mennonite church in Ghana was in existence before American missionaries came there. It began through the work of a Mennonite layman, T. George Thompson, whose home was in Ghana, and who gathered a Christian fellowship in his home. In 1957 the first congregation was founded and a conference formed in 1964. Opportunities for mission work were plentiful, and within three years forty-five missionaries were working in the Accra area on seven stations. A strong emphasis was being placed on medical and educational work, but since the government was taking over these areas the emphasis of the work was changing in the direction of thorough training of persons for local leadership.

The Ghana Mennonite Church with seventeen congregations (more than 700 members) represents a partnership with the Mennonite Board of Missions, and maintains a close relationship with the Mennonites of Nigeria, their closest neighbors. **Teacher Erma Grove** has served in Ghana since 1957. In 1958 some fifty native churches around Uyo, Nigeria, declared themselves to be "Mennonite" before any Mennonite mission worker ever set foot in the country. These **three Nigerian church leaders** are among those who serve the thirty-seven congregations which remain in our fellowship.

The *Ghana Mennonite Church*, which had a membership of 747 in seventeen congregations in 1981, seemed unique in its teaching emphasis. The Ramseyer Training Center prepares teachers and catechists, in-service training is practiced regularly for church workers, the New Life for All program has itinerated through congregations, a Home Bible Studies (HBS) program has a normal enrollment of 700, and students are encouraged to attend both Ghana Christian College and the theological Trinity College. Several leaders have also studied in North America. Close ecumenical relations are maintained with the Bible Society and the Christian Council of Churches in Ghana. In the late 1970s the Mennonite Church was also involved with a number of churches in union negotiations through the Ghana Christian Union Committee.

In addition to these activities MEDA has helped fund farmers, traders, and other small businesses. A bookstore ministry is maintained. Every other year fraternal delegates are sent to visit sister churches in Nigeria.

In 1958 a call for help came to the Mennonite church in Ghana from *Nigeria*. A considerable number of Christian congregations in Calibar Province asked for leadership and for medical and educational help. Missionaries from Ghana responded to the call, investigated, and proposed that help be sent. The story of this help is eloquently told by Irene and Ed Weaver in *The Uyo Story*. As they neared Uyo, which was to be the center of their work, they saw a roadside sign which read *Mennonite Church, Nigeria, Inc.* What a story! Some forty to fifty congregations of Christians already awaiting the first missionary! What a change from the early days of missionary work in Nigeria!

But if there was a church already there, the first missionaries wondered if it was a burden or a blessing. For these were congregations that had broken away from the older Presbyterian and Methodist churches for various reasons. They were in charge of leaders who were poorly trained; their religion was a mixture of Christian faith and animism. And yet they wanted to be Christians; they wanted Bible schools so that they could know more about what it means to be a Christian. On the other hand, the older missions did not welcome the Mennonite intention of starting work there. It would merely increase the confusion of Christian fragmentation further, they said. Other denominations had come and gone; these churches had been known by various names. Now they would be called Mennonite for a while and a few years later something else. What these churches needed to do was to repent and return to the established churches. A lot of heart-searching, conversation with older missionaries, praying, and agonizing took place. The people clearly needed help, but there was the bitterness of long division between Christians. What added to the disquiet and uncertainty was that the Nigerians seemed to be interested more in the social and religious respectability of association with an established church denomination than in the gospel. They seemed to be more anxious about the benefits of Western civilization than about being disciples of Christ. And yet there was that longing for schools so that they might know.

It was finally decided to stay and begin work in this complicated and difficult situation. A real ministry of reconciliation began to unfold between these believers and the older missions. Medical work was begun in cooperation with the Presbyterians and leadership training began immediately. By 1981 the Nigeria Mennonite Church numbered 4,194 members in thirty-six congregations and a new seminary was ready to begin the task of leadership training. Mennonite Board of Missions workers served as needed and requested by the Nigerian Church and under their direction.

The Church of God in Christ, Mennonite also began mission work in Nigeria in 1963. Literature distribution has been emphasized particularly, together with an attempt to direct all teaching and training of new Christians in such a manner as to make them ready, in their turn, to work effectively in evangelism. Membership in 1978 was approximately 200.

Zimbabwe and Zambia: The Brethren in Christ Church began mission work in Zimbabwe, then known as Rhodesia, in 1898. Zambia was part of Northern Rhodesia at that time and included in the same field of work. By 1924 the mission had expanded to include three stations, Matopo, Mtshabezi, and

Wanezi, and which has remained the general field to the present, except for the Gwaai area in the northwest, where work began in 1954. Particular attention was given to educational institutions and medical work. From the present perspective the missionary approach has been criticized as having been too institutional and too legalistic in its regulations, but leaders who have themselves arisen in the church under this system defend it as the only way whereby the present healthy state of spiritual life and numerical growth could have been reached. The approach has changed as a mature and autonomous church reaches out to new areas in Salisbury, Victoria Falls, and in the area north of Bulawayo. All foreign missionaries were withdrawn in 1977, but some financial support from North America continues.

The internal political tensions in Zimbabwe made church work extremely difficult during the 1970s. Nevertheless, evangelism continued, supported by the Bible Institute and a Theological Education by Extension (TEE) program which is a traveling Bible school moving through the districts. The departure of missionary personnel, while prepared for and anticipated, accented the need for leadership training at all levels of church work, including Sunday schools, youth activities, and counseling. Since the school programs have continued there is also constant need for Christian teachers in science, math, history, and all subjects. Though Zambia has enjoyed political stability these same needs are also underscored there. During the 1960s and 1970s MCC has been of significant aid in meeting this need through its Teachers Abroad Program (TAP).

In 1981 church membership in Zimbabwe was listed at 3,843 with a total community of about 7,000, and 3,115 members in Zambia in a community of about 8,000. While there were no missionaries in the former nation, some thirty-seven continued to work under the direction of the Brethren in Christ Church in Zambia. A report from Zambia summarizes many of the concerns in this crucial area of Africa, concerns not too different even from those in North America, when it states:

> Economic prosperity, promotion, materialism, tribal and ideological clashes, culture, tradition, modernism and in-

dustrialization, poverty, corruption and injustice, liberation, freedoms, education and international travel, and self-reliance all bear heavily upon the lives and emotions of our people.[6]

Yet the church was continuing actively in the midst of these pressures. New congregations were being founded, a witness through Trans World Radio in Swaziland had begun, the Ekuphileni Bible Institute was playing an increasing role in preparing leaders, patience was being exercised in the face of crucial political issues. Clearly the Spirit of God was at work among His people.

The African Independent Churches (AICs): Perhaps the most powerful Christian movement in Africa in the 1960s and 1970s was not related to any denomination or any unique new strategy for mission effectiveness. They were the AICs which were arising across the land by the hundreds, even thousands. Sometimes they were schisms from established congregations, sometimes described best by the woman who said, "I go to worship in the big church on the corner over there. But when I have sickness I go to a spiritual church; they know how to pray."[7] Sometimes they arise where there is no church at all, but where a prophet is raised up to prophesy and heal and pray. In some ways it is more correct to refer to them as *spiritual churches* rather than as independent churches, though the latter term points out their autonomy and uniquely African nature.

For a time missions from the West, and churches established by them, saw the AICs as a threat because of their strong appeal to the people, their uncontrollable dynamic and power in the lives of people, their thoroughly un-Western ways of worship, their seeming lack of concern about "right" theology, the selfish objectives of some of the prophets, and other reasons. Most have come to see, however, that many of the AICs are profoundly Christian in their reliance upon the Holy Spirit, in the simplicity of their faith, in their commitment to Christ, and in their daily living. One of the groups, which is well known because it has been so thoroughly analyzed by sociologists, anthropologists, and theologians of the West, is the *Church of the Lord (Aladura),* but there are hundreds, likely thousands of others.

Over 6,000 new religious movements have been documented in Africa, but not nearly all of them are AICs.

At the center of an AIC stands the prophet, called only by God. Some may be imposters, but they soon lose their following because they lack spiritual power to have visions, to heal, to "bring God close." One of the well-known prophets of Ghana, F. A. Mills, who has also traveled in North America, once told his story as follows:

> In the year 1965, on September 14, I went to Mount Gemi at Amedzofe for fasting and prayer. I arrived at 4:30 in the afternoon and went first to greet the chief. That evening I started my fasting of seven days without food or water. I stayed at the foot of the cross day and night, through sunshine and rain, fasting and praying. In the presence of God, one is not conscious of cold or wet or hunger.

> On the third day a woman brought her mad child and by the grace of God he was healed. This wonder brought the whole village trooping up the mountain for healing and messages. To my surprise other surrounding villages were informed and they also came up to the mountain to test the power of God.

> I wish you had been there to see things for yourself. They brought the blind and crippled children and in the name of the Lord Jesus they were healed. The chief of the village also came with some problems and those were solved.

> I left there on the eighth day and returned to Accra with joy and happiness. May the name of God be praised.[8]

Mennonites have been relating to the AICs as Bible teachers—when and where they are asked. There is a great longing for more biblical knowledge, and many more teachers are needed, though some prophets have been known to leave Bible study groups because they felt study diluted their spiritual power. Some AICs have been drawn close to Mennonites, but it has not been the intention of Mennonite Bible teachers to make Mennonite churches out of the AICs. Instead of establishing institutions of learning, the itinerant Bible teacher is free to meet a given need when and where it arises. He or she is available as the Spirit leads. Hundreds of lay teachers have been and are be-

Some of the **African Independent Churches** (AICs) are closely associated with the Mennonites although they have not officially become part of the denomination. Mennonite Bible teachers serve the movement when and where they are asked. A **special prayer session** is held in behalf of a witch doctor who accepted Christianity and destroyed his juju.

ing trained, particularly in West Africa but also across the length and breadth of the continent. The Bible teachers invariably report that they learn at least as much as they are able to teach about the faith and power of God.

There were other significant Mennonite involvements in Africa, from MCC volunteers in nearly every country in Africa at some time during the 1960s and 1970s and continuing, to the July 1979 meeting of over 6,000 Christians of all persuasions in Pretoria, at the South Africa Christian Leadership Assembly (SACLA), where two Mennonites and a Brethren in Christ person addressed the meetings. One person continued a witness in *Algeria* begun by the Mennonite Board of Missions in 1956. The same board began new work in the *Ivory Coast* in 1978. The Eastern Board and MCC were together involved in both *Swaziland* and the *Sudan* in relief and witness ministries in 1978, and MCC continued to be involved in *Lesotho* and the *Transkei*. Reference has already been made to AIMM's involvement in *Botswana, Lesotho*, and *Upper Volta*. The French Mennonites were involved in *Chad*, working together with the Sudan United Mission. And we might add *Morocco* and *Burundi* for MCC work and *Uganda*, after the rule of Idi Amin, and other areas in a constantly changing, dynamic attempt to show compassion, to break down the barriers of racial prejudice, of economic injustice "to preach good news to the poor ... to set at liberty those who are oppressed" (Lk. 4:18).

All of these developments and concerns were already anticipated and, in a sense, climaxed long ago at Limuru, Kenya, in 1962 when representatives from all Mennonite and Brethren in Christ groups in Africa met together for the first time. While the conference had been convened primarily to discuss the peace testimony Mennonites could give in volatile Africa, it soon became apparent that the representatives had many other problems they wished to share with each other. A second conference was therefore convened at Bulawayo, Rhodesia, in 1965, under African leadership, to provide opportunity of discussion on some of the critical issues facing the church in Africa. The following five problems emerged as common to all nations and groups present at the conference:

1. There is a growing awareness of the fact that Christianity must speak to all of life and must be relevant to everyday needs and problems.

2. The church is stretched far beyond its means and so has great difficulty expanding. It takes the full tithe of many, many members to support one highly trained pastor. Yet there is a reluctance to ask Western churches for large subsidies, and Western churches are honestly asking whether this is the way.

3. There is growing unrest on the part of the masses because, even after independence, they see their condition as wretched as compared to industrialized nations, and things are not improving. They wonder why. Can the rich Christian brother turn his back on the poor one, even though separated by an ocean?

4. Since independence the new nations find themselves in the East-West struggle. This arises out of their need for foreign capital. Also some non-African nations are still in Africa, speaking from a lofty position of power, and showing that power when necessary.

5. The problem of race relations is far from settled in Africa, and the rest of the world, for that matter. Africa is disturbed by what she sees in the world. How long are her children destined to be second-class citizens, at home and abroad?[9]

The conference decided also to continue its meetings in the future and organized the African Mennonite and Brethren in Christ Fellowship (AMBCF) to aid in coordinating interchurch activities and to serve the churches when unified action is required.

It has become clear from our discussion of Latin America, Asia, and now Africa, that the fellowship of Mennonite and Brethren in Christ churches circles the globe. Its members belong to many nations and races. In Asia and Africa alone there are some 76,000 and 86,000 church members respectively, for a total of 162,000 *nonwhite* members in the Mennonite family, not counting at least 15,000 in North and South America. In Africa and Asia nearly all are citizens of nations which have achieved political independence since 1945.

This has had its effect on the church. Today it is no longer a matter of home churches—European and North American—and foreign missions. The fact is that Mennonite congregations throughout the world are working at witnessing to the reconciling love of God as partners, as fellow workers, sharing the resources, and bringing to the one task the special gifts given to each by Christ, the Head of the church. The question of whether increasingly affluent North American and European Christians could still be heard by the millions of poor around the world became increasingly acute. While workers were continuing to go to Africa and Asia and Latin America, it had become clear that North America and Europe too needed to hear the good news in a new, prophetic way from believers in the so-called Third World.

Chapter 20

Mennonites in Europe
Since 1815

WHEN the Thirty Years' War ended with the Treaty of Westphalia in 1648, the age of nationalism in politics and denominationalism in religion had arrived in Europe. The meaning of these new forces for the states and churches became clearer by the nineteenth century, particularly also through the French Revolution, which was both a sign and a product of the new age.

The French Revolution (1789-99) was initially a struggle between the French people on the one hand and the king with his nobles on the other. The ideals of the Revolution had strong appeal to the masses and were embodied in the slogan *Liberty, Equality, Fraternity*. They seemed to agree with Christian teaching, but in the French context came more from social and political reformers who based their theory on natural law which said that since all men are born equal, no one has the right to make them unequal or enslave them.

When these ideals were combined with Napoleon's military and political plans, they brought both hope and new problems for the Mennonites. Persecution by death or imprisonment had ended, but the Mennonites were still second-class citizens whose privileges were restricted beyond those of others in most of Europe. Because of this they had withdrawn to isolated rural areas, where they remained unmolested as long as they remained "the quiet in the land." There were exceptions, of course, as we saw in Chapter 9.

The ideal of equality brought full citizenship to most people, but the granting of equal rights also meant accepting equal responsibilities, and among the latter military service was a primary duty. Mennonites had always faced this requirement in some form, and had tried to meet it—sometimes by working out special exemptions, sometimes by cash payments, sometimes by hiring substitutes, sometimes by emigration, sometimes by dying for their faith. By the time Napoleon introduced universal military service, however, the first three options were becoming almost impossible to obtain. Some forms of alternative service were available in several countries, but they were related to the military and therefore usually unacceptable to the Mennonites. As defined in the nineteenth century, equality did not include freedom of conscience when it conflicted with the demands of the majority, and liberty was more national than personal.

In 1803, and again in 1805, the South German Mennonites decided, after much prayer and fasting, to ask Napoleon for some acceptable form of alternative service. Pastor Möllinger of the Ruchheim congregation was sent to begin negotiations with him to that end but was unable to even get to see him. Early in the nineteenth century the French Mennonites made five appeals to secure acceptable alternatives, in 1809, 1811, 1812, 1814, and 1829, but without any success. A regulation made in 1793 would actually have given them relief, but it was not observed by the authorities. Some Mennonites were still able to hire substitutes, but conscription left few available men at large, and the cost of paying a substitute soon became a heavy burden also. Some Mennonites doubted the virtue of the practice as well.

A course still open to many was the fourth option listed above—emigration, but many had come to love their environment and found it difficult to leave. We have seen from Chapters 10 and 11, however, that large numbers chose the fourth option. Only one group left from the Netherlands; in 1854, most of the members of the Balk, Friesland, congregation, consisting of fifty-two persons, settled near New Paris, Indiana, not far from Goshen. The large Amish migration and the Swiss migration described in Chapter 11 were motivated primarily by these military pressures. The migration of large numbers of Mennonites from Prussia after 1789, and from Russia after 1870, was also caused in large measure by this problem, though other social and economic factors were also involved.

There were other Mennonite beliefs, in addition to nonresistance, which came to be seen differently by others because of the ideals of the French Revolution. Equality tended to mean uniformity; why should Mennonites be different from others and refuse to swear an oath, or believe in the lay ministry? On the other hand, however, the lay ministry appealed to those who had imbibed something of the Revolution's anticlericalism, and to many equality also meant trusting each other—so why swear an oath at all? Most countries were still willing to make exceptions to the swearing of the oath, Switzerland by substituting a handclasp for it, France by requiring only the simple statement that one would tell the truth.

Migration siphoned off those who held most strictly to traditional Mennonite beliefs. The constant demands for conscription and for conformity in other ways nibbled away at the consciences of many until few Mennonites living in Western Europe in late nineteenth century were willing to make an issue of military service any longer. In Switzerland noncombatant service became the rule for Mennonites, which had been provided in the constitution of 1848, and which Mennonites felt to be a recognition of their principles. The fact that Switzerland did not take part in either World War I or II has helped to support the idea that service in the Swiss military does not involve them in any real conflict.

In Germany and the Netherlands, where Mennonites were more fully accepted in industry, politics, and culture, more young men have willingly accepted military service as a duty. In 1848, a Mennonite deputy from Krefeld opposed in Parliament a request for special exemption from military service for the Mennonites, when it was introduced by a non-Mennonite from Danzig. The congregation at Emden had among its members Isaac Brons as president of the East Friesland Navy League in 1861, a major general in the army, and an admiral in the navy during World War I. By World War I, nonresistance was largely a historical memory for the Mennonite churches in Western Europe. It was no longer a living conviction. Most other distinctive Mennonite teachings and practices were in danger of suffering the same fate, or had already been lost.

The Netherlands

The Dutch Mennonites had suffered a steady drop in membership during the eighteenth century. From an approximate high of 160,000 members in 1700, they dropped to less than 27,000 by 1808, or about one sixth of what they had been a century earlier. The Haarlem congregation, for example, had about 3,000 members in 1708, but only 488 in 1834. Also in rural Friesland membership dropped from 20,000 in 1666 to 13,000 in 1796. It was not until after 1830 that the decline was stopped. Later in the nineteenth century, beginning in 1855, but especially after 1880, the direction changed to where they again increased to 39,000 by 1960 but declined to 25,589 members in 1981.

Much of this loss must be attributed to the impact of the Enlightenment on all of Europe, and including the Mennonites. The Enlightenment was an eighteenth-century movement characterized by love for the scientific method and a consequent questioning of anything which seemed irrational, including the authority of the Bible, the church, and tradition. The movement was strongest among the educated classes, and this included the Mennonite seminary in Amsterdam which had been established in 1735. Soon a reaction against traditional Anabaptist-Mennonite ideas and practices as old-fashioned set in among the congregations. Particularly noticeable among the Mennonites was also the individualism which the Enlightenment brought; people were free to do their own believing, to write their own confession of faith, and to interpret the Bible for themselves and by themselves.

There were, nevertheless, those among the Mennonites who were not swept away by the flood of Enlightenment thought, though they could not stop its eroding effects in the church. A leader among these was Samuel Muller (d. 1875), a professor at

The historic Singel Mennonite church of 1608 is considered the symbolic center of Dutch Anabaptism. Here the congregation gathers around a half circle of **baptismal candidates.** The long-standing Mennonite concern for the welfare of the elderly and the needy—their own and others—finds modern-day expression in the **Menno Simonszhuis** in Amsterdam.

the Mennonite Seminary and an able preacher. D. S. Gorter, another minister, wrote in 1856: "I do not want to be either liberal or orthodox ... but only biblical." A revivalistic movement called the *Reveil* found support among some of the Mennonites. Unfortunately the so-called orthodox were at odds among themselves over the kind of orthodoxy they felt ought to prevail. Some of these later organized an "Association for the Maintenance of God's Word in the Mennonite Congregations." Seeing this confusion, the enlightened rationalists were confirmed in the wisdom they believed they had shown in rejecting the church.

A prophet arose in Jan de Liefde (d. 1869), but his voice went unheard—perhaps because it was too true. He charged that the Mennonites tolerated every heresy except infant baptism. In graphic language he wrote of a fishing boat driven before a storm and in danger of sinking, while some on board saw no danger, and the others could not agree on how to save themselves. He entitled the 110-page pamphlet. *Danger, Danger, and No Peace*, with the subtitle "A Word to Those Sleeping and Lulled to Sleep," but it went almost unnoticed. In desperation de Liefde left the Mennonites, and nobody responded to that protest either, but recent scholarship has finally recognized what it was that de Liefde tried to do.[1] There were others like Assuerus Doyer of Zwolle, Taco Kuiper of Amsterdam, and Jan Hartog of Utrecht, who tried to maintain a more traditionally Mennonite position.

Interestingly enough, it was the Enlightenment spirit itself which helped to bring unity and recovery to the Mennonites in due time. Some of the increase in membership came from the Reformed Church, whose members were restive under an increasing stress upon confessions as tests of orthodoxy; but it was the tolerance of liberalism which finally brought the Dutch Mennonites together for the first time, ending divisions which had begun in the time of Menno Simons. This new unity marked a turning point in their life, leading to the organization of the ADS *(Algemeene Doopsgezinde Societeit)*, a general conference of all congregations, in 1811. The growing unity and the financial needs of the seminary and small congregations were the reasons for its founding. The ADS immediately set about strengthening the training of ministers, giving financial support to small congregations, and in other ways working for the health of the members of the conference.

Although many of the Dutch Mennonites had no interest in missions because of their liberalism, a small group was interested enough to organize the Mennonite Missionary Association in 1847. Many of these had already been instrumental in founding the Dutch section of the British Baptist Missionary Society in 1821 and now decided to transfer the assets to the Mennonites and to change the name, since they were almost the only supporters. They soon gained support from other European Mennonites, especially those in Germany and Russia. In 1851 P. Jansz was sent to Java to open the first field. The mission soon encountered difficulty because converts found it too difficult to live as Christians in a society run by Muslims. The mission continued, but new methods of approach were used after 1879, especially the establishing of an agricultural colony for the converts as discussed earlier in connection with Indonesia.

The Dutch opened a second field in Sumatra in 1871. It had only moderate success, and when financial difficulties came after World War I, it was turned over to a German mission society in 1928. The General Conference in America contacted the Dutch Mennonite Missionary Association when it first became interested in foreign missions. Some contributions were sent to that work by the General Conference and for a time the first American Mennonite missionary, S. S. Haury, considered going to Java under the Dutch Association.

The Mennonites in Holland have a long history of charity and service. During the nineteenth century they were in the forefront of a number of welfare activities. An Association for the General Welfare *(Maatschappij tot Nut van't Algemeen)* worked for improvement of the school system, as well as for a system of savings banks. Special efforts were being made to care for the old, the sick, and others in need, with some congregations adding social workers to their staff as these became available.

The Dutch story takes a new turn with the coming of World

War I, though not directly related to it. During the war three young Mennonite ministers went to a Quaker center in England. The Quakers had experienced a spiritual decline in the nineteenth century and had established the center as a source of renewal among them. Though at least one of the Dutch ministers did not really expect much to happen, they all came back fired with a new idea for awakening in the church. Their work led to the *Gemeentedagbeweging,* a Church Day Movement. On August 2, 1917, a conference in Utrecht launched the effort, with far-reaching results. A series of retreat houses have been built. Conferences, meetings, and vacations together have afforded new fellowship and the opportunity to work in bringing new life to the churches. An active program for youth grew out of a youth day held in 1922, leading also to renewed interest in the peace witness, in missions, in student work, and in other avenues of service and witness.

During the years between World War I (1914-18) and World War II (1939-45), a new direction was given to European theology as the weaknesses of nineteenth-century theology were discovered. Older beliefs were reexamined and put in terms understandable to twentieth-century people. The Dutch Mennonites have had leaders who shared in these efforts and agreed with many of them. They have helped to check the movement that led many out of the church. Mission work has become a part of the work of the entire conference. A relief organization for "special needs" collects money and goods and supports a variety of projects. A Fellowship for Mennonite Brotherhood Work acts as a clearinghouse for much lay activity sparked by the Church Day Movement. A weekly paper, the *Algemeen Doopsgezind Weekblad,* serves a variety of needs, carrying special inserts from the different groups such as missions and peace work, as well as church news and announcements.

In 1922 the Dutch Mennonites organized a Work Group of Mennonites Against Military Service and reorganized its work after 1945. They hold regular conferences, orientation meetings for prospective conscientious objectors, camps for young people, and service projects. In 1963-64 they built their own camp on the island of Texel. A strong testimony was given against the

Vietnam War and against the continuing arms race, but the peace group is not united on how political its witness ought to be. The work of the peace group extends far beyond the Mennonites only and is related to the most important peace movements in the Netherlands. Meanwhile a Concern Group for Development Cooperation has been organized to help developing nations and sensitize Western Christians to world need in the areas of economics, justice, and social growth.

A director and four regional consultants work with the Central Organization for Mennonite Youth, serving as consultants for church programs, service opportunities of relief and mutual aid, and helping in strengthening a sense of their identity and heritage. One of the strongest groups in the ADS is the Federation of Mennonite Sisters Circles, organized in 1952. This organization not only works with traditional women's programs in congregations, but stimulates many of the developments occurring in other areas of the ADS. A *Historische Kring* (Historical Society) was organized in 1975, after a lapse of sixty years, and in 1975 resumed publication of the *Doopsgezinde Bijdragen,* a historical journal which had been published from 1861-1919. The society also undertook sponsorship of a major sixteenth-century sources publication project. The Dutch Mennonites carry a strong concern for Christian unity and continue vigorous support of MWC. They are also members of the World Council of Churches.

Though membership has been declining, 7,800 catechumens were listed in 1978 and a total community of 43,345. In the late 1970s an experiment in lay education for ministry in fifteen congregations of northeast Holland received strong support as a pilot program and held good promise for the future. As the largest group of Mennonites continuing in one geographical location since the sixteenth century, their life and thought and history was being studied with particular interest by other Mennonites for whatever lessons it might hold for them also.

Germany
The Mennonite churches in Northern Germany had much in common with the Dutch and differed very little from them in

their activities and spiritual direction. They maintained close contact with the Dutch congregations and reflected the same influences which had shaped their coreligionists in the Netherlands. In Southern Germany, on the other hand, Mennonites continued to be a rural people with quite different attitudes and values. The nineteenth century brought more toleration for them, but migrations continued because of military conscription and because of economic needs. In addition to the steady flow to North America, some moved to the east along the Danube, settling as far away as Galicia in Poland.

In addition to the long-standing influence of pietism among the southern congregations, the Baptists also began to influence the Mennonites. They appealed to them because of their warm personal religious life and their stress upon the Scriptures. Adult baptism, and the belief that the church is composed only of believers, also agreed with Mennonite views. On the other hand, the Baptists did not stress discipleship in the way Mennonites had been taught, nor did they believe in nonresistance. By mid-nineteenth century congregations in the Palatinate were employing salaried ministers, but in other parts of south Germany many congregations continued to use the lay ministry pattern to the present time. A few of these ministers had received their training at the Mennonite seminary in Amsterdam, but more were trained in Baptist and related pietistic schools in South Germany and Switzerland.

During this entire period the *Weierhof* came to be a most significant center of south German Mennonite life. Michael Löwenberg (d. 1874) was minister and teacher on this estate, also establishing a training course for ministers. He had a vision for the founding of a secondary school and seminary and became a pioneer in Mennonite education in South Germany. After 1884, Ernst and Gustav Göbel carried on the work with such success that the *Weierhof* became the largest private school in the Palatinate—a boarding school which also accepted non-Mennonite students. From it came a host of church leaders, and the school itself provided a center for congregational renewal activites.

One of the outstanding leaders who worked from this center was Christian Neff (d. 1946). Neff was ordained at the *Weierhof* in 1887 and soon became known for the depth of his spiritual concern and his vision for the Mennonites of Germany. In addition to his pastoral and conference duties, he was an earnest and able scholar. It was he who first envisioned the compilation of an encyclopedia about the Mennonites, beginning the *Mennonitisches Lexicon* in 1913. It was Neff also who first envisioned a conference of Mennonites around the world and called the first meeting of the Mennonite World Conference in 1925, in Switzerland. He was constantly active in historical writing and research, in editing journals, hymnbooks, and other literature for the needs of his people, while at the same time teaching in the *Weierhof* school and serving as pastor of the *Weierhof* congregation for nearly fifty-five years.

Under his influence, and together with others of like mind, the German Mennonites also showed signs of renewal, even as the Dutch. In 1924 a relief agency called *Christenpflicht* (Christian Duty) was organized by them to help the Mennonites in Russia. A Mennonite historical society was founded, which began publishing a periodical in 1936. A retreat and Bible study center called the *Thomashof* was founded near Karlsruhe in 1920. The *Gemeindeblatt der Mennoniten*, a church paper founded in 1870, continued to serve the congregations, and a youth paper called *Junge Gemeinde* was founded in 1948. Support was given regularly to the German missions committee, and through it to the international Mennonite missions committee (EMEK). Mennonite students from Germany regularly found their way to the Bienenberg Bible school in Switzerland, an international school which the German Mennonites helped to support.

World War II took a heavy toll of the German Mennonites. All of those living east of the Oder-Neisse rivers were driven west and now live in West Germany or emigrated to Uruguay and Canada. Their own poverty, however, did not keep the German Mennonites from helping refugees from Russia and other eastern areas, together with MCC. During the 1960s and 1970s some 10,000 immigrants *(Umsiedler)* from Russia and South America have been helped in resettling in West Germany, particularly in Espelkamp, Bechterdissen, and Neuwied, but

also Backnang, Enkenbach, Torney, and Wedel. For this purpose
an International Mennonite Organization (IMO) was established
in cooperation with the Swiss, French, and Dutch Mennonites
and MCC. Material and spiritual aid was given to the immigrants as needed. Frequently they preferred to establish their
own congregations rather than join existing ones. New interest
has been taken in youth work, Bible study retreats at the
Thomashof and other places, and dialogue with non-Mennonite
Christians through local and regional organizations. A vigorous
historical society continues to publish the *Mennonitische Ges-
chichtsblätter* and encourage studies in Mennonite history and
identity. Nonresistance has again become a live option for some
young people, who are also asking penetrating questions of their
elders about Mennonite attitudes and experiences during the
years of Hitler and World War II.

The traditional north-south separation of conferences
continued, with some differing theological emphases as indicated but working together in mission, relief, youth activities
and other concerns. In the north the *Vereinigung* (United
German Mennonite Congregations) listed thirty-five congregations with a membership of 7,300 while in the south the *Verband*
(Union of Mennonite Churches in Germany) listed 1,700
members in 23 congregations, but these figures did not include
the immigrant groups. The official publication of the
Vereinigung is *Mennonitische Blätter*, and of the *Verband* the
Gemeinde Unterwegs. An annual yearbook is published jointly.

There are also an unknown number of Mennonites scattered
through East Germany (German Democratic Republic, DDR),
with a congregation of 285 members meeting in (East) Berlin.
Two or three times a year services are also held in cities scattered throughout the DDR. Communication between them and
the congregations in West Germany is minimal. The combined
membership in Germany would therefore be 9,000 and 10,000
Umsiedler, with the latter figure including children and persons
who had not joined any congregation by 1981.

France

The French Mennonites had a troubled history in the

Following World War II North American MCC workers, Pax men, and European volunteers cooperated in the construction of refugee settlements at Enkenbach, Espelkamp, Backnang, Neuwied, and elsewhere. **The Mennonitenstrasse** in Neuwied-Torney is typical of the new towns.

nineteenth century. Most of them had come from the Berne district of Switzerland, settling in the more isolated areas of the Vosges Mountains in the province of Alsace, although some moved on northwest to Lorraine, and some later moved to the interior of France. Montbeliard became an early refuge. Since 1912 it has been the largest and most compact Mennonite settlement in France.

Being few in number, and scattered over these regions, the French Mennonites were hard put to retain their faith. They were often surrounded by French Catholics who envied their prosperity and took numerous occasions to molest them. They also suffered because of the wars which swept over their area. While they were not heavily affected by the Napoleonic wars except through the conflict over military service, the wars of 1870, 1914, and 1939 all ravaged their lands. Most difficult of all was the changing political status of Alsace and Lorraine, whereby its ownership was thrown back and forth between France and Germany, accompanied by all the hatred engendered by the wars.

By the end of the nineteenth century French Mennonitism was at a low ebb. Available statistics place the number of French Mennonites at 4,450 in 1810. An official government source listed them as numbering 5,044 in 1850, undoubtedly including children. A German source gives their numbers as 3,143 in 1892. Intermarriage with non-Mennonites, French nationalism, and continuing migrations added to the problems already mentioned. The Mennonites in German-speaking France tried to retain the German language. Those among them who felt more French than German, as well as their non-Mennonite neighbors, resented the German invasions of 1870, 1914, and 1940. This expedited the transition from German to French.

By the turn of the century several factors and the work of two men began to lead to a strengthening of spiritual life among the French Mennonites. There was, first of all, the influence of other groups such as the Salvation Army and the Baptists, to which the Mennonites had always been open. The immigration of a number of Swiss Mennonite families into Alsace also brought fresh life among them. It ended those distinctions in dress which had still prevailed, and with it the external evidences of the Amish background of the group. To these influences must be added the work of Valentin Pelsy (d. 1925) and Pierre Sommer (d. 1952). Sommer had been deeply influenced by Christian Neff at the *Weierhof*. In an effort to unite the scattered groups these two men initiated the organization of the French Mennonite conference in 1901. In the same year Sommer founded a paper first called *Bulletin de la Conference* and *Christ Seul* (Christ Alone) since 1907, promoting Christian living and meaningful congregational activity. Though its publication was interrupted several times, it became a major organ of renewal, with Sommer editing it until 1941.

Other activities followed the work of these two men. First one and then a second minister was employed to visit the scattered families and congregations, a mission committee was formed, a youth committee and a relief organization were set up. Two orphanages were operated together with MCC but without outside help since 1959. A retirement center and care for persons who are mentally ill have been added. A mission committee was formed in 1951, which supports EMEK, work in Chad, and other efforts. Home mission work is also carried on, in some locations in cooperation with American Mennonites. Conscientious objector status is now legal in France, and some young people are choosing civilian work as an alternative to military service. A historical society was formally established in 1979.

For many years the French Mennonites were organized into two conferences, the *Association* or primarily German speaking conference, and the *Groupe* or French speaking one. In 1980 these two conferences merged to form the *Association des Eglises Evangéliques Mennonites de France* with a membership of approximately, 2,000 in twenty-five congregations. By 1979 a French Mennonite teacher, a woman, was also on the faculty of the Bienenberg Bible School in Switzerland. Jean Séguy, not a Mennonite, had published a rather definitive 904-page study of the French Mennonites—*Les assemblées anabaptistes-mennonites de France* (Paris: Mouton, 1977).

Switzerland

The story of the Swiss Mennonites from the time of Napoleon to the present is quickly told; the effects of toleration on the practice of nonresistance have already been told, and much of the rest of the story is included in the chapters telling of their emigration to France and America. Those who did not emigrate had withdrawn to remote mountain regions, where they developed thriving farming communities. Except for nonresistance, they were able to preserve much of the heritage of their Anabaptist ancestors, which continued to make them suspect in the eyes of their neighbors. A number were able to keep a kind of nonresistance through accepting medical corps service. At times their relative prosperity also caused them to be envied and discriminated against even in the twentieth century. By the 1970s urbanization had led to the establishing of numerous congregations in cities also. Officially they are not known as Mennonites, but as *Die Altevangelische taufgesinnte Gemeinden der Schweiz* (the old evangelical, baptism-minded congregations of Switzerland). All of the congregations are united in a conference organized in 1780, which had a total membership of 2,626 in sixteen congregations in 1978.

From 1946 to 1952 the Swiss Mennonites had much contact with the North American Mennonites through MCC which had located its European headquarters in Basel. In 1951 Basel became the location of a European Mennonite Bible school, which relocated to the *Bienenberg,* a huge building at Liestal, near Basel, in 1957. The fifth meeting of the MWC was held at St. Chrischona, near Basel, in 1952. The conference also held a memorial service for Felix Mantz, who became one of the first known Anabaptist martyrs at the hands of the Reformed when he was drowned in Zurich in 1527.

The Swiss Mennonites participate in EMEK with other European Mennonites and have founded their own relief agency, the Swiss Mennonite Organization for Relief Work (SMO), which cooperates with IMO and MCC as necessary. A youth retreat center in Les Mottes serves as activities center, with non-Mennonite youth also participating. Sunday schools are operated in all congregations. Most Swiss Mennonite congregations are rural and are served by lay ministers, but some urban churches have also been planted. The greatest loss of membership seems to be due to upward social mobility coming with success and affluence. Nevertheless, the Swiss Mennonites are conscious of the fact that many European and North American Mennonites trace their roots back to their own land. A Swiss Association for Anabaptist History was founded in 1974 and by 1978 had a membership of 200. Its expressed intention was not only to recover an almost lost heritage, but to transmit it to the coming generation.

Between 1832 and 1835 Samuel Fröhlich (d. 1857), a

Reformed minister, organized a new group called the Neu-Taufer (New Baptists) or Fröhlichianer. About half of his initial membership came from Mennonites in the Emmental region who were dissatisfied with the low spiritual life in their congregations. Emigration soon scattered the new group, however, many moving to Hungary and Yugoslavia, while others moved to Ohio, New York, and Illinois, from where they scattered to other states and Canada. The groups in Hungary, Czechoslovakia, and Yugoslavia have grown to several thousands in number and manage to retain many of the early Anabaptist emphases in a remarkable way. They are called *Nazarenes*. They are the only Slavic people knowing Anabaptist doctrine and seeking to follow it, except for the Baptists in Czechoslovakia, who are also quite interested in and informed about Anabaptism.

The groups which came to America in 1846 and later have been known as "New Amish" or *Apostolic Christians*. Two or three families also came from the German-speaking area of Lorraine and settled in Canada. They have no direct connection with the Amish but in their attempt to reform the church on the apostolic pattern have many practices which Jacob Ammann and his followers brought from the same area of Switzerland.

Luxembourg

There were about 100 baptized members in the Mennonite church in Luxembourg in 1981 and most of these were descendants of three families which had come there in the nineteenth century. Several meeting places had been established, including a small stone chapel built on a farm with the help of a voluntary service camp in 1953-54. In 1946 these groups started an annual Bible conference, which helped to keep the faith alive among them and served as outreach center to others. In most of their activities they worked closely with the Association Mennonites in France.

Other Developments

The life of the nearly 55,000 Mennonites in the USSR has been discussed in Chapter 10, and in this chapter reference has been made to those who come from the USSR to settle in West Germany. Many more would like to leave but are not permitted to do so. Along with other Soviet citizens they have petitioned the United Nations to intercede on their behalf to allow them to leave the Soviet Union. Those who can come are commonly referred to as *Umsiedler* (repatriates) and have received major financial help from the German government. In church and spiritual affairs they have been helped by IMO and the MCC, the latter working particularly through Canadian Mennonites. The *Umsiedler* find it extremely difficult to adjust to the church in the West. After expressing his appreciation for all the help received, one person from the USSR said, "but spiritually speaking, God has now led us into a desert."

North American Mennonites have been active in mission work also in Europe after 1945. The Mennonite Brethren have been particularly active in ministering to the *Umsiedler*, including some who came to West Germany from South America, and have established nine congregations with a membership of 812 in 1978 in Germany and Austria. These congregations include many new members from the national communities in which they live and witness. In 1976 some of these joined the Mennonite Brethren of North America in beginning work in Spain.

Through several of its mission boards the Mennonite Church began work in *Sicily* in 1949, *Belgium* in 1950, *Luxembourg* in 1951, *England* in 1952, and *France* in 1953. Most of the work in these countries grew out of the relief activities of MCC. The work in Luxembourg and France has already been mentioned. The membership of about 100 in Belgium is similarly related to the *Groupe* conference in France and included in its work. The work in Italy has grown to include Florence, with membership in *Italy* being forty-nine in 1978. There was little communication, however, with the 20,000-member Waldensian Church in Italy, though historically and theologically the Anabaptists had much in common with them. A growing witness was being felt in England through the work of the London Center and plans were progressing for a peace witness ministry in *Ireland*, where Michael Garde, the only known Mennonite thus far, could say in 1978, "Greetings from the Mennonite

Church in Ireland. I am the Mennonite Church in Ireland."

European Mennonite Evangelism Committee: Known from its German title as EMEK, this committee was set up in 1952 to coordinate the mission work of the churches in the Netherlands, Germany, France, and Switzerland. It continued the mission cooperation begun among the Mennonites in the nineteenth century. Particular support has been given to the Dutch work in Indonesia and New Guinea. The French have shown particular interest in the Chad in Africa. A Dutch family was also sent to Ghana to work in the Islam project, a joint undertaking of many mission groups. References have been made in preceding pages to other EMEK activities. It is also serving increasingly as liaison office with North American and other Mennonite mission agencies in an increasingly unified worldwide believers' church witness.

International Mennonite Peace Committee: The IMPC was organized in 1936 in the Netherlands, immediately following the third MWC. In 1949 representatives of most of the European and American Mennonite groups met in the Netherlands to reorganize this committee, in order that the cause of peace might be promoted more effectively. Annual meetings were projected and have been held since 1961, an information bulletin was begun, and aid was given to conscientious objectors having difficulty with their respective governments.

Relatively few Mennonites in Europe had chosen nonresistance in the twentieth century. In World War I Pierre Kennel, a French Mennonite, refused the call to army service and was dismissed from his teaching position at the University of Geneva as a result. His own congregation did not support him in his stand. There were a handful of conscientious objectors in World War II, several of whom were executed for their stand, but these were led more by individual conviction than historic roots. Active peace groups have now arisen, as indicated, and legal provision has been made for conscientious objectors in the Netherlands, France, and Germany.

The IMPC is not active now, but on a standby basis. The annual meetings have been discontinued. Meanwhile a worldwide peace committee is in process of formation under MWC with representation from each continent. The Peace Section of MCC has been asked to provide staff services for this committee for the present.

In review it may be said that persecution had driven most of the Mennonites in Western Europe to the farms and mountains. Except for the Mennonites in the Netherlands and Northern Germany, they had been isolated from the main stream of history. Persecution and isolation led them to a formalism which centered primarily in the attempt to preserve the faith among themselves. The greater freedom of the nineteenth century exposed them to other influences around them. In the south and east, pietistic influences were strong, while the theological liberalism of the Enlightenment made its inroads in the north and west. Nationalism and cultural influences also had a bearing on their development.

Despite these weaknesses, the Mennonites in the isolated byways of Europe did preserve a memory that might otherwise have been lost. When they were either isolated, or too much a part of a nation, they tended to decline in numbers and lost their vitality. Meetings with other Mennonites and a study of the past stimulated new life among them all. The disappearance of divisions was sometimes simply the result of a lack of conviction, and such unity did not greatly help the church, but when differences were overcome to achieve a larger goal, the unity became fruitful. Similarly, contact with other Christian groups stimulated the Mennonites, but sometimes it led to divisions, sometimes to the loss of their heritage. It seems that those groups were most in danger of outside influence which had become formal and rigid in their own internal life.

In 1981, the total number of baptized Mennonites in western Europe was approximately 40,000 and the nearly 10,000 *Umsiedler* which, with about 55,000 in the USSR meant a total of over 100,000 members. There was growth numerically in some areas but loss in others. EMEK, IMO, the Bienenberg Bible school, and other developments were solid reminders of increasing unity and cooperation. New interest was apparent in their Anabaptist origins and Mennonite identity. New centers and methods of witness were developing. One might say that though the European Mennonites seemed at times to be asleep the Spirit of God could bring new life to them in a new age through the influence of other Mennonites and non-Mennonites, through the forces of their environment, through suffering, through dedicated leaders, and through a remembering of their past. Numerically they had declined during the 1960s and 1970s, but can the life of the spirit be measured? They were entering the decade of the 1980s with significant opportunities and challenges. Only time would tell what the response would be.

Chapter 21

Mennonites in the North American Environment

SINCE MENNONITES came to North America from many different regions of Europe and over a period of more than two hundred and fifty years, from 1683 to 1950, as we have seen in earlier chapters, they naturally brought with them a variety of cultural forms and religious concerns. Their subsequent choice of location in the vast lands of the United States and Canada further determined their development and added to the variety among them. Yet in spite of these historical and geographical differences Mennonites have much in common because of their faith and because they have been a cohesive and homogeneous ethnic group throughout much of their history. The following description of their life in the North American environment, therefore, deals briefly with some of their common experiences and concerns in an attempt to see them in their present context from the perspective of their Anabaptist heritage.

The North American Way of Life
Most Mennonites came to the United States and Canada to escape European intolerance and persecution. It was difficult for them to leave their homes in Germany, Switzerland, France, Prussia, and Russia but force of circumstances *pushed* them into the New World to preserve their faith. Yet there were also *pull-*

ing forces which attracted them—economic opportunity, relatives, and most of all the prospect of establishing the ideal Mennonite community on the frontiers of civilization. They yearned for freedom without having the vision of a democratic society, desiring only to be left alone to worship God according to their conscience and their tradition. For most of them being a Mennonite was something they inherited, rather than being a deliberate choice made by each individual between several religious options. All members of the relatively closed Mennonite community were considered either actual or potential members of the church also. For many of them non-Mennonites were a threat to the faith, necessitating withdrawal from the "world" with its temptations and sin. Marriage with non-Mennonites, for example, was strongly opposed and sometimes led to excommunication because the new partner was considered to be worldly and an outsider, usually designated by the terms *Weltmensch* and *Engländer*.

Economics: From this perspective the agricultural economy was long considered ideal by the Mennonites. For three hundred years farming was considered to be *the* Mennonite way of life and the rural community the indispensable form of organizing their common life. Initially, to be sure, Anabaptism had been an urban movement but under the pressure of persecution it quickly became rural, surviving best in small, isolated ethnic communities. Throughout most of the seventeenth, eighteenth, and nineteenth centuries to be a Mennonite almost invariably meant to grow up in an agricultural community. So strong was this heritage that many believed Mennonites could not survive in the cities; they would either be lost to the church, or compromise the essentials of Mennonite doctrine.

All this began to change in the twentieth century. Following World War II, urbanization took place on an unprecedented scale in North America. As farms became more difficult to acquire and to operate profitably, Mennonites too found their way to the cities, serving in the professions, in business, or attending schools of higher learning. While the degree of urbanization varied from group to group, the phenomenon itself was common to all but the most conservative groups and the Amish. By 1959, for example, the General Conference Mennonites had more members in city churches than in either country or town churches.[1] According to the 1963 family census in the Mennonite Church only 38.9 percent of 4,139 employed heads of homes were farmers. Another illustration of this movement was the city of Winnipeg which, by 1981 had over two dozen churches representing all of the Mennonite groups in the area. By this time, too, most of the churches being received into membership of the various Mennonite conferences in North America were urban churches.

This movement to the cities and consequent shift in the vocations of many Mennonites tested their faith and moral values in a new way. As tensions increased between inherited values and the common social values of their environment, some gave up any pretensions of having a unique faith and left the Mennonite church. Others became what might be called *marginal* Mennonites, retaining a certain nostalgic love for the tradition which nurtured them but discarding most of its claims upon them as outmoded and narrow limitations upon their freedom. Many, however, took up the challenge of relating their heritage in a meaningful way to their environment and to the world in the second half of the twentieth century. Some of the most penetrating critics of Mennonitism were among this last group, appealing to the biblical and early sixteenth-century Anabaptist models in their call for renewal. The recovery of interest in what the biblical and Anabaptist leaders had really been saying, a recovery in which the work of Harold S. Bender and others played a significant role, became a major source of renewal together with a new interest in biblical studies.

It may, therefore, be said that the history of North American Mennonitism in the twentieth century was in part a history of their accommodation to the American environment. Sometimes this accommodation was only an adding or recognizing of the values of others around them, sometimes it led to full secularization with a rejection of the heritage of faith. But in part this history was also one of spiritual renewal which made the Mennonites conscious of the unlimited opportunities for witness and service in the cities.

Winnipeg, Manitoba, has the largest urban Mennonite population in the world. Mennonites minister through **twenty-six congregations in Winnipeg,** as well as two colleges, two collegiate institutes, a hospital, a credit union, the offices of MCC Canada, an archives and heritage center, two conference headquarters, and the Christian Press.

Language: Many of the Mennonite immigrants to North America believed the preservation of the German language to be necessary for their survival as a church. This was particularly true of the Mennonites from Russia, where they had become accustomed to including instruction in the Bible and in the German language under the term *religion.* One of the primary reasons for the establishing of their own schools was, in fact, the need to preserve *both* the faith and the language. A minute of a conference meeting in Kansas in 1879 showed how inseparable the two appeared, when it stated, "A fundamental religious instruction must be given in the German language in order that in the future our congregations may find resources prepared to maintain religion."[2] As late as 1960, the following words appeared in the Mennonite paper *Der Bote:*

> What will happen if we lose our German language? Our spiritual position will decline. In our churches quarreling and fighting develop and lead to splits. So it has been and so it will happen again. New churches will have to be built.... What, then, shall we do? The German language is our mother tongue, the inheritance from our fathers which we are obliged to pass on to our children.... We have the important assignment of transmitting to our children the inheritance of our fathers, which is our mother tongue....[3]

In spite of this concern and protest, the language transition from German to English was in full progress among the churches in Canada in the 1960s and 1970s, though slowed here and there by the presence of the immigrants from Europe and South America. The transition had been completed much earlier and without causing serious problems among the Swiss Mennonite groups in the United States, except the Old Order Amish. English gained the ascendancy late in the 1920s among the immigrants who had come from Russia in the 1870s. With the change to the English language came an increasing desire to see other than ethnic Mennonite names on church registers. New experiments in evangelism and church extension were common. Membership in the church was coming to be more in terms of a voluntary decision, as in early Anabaptism, rather than as a birthright, but American evangelicalism may have been more responsible for this than the influence of Anabaptism. The German language continued to be promoted as a cultural asset and as the international Mennonite "Latin" or universal language, but it was no longer seen as inseparable from the historic faith of the fathers.

Nonresistance

The wars of North America naturally also involved the Mennonites in one way or another. In the United States this included particularly the War of Independence (1775-83) and the

Civil War (1861-65), World Wars I (1914-18) and II (1939-45), in which Canada was also involved, as well as the Korean War (1950-53) and the Vietnam War which ended in 1975.

During the War of Independence the Colonial Assembly was most cordial in its treatment of Mennonites and Quakers, warning zealots against violating the rights of the conscience of others, while at the same time encouraging nonresistant people to "... cheerfully assist in proportion to their abilities..." those who were suffering from the war. The same year, on July 18, 1775, the Continental Congress passed the following resolution:

> As there are some people who from religious principles can not bear arms in any case, this Congress intend no violence to their consciences, but earnestly, recommend it to them to *Contribute Liberally*, in this time of universal calamity, to the relief of their distressed brethren in the several colonies, and to do all other services to their oppressed country which they can, consistently with their religious principles.[4]

Beginning in November 1775, a special fee was imposed on those not in the military services. In addition to this all people had to pay a war tax, but many Mennonites refused and it was consequently collected by confiscating their goods. Some Mennonites believed strongly that Jesus would have paid the tax, and a schism came to the church over this issue.

The Mennonites were also often accused of being Tories or Loyalists, and some did leave for Ontario in order to remain true to the British crown. Their motivation, however, was usually not political but stemmed from their being asked to renounce the British government to which they had given their pledge of obedience, which they did not wish to break. Some, perhaps, may have felt more comfortable under a monarchy than under a democratic form of government, but most of them soon were giving full obedience to the new American government.

During the Civil War (1861-65) a system of hiring substitutes was available to the Mennonites both in the Union (North) and in the Confederacy (South). Most Quakers and some Mennonites objected to hiring others to do what they would not do themselves, but the majority of the Mennonites were content with the arrangement. Some opportunity for hospital service was also provided in the North, but very few took advantage of it. Because of a decline in the teaching on nonresistance in the churches, Mennonite young people were poorly prepared for the war and its demands, and "to judge from the records, many men from Mennonite and Amish homes must have entered the ranks of the Union Armies."[5] In the South the Mennonites had a rather difficult time since they were not only nonresistant but also opposed to slavery. Some fled to the free Northern states; others hid in the mountains of Virginia. Some were drafted under protest and decided among themselves, together with other peace church men, that they would not shoot. This became enough of a problem for General T. F. (Stonewall) Jackson to say:

> There lives a people in the Valley of Virginia, that are not hard to bring to the army. While there they are obedient to their officers. Nor is it difficult to have them take aim, but it is impossible to get them to take correct aim. I, therefore, think it better to leave them at their homes that they may produce supplies for the army.[6]

Some served as teamsters and cooks for the army. Many suffered hardship, as did the Mennonite communities of Virginia, where many of the battles of the war were fought. It was a very difficult time for the church, and there were many failings, but the church itself never sanctioned participation in the military either in the Union or in the Confederacy.

World War I found the church better prepared and more creative in thinking through the issues involved. Conscientious objectors were legally exempt from military service, but they were subject to the draft and being taken to military camps. There some of the men were abused, and a few died of injuries inflicted on them by antagonistic officers and enlisted men. Misunderstandings also occurred in the home communities; some church buildings were painted yellow, and several ministers were tarred and feathered and abused in other ways. One was hanged from a telephone pole by a mob but rescued before he died. But the war forced the Mennonites to clarify their stand on several issues, including noncombatant service

Inter-Mennonite cooperation has been most visible in response to man-made and natural calamities around the world. All groups have donated generously to **Heifer Project,** the brainchild of Dan West of the Church of the Brethren. Since 1920 **Mennonite Central Committee** has distributed food, clothing, and services around the world "In the Name of Christ."

and the purchase of war bonds, both of which were rejected. In place of the bonds a new zeal for relief ministries gripped the Mennonite churches, which led to real sacrifices on the part of many. While the motive of compassion was clear, there may well also have been a hidden desire to prove that Mennonites were also good citizens, but motives are usually hard to identify clearly. In 1920, two years after the war, the MCC was formed to serve as their relief agency. During the war most of the eligible Mennonite men were assigned to significant farm projects, which marked the beginning of the full-scale alternative service program of World War II.

As World War II aprroached, leaders of the Historic Peace Churches (HPC) (Mennonites, Brethren, and Friends) approached the United States government with the plea that no law establishing universal military training be adopted, but if it was, that provision be made for those conscientiously opposed to all forms of military service. The Selective Training and Service Act of 1940 granted this request, assigning conscientious objectors to work of national importance under civilian direction. This led to the setting up of Civilian Public Service (CPS) camps where such men did work in soil conservation, dam building, and other projects. A similar program was provided by the Canadian government. The cost to the churches of supporting the CPS camps in the United States amounted to over three million dollars. Overseas relief ministries were proposed for draft age men, some actually leaving for the Far East, but they were recalled while on board ship because of new government regulations and returned to service in the United States, including also Puerto Rico. Eventually many men volunteered to serve as attendants in mental hospitals, where they gave distinguished service and helped to bring about a revolution in the treatment of the mentally ill. The regional psychiatric centers established by the Mennonite churches during World War II were a direct outgrowth of this earlier involvement.

By the end of World War II in 1945, the Mennonite churches were more than ever convinced that the doctrine of love and nonresistance meant for them a continuing relief and service ministry around the world. These continuing services included

In addition to food and clothing distribution, MCC has been involved in refugee resettlement, village reconstruction, **youth and adult literacy programs,** agricultural education, vocational schools, medical services, drug and alcohol abuse counsels, native ministries, and similar programs designed to move persons from dependency to self-sufficiency.

emergency food, clothing, and medical aid, as well as agricultural development programs, work in the field of education, and a host of other areas of human need. By the 1960s it was almost taken for granted that all dedicated young people would include voluntary service of some kind in their life plans. In 1965, a total of 300 workers were serving abroad under MCC in thirty-six countries, while an additional 481 workers were serving in twenty-six locations in the United States and Canada. To these were added over five hundred persons annually, who entered voluntary service directly under their conferences for shorter or longer periods, in areas of racial tension, poverty, and other places of human need in North America. Others chose to work overseas in the peace (Pax) and Teachers Abroad Programs

(TAP) of MCC. In 1980, a total of 809 persons were serving through MCC with a budget of approximately 17 million dollars. Of these workers over 200 were in Africa, some 80 in Asia, 20 in the Middle East, 19 in Europe, 135 in Latin America, and around 300 in North America. A unique program known as the Exchange Visitor or Trainee Program providing for one year of work in another country, was begun in 1950. In 1978 there were 57 persons from 19 countries serving in North America, while 53 North American young people were abroad.

These ministries were made possible through new life in the congregations, a new sense of social responsibility, more inter-Mennonite cooperation, and increasing economic abundance. While some continued simply to enjoy what they had, many others were becoming increasingly concerned with what they saw as they entered the 1980s. There was the global arms race and the possibility of a nuclear holocaust. How could nonresistant Christians witness to this madness? Should they allow their taxes to be used for war purposes, or was the use of tax funds the sole responsibility of government? How could Mennonites work to relieve racism in their own communities and in the nation? Were the churches doing all they could to help minorities overcome personal and institutional injustice? Could they become agents of social change in offender ministries like they had in mental health after 1945? What about world hunger and overpopulation and the deep socio-economic needs of the developing nations? What about North Americans' exploitation of global natural resources? The Mennonite response in the face of these issues tended to be to work at the local levels, in small ways, through personal witness and sacrifice rather than through formal pronouncements or political processes, though an increasing number of North American Mennonites were becoming politically involved.

Movements of Spiritual Renewal

For about 150 years the Mennonites in North America remained largely isolated from each other and from other churches by a strong sense of loyalty to their heritage and by their use of the German language, but the protective walls were crumbling and new life did come. The spiritual renewal which came in mid-nineteenth century was initiated and promoted in large part by John F. Funk (1835-1930), who as a young man worked with evangelist Dwight L. Moody in Chicago. Soon after his conversion in the winter of 1857-58 Funk found his way to Elkhart in Indiana, from where he began to wield great influence for good among the Mennonites for many years, particularly through his publishing of a paper—the *Herald of Truth*—beginning in 1864.

This does not mean that Mennonitism in the Colonial Period had been without spiritual life. As early as 1690 the Germantown Mennonites had chosen William Rittenhouse as minister. Other leaders continued to be called in increasing numbers until a report written to Holland in 1773 said the ministers were too many to count. Some, like Hans Herr in 1710, came to America with many years of experience in church work.

The pioneers were also not without literature. In 1712 the Dutch Mennonites translated into English and printed the 1632 Dordrecht Confession of Faith for the colonies. By 1749 the *Martyrs Mirror* had been translated from the original Dutch into German and printed at Ephrata, Pennsylvania. Devotional writings like J. P. Schabaelje's *The Wandering Soul,* Gerrit Roosen's *Spiritual Dialog,* and others were in circulation, including particularly the *Ausbund* hymnal. By early nineteenth century more and more literature began to be published in the English language.

One of the major movements for renewal among Mennonites was the Sunday school, but it also helped to dilute Mennonite identity and uniqueness. The Sunday school had come to America from England during the era of the Second Great Awakening late in the 18th century, together with numerous other innovations like the Bible, tract, and temperance societies and the new interest in missions. Mennonites resisted Sunday schools from coming into their churches until it became obvious that they were losing hundreds of their own young people who attended the schools of other denominations in the community and enjoying the new spiritual vigor they found there. Frequently the schools were union efforts of many denominations in a given community and Mennonite leaders soon found many of their lay members actively helping in teaching and even leadership.

The first Mennonite Sunday school was probably held at the Wanner and Bechtel meetinghouses in Waterloo County, Ontario, in 1840. In the United States it may have been the school at the Masontown (Pa.) church in 1842. John H. Oberholtzer, who broke with the main body of Mennonites in 1847, was convinced of the importance of the schools for the future of the church. Many arguments were brought against the schools by their opponents and some schisms resulted because of them. They did, in fact, promote a piety foreign to Mennonites and, in the absence of Mennonite materials, introduced literature not in harmony with Mennonite doctrines of nonconformity, nonresistance, the meaning of conversion and church membership, and other basic issues. The Sunday schools became one of the major avenues through which Mennonites were drawn into the main stream of American evangelicalism.

Revivalism was another renewal movement which affected the Mennonites both negatively and positively. It was a uniquely North American way of winning new church members in contrast to the European state church system with automatic membership and state financial support. The first Great Awakening, ca. 1725-50, had come quite unexpectedly, leading the Puritan Jonathan Edwards to write about it as a "surprizing work of God" (1737), but by the time of the second Great Awakening, ca. 1790-1830, the leaders were learning to program their approach to increase effectiveness. By the time of Charles Finney (d. 1875) and Dwight L. Moody (d. 1899), revivalism had become a highly specialized evangelistic method with predictable results in terms of souls saved, and specific styles of preaching and doing theology. Unfortunately, it also became a highly divisive issue within most denominations and congregations.

It also became a divisive issue among Mennonites. The period of 1800-1860 has sometimes been described as one of "stress and strain" among them, but we might well include the entire nineteenth century under this theme. Until the twentieth century Mennonites in North America were largely a rural people, conservative in both their theology and social views, suspicious of the urban methods for spiritual renewal. Revivalism was suspect for its enthusiasm, for its stress upon one specific form of conversion, for its prayer meetings, frequent theological oversimplification, and the close contact it gave Mennonites with all kinds of persons of unknown values and theology.

While Mennonites had not worked this way before, they were actually not strangers to revivalism. Many of the immigrants of the 1870s from Russia had become familiar with this method through the work of Eduard Wuest in mid-century, which had led to the founding of the Mennonite Brethren Church in 1860. American Mennonites also knew about it through John F. Funk, who had greatly appreciated the work of Moody, and had held some revival meetings among Mennonites. But Funk's work was not encouraged by the church leadership, nor were the responses of the people encouraging.

It remained for John S. Coffman to make the long meetings for decision, the altar call, the appropriate hymns of invitation acceptable to Mennonites. His gentle and irenic spirit overcame most opposition and the results were most encouraging. Consequently, he worked effectively as evangelist from 1881 until his death in 1899. By then revivalism had been legitimized as a method Mennonites could use. His work led to new life in many places, to new interest in missions and even in education, but through the literature it introduced and the association it provided with other revivalists, it opened the Mennonite door wider to the impact of alien theologies, particularly Fundamentalism. It was to take to mid-twentieth century before Mennonites would overcome these influences, partly through the work of Harold S. Bender, and return to the apostolic roots as pioneered in sixteenth-century Anabaptism.

There were other sources of renewal. The coming of the Russian Mennonites to the Canadian and American Midwest in the 1870s brought new life to mission interests and to education, as well as simply numerically. Bethel College, North Newton, Kansas, was founded in 1887, Bluffton (Ohio) College in 1889, Goshen (Ind.) College in 1903 as an outgrowth of the Elkhart Institute, and Tabor College, Hillsboro, Kansas, in 1908. Winter

Bible schools were popular both among the "American" Mennonites and the immigrants. Mennonite high schools proliferated. Other colleges emerged. In the twentieth century education seemed to be a very major thrust among Mennonites in North America.

Twentieth-Century Developments

One of the significant developments of this century has been the growth of Mennonitism in Canada, numerically as the statistics in this volume indicate, but also in their strength and influence in church and society. In the field of education, for example, the number of strong high schools and Bible schools is significant as is the establishment of two Bible colleges in Winnipeg, Manitoba, and a college of arts in Waterloo, Ontario. Numerous Mennonites can be found on the faculties of most of the major universities across the land and in responsible administrative positions in public education.

Equally significant has been the phenomenal growth of MCC activities in Canada on both the provincial and national levels, and the way different conference bodies have been able to join forces in MCC for the achieving of common goals. So also the Canadian government has found it expedient to use MCC channels for some of its overseas development programs. Many Mennonites in Canada have been able to identify closely with their government and its goals, including greater independence from their giant southern neighbor. Through historical development many of the schools, administrative offices, and other centers of Mennonite denominational life are located south of the 49th parallel. These situations have led to questions of nationalism and its meaning on both sides of the 49th parallel, particularly among some conference bodies, resulting in some pressure for a realignment of denominational structures along national lines. The need for changing inherited institutional patterns is shared by many, as is the conviction that nationalism has no place in the church of Christ. The issues involved constitute continuing agenda.

In sharp protest against the rapid acculturation of Canadian Mennonitism have been small groups of emigrants who, beginning in the 1920s, migrated to Mexico, Paraguay, Bolivia, Central America, and other places in an attempt to preserve their religious identity. These movements have, for the most part, not been interpreted by Mennonites as genuine attempts at counter-culture faithfulness, but the question of their deeper spiritual significance remains. On the other hand, attempts to understand and work with native Canadian (Indian) concerns have been significant and encouraging.

Perhaps one of the most reliable approaches to interpreting North American life and thought is to cite some of the findings of a study published in 1975 under the title *Anabaptists Four Centuries Later* (Scottdale: Herald Press). The study was commissioned by four Mennonite conferences and the Brethren in Christ to serve as guide in the preparation of Sunday school and other church materials. It was carried out by J. Howard Kauffman and Leland Harder, and represents a remarkable profile of who the Mennonites and Brethren in Christ are in terms of beliefs and practices. The norm against which the findings were measured was sixteenth-century Anabaptism as defined by relative consensus. Church members, 3,591 scientifically chosen in both Canada and the United States, completed a massive questionnaire to provide this cross-section.

To begin with, the study found that about one third of the Mennonites in North America live on farms and another third in rural but nonfarm places. Educationally, they are about equal with the national populations, as are age and sex distributions. Their economic level is slightly above the national average. Since the primary interest of the study was with religious characteristics, of which some 34 areas were measured, this concern forms the heart of the study. Only a brief sampling of the findings can be shared here.

The study shows Mennonites and Brethren in Christ to be among the most conservative groups, with about 90 percent choosing the most orthodox response on the questionnaire. The authors state: "Contemporary Anabaptists seem to have emerged from the first half of the twentieth century relatively unaffected by the theological development of that period referred to as 'modernism'! They were affected substantially, however, by the movement called 'fundamentalism' " (p. 335).

About four fifths of the respondents reported a definite conversion experience, with over one half of those reporting two experiences and some reporting four or more experiences. Two thirds of these experiences occurred in a public church meeting. Measuring what the researchers called "devotionalism," that is participation in worship, Bible study, and prayer, they found that those who scored high in this area also scored high on participation in church activities, doctrinal orthodoxy, moral attitudes, stewardship, and evangelism. A significant finding was that during the preceding three years at least half of the members had been involved in some type of leadership responsibility in the congregation.

Regular Sunday school participation was reported by over 80 percent, with teenagers having the highest attendance rate, but the study also showed that while this participation led to more Bible knowledge it was less influential in promoting social ethics and concern for minorities and the poor. Marriage is taken as binding for life by three fourths of the members. Less than 2 percent have experienced divorce or separation. Opinions on whether divorced and remarried persons should be received into the church varied widely. Three fourths of the members chose their spouses from the same denomination/conference. "A substantial minority evidence racial prejudice in opposing interracial marriage even if both persons are Christians" (p. 336). Eighty-five percent of the respondents view sexual intercourse outside of marriage as "always wrong."

The commitment to sixteenth-century Anabaptist norms is a particularly interesting part of the study. From 60 to 80 percent expressed basic agreement with Anabaptist principles, 10 to 20 percent were uncertain, and 10 to 20 percent definitely disagreed with them (p. 337). Further, while affirming the priesthood of all believers, the majority believed a congregation would not be complete without an ordained minister. Traditionally conservative views on women's roles in church and society prevailed among both men and women. Those high on the scale favoring Anabaptist values showed slightly more prejudice against Catholics and Jews than the others, as well as more

For a relatively small denomination, Mennonites have an unusually ambitious publishing program of books and periodicals. Some Mennonite authors such as Barbara Claassen Smucker, Rudy Wiebe, and the late **Doris Janzen Longacre** *(More-with-Less Cookbook* and *Living More with Less)* have won national and international acclaim.

negative views about relationships with other non-Mennonite denominations. They were also more opposed to labor unions.

Finally the authors reflect on some of their interpretations under the heading of "Some Unresolved Tensions" (p. 338 f.). The reluctance of Mennonites to become involved ecumenically has already been referred to. In another area, while 3 percent reported having held political office, the study reveals real Mennonite caution about becoming involved in political issues. In yet another area, that of social concern and personal piety, the study showed that while great activity occurred in the area of relief and missions abroad, those with the highest concern for piety tended to score low on local social concerns. The study finds some correlation of this with what it calls "The Enigma of Fundamentalism" (p. 341 f.). There is no clear indication that present trends to urbanism are undercutting Anabaptist values.

The authors are right in their concluding comments when they state: "If Anabaptism is to speak with freshness and relevance to the here and now, it cannot be freighted with too much cultural baggage from the past. The younger generation is looking for a message that will speak to the latter part of the twentieth century" (p. 343).

It is clear from this study that there is great diversity among Mennonites in North America but that there also exists an amazing unity on many of the basic issues of faith and life. The numerous Mennonite conferences are not so much *divisions* as historically shaped differing emphases upon a common central theme. The unity of most of these conferences, including the Amish, in the MCC "family" illustrates this point. The movement is in the direction of spiritual and working unity rather than of separation. A mid-1970s survey counted over seventy projects in which Mennonites cooperated with each other, not including many regional programs nor the increasing number of congregations with affiliation in more than one conference.

Mennonite activism continues unabated. Church budgets are increasing annually, missionary activity at home and abroad continues strong in funds and personnel with a gratifying flexibility and willingness to adjust to changing global and social problems. Educational institutions continue to receive strong support, beginning with over 200 elementary schools to high schools, colleges, and four seminaries, even though a rather small percentage of Mennonite youth attend church high schools and colleges. Since its inception in 1920 MCC continues to receive the confidence and support of its constituency who see it as a gift of God for their use and for all who would meet it around the world.

Coupled with this activism, or perhaps in counterpoint to it, is a new search for meaningful relationships and deeper spiritual roots. There is manifest a strong new interest in Bible study, in marriage and family enrichment retreats, in seminars on the meaning of obedience in the face of war taxes. Most congregations have numerous small groups meeting regularly for Bible study, prayer, and mutual support. Intentional communities have arisen here and there embodying some of these

Meetinghouse architecture workshops, visual arts conferences, Christian writers seminars, music weeks, heritage tours, and art exhibits of high caliber are made available by church-owned institutions and by independent associations. Mennonite authors Katie Funk Wiebe, Rudy Wiebe, and Merle Good answer questions at a **writers workshop** sponsored by the People's Place in Lancaster.

concerns, and the charismatic movement has helped to bring new freedom and joy to many congregations without, for the most part, causing serious division. Fellowship with Christians of other denominations is no longer feared, and the MWC is generally given warm support. More and more non-Germanic names are appearing on Mennonite church rolls, as well as in responsible committee and board memberships. Serious efforts are being made to understand and respond to minority concerns, including the role of women in the life and work of congregation and conference.

Accommodation to the surrounding culture continues. In terms of net worth, if not in liquid cash, many Mennonites hardly realized how affluent they had become. But again, many were deeply conscious of the responsibility which wealth brings in relation to the needs of many people at home and especially in developing countries, including Mennonites. Mennonites were becoming more sure of who they were and love was increasing among them. Most seemed seriously to want to "grow up in every way into him who is the head, into Christ . . . " (Eph. 4:15).[7]

Chapter 22

The Continuing Vision

IN THE PRECEDING CHAPTERS the history of the Anabaptists and the Mennonites has been told from earliest beginnings to the present time. It is a history of obedience and disobedience, of human strength and weakness, and of the grace of God. It is human history, in which by faith we see the hand of God.

Having studied this history, it is in order to ask questions about its meaning for the individual, the church, and the world today. Does the Anabaptist-Mennonite faith have a contribution to make to our own day which would not be made without it and, if so, what is it? If it has vital significance for people today, why is it that the Mennonites have remained a small denomination of some 620,000 members worldwide? We know that statistics are not a measure of faithfulness, but the question is still there: have Mennonites "kept the faith," and how is it being expressed? In an article entitled "Influenced but Not Imprisoned by Our Heritage" Robert S. Kreider writes:

> A few months ago a middle-aged Mennonite university professor commented to me: "I am working on the spiritual capital of my parents. They gave me a powerful heritage—a memory of suffering in Russia, exodus, tragedy and deliverance, and then an ethnic thing (German language and all) to rebel against; what spiritual

capital am I building into my kids? . . . We can't live for long on the
heritage of the early 1920s."

Nor, we might add, on the heritage of the sixteenth century, unless we reinterpret it and find fresh applications for it in our
own experience. Kreider goes on to say:

> I am of the conviction that our Mennonite heritage speaks to the
> sickness of our society. Here are people who take seriously the bib-
> lical record and their dramatic Anabaptist-Mennonite heritage.
> This heritage expressed in the language of family, smallness,
> neighborliness might offer answers to the ills of our society with its
> vacuum of the soul, its value-free chatter, its rootlessness, its rest-
> less movement, its mindless conformity, its buy-use-and-throw-
> away approach to things and people, its dreary sameness, its tem-
> porariness, its bondage to public opinion, its pressures "to be with
> it," its manipulation of images.[1]

With these comments in mind let us return once more to the
Anabaptists, with whom we are now familiar, to see how they
fitted into their time and served the people of their day. In so doing we may see more clearly the issues and possibilities facing
Mennonites and all believers' church people in the last two
decades of the twentieth century. Let us do this by seeing the
Anabaptists both as others saw them and as they saw
themselves as individuals and as a people. Let us place these
images into the context of our contemporary life to see if they
belong and how they might be applied. Times have changed, but
in doing this we should be alert to (a) the unchanging nature of
the good news of Jesus Christ, (b) the sinfulness of human nature, which has not changed with increased knowledge, and (c)
the continuing tension between the church as the people of God
and the world as the city of man.

Revolutionaries

In turning to the sixteenth century we are struck by the
extremely harsh names with which the Anabaptists were
identified by some of their contemporaries, who honestly
considered them to be tools of the devil. Surely such hatred must
have shriveled the souls of those who felt it and closed their eyes

to new truth. For the most part, however, these were persons in authority in Catholic or Protestant churches, or in the state. The common people were not unfriendly to the Anabaptists, unless they were aroused by the authorities. The hatred of officials was, in fact, poured out upon the Anabaptists precisely because they were so popular with the people.

When we search for the reasons for this popularity, we soon discover that the clean living and simple faith of the Anabaptists met a deep longing in the hearts of the people who were disgusted with the corruption of the church and the oppression of the state. In redefining the nature of the church to consist of believers only, the Anabaptists were also redefining the nature of the state, since church and state were one society which all were expected to enter through infant baptism. As heretics they were thus also considered to be revolutionaries, people intent on undermining the state. The charge of sedition, of being revolutionaries, is very common in the records of the court hearings available to us.

There were other reasons for this charge in addition to their rejection of infant baptism. They refused to swear an oath of any kind, including the required oath of loyalty to the state; they would not serve as soldiers and generally believed a Christian should not be in government; because of persecution they frequently met at unusual times and places, giving the further impression of secrecy and subversion. Besides this, they were extremely zealous promoters of their cause, ignoring all risks for the sake of spreading their faith. Felix Mantz was one of the first of many who died because they would not promise to keep quiet about their faith. When they were caught and tortured and burned, they died as victors, not as victims of a cruel age, confident to the end that their cause would ultimately triumph. All of these signs convinced the authorities that they were dealing with dangerous revolutionaries for whom the only answer was death.

There was a final major reason for calling the Anabaptists revolutionaries. Revolution meant violence to the authorities; the tragic events of the Peasants' Revolt under the leadership of Thomas Müntzer (Chapter 1) and the equally tragic Münster episode a few years later (Chapter 6) convinced them that all Anabaptists were revolutionary at heart. Even the most peaceful, they said, were no more than wolves in sheep's clothing waiting for the right moment to overthrow all government and order: "For although Müntzer is thrown down, yet his spirit is not; it lives even yet, indeed rules in many corners—especially in the Anabaptist sect which was planted by Müntzer in this part of the land—and it has been impossible up to now to root it out."[2]

This interpretation of Anabaptism as being related to the revolutionary violence of Müntzer and Münster was accepted by many scholars almost to the present and is still used by Marxist historians. Because of this others spent much time and effort in research to show that the Anabaptists actually had very little to do with these movements, and that they cannot be understood as anything but a peaceful movement seeking as disciples to follow the example of their Master. This legitimate goal of showing the peaceful nonrevolutionary nature of Anabaptism has been reached, but in the process the radical nature of the first generation of the movement has been obscured. They have emerged as unfortunate victims who were born before the world was ready for them, as quiet and timid people who wanted only to be left alone. But this is not a faithful reading of the sources and was not the image most of the early Anabaptists had of themselves. They did not want pity; they were out to change the lives and destinies of people at any cost. In a way they were indeed revolutionaries, and history has shown that they did succeed in changing the church and even society at numerous points.

It is clear that the Anabaptists were peaceful to the point of nonresistance. Instead of violence their method of revolution was love, witness, and faithful discipleship; but this method was already so revolutionary that it threatened the foundation of church and state enough for the authorities to execute all the Anabaptists they could find as a measure of self-defense. The Anabaptists did not have a revolutionary program for society; their message was a call to repentance and faith and obedience, but they knew that those who responded would need to make a radical break with the old church and with society in a way similar to the response of those who followed Jesus during His ministry on earth. With the Apostle Paul they were announcing a new order (2 Corinthians 5:17) and like him, were accused of turning the world upside down (Acts 17:6). It was revolutionary to propose the complete separation of church and state as they did, together with freedom of religion, and a church composed of adults who would freely decide whether to join it or not. In talking thus about the church they were, in effect, saying that the existing church was no church at all. All of this seemed decidedly revolutionary, though the Anabaptists insisted it was simply what the Bible had taught from the beginning.

In the history of mankind the nonviolent revolutions promoted by people like the Anabaptists have usually been more effective and have changed the course of society more permanently than violent political or other revolutions. The means used to achieve a given end cannot be separated from the end itself. We think of the deep changes over the centuries in the history of ideas, of science and its Copernican Revolution, of the Industrial Revolution and the revolutionary developments in contemporary technology. Revolution in itself is not a bad word but has come to be so interpreted because of its association with violence and because it brings many rapid changes which threaten the established order of things.

To accept the label of *revolutionaries* for the sixteenth-century Anabaptists, therefore, means to associate with them a great vision and courageous witness in the face of severe resistance from church and state. It means a willingness to pay the highest price anyone can pay, life itself, to see the vision realized. Normally people resist change today as much as they did 450 years ago. They still confuse the church with their cultural environment and are still unable to distinguish between church and world. Society will go to great lengths to defend itself against those who threaten the established order of things. It is much easier and safer to conform. Whether the heirs of the Anabaptists can in their turn be revolutionaries in the highest sense of the word also, speaking and acting where it counts, depends on the extent of their recovery of the biblical witness and identity in our day as the Anabaptists did long ago.

Socialists

Related to the charge of being revolutionaries was the interpretation of the Anabaptists as socialists or even communists. It was believed that they came from the lower classes of society, and that all of them practiced community of goods, a system which they hoped to impose on everyone eventually. Court hearings and inquisitions in torture chambers often centered around this issue, showing how afraid the privileged classes were of losing their wealth and status. There have also been attempts by modern socialists to identify the Anabaptists as pioneers of economic and social equality.

Actually neither of the two charges was true. Research has shown that Anabaptism did not arise among the poor and disinherited and friendless primarily but counted among its members persons from all classes of society—laborers, nobles, priests, artisans, fishermen, theologians, and others. It is also well known that only a small number of Anabaptists—the Hutterites—practiced complete community of goods, and that none of them ever believed it could or should be practiced among any except believers who agreed to do so voluntarily. But they did teach that the Christian has no moral right to a selfish enjoyment of goods while others suffer want. While being severely tortured one Anabaptist said:

> ... And as to community of goods, no one is forced among us to put his property in a common treasury and we have no intention of making it common by force. But he who possesses and then sees his brother or sister in need, he is duty bound in love and without constraint to help and to succor.[3]

But they refused to believe him as they refused to believe the others, and suspected him of communism. Under further torture they told him, "... though you say that this community of goods is meant for you and your people only, yet your heart and ambition are far different, in actuality to have the goods of all men in common."[4]

As with the former charge of being violent revolutionaries, so here the charge of communism against them was false, but underlying it was a deep insight into the nature of Anabaptism nevertheless—that Christians must not attach themselves to things of this world, using them only as instruments in the service of God for the welfare of others. Their persecutors were puzzled and suspicious of Anabaptist indifference to material possessions, an attitude which struck them as unnatural and demonic. In a time when the majority of the people of the world are poor and suffer malnutrition, and when an underlying factor in many revolutions of our day is a struggle between those who have and those who do not have possessions, it goes without saying that the Anabaptist concern for sharing with the less fortunate is a vital part of Christian obedience. Modern Mennonites have a good record of service and relief ministries around the world, but even that is no more than a fraction of what they could do if the Anabaptist sense of responsibility for their neighbor really gripped them as a people. With the Anabaptists this sense of responsibility arose out of their great joy over what God had done for them in Jesus Christ. To help the needy physically as well as spiritually was an integral part of the good news of salvation.

Salvation by Works Christians

The Anabaptists were also often accused of trying to earn their own salvation instead of relying on the free grace of God because they stressed the importance of obedience and moral purity. Luther and the other Reformers also wanted clean living and church discipline, but they wanted even more to have everyone in the church in order to be saved. To them the church was like the ark of Noah, a place of refuge and salvation, while the Anabaptists saw the calling of the church to be a city set on a hill as an example for all men to see. To the former grace was first and last, and while good works would hopefully grow out of faith, it was grace that really mattered. To the Anabaptists faith without works was dead, meaning that the way a person lived showed how and what he believed.

Because of this, unfortunately, almost anyone living a clean life was suspected of being an Anabaptist. It was reported at the trial of Hans Jeger, for example, that "... because he does not swear and because he leads an unoffensive life, therefore men

suspect him of Anabaptism.... He has for a long time passed
for such, because he did not swear, nor quarrel, nor did other
such-like things."[5] Some even considered good works a hin-
drance to salvation and pointed to the disciplined life of the
Anabaptists as a further sign of the work of the devil. So Bullinger wrote about good works that "This is an old trick of the
devil, with which he has in all churches, from the days of the
Apostle Paul, sought to catch his fish." So synonymous did good
works become with Anabaptism that historians have frequently
been tempted to identify as Anabaptist any movement which
stressed moral uprightness in any period of history.[6]

It must have been a wicked age if anyone who lived a clean
moral life was suspected of being a heretic, an Anabaptist, because of it. For them, however, it was not work-righteousness,
but holiness brought about through faith, by the power of the
Holy Spirit. The first article of the Schleitheim Confession of
1527 speaks of the candidate for baptism as one who "desires to
walk in the resurrection of Jesus Christ." Menno Simons wrote
much about the relationship between grace and good works,
including the following:

> The regenerate, therefore, lead a penitent and new life, for they are
> renewed in Christ and have received a new heart and Spirit....
> And they live no longer after the old corrupted nature of the first
> earthly Adam, but after the new upright nature of the new and
> heavenly Adam, Christ Jesus.... Their poor weak life they daily
> renew more and more, and that after the image of Him who created
> them. Their minds are like the mind of Christ: they gladly walk as
> He walked; they crucify and tame their flesh with all its evil
> lusts.... They put on Christ and manifest His Spirit, nature, and
> power in all their conduct....[7]

This emphasis on obedience has been described by the word
discipleship. The Anabaptists were convinced that Christians
need not lightly resign themselves to the necessity of sinning;
sin could be overcome by the grace of God. Thus their refusal to
baptize infants was not because they believed that little children
were not sinners. They were optimistic about the possibilities of
man and assured of the salvation of infants because of the power
of God as they knew Him in Jesus Christ. It has been suggested

that they were able to achieve holiness in living because (i) they insisted on conversion and personal commitment of every member of the church, (ii) they worshiped in small groups where everyone knew each other and could admonish and help each other, (iii) they had high standards for the Christian life, (iv) they practiced church discipline, and (v) they were able to keep themselves separated from the evil influences of society around them.[8]

If the Anabaptist vision and witness is to continue among the Mennonites, this description of the church and discipleship might well serve as a model for today. Words are easily spoken, but often mean little. People need to see the love of God in order to believe. Christ was the Word of God made flesh, setting the pattern for His disciples to follow with His help. If the Mennonite faith can produce such disciples, then it has an urgent and continuing calling indeed.

Bible Christians of the Reformation

In recent times two images of Anabaptism have emerged which may help us in understanding them. The first of these is that they were the Bible Christians of the Reformation. In 1931 Walther Koehler (d. 1948), the well-known church historian of Heidelberg, wrote that "The Anabaptists are the Bible Christians of Reformation history ... seeking to restore the Early Church of Jerusalem as a holy people, strictly separated from the world."[9] Before him an Old Catholic historian C. A. Cornelius had called them *eine Kirche der Radikalen Bibelleser*—a church radically committed to the reading of the Bible. More recently it has been said that the rediscovery of the Bible was *the* great and all-inclusive contribution of the Anabaptists, as seen in their attitude to the Scriptures:

> Thus, the inspiration, infallibility, unity, and authority of the Bible was fervently affirmed. Yet, they maintained the basic distinction between the old and new covenants; and they did this without denying the inspiration of the Old Testament. . . . [10]

There is no doubt that Anabaptism arose because there were those who believed that the Scriptures meant what they said, and ought to be obeyed. Some of the early Anabaptist leaders had received an excellent university education and had come under the influence of humanism. One of the major contributions of humanism to the Reformation, including the Anabaptists, was its stress upon the importance of studying the sources. Its slogan *ad fontes* (to the sources) led to a new interest in and recovery of the Scriptures, which in turn led to the Reformation. All of the major Reformers had been deeply influenced by humanist biblical studies in their earlier years, but where they insisted that only a trained minister could really interpret Scripture, the Anabaptists believed with Menno Simons that "The Word is plain and needs no interpretation." Not that they understood it all, but they were troubled at how the learned were able to twist Scripture to suit their own purposes. So they became convinced that what was needed was not more knowledge but more obedience.

It was from the Scriptures that they also received their model of what the church should be like. Instead of a reformation they wanted *restitution*—to restore the church as described in the Bible. The church had fallen by becoming a state church under Constantine in the fourth century and could be restored only by returning to a point before the fall. It was with the fall, they believed, that infant baptism, militarism, clericalism, and all the un-Christlike characteristics had come into the church. The true church, according to Menno Simons, should have (i) pure doctrine, (ii) Scriptural use of the Lord's Supper and baptism, (iii) obedience to the Word, (iv) love, (v) a willingness to witness, and (vi) a willingness to suffer. This desire to restore the New Testament church has sometimes been called *primitivism*, meaning a return to the first or primary model.

It is this faithfulness to the Scriptures, seeking to apply its message to the needs of our time, which makes the church more than just another organization set up by people to serve their own interests. Often the Scriptures are used by the Holy Spirit to bring under judgment the things people do and fail to do. Because of this no great renewal has ever occurred in the history of the church without a recovery of the Scriptures and a willingness to listen to what God is saying through them. The Bible is

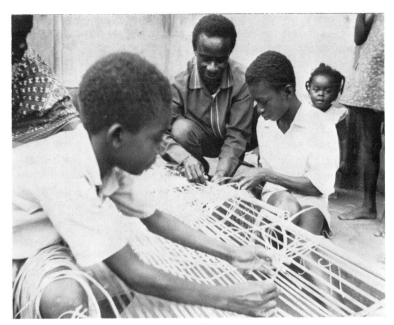

Originally founded to help Paraguayan Mennonite pioneers become better established economically, Mennonite Economic Development Associates (MEDA) has grown into a worldwide organization. Their projects include a credit union in Colombia, well drilling in Haiti and the Central American nations, encouraging **home industries** in the less developed countries; a shoe factory in Paraguay, a public transit system in Indonesia, land development in Belize and Bolivia.

not God; it points to God and His saving work in the lives of those who follow Him. Mennonites are not the only ones who love the Bible and seek to follow its teaching, but many Christians still do not read it as seriously as the Anabaptists did who believed it meant what it said about love, peace, swearing of oaths, and other emphases which are contrary to human nature, and therefore, unpopular in any society. But if, as the Anabaptists believed, God is in control of the destinies of persons and nations, then those who know and do His will with the help of the Scriptures also serve the best interests of all as they serve God. The calling to be Bible Christians of the twentieth century in the full sense of the term as the

Anabaptists understood it is a major challenge and holds great promise. Whether the Mennonites can indeed become this more fully, and witness to its power, remains to be seen.

People Ahead of Their Time

The second image which has emerged in recent years has been that the Anabaptists were far ahead of their time, advocating principles which it was to take further centuries to make acceptable, and some principles which still seem to be unacceptable to society. One of the men saying this was the German sociologist and historian Ernst Troeltsch (d. 1923), who ended his discussion of Anabaptism with the words, "The whole movement was an early premature triumph of the sectarian principles of the Free Churches." Among those who agreed with this view was the Quaker Rufus Jones, who wrote:

> And yet, as has happened many times before and since, with movements that have been showered with scorn and opprobrium, the conquered and defeated became in the end the conqueror . . . when nearly every one of the constructive principles of the Anabaptists got written into the Constitution of the United States, or got expressed in some important branch of American Christianity.[11]

By the "sectarian principles of the Free Churches" Troeltsch meant what Jones also implied, the separation of church and state, freedom of religion, and voluntary church membership. In contrast to these principles, much of the history of Europe has been characterized by a power struggle between church and state and the domination of one or the other; church membership has not been voluntary, and consequently there has been little freedom of religion. The Anabaptist vision of a church composed only of believers, and free from interference by the state, was completely opposed to the idea of a state or people's church which included everyone from birth to death.

While these tributes are indeed encouraging, it is doubtful whether the Anabaptists deserve all the credit. Historian Roland H. Bainton has suggested that the principles of the voluntary church, the separation of church and state, and religious liberty came into North American life and thought more

Following British Quaker example, the Dutch Mennonites established their church camps and retreat centers during the 1920s. The first Mennonite camp in North America, Men-O-Lan, was established in 1938. Several of these "summer only" camps have evolved into year-round church centers. For a number of years Laurelville Mennonite Church Center hosted a **Christmas International** for the foreign students of various large university campuses.

through the Puritans and the influence of the French Revolution than through the Anabaptists, though the latter were the first to hold them in the western world. Bainton does not deny the influence of Anabaptism in these areas, but limits it.[12]

Though these three principles are now generally accepted in the Western world, they are often misunderstood. The right of a person to believe or not to believe in Christ, as the principle of freedom of religion affirms, is often taken into the church by believers to claim "what I believe is my business" which, in a believers' church, is not adequate. Many Mennonite young people do not really make a free and independent, voluntary decision to be baptized and join the church; they do this because they are "old enough," or because their friends do, or their parents wish them to, or for other reasons. These reasons are important, but not primary. Similarly it is difficult to keep the demands of the state separate from the claims of Christ and His church, as indicated in the taxes for war issue, in business, in teaching in public school systems, and like situations.

A great contribution can be made to church and society by Christians who seriously hold these principles to be true and put them into practice. To believe in the separation of church and state then, for example, means to let word and deed speak to vital issues, to turn back nationalism in the church; to believe in freedom of religion then means to love those who believe differently and those who do not believe, while at the same time witnessing to the power of God in history and in one's own life; to believe in voluntary church membership then is the end of traditionalism, practicing believers' baptism rather than adult baptism, and restoring the meaning of covenant in the congregation.

What Shall We Do with It?

Now that we have considered some of the possibilities of recapturing in a new way the biblical vision as the Anabaptists did in the sixteenth century, what shall we do with it? There seem to be at least five choices before us, in addition to a variety of combinations of several of them:

First, we can choose to do nothing with it if we are Mennonites. Since a Mennonite has traditionally been defined as one who is born into a Mennonite family, there is really nothing those who are so born can or ought to do about it. Being a traditional Mennonite has become quite respectable by now—Mennonites have the reputation of being good farmers and honest businessmen. If difficult questions are asked about the faith, we can always quote a text, or say that this is what our church teaches, without really knowing much about it ourselves.

Second, we have the choice of rejecting the claims of this history upon us as meaningless and irrelevant to our day and age. While the accounts of faith and martyrdom inspire us, these are all history. As a faith Mennonitism is then considered unrealistic and outdated in a time in which people struggle with poverty, the arms race, racism, ecology, and population growth. But since it takes a good deal of courage to announce publicly that one is rejecting the faith, and raises a lot of fuss, a simpler way is to limit and finally avoid participation in the life of the church and drift away little by little.

Third, we can acknowledge the great contribution of the Anabaptist-Mennonite tradition to church and society, but also feel that the time has come to let Mennonitism die—either by changing the name to something more acceptable in our culture, or by becoming nondenominational Christians, or by merging with other Christians. Such choices might be motivated by a feeling of sacrifice, or inferiority, or simply frustration with the organized church and a desire to get rid of all the traditionalism by starting over. If such a new beginning is made in small groups, discipline could become possible, and one might hope to prevent the old hardening of the arteries from repeating itself.

Fourth, in frustration over the sad state of the church as we may know it, we can select some period of the past, either in Anabaptist or earlier history, as the *Golden Age* and spend our time talking about how wonderful it would be if everyone would catch that vision of the church. All the while, however, we would continue to be conscious of the humanness of people even in the church of Christ, and we would recall the impossibility of turning back the pages of history to reproduce the past. Positively, the holding up of such a model for the church to imitate would remind Christians of their high calling in Christ; negatively, it could become an excuse for not becoming involved in the life and work of the church.

Fifth, we can choose the Anabaptist-Mennonite heritage as the faith which seems to us to be a most faithful interpretation of the biblical message and by making it truly our own, testify to its truth and power in word and deed. The glory and obedience of our ancestors then becomes our history also, as does their stumbling and disobedience. In studying them we learn to understand ourselves better and become more able to discern where we are going, both as individuals and as a church. Instead of seeking to start all over with the church we begin where we are. By accepting our past we become free to change, adapt, and relate in new ways to the needs of our time without being bound by traditionalism on the one hand, or by the emotional effects of rejecting the heritage. This choice means we then have nothing to defend—neither ourselves nor the church, nor a rejection of the church nor even the Gospel; we have

436 An Introduction to Mennonite History

then only to testify to the power of Jesus Christ in the past and in our own living experience.

In July of 1978 over 16,000 Mennonites gathered together in Wichita, Kansas, for the tenth Mennonite World Conference (MWC). Nowhere has the life of Mennonitism around the world become more visible in a single event than in those sessions. Here was a sign of what the Anabaptist-Mennonites, a small part of the people of God, may yet become.

MWC had a small beginning in Switzerland in 1925 when approximately 100 Mennonites, including one North American, met to remember the 400th anniversary of the founding of the Swiss Brethren (Anabaptist) movement. It was a gathering of Germanic Mennonites expressing gratitude for a rich heritage. Later conferences continued in this tradition, but gradually the meetings began to mirror the rising up of a believers' church people around the world, sometimes called Mennonites, sometimes not, but always standing in the biblical stream of faith pioneered by the Anabaptists. More and more non-Western participants become involved until the ninth conference was held in Brazil in 1972, the first meeting away from Europe and North America.

And then came Wichita. Mennonites were still ethnic, of course, but now ethnic Africans, ethnic Asians, ethnic Cheyennes, ethnic Latin Americans, and yes, ethnic Germanic Mennonites too, but all together a new family in Christ which the Spirit had raised up in the East and West and North and South. There was Bible study, and lectures, and preaching, and prayer, and carefully rehearsed drama, but the biggest drama was the unity of minds and hearts, and love expressed across national, racial, and cultural boundaries as participants discovered who they really were all together. From this large new family a new identity emerged for each individual. They came from forty-four countries but were one family in Christ. Mennonites a family church? Yes indeed, but with global dimensions vastly extending the experience of the early church recorded in Acts 2. In the sixteenth century there had been suffering and persecution of the Anabaptists in Europe, now it was happening in other places

The **First Mennonite World Conference,** suggested by Christian Neff, was held in Basel, Switzerland, in 1925 to commemorate the 400th anniversary of the Anabaptist-Mennonite tradition. Attendance at this first conference was small, with only one delegate from America. By contrast **the Tenth Mennonite World Conference** brought together 16,000 Mennonites from around the world. The **Eleventh Mennonite World Conference** is scheduled to be held in Strasbourg, France, in 1984.

too. There had been faithfulness then and there was now, worldwide.

And so to the question of "What shall we do with it?" we need to add "What is the Spirit doing with it—with the Mennonites as a part of His people?" The future seemed to be as bright as the promises of God.[13]

Notes

Chapter 1

1. *Apology*, 37:4.
2. Quoted in Leonard Verduin, *The Reformers and Their Stepchildren.* Grand Rapids: Eerdmans, 1964, p. 143, note 1.
3. Quoted in *ibid.*, p. 173.
4. Quoted in Matthew Spinka (ed.), *Advocates of Reform*, Vol. XIV, *The Library of Christian Classics.* Philadelphia: Westminster Press, 1953, p. 26.
5. Quoted in Elgin S. Moyer, *Great Leaders of the Christian Church.* Chicago: Moody Press, 1951, p. 296.
6. Quoted in Harry E. Fosdick, *Great Voices of the Reformation.* New York: Modern Library, 1952, p. 41.

Chapter 2

1. The story of these earliest beginnings is told more fully by Fritz Blanke in *Brothers in Christ* (Scottdale, 1961), and by John H. Yoder in "The Turning Point in the Zwinglian Reformation," *Mennonite Quarterly Review,* XXXII (April, 1958), pp. 128-40.
2. "Letters to Thomas Müntzer by Conrad Grebel and Friends" in *Spiritual and Anabaptist Writers*, Vol. XXV of *The Library of Christian Classics*, edited by George H. Williams and Angel M. Mergal. Philadelphia: Westminster Press, 1957, pp. 73-85.
3. No. 22, page 33 in *Quellen zur Geschichte der Täufer in der Schweiz.* Vol. I, Zürich. Edited by Leonhard von Muralt and Walter Schmid. Zurich: S. Hirzel Verlag, 1952.
4. Carel van Ghendt, *Het Beginsel Der Scheuringen enz.* in *Bibliotheca Reformatoria Neerlandica,* VII ('s-Gravenhage: Martinus Nijhoff, 1910), pp. 515-516.

Chapter 3

1. The quotations of the Schleitheim meeting and of the trial and martyrdom are taken from the translation prepared by John H. Yoder in *The Legacy of Michael Sattler.* Scottdale: Herald Press, 1973, pp. 34 ff.

Chapter 4

1. *The Mennonite Encyclopedia,* I, p. 193, quoting from Wolkan, 63.
2. Sendbrief, 1652, in *The Mennonite Encyclopedia,* I, p. 660.
3. *Chronicle,* in Robert Friedmann, *Hutterite Studies.* Goshen, Ind.: Mennonite Historical Society, 1961, p. 79.

Chapter 6

1. Williams and Mergal. *Spiritual and Anabaptist Writers,* pp. 209, 210.
2. T. J. van Braght, *Martyrs Mirror.* Scottdale: Mennonite Publishing House, 1951, p. 422.
3. J. C. Wenger (ed.), *The Complete Writings of Menno Simons.* Scottdale: Mennonite Publishing House, 1956, p. 1019.
4. *Martyrs Mirror,* p. 445.
5. *Martyrs Mirror,* p. 579.

Chapter 7

1. Pages 1008-24. See also Irvin B. Horst, *The Radical Brethren.* Nieuwkoop: B. De Graaf, 1972.
2. *The Mennonite Encyclopedia,* II, p. 218.

Chapter 8

1. First printed in *Church History* XIII (March, 1944), pp. 3-24. This very basic article has been reprinted numerous times and widely accepted as an accurate and authoritative statement. See, e.g., Guy F. Hershberger, *The Recovery of the Anabaptist Vision.* Scottdale: Herald Press, 1957, pp. 29-54. Also available as a separate pamphlet from Herald Press. Scottdale, Pa. 15683.
2. Ulrich Zwingli, *Works,* III, p. 407.
3. Matthew 18:15-18.
4. From Grebel's letter to Müntzer, September 1524.

Chapter 10

1. Quoted in David G. Rempel, "The Mennonite Colonies in Russia: A Study of Their Settlement and Economic Development from 1789 to 1914." Unpublished PhD dissertation, 1933, Appendix II.
2. Gerhard Lohrenz in *A Legacy of Faith,* C. J. Dyck (ed.) (1962), p. 173.
3. Heinrich Franz, ed., *Geistliche Lieder und Gelegenheitsgedichte* (1888), and P. B. Harder, ed. *Kleines Liederbuch: Geistliche Gelegenheitslieder* (1902).
4. Fred R. Belk, *The Great Trek of the Russian Mennonites to Central Asia,* 1880-1884. Scottdale: Herald Press, 1976.
5. Adolf Ehrt, *Das Mennonitentum in Russland.* Langensalza: Julius Beltz, 1932, pp. 91-95.

6. P. M. Friesen, *Die Alt-Evangelische Mennonitische Bruderschaft in Russland* (1789-1910). Halbstadt: Raduga, 1911, pp. 500, 501.
7. *Ibid.*, p. 501.
8. A. A. Toews, *Mennonitische Martyrer*, I (1949), and II (1954).

Chapter 11

1. Quoted in C. J. Dyck, "For Conscience Sake?" an unpublished paper (1965), from J. M. Hofer (ed), "The Diary of Paul Tschetter, 1873" *Mennonite Quarterly Review*, V (July, 1931), p. 204.
2. Quoted in Dyck, *ibid.*, p. 24, from E. K. Francis, *In Search of Utopia.* Glencoe, Ill.: Free Press, 1955, p. 79.
3. Quoted in Dyck, *ibid.*, p. 25, from Helen B. Shipley, "The Migration of the Mennonites from Russia, 1873-1883, and Their Settlement in Kansas," MA thesis (1954), p. 184.
4. In S. C. Yoder, *For Conscience' Sake*, Goshen, Ind.: Mennonite Historical Society, 1945, p. viii.
5. *Ibid.*, p. 234.

Chapter 12

1. *Mennonite World Handbook.* Paul N. Kraybill, editor. Lombard, Ill.: Mennonite World Conference, 1978, p. 357.

Chapter 13

1. John A. Hostetler, *Amish Society.* Baltimore: The Johns Hopkins Press, 1963, p. 55. An older form added "whether it be for life or death" at the end of questions three and four as part of the commitment.
2. Levi Miller, "The Amish Word for Today," in *The Christian Century*, Vol. XC, No. 3, January 17, 1973, p. 71.
3. Quoted in *ibid.*, from John A. Hostetler and Gertrude Enders Huntington, *Children in Amish Society.* New York: Holt, Rinehart, and Winston, 19, p. 2.
4. *Mennonite World Handbook*, p. 369, by Ervin N. Hershberger.
5. Recounted in John A. Hostetler, *Hutterite Society.* Baltimore: The Johns Hopkins University Press, 1974, pp. 128 ff. from the original account in A. J. F. Zieglschmid, *Das Klein-Geschichtsbuch der Hutterischen Brüder.* Philadelphia: Carl Schurz Memorial Foundation, 1947, pp. 477-489.
6. Hostetler, *Hutterite Society*, p. 134-135.
7. Ibid., Appendix VII, pp. 337-38; reprinted from Peter Hofer, *The Hutterian Brethren and Their Beliefs.* Starbuck, Man.: The Hutterian Brethren of Manitoba, 1955, pp. 26 ff.
8. John A. Hostetler and Gertrude Enders Huntington, *The Hutterites in North America.* New York: Holt, Rinehart, and Winston, 1967, p. 110.
9. Paul S. Gross in *Mennonite World Handbook*, p. 356.

Chapter 14

1. S. F. Pannabecker, *Open Doors, A History of the General Conference Mennonite Church.* Newton, Kan.: Faith and Life Press, 1975, p. 14.
2. James C. Juhnke, *A People of Mission.* Newton, Kan.: Faith and Life Press, 1979, p. 4.

3. S. F. Pannabecker, *The Development of the General Conference of the Mennonite Church of North America in the American Environment.* Unpublished PhD dissertation, Yale University, 1944, p. 204.

4. J. C. Wenger, quoted in "General Conference Mennonite Church." *The Mennonite Encyclopedia,* II, p. 465.

5. Pannabecker, *Development . . .* p. 219.

6. E. G. Kaufman, *The Development of the Missionary and Philanthropic Interest Among the Mennonites of North America.* Berne, Ind.: Mennonite Book Concern, 1931, p. 103.

7. See Juhnke, *A People of Mission.*

8. Quoted in Pannabecker, *Open Doors,* pp. 399-400.

9. *Ibid.,* p. 401.

10. *Ibid.*

11. *Ibid.,* pp. 404-405.

12. *Ibid.,* p. 397.

13. J. Howard Kauffman and Leland Harder, *Anabaptists Four Centuries Later.* Scottdale: Herald Press, 1975, p. 142.

Chapter 15

1. *Yearbook.* 54th Session General Conference of Mennonite Brethren Churches. Hillsboro, Kan.: Mennonite Brethren Publishing House, 1978, p. 94.

2. J. A. Toews, *A History of the Mennonite Brethren Church.* Hillsboro, Kan.: Mennonite Brethren Publishing House, 1975, p. 367, quoting Frank C. Peters.

3. For the following grouping of subheadings I am partly indebted to the above-mentioned volume by J. A. Toews, pp. 367-379.

4. *Toews,* History . . . p. 370.

5. *Ibid.,* p. 372.

6. *Ibid.,* p. 376-77.

7. *Ibid.,* p. 379.

8. Waldo Hiebert in *Ibid.,* p. 307.

9. John E. Toews, "The Meaning of Anabaptism for the Mennonite Brethren Church," in Paul Toews, Editor, *Pilgrims and Strangers.* Essays in Mennonite Brethren History. Fresno, Calif.: Center for Mennonite Brethren Studies, 1977, p. 167-68. In his *History* . . . J. A. Toews cites B. B. Janz as saying: "Never use the gospel-horse to pull the culture-wagon; but hitch culture to the gospel and let it promote the cause of Christ," p. 341.

Chapter 16

1. Based on correspondence with Amos B. Hoover, Denver, Pennsylvania, as well as on an article by him and others in Kraybill, *Mennonite World Handbook,* pp. 373-381.

2. See Kraybill, *Mennonite World Handbook,* pp. 321 ff., 370 ff., and especially Calvin W. Redekop, *The Old Colony Mennonites.* Baltimore: The Johns Hopkins Press, 1969.

3. J. A. Huffman, *History of the Mennonite Brethren in Christ Church.* 1920, p. 34.

4. See the essay "General Conference of the Brethren in Christ" by Carlton O. Wittlinger in Kraybill *Mennonite World Handbook,* pp. 330-36, and especially Wittlinger's definitive *Quest for Piety and Obedience.* The Story of the Brethren in Christ. Nappanee, Ind.: Evangel Press, 1978, pp. 580.

Chapter 17

1. The statistics for this chapter are based on a large number of sources including private correspondence, published yearbook, and other reports, such as: M. W. Friesen, *Kanadische Mennoniten Bezwingen eine Wildnis.* Chaco, Paraguay: Kolonio Menno, 1977. G. S. Koop, *Pionier Jahre in British Honduras (Belize).* Belize City: National Printers, 1977, and others. Particularly helpful were Kraybill, *Mennonite World Handbook,* pp. 189-280, and James E. Horsch (Editor), *Mennonite Yearbook and Directory,* Scottdale: Mennonite Publishing House, 1978.

2. J. W. Shank, "Argentine Mennonite Mission," *The Mennonite Encyclopedia,* I (1955), pp. 154-56.

3. See Calvin W. Redekop, *Strangers Become Neighbors: Mennonite and Indigenous Relations in the Paraguayan Chaco.* Scottdale: Herald Press, 1980.

Chapter 18

1. C. J. Dyck (ed.), *The Lordship of Christ.* Scottdale: Mennonite Publishing House, 1962, p. 273.

2. Jim Bowman in *The Mennonite Reporter* (Waterloo, Ont.), Vol. 9, No. 2, January 22, 1979.

3. Hiroshi Yanada in Kraybill, *Mennonite World Handbook,* p. 169.

4. Santiago Bulfa, Sr., in *ibid.,* pp. 178-82; James E. Metzler, "Partners for Christ in the Philippines," *The Mennonite* (Newton, Kan.) 89:35, October 1, 1974, p. 564.

5. Foppe Brouwer, "Australia" in Kraybill, *Mennonite World Handbook,* pp. 43-44. See also the article by LaVerna Klippenstein, "A Church Is Being Born in Australia," *The Mennonite.* 94:06, 6 February, 1979, pp. 84-85.

6. "Temple" in *The Mennonite Encyclopedia,* IV, pp. 693-64.

7. P. B. Arnold in Kraybill, *Handbook,* p. 140.

8. Cited in *ibid.,* p. 144.

Chapter 19

1. James C. Juhnke *A People of Mission.* Newton, Kan.: Faith and Life Press, 1979, pp. 67 f.

2. *Ibid.,* pp. 180-182.

3. Alemu Checole, in *Mennonite World Handbook,* p. 80.

4. The biography of Merlin Grove is told in *A Whisper in a Dry Land,* by Omar Eby. Scottdale: Herald Press, 1968.

5. Helen Amolo and Meshack Osiro, in *Mennonite World Handbook,* pp. 85-90.

6. H. Frank Kipe, in *ibid.,* p. 120.

7. Edwin and Irene Weaver, *From Kuku Hill, Among Indigenous Churches in West Africa.* Elkhart, Ind.: Institute of Mennonite Studies, 1975, p. 121.

8. *Ibid.,* pp. 53-54.

9. *Messages and Reports, Africa Mennonite Fellowship.* Bulawayo, Rhodesia, March 3-10, 1965, pp. i, ii.

Chapter 20

1. Frits Kuiper, "The Discordant Voice of Jan de Liefde," in *A Legacy of Faith.* C. J. Dyck (ed.), pp. 159-168.

Chapter 21

1. Leland D. Harder, "The Quest for Equilibrium in an Established Sect: A Study of Social Change in the General Conference Mennonite Church." A PhD dissertation, Northwestern University, 1962, p. 253.
2. *Ibid.*, p. 310.
3. Quoted in *ibid.*, p. 113 from *Der Bote*, December 20, 1960, p. 3.
4. Wilbur J. Bender, "Pacifism Among the Mennonites, Amish Mennonites and Schwenkfelders of Pennsylvania to 1783," *Mennonite Quarterly Review*, I (October, 1927), p. 23.
5. Quoted in Guy F. Hershberger, *War, Peace, and Nonresistance* (1946), p. 101.
6. *Ibid.*, pp. 107-108.
7. The section on "Spiritual Movements of Renewal" has been adapted from the editor's article on North American Mennonitism in Kraybill, *Mennonite World Handbook*, pp. 58-62. Used by permission.

Chapter 22

1. *The Mennonite*. 88:34 September 25, 1973, pp. 539, 540.
2. Justus Menius, Von dem Geist der Wiederleuffer (1544), quoted in Franklin H. Littell, *The Anabaptist View of the Church*. Second edition. Boston: Starr King Press, 1958, p. 145. Reprinted as *The Sectarian Origins of Protestantism*. New York: The Macmillan Co.
3. *Quellen* II, p. 238, quoted in Leonard Verduin, *The Reformers and Their Stepchildren*. Grand Rapids: Wm. B. Eerdmans Publishing Co., 1964, p. 235. Used by permission.
4. *Ibid.* Used by permission.
5. *Ibid.*, pp. 108-9. Used by permission.
6. For example the work of Albrecht Ritschl (d. 1889) on Pietism, Ludwig Keller (d. 1915) on old evangelical brotherhoods, and the recent work by Leonard Verduin, *The Reformers and Their Stepchildren.*
7. *Menno Simons, Complete Works* (1956), quoted in Harold S. Bender, "Walking in the Resurrection," *Mennonite Quarterly Review*, XXXV (April, 1961), p. 100.
8. *Ibid.*, pp. 108-9.
9. *Die Religion in Geschichte und Gegenwart* (1931), 5:1916-17.
10. Donovan E. Smucker, "The Theological Triumph of the Early Anabaptist-Mennonites," *Mennonite Quarterly Review*, XIX (January, 1945), p. 10.
11. *Mysticism and Democracy in the English Commonwealth*. Cambridge: Harvard University Press, 1932, pp. 32, 33.
12. "The Anabaptist Contribution to History," in *The Recovery of the Anabaptist Vision*, Guy F. Hershberger, ed. Herald Press, 1957, pp. 317-26.
13. For a discussion of MWC developments see Cornelius J. Dyck, "The History of the Mennonite World Conference," in Kraybill, *Mennonite World Handbook*, pp. 1-9.

Select Bibliography

Armour, Rollin Stely. *Anabaptist Baptism.* Scottdale, Pa.: Herald Press, 1966.

Augsburger, Myron S. *Pilgrim Aflame.* Scottdale, Pa.: Herald Press, 1967.

_____. *Principles of Biblical Interpretation.* Scottdale, Pa.: Herald Press, 1967.

Bainton, Roland H. *Women of the Reformation in Germany and Italy.* Minneapolis: Augsburg Publishing Company, 1971.

_____. *The Reformation of the Sixteenth Century.* Boston: The Beacon Press, 1952.

Belk, Fred R. *The Great Trek of the Russian Mennonites to Central Asia, 1880-1884.* Scottdale, Pa.: Herald Press, 1976.

Bender, Harold S. and Smith, C. Henry, eds. *The Mennonite Encyclopedia.* Vols. 1-4. Scottdale, Pa.: Herald Press, and Newton, Kan.: Faith and Life Press, 1955-59.

Bennett, Lerone, Jr. *Before the Mayflower: A History of the Negro in America, 1619-1964.* Baltimore: Penguin Books, 1962.

Brown, Hubert L. *Black and Mennonite.* Scottdale, Pa.: Herald Press, 1976.

Davis, Kenneth R. *Anabaptism and Asceticism.* Scottdale, Pa.: Herald Press, 1974.

Durnbaugh, Donald F. *The Believers' Church.* New York: Macmillan, 1968.

_____. *Every Need Supplied: Mutual Aid and Christian Community in Free Churches, 1525-1675.* Philadelphia: Temple University Press, 1974.

Dyck, Cornelius J. (ed.). *A Legacy of Faith. The Heritage of Menno Simons.* Newton, Kan.: Faith and Life Press, 1962.

―――――. *The Mennonite Central Committee Story. Vol. 1, From the Files of MCC. Vol. 2, Responding to Worldwide Needs. Vol. 3, Witness and Service in North America.* Scottdale, Pa.: Herald Press, 1980.

Epp, Frank H. *Mennonite Exodus. The Rescue and Resettlement of the Russian Mennonites Since the Communist Revolution.* Altona, Man.: D. W. Friesen & Sons, Ltd., 1962.

―――――. *Mennonites in Canada, 1786-1920.* Toronto: Macmillan, 1974.

Estep, William R. (ed.) *Anabaptist Beginnings (1523-1533).* A Source Book. Nieuwkoop: B. de Graaf, 1976.

―――――. (Ed.). *Balthasar Hubmaier. Anabaptist Theologian and Martyr.* Valley Forge, Pa.: Judson Press, 1978.

Falk, Peter. *The Growth of the Church in Africa.* Grand Rapids: Zondervan, 1979.

Fretz, J. Winfield. *Pilgrims in Paraguay.* Scottdale, Pa.: Herald Press, 1953.

Friedmann, Robert. *The Theology of Anabaptism.* Scottdale, Pa.: Herald Press, 1973.

―――――. *Mennonite Piety Through the Centuries.* Scottdale, Pa.: Herald Press, 1942.

Friesen, P. M. *The Mennonite Brotherhood in Russia (1789-1910).* (Translated.) Fresno, Calif.: Board of Christian Literature, General Conference of Mennonite Brethren Churches, 1978.

Gross, Leonard. *The Golden Years of the Hutterites: The Witness and Thought of the Communal Moravian Anabaptists During the Walpot Era, 1565-1578.* Scottdale, Pa.: Herald Press, 1980.

Handy, Robert T. *A History of the Churches in the United States and Canada.* New York: Oxford University Press, 1977.

Hershberger, Guy F. *Recovery of the Anabaptist Vision.* Scottdale, Pa.: Herald Press, 1957.

―――――. *War, Peace, and Nonresistance.* Scottdale, Pa.: Herald Press, 1969.

Horst, Irvin B. *The Radical Brethren. Anabaptism and the English Reformation to 1558.* Nieuwkoop: B. de Graaf, 1972.

Horst, Samuel. *Mennonites in the Confederacy: A Study in Civil War Pacifism.* Scottdale, Pa.: Herald Press, 1967.

Hostetler, John A. *Amish Society.* Baltimore: Johns Hopkins Press, 1963.

―――――. *Hutterite Society.* Baltimore: Johns Hopkins Press, 1974.

Jeschke, Marlin. *Discipling the Brother.* Scottdale, Pa.: Herald Press, 1972.

Juhnke, James C. *A People of Two Kingdoms: The Political Accultura-*

tion of the Kansas Mennonites. Newton Kan.: Faith and Life Press, 1975.

Kauffman, J. Howard, and Harder, Leland. *Anabaptists Four Centuries Later: A Profile of Five Mennonite and Brethren in Christ Denominations.* Scottdale, Pa.: Herald Press, 1975.

Keeney, William. *Dutch Anabaptist Thought and Practice, 1539-1654.* Nieuwkoop: B. de Graff, 1968.

Kennel, LeRoy. *Mennonites: Who and Why.* Scottdale, Pa.: Mennonite Publishing House, 1963.

Klaassen, Walter. *Anabaptism in Outline: A Collection of Primary Sources.* Scottdale, Pa.: Herald Press, 1981.

——————. *Anabaptism: Neither Catholic Nor Protestant.* Waterloo, Ont.: Conrad Press, 1971.

Klassen, William, and Walter Klaassen. *The Writings of Pilgram Marpeck.* Scottdale, Pa.: Herald Press, 1978.

Krahn, Cornelius. *Dutch Anabaptism: Origin, Spread, Life and Thought.* The Hague: Martinus Nijhoff, 1968, and Scottdale, Pa.: Herald Press, 1981.

Kraus, C. Norman. *The Community of the Spirit.* Grand Rapids: Eerdmans, 1974.

Kraybill, Paul N. (ed.) *Mennonite World Handbook.* Lombard, Ill.: Mennonite World Conference, 1978.

Lapp, John A. *The Mennonite Church in India, 1897-1962.* Scottdale, Pa.: Herald Press, 1972.

MacMaster, Richard K., with Samuel L. Horst and Robert F. Ulle. *Conscience in Crisis: Mennonite and Other Peace Churches in America, 1739-1789.* Scottdale, Pa.: Herald Press, 1979.

Moquin, Wayne (ed.). *A Documentary History of the Mexican-American.* New York: Bantam Books, 1971.

Oyer, John S. *Lutheran Reformers Against the Anabaptists.* The Hague: Martinus Nijhoff, 1964.

Pannabecker, S. F. *Open Doors: A History of the General Conference.* Newton Kan.: Faith and Life Press, 1975.

Redekop, Calvin. *Strangers Become Neighbors: Mennonite and Indigenous Relations in the Paraguayan Chaco.* Scottdale, Pa.: Herald Press, 1980.

Ruth, John L. *Conrad Grebel: Son of Zurich.* Scottdale, Pa.: Herald Press, 1975.

Sawatsky, Walter. *Soviet Evangelicals Since World War II.* Scottdale, Pa.: Herald Press, 1981.

Schlabach, Theron F. *Gospel Versus Gospel: Mission and the Mennonite Church, 1863-1944.* Scottdale, Pa.: Herald Press, 1980.

Sider, Ronald J. *Rich Christians in an Age of Hunger.* New York: Paulist Press, 1977.

Smith, C. Henry. *The Story of the Mennonites.* Newton, Kan.: Faith and

Life Press, 1981 ed.

Springer, Nelson P., and Klassen, A. J. *Mennonite Bibliography, 1631-1961.* 2 vols. Scottdale, Pa.: Herald Press, 1977.

Studer, Gerald C. *Christopher Dock: Colonial Schoolmaster.* Scottdale, Pa.: Herald Press, 1967.

Toews, J. A. *A History of the Mennonite Brethren Church.* Hillsboro, Kan.: Mennonite Brethren Publishing House, 1975.

Toews, Paul (ed.). *Pilgrims and Strangers: Essays in Mennonite Brethren History.* Fresno, Calif.: Mennonite Brethren Biblical Seminary, 1977.

Van Braght, Thieleman J. *Martyrs Mirror.* Scottdale, Pa.: Herald Press, 1951.

Verduin, Leonard. *The Reformers and Their Stepchildren.* Grand Rapids: Eerdmans, 1964.

Verheyden, A. L. E. *Anabaptism in Flanders, 1530-1650.* Scottdale, Pa.: Herald Press, 1961.

Vogel, Virgil J. *This Country Was Ours.* New York: Harper, 1972.

Weaver, Ed and Irene. *From Kuku Hill. Among Indigenous Churches in West Africa,* Scottdale, Pa.: Herald Press, 1975.

Wenger, J. C. (ed.). *Complete Writings of Menno Simons.* Scottdale, Pa.: Herald Press, 1956.

_____. *Even unto Death.* Richmond: John Knox Press, 1961.

_____. *The Mennonite Church in America.* Scottdale, Pa.: Herald Press, 1966.

_____. *Glimpses of Mennonite History and Doctrine.* Scottdale, Pa.: Herald Press, 1940.

Williams, George H., and Mergal, Angel M. *Spiritual and Anabaptist Writers. Documents Illustrative of the Radical Reformation.* Philadelphia: Westminster Press, 1957.

Wittlinger, Carlton O. *Quest for Piety and Obedience. The Story of the Brethren in Christ Church.* Nappanee, Ind.: Evangel Press, 1978.

Yoder, John H. *The Legacy of Michael Sattler.* Scottdale, Pa.: Herald Press, 1973.

_____. *The Politics of Jesus.* Grand Rapids: Eerdmans, 1972.

Zeman, Jarold K., Klaassen, Walter, and Rempel, John D. *The Believers' Church in Canada.* Winnipeg: Mennonite Central Committee, 1979.

Index

Janz, B. B., 256
Janzen, Cornelius, 256
Janzen, Wilhelm, 274
Japan, 244, 263, 341
Java, 336ff.
Johnson, Anthony H., 194
Joris, David, 105, 110f., 126, 145
Jung-Stilling, J. H., 150

K
Kauffman, Daniel, 209, 221-223
Kenya, 368
Kessler, John, 52
Kimbanguism, 362
Klassen, C. F., 256f.
Kleine Gemeinde, 175, 201, 283, 286,
    306, 315
Kliewer, J. W., 258
Koehler, Walther, 429
Kratz, Clayton, 184
Krehbiel, Jacob, 247f.
Krimmer Menn. Brethren, 282ff., 286
Ku Klux Klan, 194

L
Leiden, Jan van, 104
Lenzmann, August, 271
Lesotho, 376
Liefde, Jan de, 384
Luther, Martin, 15, 20, 25, 27ff., 38, 39,
    44, 86, 106
Luxembourg, 395
Luyken, Jan, 134

M
Machno, Nestor, 182 ff.
Mander, Carel van, 134
Malagar, P. J., 357
Mantz, Felix, 42, 44ff., 55, 423
Marpeck, Pilgram, 83-98, 145
Matthijs, Jan, 102ff.
MCSFI, 352
MEDA, 320-321ff., 348, 431
Menno Colony, 317ff.
Mennonite Biblical Seminary, 263
Mennonite Brethren Biblical
    Seminary, 285
Mennonite Brethren Bible College, 294
Mennonite Brethren Church, 176ff.,
    270-294

Mennonite Brethren in Christ Church,
    see Missionary Church
Mennonite Church, 208-229, 341
Mennonite Collegiate Institute, 258,
    387, 398, 420, 436
Mennonite World Conference, 226,
    229, 341, 387, 398, 420, 436
Mexico, 206f., 295, 298, 304, 315ff., 333
Micron, Martin, 109, 123
Missionary Church, 307-309
Missionary Church Association, 307f.
Moellinger, David, 150
Molotschna, 169ff., 273ff.
Moody, D. L., 218, 412
Moravia, 66
Moravians, 190
Muller, Samuel, 382
Mumaw, Henry A., 221
Münster, 101ff.
Müntzer, Thomas, 34, 35, 44, 63ff., 139,
    140, 423

N
Nafziger, Christian, 232
Neff, Christian, 389, 437
Nepal, 357
Netherlands, 382ff.
Neuland Colony, 287, 319ff.
Nicaragua, 332
Nicholsburg, 72f., 143
Nigeria, 368ff.

O
Oath, 59
Oberholtzer, John H., 209, 249ff., 259,
    412
Oecolampadius, Johannes, 52, 62ff.
Old Colony Mennonites, 302-305, 315ff.
Old Order Mennonites, 300ff.
Oncken, J. G., 281
Ophoorn, Jan van, 129
Otterbein, Philip, 309f.

P
Panama, 332
Pacific College, 294
Paraguay, 206, 241, 256f., 263, 287,
    304, 317
Pastor, Adam, 110f., 126
Pastorius, Francis Daniel, 190

Anabaptists in 1550 CENTRAL EUROPE

Main areas of Anabaptist concentration

• Main cities related to Anabaptist movement

Only the larger political divisions which had a significant number of Anabaptists are shown; smaller areas are not marked.

Jan Gleysteen '67

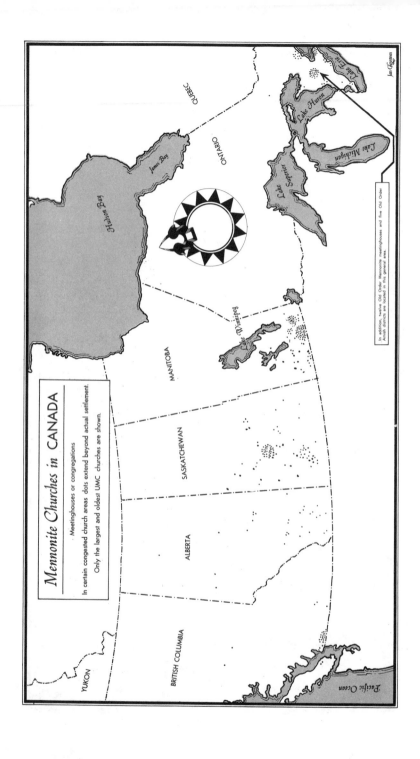

Mennonite Churches in CANADA

Meetinghouses or congregations

In certain congested church areas dots extend beyond actual settlement.

Only the largest and oldest UMC churches are shown.

In addition, twelve Old Order Mennonite meetinghouses and five Old Order Amish districts are located in this general area.

Jan Gleysteen

YUKON

BRITISH COLUMBIA

ALBERTA

SASKATCHEWAN

MANITOBA

ONTARIO

QUEBEC

Hudson Bay

James Bay

Lake Winnipeg

Lake Superior

Lake Huron

Lake Michigan

Lake Erie

Pacific Ocean

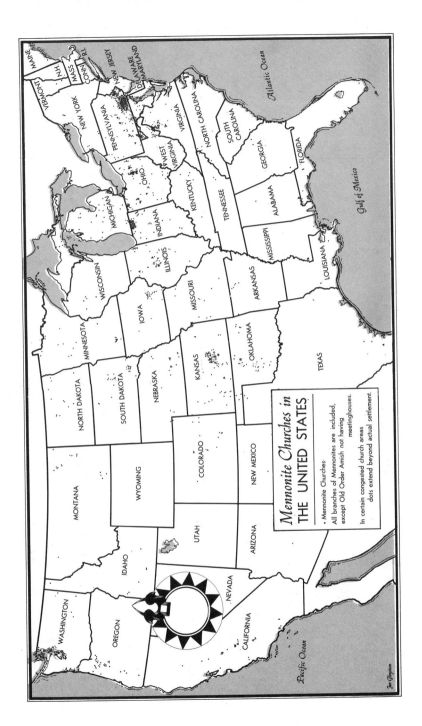

Mennonite Churches in
THE UNITED STATES

- Mennonite Churches:
  All branches of Mennonites are included,
  except Old Order Amish not having
  meetinghouses.

  In certain congested church areas
  dots extend beyond actual settlement.

Mennonites in LATIN AMERICA

MCC   Mennonite Central Committee
MC   Mennonite Church
MB   Mennonite Brethren Church
GC   General Conference Mennonite Church
C of G Church of God in Christ Mennonite
EMC   Evangelical Mennonite Church

MCC

MCC
MC

Mediterranean Sea

MOROCCO

SPANISH
SAHARA

TUNISIA

ALGERIA

LIBYA

EM

MCC

MAURETANIA

SENEGAL
GAMBIA

GUINEA

SIERRA
LEONE

LIBERIA

IVORY
COAST

GHANA

MALI

UPPER VOLTA

TOGO
DAHOMEY

MC

MC
C of G
TAP

NIGER

Niger

NIGERIA

EGYPT

Nile River

CHAD

Red Sea

BR. CAMEROUN
RIO MUNI

CAMEROUN

CENTRAL AFRICAN REPUBLIC

SUDAN

Atlantic Ocean

GABON

CONGO

Congo River

ZAIRE

MB
AIM

ETHIOPIA

SOMALIA

UGANDA

RWANDA
BURUNDI

KENYA

MC

ANGOLA

TANZANIA

NAMIBIA

Zambezi River

ZAMBIA

MALAWI

MCC

TAP

Indian Ocean

BOTSWANA

ZIMBABWE

MOZAMBIQUE

B in C
MCC

Orange River

Limpopo River

MADAGASCAR

LESOTHO
TRANSKEI

SWAZILAND

MCC

Jan Gleysteen
/67

Mennonites in AFRICA

MCC	Mennonite Central Committee
MC	Mennonite Church
EM	European Mennonites
TAP	Teachers Abroad Program
MB	Mennonite Brethren Church
AIM	Africa Inland Mission
C of G	Church of God in Christ Mennonite
B in C	Brethren in Christ

Cornelius J. Dyck comes to the writing of this history from a wide background of service in the church. Born in Russia, he grew up in Canada, but later made his home in the United States. From 1945-51 he served with the Mennonite Central Committee (MCC) in Europe and South America and, more recently, as a member of the MCC Executive Committee. From 1951-55 he pastored a Mennonite church in Kansas. In addition to membership on numerous conference and community boards and committees over the years, he served as executive secretary of Mennonite World Conference from 1962-73.

He received his PhD degree from the University of Chicago, and has served as Visiting Fellow at other centers and universities in the United States and Europe. In addition to teaching at the Associated Mennonite Biblical Seminaries since 1959, Dyck was for two decades director of the Institute of Mennonite Studies, a research agency of the seminaries. He is the author and editor of numerous books, chapters of books, and articles in professional journals, including *The Encyclopaedia Britannica* and other scholarly publications.

Dyck is married to Wilma L. Regier of Laird, Saskatchewan, and they have three children. He is a member of Hively Avenue Mennonite Church of Elkhart, Indiana.